"This book is an invaluable resource for anyone who opposes the violence and waste of Canadian mining operations. While many studies have assessed the impacts of mining, Kuyek goes deeper in explaining how the mining industry works at every level, providing a richness of analysis that is uncommon and much-needed. This is an urgent and informative read."

—Tyler Shipley, professor of culture, society, and commerce, Humber College, author of *Ottawa and Empire: Canada and the Military Coup in Honduras*

"*Unearthing Justice* reveals the false equation between mining and prosperity in stories of mine disasters, toothless regulation, and environmental contamination. Kuyek illuminates the legal and financial contexts of mining development, providing practical advice to help readers challenge the promises and legacies of mining in their communities."

—Dr. Rachel Ariss, Ontario Tech University

"When it comes to offering support to communities fighting against mines and the international mining industry, there's no one I know who's quite like Joan Kuyek. She combines a sophisticated researcher's nose for how and where to find the information that will increase the odds of stopping a mining corporation in its tracks with a grassroots organizer's strategic savvy for how best to help endangered communities fight to preserve what's theirs. In Musicians United's work to help stop the proposed Pebble Mine in Alaska's Bristol Bay, Joan's knowledge and experience were among our most important assets. In *Unearthing Justice*, she shares her lifetime of earned experience and hard-won knowledge. This book will help rebalance the scales of justice in favour of people and communities."

—Si Kahn, civil rights, labour, and community organizer and musician; co-founder, Musicians United to Protect Bristol Bay

"In *Unearthing Justice*, Joan Kuyek pulls into sharp focus the fuzzy ideas that shape most Canadians' understanding of what it means to live in a 'mining country.' For over a century, Canadians have largely accepted Canada's mining practices without acknowledging the long-term costs. However, as Kuyek shows us, the threads of colonial violence that run through the fabric of Canada's mining history reappear in modern-day Canadian mining projects from Vancouver Island to Guatemala to isolated northern Indigenous communities. *Unearthing Justice* provides the tools to prevent, disrupt, or reshape inherently destructive mining projects and put a true price on mining."

—Tara Scurr, business and human rights campaigner,
Amnesty International Canada

"This book is essential reading for anyone who wants to understand the mining industry. Kuyek's experience and analysis shine through the stories she tells."

—Jamie Kneen, co-manager, MiningWatch Canada

"A very informative and disturbing book. *Unearthing Justice* shines a light on how Canadian mining companies operate and how Canadians and the environment end up suffering as a result. More to the point, it outlines how to oppose mines, how to force mining companies to improve their operations, and how we as Canadians can hold these corporations accountable for their actions."

—Lewis Rifkind, mining analyst, Yukon Conservation Society

"Joan Kuyek has written an excellent book, describing in layperson's terms all aspects of mining, from exploration to reclamation, as well as the laws, operations, and financing of the mining industry. Even though I have worked with two Indigenous communities to stop mining exploration, I didn't understand the whole process or industry. This book provides clear advice on how to hold the mining industry in check and how to stop a mine. I highly recommend this book for anyone having to deal with potential or existing mines."

—Russ Diabo, Kahnawake Mohawk, Indigenous policy analyst,
editor and publisher of the *First Nations Strategic Bulletin*

"Joan Kuyek is an authority when it comes to researching and organizing against destructive mining projects. This book provides a detailed understanding of many different types of mineral extraction and shares strategies for opposing them. Filled with dozens of examples drawn from decades of experience, this book is essential for understanding this powerful industry."

—Sakura Saunders, co-founder, Mining Injustice
Solidarity Network

"Kuyek thoughtfully weaves together facts with her own experience and immense wisdom to expose what the mining industry would prefer stay buried. A community organizer renowned for her knowledge of mining in Canada and abroad, Kuyek reminds us of the many brave people who have resisted, sometimes triumphantly, destructive extractivism."

—Tracy Glynn, activist, instructor of critical development studies,
University of New Brunswick

"When a mining company comes to your town it brings its imperialist ideology, its private militia, its army of lawyers, its lobbyists, its public relations experts, its tax haven–connected accountants, and the various levels of government it has purchased. It will threaten your community's living conditions, its ecosystems, its agriculture, its security, and its culture. You will have to pour all of your energy into an entirely uphill battle. But Joan Kuyek's book reminds you that your community is not nearly as alone or as isolated as it may seem, that bonds of solidarity are as possible as they are necessary. Above all, her book shows us why we must tear down the institutions that make Canada a legal and regulatory haven for the global mining industry."

—Alain Deneault, co-author of *Imperial Canada Inc.: Legal Haven
of Choice for the World's Mining Industries*

"A clear and helpful overview of the mining industry from a Canadian perspective that includes powerful observations about colonial violence, perpetual care, and sacrifice zones."

—Jen Moore, former Latin American coordinator for
MiningWatch Canada

UNEARTHING JUSTICE

JOAN KUYEK

UNEARTHING JUSTICE

HOW TO PROTECT YOUR COMMUNITY FROM THE MINING INDUSTRY

FOREWORD BY
JOHN CUTFEET

BETWEEN THE LINES
TORONTO

Unearthing Justice
© 2019 Joan Kuyek

First published in 2019 by
Between the Lines
401 Richmond Street West
Studio 281
Toronto, Ontario M5V 3A8
Canada
1-800-718-7201
www.btlbooks.com

Library and Archives Canada Cataloguing in Publication

Title: Unearthing justice : how to protect your community from the mining industry / Joan
  Kuyek ; foreword by John Cutfeet.
Names: Kuyek, Joan, 1942- author. | Cutfeet, John, writer of foreword.
Description: Includes bibliographical references and index.
Identifiers: Canadiana (print) 20190139374 | Canadiana (ebook) 20190139382 | ISBN
  9781771134514 (softcover) | ISBN 9781771134521 (EPUB) | ISBN 9781771134538 (PDF)
Subjects: LCSH: Mineral industries—Canada. | LCSH: Mines and mineral resources—Can-
  ada. | LCSH: Environmental policy—Canada—Citizen participation. | LCSH: Environ-
  mental protection—Canada—Citizen participation. | CSH: Native peoples—Canada—Pol-
  itics and government.
Classification: LCC HD9506.C22 K89 2019 | DDC 338.20971—dc23

Cover and interior illustrations by Nicole Burton
Designed and typeset by DEEVE
Printed in Canada

We acknowledge for their financial support of our publishing activities: the Government of
Canada; the Canada Council for the Arts, which last year invested $153 million to bring the
arts to Canadians throughout the country; and the Government of Ontario through the Ontario Arts Council, the Ontario Book Publishers Tax Credit program, and Ontario Creates.

   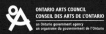

For Donna and all the water and land protectors
challenging the Canadian mining industry.

CONTENTS

PART V
HOW TO PUT MINING IN ITS PLACE

FOREWORD

Finally, a long overdue book that shines a light into the oftentimes dark, murky world of mining, exposing a tradition that has always been cloaked under economic prosperity without taking into consideration the real costs to human health and the environment. This book brings to the surface the process of mining and its very real impacts on people who live close to the land.

In a world often far removed from the view of mainstream society, and as mining companies and shareholders celebrate the financial gains reaped by operating mines, communities, and particularly Indigenous communities, are faced with the potential destruction of lands and waters that have sustained their cultures for centuries, leaving them with what is referred to as a "culture of contamination."

From the effects of the Mount Polley disaster—and it was a disaster, not only for the millions of salmon that use those waterways to reach their spawning grounds, but also for the people and communities that use the salmon to sustain life—to the struggle of both settler and Indigenous communities dispossessed of lands and waters, Joan Kuyek shines truth onto the fallacies perpetuated by government and industry that mines are "little holes in the ground" and a "temporary use of land."

There is nothing "temporary" about the impacts of mining on ecosystems, many of which have been used for generations by people who live close to and survive off these lands.

I first met Joan in her role as national coordinator of MiningWatch Canada during a difficult period in the history of my home community of Kitchenuhmaykoosib Inninuwug (KI, to those who cannot pronounce the official title for our community). A junior exploration company had come onto Kitchenuhmaykoosib *Aaki* (land) in 2006 without the knowledge or authorization of Kitchenuhmaykoosib Inninuwug as a collective. In the struggle that continued well into 2008, culminating in the courtroom drama of having to release the KI leadership from incarceration, Joan's support and vast knowledge of mining (reflected in this amazing book)—and including other resources at her disposal—were available to KI during this time of great turmoil and conflict in this remote community of just over 1,500 people.

Joan worked tirelessly to assist KI by attending court hearings after we were sued for $10 billion when KI protested a proposed drilling program. Joan's support was evident as she brought awareness to the main issue: the need to reform the antiquated *Mining Act* in Ontario. As Joan has said, "The problem here is the antiquated 'free-entry' system that allows mining and exploration without consultation with affected First Nations communities or consideration of other values such as ecological values, trapping, hunting, clean water or even consideration of climate change impacts."

When six members of KI (including five members of Chief and Council) were sentenced to six months of incarceration for not allowing the mining company access to KI homelands in contempt of a Superior Court ruling to provide immediate access, Joan continued her support of KI through letter-writing campaigns, media releases, and the mobilization of support networks. Joan came to KI to decipher the technical jargon mostly unheard of at the community level and was able to paint a clear picture of the mining industry to Kitchenuhmaykoosib Inninuwug.

She understood the concept of *Kanawayandan D'aaki*, the spiritual mandate provided to KI to protect and steward the lands and resources—and the need for alternative economies that are sustainable to ensure the survival of Kitchenuhmaykoosib Inninuwug and its future generations. This book provides the same insight for people who are looking at ways to develop strategies that move beyond the core sampling and mine tailings.

As she so generously shared and supported KI in times of strife, Joan shares her fifty-plus years of experience, her knowledge and wisdom in these pages, allowing us a glimpse into an industry that she has explored for most of her working life. From policies and legislation, boardrooms and stocks markets, to the coal mines of Nova Scotia and the dumping of mine tailings into the Rose Creek, which flows into the Pelly River system in the Yukon, this book paints a picture of the true costs and impacts of the mining industry on the environment and, more importantly, the lives of the people it touches, be they positive or negative, short or long term.

Joan breaks down the impacts of chemicals used in the mining industry and their effects on humans and wildlife. She describes how cyanide, sulphuric acid, ammonia, chlorine, and hydrochloric acid impact humans and the environment. The price of prosperity is measured against the cost of human health, wildlife, the environment, and the future.

This tool developed by Joan will provide many with access to the experience and knowledge that we had during the conflict in KI. If you are facing uncertainties from mining and are looking to gain insight into a complex industry whose impacts are felt in a huge way on the ground, Joan's unique insight can support the development of strategies that can help you put mining in its place.

With government and industry pushing to mine, mine, and mine, in often impoverished Indigenous and settler communities alike, Joan's book is a solid rock on which to build to protect what is yours and mine.

—John Cutfeet, Kitchenuhmaykoosib Inninuwug,
December 2018

INTRODUCTION

MINING AND COMMUNITY RESISTANCE IN CANADA

This book is intended to help communities, organizations, and individuals who find themselves defending the land, waters, and people they cherish from the impacts of mining. As Jacinda Mack says in her presentations about the effects of the Mount Polley Mine disaster in 2014, "This is a love story": a story about how we can protect those places we love "to clear the path so our children don't have to carry as much."[1]

Maybe you are defending a watershed against a new mine. You might be trying to deal with the toxic by-products of an existing mine and/or smelter. Maybe your town is facing the closure of a mine that is your major source of income. Your community might be affected by the legacy of waste and unpaid property taxes from an abandoned mine. It might be that you are upset by the tales of murder and pillage linked to Canadian mining companies operating internationally. Maybe you are just curious.

This is a personal story, in which I want to share what I have learned through decades of experience working to limit the damage caused by the mining industry in Canada. I spent thirty years as a community organizer in Sudbury (the largest mining community in Canada), ten years as the founding national coordinator of MiningWatch Canada, and the past ten years (and counting) working as a consultant to communities affected by mining in Canada. I also developed and taught a course called Mining Law, Policy, and Communities at Algoma University, which I later co-taught with a legal practitioner at Queen's University Law School. In this time, I have been up close and personal with some of the worst and best of mining. The book is anchored in this experience, and in the stories I have been privileged to hear from people and organizations on the front lines.

Daniel Ashini, the chief negotiator for the Innu with the Voisey's Bay Mine,[2] said in 1999:

> As I'm sure you all know very well, dealing with industrial developments such as mines involves much more than protesting. It also involves participating in environmental assessments, attending co-management meetings, and having big arguments with the governments over things like the definition of consultation.
>
> I have a lot of experience in these matters, but I wish it weren't so. I wish I had never heard of these things that I am going to talk to you about. I wish I could use my time to try to solve the problems of my community instead of always fighting these developments. This takes up a lot of my time, time that I could be spending with my family and friends in the community or in the country.

Mining is the story of loss. All kinds of loss. Of lives. Of land. Of water. Of livelihoods. Of good governance. Of future possibilities. In Canada, we have created an economy that is dependent on extraction, that creates profits from loss.

The powerful mining industry controls information about its costs and benefits; propagates its own myths about its importance and history; shapes government law, regulation, and policy; and ensures that Canadian and Indigenous peoples pay so it may succeed.

Of course, we depend on metals. Of course, mining, smelting, and metal manufacturing create jobs and contribute to Canada's GDP. I am writing this book with equipment made from petrochemicals and metals, in a home where metals have been used for the stove, the fridge, and the furnace, and I get around with a car, buses, trains, and a bike. That said, we need to treat these metals we take for granted with respect. We need to understand their awesome cost: in terms of workers' lives, Indigenous displacement and dispossession, environmental degradation and destruction, inequality and political distortions.

Minerals are not inexhaustible. Deposits that we can afford to mine are being depleted, and the environmental and social costs of extracting them are increasing. The waste left behind will burden future generations forever.

For centuries, miners have been proud of the sacrifices they make to produce the minerals on which we depend. Like the rest of us, people who work in the mining industry want to feel that the work they do every day helps not only their families, but also their community, the environment, and the planet.

The owners of mining companies know full well that the willingness of people to work for them is not easily got. These days, most "mining as good citizen" hype is directed as much at workers as at governments.

If we were to respect the full costs of producing metals and diamonds, we would ask: Do we really need this metal or gem? What will it be used for? Can it be obtained by recycling? Can it be reused? What damage will its production do to the environment? To democratic governance? To future generations? Are there less damaging ways in which it may be produced? How dangerous is its production and transport to workers? How will it contribute to healing the earth and to greater equality? How will the benefits and costs from producing it be distributed? How much will taxpayers be required to subsidize it? How long will the benefits last, and what costs and legacy will remain post-extraction? What opportunities to do something different now or in the future are lost or overlooked?

Mining is the ultimate expression of the violence of colonialism. Pillaging the earth for minerals and gems in order to build our industrial and unequal society, mining takes place on lands that are being stolen from Indigenous people both directly and indirectly through a flawed treaty negotiation, interpretation, and enforcement process. Dispossessed by the Canadian state of their lands and resources, many Indigenous people are deeply impoverished and forced to take what jobs and revenues the corporate masters are willing to share. After the minerals and gems are gone, the land remains despoiled, home to toxic wastes that will have to be managed forever.

HOW THIS BOOK IS ORGANIZED

This book is organized into five parts.

Part I, What Mining Looks Like, is intended to help understand this complicated industry: the physical footprint of an operating mining camp and the sequence of mining operations through prospecting, development, operations, smelting, and closure, and key environmental impacts on water and air.

Part II, What It Costs, opens with a brief overview of mining's colonial context and discusses the key social impacts. Within this part, there are chapters on working for the mining industry and what happens after the mine is closed.

Part III, Profits from Loss, provides an overview of the structure of the industry and its relationship to financial markets and discusses mining as an externalizing machine.

Part IV, Justice or Just Us, describes the relationships among the mining lobby, the regulatory system, and the tax regime in Canada, and provides a synopsis of Canada's role in mining internationally. A chapter on uranium mining in Canada provides a case study.

Part V, How to Put Mining in Its Place, is all about organizing for change. It provides stories and some learnings from community struggles at each stage of the mining sequence. There are chapters on effective international solidarity work, corporate research and campaigns, and discussions of what it takes to change law, regulation, and policy. The concluding chapter, Creating a New Story: Putting Mining in Its Place, summarizes key strategies to limit the power of the mining industry in Canada, and to respect the awesome cost of the minerals we take for granted.

The endnotes to each chapter offer a few key resources for those wanting more information.

In order to keep this book "user-friendly," I have had to limit stories and explanations that could be much more detailed. I am well aware that there are many other stories that could be told, many more activists that could be celebrated, many other aspects of mining that could be explored. The book is also largely limited to metal and diamond mining and does not have space to talk about the differences in the mining and processing of industrial minerals such as potash, coal, and asbestos.

Sections of this book are based on materials that have been previously published by MiningWatch Canada. Although I have tried to tell the reader where this is the case, my history is so bound up with that organization that I may have missed some instances. I am deeply indebted to the board and staff at MiningWatch for the permission they have given me.

In addition, I acknowledge that some parts of *Unearthing Justice* incorporate analysis from two previous books I wrote on community organizing: *Fighting for Hope* (Black Rose, 1990) and *Community Organizing* (Fernwood, 2011).

I also want to thank those who read early drafts of the book and made helpful suggestions, including Jen Moore, Sakura Saunders, Donna Ashamock, David Peerla, Susan Kennedy, John Cutfeet, and Bessa Whitmore. Opinions and mistakes in this book are entirely mine. Thank you to Nicole Marie Burton for her wonderful drawings. I owe a huge debt to my editor and others at Between the Lines. I also want to recognize the support I received from the Ontario Arts Council for this work.

Of course, this book would not have been written without the stories, activism, and analysis of dedicated people all over Canada and around the world who spend their lives putting mining in its place. Thank you.

PART I

WHAT MINING LOOKS LIKE

The chapters in this section are a tough but essential read. They describe the physical impact of mining, starting with the enormous environmental footprint of an operating mine in chapter 1.

The next chapter describes how mining and smelting actually happen, from the staking of a claim through construction and operations to the mine's closure. The operations of the mine include a description of how the desired metals and gems are removed from the host rock, and what happens to the wastes after their removal.

Next, the key environmental impacts on water, air, and land at different stages of mining are discussed.

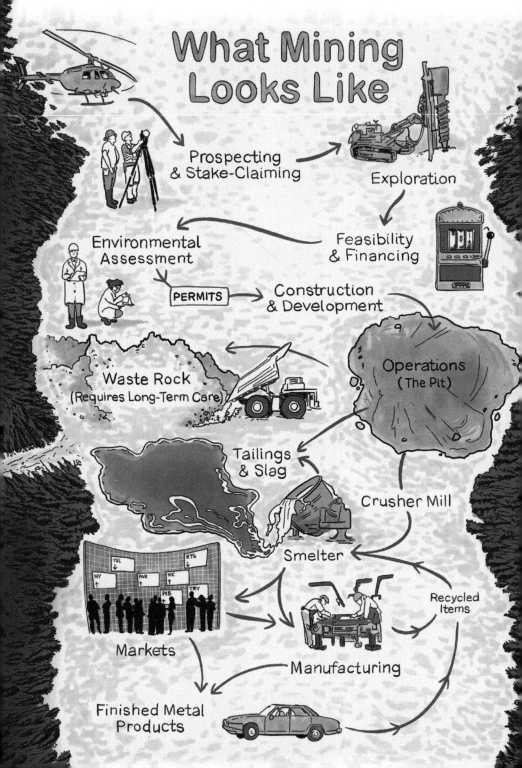

1

THE PHYSICAL FOOTPRINT OF A MINE

I am flying over Sudbury on a clear autumn day. I can see the city and the surrounding towns, the roads and railways, power lines, rivers, lakes, and hills. But I also see three huge turquoise and rusty-orange tailings lakes (one thirty-five square kilometres in size), the Glencore and Vale smelters, and the old refineries. Everywhere there are blackened slag heaps and waste rock piles. A number of open-pit mines dot the surface, as do the head frames of underground mines. Smoke streams from the superstack. From this height, I am aware of how much the footprint of these mines has grown since my last flight just a few years ago. Despite reclamation and re-greening programs, the mines and their wastes are quickly devouring the landscape.

The mining industry likes to say that mines are just "a little hole in the ground"[1] and are a "temporary use of the land."[2] This is not true. This chapter provides an overview of the extent of the footprint of an operating mine and offers some important definitions for understanding mining.

The minerals and gems we mine are the product of movements of the earth's crust over billions of years. Although they are scattered in various concentrations everywhere in the earth's rocks, to be concentrated into deposits that are economically viable, they have undergone dramatic heating, cooling, and gravity separation. Metals have different weights and different specific gravity. As the earth's crust dances with the shifting of tectonic plates, the eruption of volcanoes, the impact of meteorites, and the cooling effects of water, mineral deposits—of gold, copper, uranium, zinc, diamonds—are formed.

We call these deposits *ore bodies*.

To get to the ore body, the mining company will have to displace any people from the land where the mine will be built, then remove the overburden—the trees, plants, and soil—covering it, and then remove the rock surrounding or covering the ore body.

The amount of desired metals or gems in the ore body is called the *grade*. Depending on what metal or gem you are talking about, this may be shown as grams per ton or ounces per ton (for gold), a percentage of the metal in the ore body (copper), or carats per ton (diamonds). In Canada and elsewhere, the grade of ore has been decreasing as deposits that are profitable to mine are being used up. It used to be that copper grade had to be 4 to 5 percent and gold grade 5 grams per ton (gpt) before it was considered worth mining. But now the Gibraltar Mine in British Columbia has ore with a copper grade of 0.26 percent and a molybdenum grade of 0.008 percent; the Mount Milligan Mine (also in British Columbia) grades 0.19 percent for copper and 0.3 gpt for gold.

Mining is a waste management industry. The process creates an extremely high volume of waste: the overburden, the waste rock that is removed to get to the ore, and the ore body that has been crushed into powder at the mill and rejected, called *tailings*. Some mines dispose of almost 100 percent of the rock they smash up, along with various chemicals that are added in the course of extracting the minerals. The volume will definitely be larger than it was before mining because of the blasting and milling process.

Mining is a rapid, ferocious, and continuous assault on the earth. A mine's footprint gets bigger every day it operates. Although it may take a long time to get permits, financing, plans, and equipment in place to start operating (something the industry complains loudly about), once the company has all this, a new road and a few holes in the ground can become a two-kilometre-wide, five-hundred-metre-deep open pit within a few years. In ten to fifteen years, the deposit will likely be mined out and the mine will be closed. Unless, of course, the company discovers a new ore body nearby, and then the process will continue.

Mining happens in two main ways: underground mines and open pits (or a combination of the two). The type of mine is determined by the nature of the ore body. If the ore body is concentrated, then underground mining may be possible. If, however, it is dispersed and low grade, an open pit is the only economic option for the company.

The tunnels and shafts of underground mines can extend for kilometres under old mining districts like Timmins and Sudbury, and will go down until the ore runs out or until heat from the centre of the earth makes it impossible to continue. The Kidd Mine in Timmins is the world's deepest base-metal mine below sea level, with a mine that is almost three kilometres deep.

Open-pit mines are among the largest human-made structures on earth. The Bingham Canyon Mine, located southwest of Salt Lake City, Utah, in production since 1906, is the deepest open-pit mine in the world and is more than 1.2 kilometres deep and approximately 4 kilometres wide. The Dome Mine open pit in Timmins removed over 286 million tons of gold-bearing rock over more than one hundred years to create a hole 340 metres deep and 800 to 900 metres across.

Diamonds are found in "kimberlite pipes," carrot-shaped intrusions into the earth's crust of magma from deep in the earth, where carbon from ancient forests has been trapped and compressed into diamonds. Two diamond mine complexes, Ekati and Diavik, are both located in the Lac de Gras area of the Northwest Territories, about three hundred kilometres north of Yellowknife. Ekati was the first diamond mine in Canada, and it started mining its first pipe in 1998. Just twenty years later, it has six open pits and three underground mines. The mine itself is only one part of the footprint, as the following section illustrates.

THE DIAVIK FOOTPRINT

The Diavik Diamond Mine in the Northwest Territories is one of the largest open-pit mines in the world and provides an excellent example of the awesome size of open-pit mines.[3]

Situated on an island in Lac de Gras in the Northwest Territories, the mine has produced roughly eight million carats a year since it opened in 2003. It consists of three open pits (with another being developed).

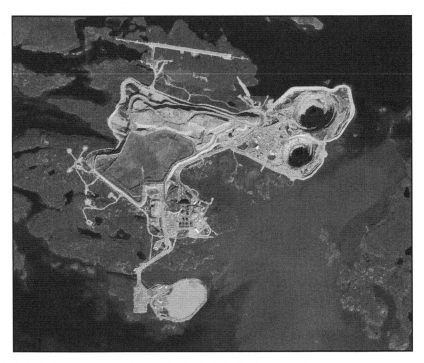

Satellite image of the Northwest Territories' Diavik Diamond Mine.
Image from Planet Labs, Inc., 2016. Creative Commons 4.0 License.

The slope of pit walls is a major concern for mine engineers as the walls have to be designed so that the rock benches don't collapse or slide. Most pit walls cannot withstand an angle greater than forty to forty-five degrees from horizontal. As a result, the radius of the pit gets bigger and bigger the deeper it goes.[4] At a certain point, the mine can only be continued with underground tunnels. When Diavik faced this problem in 2012, the mine's life was extended with further mining underground.

The waste from the pits—waste rock that is not used for road and dike construction—is stored in processed kimberlite piles (tailings) and in waste rock dumps.

[To get at the kimberlite pipes under Lac de Gras specially designed dikes had to be built to hold the water back. The lake had to be dredged], placing several million tons of crushed rock into the lake to create the dikes themselves, anchoring the dikes to the bedrock, transferring fish from the enclosed areas back into the lake, and removing several million cubic meters of water from the enclosed areas. . . .

The two initial crushed-rock dikes . . . [surrounding the first two pipes] total more than five kilometers in length. They stand as high as 32 meters above the lake bed and are wide enough to allow two large vehicles to pass one another. The dikes were constructed using 4.5 million tonnes of granite waste rock.

[Located 300 kilometres northeast of Yellowknife in the Barrens of the Northwest Territories,] the mine must operate as a self-contained community. [As of 2017], the site covers 10.5 square kilometers and contains a dormitory complex, a dining area, recreational and education facilities, an office and main-tenance building, a warehouse, and an enclosed maintenance facility where even the largest hauling trucks used at the mine can be worked on year-round. Emergency response and medical services are also available.[5]

The complex also houses a processing plant, power and boiler plants, fuel tanks, and water and sewage processing facilities. An explosives plant and storage facility are also on site. It is serviced by a six-hundred-kilometre ice road built by the owners of the Ekati and Diavik mines.[6] The Diavik airport, with a 1,600-metre gravel runway, is big enough for a Boeing 737 jet. Power is largely provided by diesel generators; a wind farm provides 11 percent of the energy requirements.[7]

Like Diavik, all mines extend their physical impact beyond the mine site through roads, power lines, railways, and ports. They may require hydro dams and the creation of large reservoirs to get their power. They are major producers of greenhouse gases, and major users of water.

Roads are often the most serious problem created by a mine. They can affect animal and plant distribution, kill many animals, and create impassable barriers for others. In addition to habitat loss, roads also enable exotic species to invade and out-compete native plants. They create an "edge effect" that can change microclimates, cause blowdowns in windstorms, and change predator-prey relationships among birds and other animals.[8] They can also dramatically affect the culture and economies of previously isolated communities.

Surface mining operations and tailings impoundments create lots of dust. The dust is frequently toxic. Open-pit mine projects, many of which operate twenty-four hours a day, create high levels of noise and light pollution. Blasting in mines, both open pit and underground, can affect the local water table and local well conditions, as well as the structural integrity of buildings. In Sudbury, blasting in underground mines shook nearby houses. In Malartic, Quebec, residents living in houses beside an open pit that expands on a daily basis are subjected to flying dust and debris, noise, and shaking. In communities with underground mines, tunnels can collapse, creating huge sinkholes.

During a mine's operational period, for both underground and open-pit mines, managing water is a serious issue. Water is pumped out to keep the mine dry and to allow access to the ore body. Pumped water may be used in the extraction process, sent to the tailings impoundments, used for activities like dust control, or discharged as a waste. The water can be very acidic and laden with high concentrations of toxic heavy metals, including methyl mercury, or with radionuclides. More on these environmental impacts, which can impair human and ecosystem health, can be found in chapter 3.

2

THE MINING SEQUENCE

Many people dealing with the mining industry do not understand the relationship between staking claims, exploration, and mine operation and closure—the mining sequence[1]—and the actual process of getting the desired minerals out of the rock. This chapter explains how this all works. Although it touches on environmental and social issues, these are explored in more depth in other chapters of the book.

Even before a prospector stakes a claim to a potential deposit, geological mapping will have been undertaken. Then, progressively detailed exploration, economic, and environmental assessments will take place. If the project looks like it is rich enough, then a mine will be built.

It has been estimated that out of ten thousand claims, only one ever becomes a mine.[2] The mine is likely to operate until the minerals are depleted and the mine is closed. It may be "abandoned" by the owner if it no longer makes money. Even after closure, the mine site will usually need to be maintained forever in order to manage the toxic wastes it will continue to generate for hundreds and—probably—thousands of years to come. Most mines in Canada are active for ten to fifteen years at the longest, although they may be part of a "mining camp" like Sudbury, a number of mines and exploration sites clustered together.

We start with a story.

THE MOUNT MILLIGAN MINE

Prospector Richard Hanslinger claimed a copper-gold deposit that he called Mount Milligan near Fort St. James, British Columbia, in 1984. A number of different owners explored the site, but it was not until February 2014 that a mine was in full production. The mine was expected to produce 81 million pounds of copper and 195,000 ounces of gold annually over a twenty-two-year mine life. At the peak of construction, there were more than one thousand people at work on the site. During regular operations it employs about four hundred people.

Before it was called Mount Milligan, the area where the proposed open-pit mine would be located was known to the Nak'azdli people as Shus Nadloh. It is a sacred area and an important watershed. It was the trapline—the *keyoh*—of the Sam family. The Nak'azdli were fiercely opposed to the mine. They knew that

> building and operating the proposed Mt. Milligan mine near Prince George meant turning a two kilometer long, fish bearing creek into a waste dump for potentially acid-leaching rock. The move to use the King Richard Creek Valley for waste disposal would result in almost three hundred million tonnes of waste rock being dumped into the creek, eliminating all fish and marine life.[3]

Even so, the mine owner claimed that the company could restore the area and replace fish habitat, and the government allowed the company to proceed.

After four years of mining, the Sam keyoh and other trapline areas are completely destroyed, and the First Nations cannot use the site. A study undertaken in 2012 by the University of Victoria, the Norman B. Keevil School of Mining Engineering, the Nak'azdli and Tl'azt'en First Nations, and the Municipality of Fort St. James detailed how, even during mine construction, the communities became a through-way for mining equipment and trucks, and how the people became dependent on a small income from the mine.[4] (A few Band members worked there.[5]) Centerra Gold, the company that owns the mine, is now demanding access to more water sources in order to continue mining.

In the following sections, we will look at a detailed description of each stage in the mining sequence.

STAKING A CLAIM

The federal government and all provincial governments in Canada undertake geological surveys: maps and reports that show mineralogic and geologic strata in their jurisdiction and reports of former exploration. Prospectors rely on these studies and also look for others' success, former mines, and rumours about "big finds."

The prospector will then claim an area that they think might have an ore body where mining could be profitable. By staking a claim, they gain the exclusive right to search for minerals on the property and to develop any discoveries.

In the past, most claim-staking of a property was physical; it involved setting posts and cutting lines to delineate the claim. These days, most provinces and territories now require map staking or Internet staking, establishing rights to minerals by identifying the area on a map and paying a small fee. The rights granted by the claim vary by provincial and territorial jurisdiction and can be the subject of considerable controversy.

Free Entry

Across the country, claim-staking takes place under a free-entry tenure system, with a few modifications.

In most jurisdictions, surface and subsurface rights to land are separated from each other, with subsurface rights held by the Crown (the federal and/or provincial government), even when the surface rights are privately held and occupied by residences, farms, or recreational properties. Surface rights holders' interests are seen as secondary to mineral, or subsurface, rights.

There are some exceptions in areas of the country that were colonized earlier, like southern Ontario and older parts of Quebec, where the land grants included mineral rights (called *patent lands* or *pioneer land grants*). Because taxes had to be paid on these subsurface rights, they frequently reverted to the Crown when the taxes were not paid.

Most "Crown land" is in fact Indigenous territory, and the rights are likely to be in dispute (see chapters 4 and 12). Staking is not allowed on land belonging to Indian reserves or on lands to which First Nations, Métis, or Inuit hold a title that includes mineral rights. For example, in areas like Nunavut and Nunatsiavut, a percentage of land is set aside as "Inuit land" and can only be staked with agreement from the Indigenous government. Under the federal Indian Mining Regulations, there is a process by which Indigenous and Northern Affairs Canada (with permission from the Band Council) can open reserve lands for exploration.[6]

The free-entry system was developed in Europe in the 1500s, largely to serve the financial needs of warring noble clans, where kings had an interest in keeping the coffers full in order to pay the military.[7] The free-entry system is based upon the following premises:

- All Crown lands are open for staking and mineral exploration unless they are expressly excluded or withdrawn by law.
- The person who stakes a claim has the right to develop a mine on the claim.
- Mineral tenures are appropriately granted on a "first come, first served" basis.
- Mineral potential is so valuable that it warrants leaving the staked area essentially unregulated and potentially unusable for other purposes.[8]

In North America, the free-entry system was introduced to keep prospectors from killing each other in the California gold fields. In Canada, it was first codified to regulate a gold rush in British Columbia and became the *Gold Fields Act of British Columbia* in 1859. As miners loved it, it spread across the country.

In 1997, the Department of Indian and Northern Affairs set out the ridiculous justification for government support of free entry, saying: "The licensed staking of mineral claims is among the least intrusive of all mining activities and causes relatively little disturbance to the land. The effects of this activity are not very different from those of many unlicensed uses of Crown land such as hunting, fishing, hiking and eco-system assessment."

While the mechanics vary slightly from one jurisdiction to the next, the way the free-entry system usually operates is as follows.

The prospector, or free miner, must obtain a prospecting licence. These are available, generally, to anyone over eighteen years of age for a small fee, usually around twenty-five dollars. Some provinces, like Ontario, require applicants to complete an online and ungraded test. The licence then gives the individual the right to prospect for minerals on any lands in the province or territory for which the licence has been granted, subject to a few exceptions. These include the very few lands with Aboriginal title, areas withdrawn by a minister's order, private lands where the mineral rights have not been severed from surface rights, a few excepted land uses such as cemeteries or occupied houses, or—in most jurisdictions—parks and protected areas.

In most jurisdictions, the prospector is required to advise the surface rights holder and/or the Indigenous government of their claim. In Quebec, the prospector needs the permission of a landholder to proceed, but, once the claim is turned into a licence, can expropriate the land from the landholder (which does not include Indigenous peoples in the *Mining Act*) for compensation if they say no. The expropriation requires permission from the province. The right of Indigenous peoples to withhold consent to exploration is disputed by the Crown in almost all jurisdictions.

There may be permits required to proceed, but most governments argue that they have no discretion to refuse the permits. The Ross River Dena in Yukon successfully challenged this argument in 2012. The judge's comments in the case are important:

> The Government of Yukon says that because the granting of a mineral claim is automatic when the statutory requirements are met, there is no duty to consult. . . . It should be noted that the statutory and regulatory scheme that is in place is not as devoid of discretion as the Crown suggests. Section 15 of the Quartz Mining Act allows the government broad discretion to prohibit the location of quartz mining claims on particular lands. . . . I do not, in any event, accept the Crown's argument that the absence of statutory discretion in relation to the recording of claims under the Quartz Mining Act absolves the Crown of its duty to consult.[9]

In Yukon, the requirement has been generally interpreted as requiring consultation before any early exploration can take place on Indigenous lands. For Ross River, consultation is required before staking. The Supreme Court of Canada refused to hear the case when the Yukon government appealed. In Ontario in July 2018, another decision quashed an exploration permit and found that the provincial government failed to properly consult the Eabametoong First Nation before Landore Resources Canada began early exploration.[10]

After having staked the mineral claim, the prospector has the exclusive right to exploit the minerals beneath the surface of the claim area, even if they damage property on the surface. In most provinces and territories, they have to get an early exploration permit before proceeding. The prospector also has to conduct a certain amount of mineral exploration—measured by expenditure per hectare or per claim—within a set time frame or forfeit the claim.

In 2018, Nova Scotia varied from this practice by deciding to ask for requests for proposals for advanced gold mining exploration in the Eastern Cobequid Highlands in northern Nova Scotia, a mostly forested area of thirty thousand hectares. The area just happens to provide the drinking water for Tatamagouche.[11]

The free-entry system creates an expectation on the part of the industry, and a practice on the part of governments, that all mining permits will be granted. The instances of mine permits being refused are few and far between.[12]

In most cases, mineral claims and leases are transferred and sold between companies—sometimes for millions of dollars—without government approval and without the consent of the Indigenous governments involved (although this is frequently a matter of dispute).

Past performance and a track record of socially and environmentally damaging practices on the part of any particular operator are not factors in the free-entry system. As a result, mine operators that have left a trail of destruction in their wake, like Peggy Witte of Royal Oak Mines, Robert Friedland of Ivanhoe Mines, or Clifford Frame of the Westray Mine disaster, are treated like any other prospector when they stake claims.[13]

The free-entry system usually prevents governments from collecting royalties and rents associated with the development of the resource unless and until a mine is developed.

By giving pre-eminence to mining interests, the free-entry system limits the land from being allocated for other uses. This is exacerbated by policies that block development of land for other uses when there are mining interests, such as Quebec's *Land Use Planning and Development Act*.[14]

Mining for Compensation

Free entry inevitably leads to conflicts. When opposition to a mining project becomes too strong, governments increasingly buy out the claims to avoid a legal challenge to the free-entry system, and thus, leave the underlying regulatory structure that led to the conflict intact.

The British Columbia *Mineral Claims Compensation Act* (1992) sets out how holders of withdrawn claims are to be compensated. It resulted from a dispute with Geddes Resources. The company held the claims at Windy Craggy, a copper-gold project on the earthquake-prone and wild Tatshenshini River on the BC–Alaska border, and the potential mine was strongly opposed by environmentalists in both countries. By 1992, the Province of British Columbia was ready to turn the site into a provincial park, but Geddes wanted millions in compensation for its mining claims.

Ultimately, a deal was struck to give Royal Oak Mines (a Geddes affiliate) the permits for their new Kemess South Mine and financial assistance to cover the infrastructure costs. This assistance amounted to $29 million cash compensation to Geddes, $20 million to an exploration fund, $50 million for on- and offsite infrastructure costs, and $49 million to cover the cost of a 320-kilometre hydro line.[15] Peggy Witte of Geddes and Royal Oak purchased the Kemess claims for $67.9 million. The First Nation upon whose land the mine was built—the Sekani—got nothing.

In Ontario, since amendments in 2011, key disputes between First Nations and exploration companies have been settled by the government withdrawing land from staking and then paying compensation to the mining companies. Platinex got $5 million; God's Lake Resources, $3.5 million. In Quebec in 2017, Copper One claims in Barriere Lake,

Algonquin territory, were purchased by Quebec's mining exploration Crown corporation SOQUEM for $8 million.

We call this *mining for compensation.*

EXPLORATION

In the provinces of Alberta, Nova Scotia, Ontario, and Prince Edward Island, anyone wishing to do mineral exploration on their claims must first apply for and obtain an exploration or land use permit. Although governments claim they do not have discretion to decide whether and on what terms they will issue permits, the Ross River decision described earlier in this chapter challenges this. Quebec has rules about surface damages around early exploration but does not require a permit until granting the mining lease (discussed later in the chapter).

The prospector (usually a mining company by this point) reviews any geochemical and/or geophysical surveys for the claim area, as well as maps and geological reports. The company undertakes helicopter surveys to look for visible mineralization and magnetic fields. If the company is looking for uranium, they will also check for radiation. Noise from helicopter fly-overs, drill rigs, and ATVs and four-by-fours is known to disrupt geese, caribou, mountain sheep, and goats, as well as people in the area.[16]

Exploring a mining claim often includes soil sampling for metals from a series of holes and "grab" samples, made up of random pieces of small rock that are believed to be representative

Exploration Sequence

- Mapping
- Surveys
- Initial Samples
- Stripping & Trenching
- Drilling
- Bulk Sampling

Mining Exploration Sequence
Source: Natural Resources Canada.

of all the material present. These samples are sent off to an assay lab for evaluation.

Exploration also includes groundwork to remove the overburden to expose any mineral-bearing rocks below. The overburden includes soils and subsoils, fungi, plants, and trees. Although rarely mentioned by the industry, it also includes the animals and the people who depend on them. Trenching, power washing, and/or stripping remove the soil and vegetation down to bedrock. Even if the trenching is done carefully—using a backhoe to remove the topsoil, then the deeper materials, and then refilling the trench using the same materials, replacing them in reverse order—the intricate community of trees and plants, soil layers, fungi, and microbial activity is disturbed. This material expands as much as 20 percent or more after excavation, which means the materials cannot all be returned to the same trench.[17]

If the claim continues to be promising, the next stage of exploration involves drilling core samples. These samples determine if the ore is economically feasible to mine. Drilling may cost from \$35 to \$120 (USD) per metre, which does not include the associated costs, like camp construction, moving the equipment, and site preparation.[18] Prior to this stage, the company needs to raise substantial investment.

Drills often go thousands of metres through solid rock to produce sample rock cores, which are then assayed for the presence of valuable minerals. If initial drill samples look promising, more drilling will be done, usually in a grid, and the results will be analyzed to create a three-dimensional map of the ore body. The drill cores will be stored at the mine site on wooden racks.

Environmental concerns related to drilling include spills or leaks of fuels, oils, and drilling fluids into soils or local water bodies.[19] Storage of the drill cores can cause problems: physical hazards as well as environmental impacts like acid mine drainage, metal leaching, or radiation. Even when exploring for other minerals, thorium and uranium may be present, and the release of radon gas to the surface is a concern to human and animal health.[20] It can be released from the drill holes themselves, but also from drill cores and rock samples.

The equipment for exploration has to be brought to the site. This may require ATV trails, roads, and stream crossings, and even airstrips. There is likely to be an exploration camp for workers at any remote site with its attendant problems. The impacts of exploration are spread over a vast area. When there is a "staking rush" the effects are multiplied, with as many as forty companies exploring in nearby areas.

Although most provinces and territories now require some kind of reclamation following exploration activity, this is poorly enforced.

BULK SAMPLING/ADVANCED EXPLORATION

If the results from early exploration look promising and the money can be raised for further work, the next step is bulk sampling or advanced exploration, with extensive metallurgical studies and test milling to see if the mine is economically feasible. Advanced exploration investigates the continuity of the mineralized zone and provides information about rock stability and structure and possible water flows.[21]

In effect, this means the creation of a small test mine: building a small open pit, and sinking a mine shaft, or driving a decline or mine adit into a hillside (a mine adit is a horizontal mine shaft). It always involves the removal of large volumes of ore. Bulk samples range from one to one thousand tons, or more. Test milling procedures may be done in laboratories using small samples, in test plants available in certain localities, or in pilot mills erected to mill pre-commercial quantities, such as one hundred tons per day. The test mine may also need a waste rock dump and a tailings impoundment.

Before undertaking advanced exploration, a company will usually convert their claims into mine leases. Leases are often for twenty-one years, although regulation varies by province. Again, in most cases governments do have discretion to decide whether and on what terms a lease can be issued.

Quebec has the most stringent rules, requiring a feasibility study and a number of other conditions before a mining lease will be granted.

Under Ontario's mining laws, bulk sampling of over one thousand tons makes an exploration project an advanced exploration project, with requirements to develop and file a closure plan with the Ministry of Northern Development and Mines and provide public notice.[22]

All of these activities—and their associated impacts—are part of a company deciding if it can go ahead with an operating mine, and except in jurisdictions that provide for environmental assessments of advanced exploration, all of this activity will take place prior to any environmental review of the mine proposal.

FEASIBILITY STUDIES, ENVIRONMENTAL ASSESSMENT, AND PERMITTING

At the advanced exploration stage, the mining company will usually undertake a pre-feasibility study (also called a *scoping study*) or feasibility study to examine questions of profitability and prepare the company to go to financiers for money to develop a mine. The studies are expected to comply with mineral estimate rules developed by investment regulators (known as *NI 43-101*). These rules are discussed in chapter 8.

The costs of actual mine development are enormous, often reaching billions of dollars, and the company will be unable to interest backers without the study. This is also discussed more in chapter 8.

Detailed engineering studies needed to build the mine will be undertaken. The studies contain conclusions about optimal design (and estimated costs) for the mine pit and/or underground shafts; design of the mill; equipment required; precise design of waste management areas for waste rock, storage for tailings, solid waste, and sewage; and location and design of administration buildings. Depending on location, mine design and development are likely to include plans for roads or rail lines, diesel farms, power lines, and exploration and mining camps.

Any mine requires a number of permits (for water taking, road building, power supply, waste disposal, etc.) before it can be developed. In most provinces and territories (with the exception of Ontario, the jurisdiction with the most mines), the mine proposal will have to undergo an environmental assessment before it can apply for the permits it needs to proceed. Some jurisdictions have exemptions for "small mines." What constitutes a small mine varies by jurisdiction and is usually defined by the tonnage of ore processed daily (for example, less than two thousand tons per day). The environmental assessment process is likely to include significant baseline environmental studies and consultation with any affected Indigenous peoples. Environmental assessment and permitting are discussed in chapter 12.

Construction of the mine infrastructure begins, often before or while the feasibility studies and baseline studies are still being done.

This includes hiring and accommodating workers (often in camps), shaft sinking, pit excavation, road building, and construction of surface facilities.

Underground mines are much more complicated to construct than open pits, as they require ventilation, underground power supply, sewage removal, transportation, and ore movement. Ensuring that the tunnels don't collapse is a paramount concern, so modern practice is to backfill the underground mine shafts with waste rock and tailings, usually mixed with cement.[23]

MINE CONSTRUCTION AND DEVELOPMENT

When it appears that money may be made from a mine, development is likely to proceed, sometimes even if the feasibility and baseline studies are not complete.

Mine site construction is an enormous undertaking lasting two to three years, and it is the high point of job creation. All the elements discussed in chapter 1 have to be put in place. Although the mine will continuously expand during its life, it is the initial construction that first shows communities how big its impact is going to be.

The construction phase will bring a wave of construction workers to the area. If the mine is close to a town, they will quickly fill available accommodation in hotels and motels and may flood the rental housing market, creating a housing crisis for low-income families living in the area. However, usually workers' camps are created. The workers will be predominately male, young, and looking for adventure, a situation that has led many people to call them *man camps*. Drugs, alcohol, and violence against women are common by-products. Dust, noise, and traffic accidents spike. These effects are discussed in more detail in chapter 5.

MINE OPERATION

An operating mine has a number of activities that continue throughout the mine life. These include removal of overburden, blasting, removal and management of waste rock, mine dewatering, beneficiation (crushing and grinding ore in mills), ore separation in flotation tanks, tailings management, tailings dewatering, water treatment, purchase and maintenance of equipment, administration, investment and stakeholder activities, regulatory reporting, marketing and transportation to smelters and markets, energy provision for the facilities, employee hiring, training, payroll and supervision, and a camp where workers live or transportation for workers from a major centre.

Once the mine is operating, it is extremely difficult to regulate the company's behaviour and to hold it to promises it made during the permitting process, because the company will argue that they cannot afford to meet the commitments without laying off workers or closing the mine.

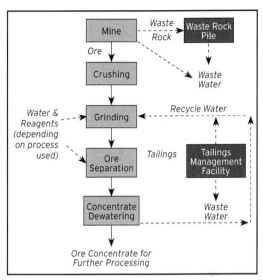

Mining Operations Sequence
Source: Natural Resources Canada.

Exploration will continue around the mine to look for more ore bodies, and the company is likely to leverage mine revenues to expand their activities through exploration or the development of other mines.

Contaminating Waste Rock

The generation and management of mine waste is a significant part of a mining operation. Waste rock comes from the need to remove a large volume of rock that is not ore-bearing in order to get to the ore body. Waste rock can also include low-grade ore, which may be stored separately in a stockpile for later processing when prices are higher or mixed with high-grade ore to provide a consistent grade for the mill. In both underground and open-pit mines, waste rock material ends up on the surface, where it and runoff water must be managed to prevent polluting streams, aquifers, and lakes in the area.[24]

Piles of mine waste rock and dumps of overburden material (soil and vegetation moved to expose the bedrock) can be some of the largest structures created by humans on the face of the earth. These immense waste dumps are often up to four hundred metres high and can contain in excess of one billion cubic metres of material.[25]

While many mines have wastes that generate acid and leach metal—resulting in massive amounts of environmental contamination—uranium mines have additional problems.

According to the Pembina Institute, in 2007, Canada's uranium mines generate nearly 600,000 tons of tailings and up to 18 million tons of waste rock each year. "Supplying a typical Canadian household with nuclear-generated electricity results in the production of 14 kg of toxic and radioactive mine tailings and up to 440 kg of waste rock every year."[26]

Waste rock management and rehabilitation are laden with both environmental and economic consequences that can significantly affect the viability of local ecosystems and the profitability of mining operations. See the discussion of environmental effects in chapter 3.

Processing

In the processing stage, extracted ore is crushed and ground in a mill, and the valued metals are separated from waste using gravity, magnetic, and/or flotation techniques. This results in two streams: concentrate that is further refined either on- or offsite, and the mine tailings, the management of which poses one of the greatest challenges to the mining industry.

Grinding and crushing—crushing the rock to the consistency of face powder—are done to create as much surface on the ore as possible, in order to expose the metals to the concentrating process. Steel balls and rods in huge metal drums crush the ore. Water and chemicals such as lime, soda ash, sodium cyanide, and sulphuric acid may be added in the grinding circuit in preparation for ore separation.

Beneficiation (physical separation processes) relies on differences in size, density, or surface area. Common processes include gravity, magnetic, chemical, and/or flotation separation. All of these processes may use some process reagents—in other words, chemicals. In flotation separation, ground ore is mixed with water, forming a slurry. Air bubbles are introduced into the slurry. Minerals that favour contact with air float to the top, and those that favour contact with water stay in the slurry.

Chemical separation processes dissolve the minerals and cause them to be deposited in solid form ("to precipitate out"). Chemical separation is commonly used for the recovery of gold, silver, and uranium, and, in some cases, copper. Gold or silver is recovered using a solution of cyanide salts. The cyanide binds to the gold ions and makes them soluble in water, thereby allowing separation from the rock. Uranium and copper can be leached using sulphuric acid. This process usually takes place inside a mill or other mining facility. When the ground ore is agitated with leach solution in large tanks, it is called *vat leaching* or *tank leaching*.

The extraction process can also take place as heap leaching, a method often used for very low-grade ore. A large outdoor mound of gold ore is sprayed with a cyanide solution (or sulphuric acid, in the case of copper) that drips through the rock over time. The resulting liquid is collected at the bottom. Heap leaching extracts less gold than processing the ore in a mill but is much cheaper.[27]

In-situ leaching is sometimes used to mine gold, uranium, and copper (although not yet in Canada). This process initially involves drilling holes and placing pipes into the ore deposit. Explosives or hydraulic fracturing are used to create open pathways within the deposit. Leaching solution is pumped into the deposit, where it makes contact with the ore. The solution is then collected through another pipe and processed.

Frequently, further refining is required if high-purity metals are to be produced. The primary types of metal recovery processes are electrolysis, gaseous reduction, and precipitation. After leaching, an electric current is passed through the solution so that the metal is deposited on an electrically charged plate, called an *anode*. Called *electro-winning*, this process is used to extract lead, copper, gold, silver, zinc, aluminum, chromium, cobalt, manganese, and the rare-earth and alkali metals. The electro-winning process is commonly called the *SE/EW process*. Uranium and copper can be leached using sulphuric acid, after which the desired metal is recovered.

The end product of ore separation is an ore concentrate. The concentrates from most ore separation processes are in the form of a slurry, which must then be dewatered prior to further processing. Concentrates are then sent to a smelter or refinery to produce a pure metal for sale, such as gold. For some metals, the concentrate will need even more processing in another refinery.

Concentrates from iron mines, such as those in Labrador, are shipped to a "pelletizing plant," where they are rolled into small balls and then compressed and fired in a kiln to force (*sinter*) the particles into hard spheres, which can be used in steel production.

Refining and smelting metals creates a number of serious air quality impacts, including the release from smoke stacks and smelter buildings of sulphur dioxide and heavy metals, which can contaminate water bodies and soil and impair human and ecosystem health. These impacts are discussed in chapter 3.

TAILINGS

Tailings are everything that is left over after primary ore separation. Tailings are a mixture of water, finely ground rock from which the valued minerals have largely been removed, and residues of all the chemicals that have been used in the processing of the ore.

Tailings are "disposed" of, or managed, in two primary ways in Canada: by returning them underground, or through tailings management areas on the surface. Because the material expands considerably during the processing stages (described above), it is generally not possible to return all the tailings underground, even if a company were to make that kind of a commitment.

There are three key environmental concerns associated with mine tailings: loss of habitat due to the huge areas required for tailings management, impacts on water quality and aquatic ecosystems, and impacts on air quality, primarily from dust.

Common minerals and elements found in tailings include arsenic, barite, calcite, fluorite, radioactive materials, mercury, pyrites/sulfide compounds, cadmium, and hydrocarbons introduced by mining and processing equipment (such as oils and greases). Common additives found in tailings include cyanide or sulphuric acid used in leaching, flotation agents, frothing agents and cleaning/descaling agents, and calcium compounds, which have been introduced as lime to aid in acid control.

Management on the surface has generally involved creating an enormous impoundment (pond) through the construction of dams made of the waste rock and/or the taking of a natural valley or lake for tailings disposal. Where the tailings are acid-generating, they will require a water cover to prevent acid mine drainage and metal leaching.[28] Often waste rock is also placed in the tailings impoundment. If the tailings are not in a slurry, then a dry cover of clay, rock, and vegetation will generally be established to control dust and direct runoff. Acid generation is discussed in more detail in chapter 3. Most Canadian mines will have a water treatment plant onsite to neutralize water flowing from the tailing facility with lime before discharge offsite. In many cases, the water treatment plant will have to function forever.

As an example of the size of these tailings impoundments, the Highland Valley Copper Mine in British Columbia has an impoundment in a valley that is 9 kilometres long, with a tailings dam at the downstream end that is 165 metres high and 3.3 kilometres wide. When I visited the site in September 2018, we were told that the company intends to expand the dam by 2026 to over 210 metres high, to hold 2.6 billion tons of tailings. The road where we were standing high above the tailings would be submerged.

Of course, these dams often fail. This is discussed in chapter 3.

The amount of tailings and waste rock generated daily by the mining industry is staggering. In 2007, I was part of a working group chaired by Environment Canada, where we were shown a chart of the ore mined and the estimated mass of tailings and waste rock produced in metric tons per day from thirty-two mines (out of a total of eighty-two mines active in Canada at that time). These mines produced 417,813 tons per day of tailings and 2.36 million tons of waste rock. This is almost 3 million tons of waste material daily to get at about 600,000 tons of ore.[29]

SMELTING

Smelting is the process of applying heat to concentrates to extract metals from their ores, including silver, iron, copper, and other base metals. Using extreme heat and a source of carbon to decompose the ore, smelting drives off unwanted elements, turning them into gases or slag and leaving the purer metal behind. *Slag* is the name for the leftover melted rock; it is what makes up the blackened rock heaps around smelter towns.

A cleaning agent (a *flux*) may also be used to provide a molten cover on the purified metal, preventing contact with oxygen while the metal is still hot enough to readily oxidize. The flux may be lime, iron, or another material, depending on the metals.

Highland Valley mine and tailings. Photo courtesy of Nikki Scuce.

Since smelting uses extreme heat and drives off toxic by-products (like sulphur dioxide), workplaces and surrounding communities often suffer greatly. The impacts are described more fully in chapter 3.

Hydrometallurgy is a method for obtaining metals from their ores, concentrates, and recycled or residual materials that uses chemicals in liquid form instead of using heat. The Argentia smelter that processes nickel ore from the Voisey's Bay Mine in Newfoundland uses this process. The waste from hydrometallurgical processes are also problematic and need to be contained and managed.

The following list shows the distribution of smelters and refineries across Canada. It should be noted that the Horne smelter in Quebec accepts a substantial amount of material for recycling.

- New Brunswick: 1 smelter
- Quebec: 9 smelters, 4 refineries, 2 secondary smelters
- Ontario: 2 secondary smelters, 3 refineries, 3 smelter/refineries, 1 conversion facility
- Manitoba: 1 smelter/refinery, 1 refinery
- Alberta: 1 refinery
- British Columbia: 1 smelter, 1 secondary smelter, 1 smelter/refinery, 1 processing plant
- Newfoundland and Labrador: 1 refinery[30]

In British Columbia and Quebec, companies also smelt and refine bauxite to make aluminum, but there are no bauxite deposits in Canada and hence, no mines. The bauxite comes from tropical countries in Africa, South America, Asia, and the Caribbean. The smelters also reprocess aluminum products. Aluminum is infinitely recyclable, making it one of the most recycled metals in the world. More than 90 percent of the aluminum used in automotive and construction applications is recycled, driving a closed-loop circular economy.[31] Secondary aluminum production requires 95 percent less energy than primary aluminum production. The aluminum industry has ten primary aluminum plants: one in British Columbia and nine in Quebec. With nearly 6 percent of world aluminum production, Canada ranks fourth in the world, after China, the Middle East, and Russia.

In the process of extracting all these metals at smelters, vast amounts of hazardous pollutants detrimental to human health and the environment are released to air, land, and water, all of which make these operations a major source of pollution in Canada. Regulation of air quality is usually a matter of provincial jurisdiction, and the regulatory regimes rarely prevent substantial releases of sulphur dioxide and other harmful substances, including arsenic, nickel, cadmium, and lead. This is discussed in more detail in chapter 3.

MINE CLOSURE

At this stage in the mining sequence, the economic ore body has been used up, and the mine has to be closed. Structures are removed, openings to the surface capped, and regrading and revegetation work done. Most often the area is reclaimed by constructing ponds, ditches, dikes, and wetlands, and by establishing vegetation over the mine site, the waste rock piles, and any mine tailings areas not under water.

There are many issues around mine closure: the standard of care that is provided; public oversight in the mine closure plan and its implementation; the long-term nature of the impacts; and the need for long-term monitoring and perpetual care. Mine closure and reclamation is an expensive and lengthy process, with uncertain results. Long-term monitoring is needed to ensure that the remediation efforts are successful and to identify any new or emerging environmental concerns. This is discussed in more detail in chapter 7.

In most jurisdictions, government policy requires that prior to mine start-up, an approved closure plan detailing all cleanup requirements must be in place, with financial securities assured by the mining company sufficient to cover the cost of implementing the closure plan. However, this policy is not necessarily reflected in regulation or in practice. The cost estimates for mine closure and long-term care are generally not publicly available, and public consultation is either limited or absent. Quebec has the most effective regulation of closure planning in Canada; a summary of Quebec legislation can be found in chapter 12.

ABANDONED MINES AND PERPETUAL CARE

After a mine has been closed—after the buildings have been demolished and most structures removed, openings to the surface capped, regrading done, and revegetation initiated—the mine moves into a state of perpetual care. This means that the site must be cared for forever, or at least into the foreseeable future.

Most major mines require perpetual care to monitor concerns such as the structural stability of the dams and structures that impound millions of tons of tailings. Many mines also require water treatment long after closure. Long-term monitoring is also required to identify new and emerging environmental issues, such as latent acid-generating potential or changes in surface water quality. The stability of underground workings and pit walls is another concern. Sludge from any wastewater treatment ponds must also be managed. This is discussed in more detail in chapter 7.

There are an estimated ten thousand abandoned mines across Canada. In the absence of sound regulations consistently implemented to make the mining companies responsible for mine closure and perpetual care, more will continue to be abandoned. If mines are created and then closed out in a manner that creates problems afterwards—or not closed at all—and if the mining companies do not maintain long-term responsibilities for the long-term hazards, the mines of today will become the mistakes of tomorrow.

3

KEY ENVIRONMENTAL IMPACTS

I think for a lot of people who haven't been to the mine site it's hard to grasp what the [Mount Polley] spill meant, but when I heard that the dam had collapsed, I felt sick to my stomach.

I opened up a video from the scene and I was almost physically ill. I started to cry, I was just like, "Oh my god, what are we going to do?"

I knew about the heavy metals, the processing chemicals, I knew about all of the treated waste and I knew about the force behind that tailings pond and that Quesnel Lake was down below.

It was a shock. All the communities around there when that happened had an emergency meeting. People were crying and talking about it like there had been a death. It was a death in our community.

We did a ceremony there on the banks of the Quesnel River in Likely. We did a ceremony you do in a time of grief, of great loss and that's exactly how our communities were all feeling.

—Jacinda Mack, reflecting on the consequences of the Mount Polley tailings dam failure, August 4, 2014[1]

Mount Polley Mine tailings pond collapse, August 2014. Photo courtesy of Cariboo Regional District.

Mining can have devastating environmental impacts.[2] This chapter looks at some of the most important environmental impacts to water, air, and soil. Chapter 1 described the enormous size of mines and the infrastructure required to service them. The physical footprint of a mine is an environmental impact in and of itself, although most environmental assessments have ignored it. The other impacts are caused by the catastrophic collapse of tailings dams, which is discussed at the end of this chapter.

The impacts to water and water bodies include:
- sedimentation
- leachate from chemical changes to mined and smelted ore and waste rock that is allowed to interact with air and rain, including acid mine drainage and metal leaching
- effects from pollutants used in the mining process, such as cyanide, ammonia, and flocculants
- impacts from water consumption
- impacts from diversion and dewatering processes
- impacts from wastewater treatment practices

The impacts to air (and to land when dust collects there) include the emission of:

- smelter fumes and dust
- arsenic trioxide
- fugitive dust
- greenhouse gases
- radon

IMPACTS ON WATER

Mining has enormous impacts on water, as we will see in the following sections.

Erosion and Sedimentation

Blasting, the removal of vegetation, the use of heavy equipment, and road, bridge, and other infrastructure construction can all cause erosion. In the absence of adequate prevention and control strategies, this erosion of the exposed earth may carry substantial amounts of sediment into streams, rivers, and lakes, where it will clog riverbeds and smother watershed vegetation, wildlife habitat, and aquatic organisms.

The degree of sedimentation is measured in "total suspended solids," or TSS. Although some sedimentation happens naturally, especially in mountainous glacial streams, mining activities can dramatically increase the amount of suspended solids in water.

Sediment affects fish and fish habitat. If the TSS level is high enough, it will kill fish directly. It can reduce the survival rate of young fish, cause fish to hatch prematurely, or can smother fish eggs.[3] At lower levels, it can cause rot in fins and retard fish growth.

Placer mining is particularly problematic. Placer is a deposit of gravel that contains particles of gold washed down from larger deposits. Placer mining occurs directly in streams and rivers. The romantic image of a placer miner is that of an old man stooped over a stream, gold pan in hand. The modern reality, however, is huge, corporate, and mechanized. Bulldozers and backhoes have replaced the pick and shovel, and a single operation can strip tens of thousands of cubic metres per season. Most placer deposits in Canada are in Yukon and northern British Columbia.

Acid Mine Drainage and Metal Leaching[4]

> Mt. Washington Copper, which operated in Vancouver Island's Comox Valley from 1964 to 1967, was abandoned along with 940,000 tonnes of waste rock. Heavy metals leaching from mine waste poisoned the Tsolum River, wiping out the salmon, steelhead and trout. . . . The provincial government estimates the surrounding community's loss in foregone recreational, tourism and commercial activities at about $2.7 million a year, a total of more than $125 million in lost revenue since the mine's closure until completion of a $4.5-million remediation project in 2010, 43 years later. . . . Unfortunately, the recovery may yet prove only palliative. A provincial background report warns that the ingenious measures—using enhanced wetlands to absorb suspended copper and covering the rock with a waterproof apron—might be effective only for 10 years before leaching polluting metals again.[5]

The metals that we mine can be found in rocks all over the earth. Undisturbed, these metals and the chemicals that are bound to them dissolve gradually and have established a long-term symbiotic relationship with the life around them. Mining destroys that relationship. It rips the desired metal from the rock that birthed it by smashing the rock to powder, and then uses chemicals and heat to break the chemical bonds; gold is taken from the arsenopyrite in the rock, nickel from the pyrites, magnesium from the asbestos.

Unwanted metals and chemicals are left behind in the extraction process and end up smashed to bits, with many surfaces exposed to air and water in waste rock dumps, tailings impoundments, mine dams and roads, and mine pits.

Most Canadian base metal, precious metal, and uranium mines work with rock that contains metal sulphide mineralization.[6] When metal sulphides in rock are exposed to air and water, there is a reaction that generates sulphuric acid. Crushing rock and grinding ore into tailings exposes infinite rock surfaces to air and water. When the water reaches a certain level of acidity, a naturally occurring bacterium called *Thiobacillus ferrooxidans* may kick in, accelerating the oxidation and acidification processes and creating sulphuric acid. As the acid flows through the waste rock and powdered tailings, it dissolves and leaches formerly dormant metals from the rock.

This phenomenon is known as *acid mine drainage* (AMD). Acid is carried off the mine site by rainwater or surface drainage and deposited into nearby streams, rivers, lakes, and groundwater. AMD severely degrades water quality and can kill aquatic life and make water virtually unusable.

Without high acidity, the same leaching process can happen in rock that does not contain sulphur, where it is called *neutral mine drainage* (NMD). While the solubility of aluminum, iron, and copper is greatly reduced in neutral drainage, elements such as antimony, arsenic, cadmium, molybdenum, selenium, and zinc remain soluble and can be leached in significantly high concentrations.[7]

The rocks determine what the contaminants will be. In Labrador, the iron ore mines are a significant source of manganese. In the Selwyn Basin mineral deposit that runs through Kaska Dene Territory in northeast British Columbia and southeast Yukon, the major concerns from the zinc ores are lead, selenium, and mercury contamination. Many gold deposits are in arsenopyrite ores, which can release arsenic and aluminum into waters.

The acidity or alkalinity of a substance is measured on the pH scale.

the numbers range from 1 to 14, with 1 being the most acidic, 7 neutral, and 14 the most alkaline. This scale, however, is not a linear scale like a centimetre or inch scale (in which two adjacent values have the same difference). It is a logarithmic scale in which two adjacent values increase or decrease by a factor of 10. A pH of 3 is ten times more acidic than a pH of 4. . . . Similarly, a pH of 9 is ten times more alkaline than a pH of 8, and one hundred times more alkaline than a pH of 7. [Pure water is neutral, with a pH of 7; battery acid is 1 on the scale; vinegar is 2; liquid drain cleaner is 14; blood is 7.5.][8]

When AMD lowers the pH of the water, it makes the water increasingly acidic and corrosive. Impacts range in severity, with toxicity dependent on discharge volume, acidity, and concentration of dissolved metals. The lower the pH, the more severe the potential effects of mine drainage on aquatic life. If the pH is low enough, the water body will be unable to support most forms of aquatic life. The overall effect of mine drainage is also dependent on the flow (dilution rate) and the buffering capacity of neighbouring rock and the receiving water body.[9] For example, a lake with a limestone bedrock has a much greater buffering capacity than a lake with granite bedrock.

Predicting the potential for and rates of acid mine drainage/metal leaching (AMD/ML) from mine waste is a complex exercise. AMD/ML may not start for decades or more, and it can persist for thousands of years. There are Roman mine sites in the United Kingdom that continue to generate acid drainage two thousand years after mining ceased.[10]

AMD can reduce the diversity and abundance (total numbers) of snails, clams, insects, and so on, and change their community structure. Most plants and animals have a well-defined range of pH tolerance. When pH falls below that range, they may die through loss of sodium ions from the blood and loss of oxygen in the tissues. Acid water also increases the permeability of fish gills to water, adversely affecting gill function.

Leaching metals increase the toxicity of mine drainage and can also act as metabolic poisons.[11] Iron, aluminum, and manganese are the most common heavy metals making the adverse effects of AMD worse. These metals are generally less toxic at neutral pH. Trace metals such as zinc, cadmium, selenium, and copper, which may also be present in mine drainage, are toxic at extremely low concentrations and may act together to suppress algae growth and affect fish and the microscopic life in the stream bed.

Some fish, such as brook trout, are tolerant of low pH, but added metals decrease their tolerance. In addition to dissolved metals in the water, coatings of iron or aluminum hydroxide solids may form in streams receiving mine discharges, where they decrease oxygen availability. They coat fish gills and body surfaces, smother eggs, and cover the stream bottom, filling in crevices in rocks and making it unfit for habitation by benthic organisms.[12]

Technologies for dealing with AMD/ML exist, but a mine that is generating or has the potential to generate AMD/ML must be monitored and treated "in perpetuity"—forever.

Treating discharges at acid-generating and metal-leaching mine sites is usually done in a water treatment plant by countering the acidity of the effluent with lime, which forces the dissolved metals to be deposited in solid form (precipitate). This sludge then has to be stored.

Most mines try to prevent AMD/ML by keeping the potentially acid-generating material away from oxygen and water. If the mine is an underground mine, up to 60 percent of the tailings can probably be mixed with cement and placed back underground. For the rest, long-term treatment means covering the mine waste with water or constructing a "dry cover"—a clay covering for the tailings.

Both kinds of covers need to remain intact for centuries, and both have serious problems in the long term. Permafrost melts; rainfall varies from year to year. Earthquakes and floods—even those caused by beaver activity—can damage the impoundments and breach the dams. With dry covers, tree roots can intrude and create pathways for water, and seismic activity can disturb them.

People may not respect the need to keep the shallow root vegetation cover intact and will run their cars, ATVs, and skidoos over them and build houses and industrial structures on them. I recently watched a TV show set in Cobalt, Ontario,[13] in which people were playing on arsenic-laden tailings (which they called *slimes*).

Pollution from Processing Chemicals

Chemical agents, such as cyanide and sulphuric acid, used by mining companies to separate the target mineral from the ore can spill onsite or in transit, leak, or leach from the mine site into nearby water bodies. They are also stored in tailings impoundments after use. These chemicals can be highly toxic to humans and wildlife. Key culprits include cyanide, ammonia, chlorine, hydrochloric acid, and sulphuric acid.[14]

Cyanide

Cyanide is used to extract gold from ore, either through heap leaching of low-grade gold deposits or as one of a series of conventional methods. Cyanide can be extremely toxic to fish, plants, wildlife, and humans. Cyanide is readily absorbed by the skin, inhaled, or swallowed; cyanide suffocates humans by blocking the transfer of oxygen across cell walls.[15]

While cyanide breaks down quickly, particularly when exposed to sunlight, it breaks down into a variety of new compounds, including some that can be harmful, such as high concentrations of thiocyanates, ammonia, and nitrate.[16]

Cyanide has to be transported to and from mine sites, risking truck accidents and train derailments. There can be serious concerns about how it is handled at the mine site. An International Cyanide Code has been developed by the mining industry that sets out rules for the handling and transportation of cyanide. Unfortunately, the code is voluntary. In 2016–17, a mine owned by Barrick Gold in Argentina (the Veladero Mine), although certified under the Cyanide Code, had three major cyanide spills in two years and polluted five rivers.[17] The transport of cyanide to the Touquoy Mine site in Nova Scotia over dangerous roads is a serious concern of people in Nova Scotia.

Two new gold mines in Yukon are planning heap leaching: the Goldcorp Coffee Project and Victoria Gold Corp Eagle Project.[18] The proposed Casino mine intended a heap leach but was turned down by the Yukon Water Board.[19]

Sulphuric Acid

Low-grade copper deposits are also leached, but with sulphuric acid, not cyanide. At Carmacks Copper, a proposed copper mine in Yukon,[20] opposition from Indigenous governments and the public resulted in it being turned down.

Ammonia

Ammonia is contributed to local streams and lakes because of its use as a process reagent, from the breakdown of cyanide wastes into ammonia, and from unspent ammonium nitrate explosives. Large mines may have explosives factories onsite, which use ammonium nitrate to make explosives for blasting. There are dangers in terms of storage and handling onsite, transportation to the mine, and disposal. The free or un-ionized form of ammonia is toxic to fish, especially at high pH and low temperatures.[21]

Toxic concentrations of ammonia in humans may cause loss of equilibrium, convulsions, coma, and death. At relatively low concentrations, ammonia in un-ionized form can interfere with fish reproduction and hamper normal growth and development. At higher levels, it can kill fish.[22]

Chlorine and Hydrochloric Acid

Chlorine chemistry starts with ordinary salt—sodium chloride—but because chlorine is so reactive, it combines quickly with organic matter to form a variety of very toxic by-products and wastes called *organochlorines.*[23] Organochlorines are persistent in the environment and are cancer-causing, either directly or by increasing the cancer-causing effects of other chemicals. Hydrochloric acid is used to lower pH and can produce acute effects on fish and other water creatures.[24]

Mixing Zones

Most tailings impoundments need to discharge excess water through effluent pipes to prevent overtopping of the dams. Mixing zones are an area of lake or river, usually immediately downstream from an effluent pipe, in which exceedances of water quality objectives are allowed by permit.

Dilution is a common approach to managing wastewater at Canadian mine sites.[25] Most jurisdictions across Canada permit the use of live water bodies as mixing or dilution zones for toxic effluent. In British Columbia, mine permits almost always allow for exceedances of water quality objectives for some contaminants in water leaving tailings impoundments. The federal Metal and Diamond Mining Effluent Regulation (MDMER) does not permit mixing zones, although it addresses only nine contaminants. (The MDMER is discussed in chapter 12.)

Water Consumption and Dewatering

Mining uses water primarily for mineral processing, covering tailings, dust suppression, slurry transport, and employees' needs. In most mining operations, the water comes from groundwater, streams, rivers, and lakes, or through commercial water suppliers. Often, mine sites are located in areas where water is already scarce and compete with local communities for supply.

According to Environment and Climate Change Canada (ECCC), the mineral sector is a major industrial user of water, following thermal power, manufacturing, and agriculture. The figure for the sector does not include water use by smelters, as ECCC includes them in "manufacturing." In 2013, the mining sector withdrew 976 million cubic metres of water and recycled (returned) 675 million cubic metres, for a total consumption of over 300 million cubic metres. However, in ECCC calculations, water removed from a groundwater source and returned to surface water is not "consumed" because when it is discharged to the surface, it is still "available for other economic uses."[26] However, this water may not return to the same water table, and it is likely to be contaminated. Clean water in, dirty water out.

Many mines, both open pit and underground, have to remove water in order to get at the ore body. The displaced water may be contaminated with heavy metals, or it might be pumped from aquifers that are saline. Pumping the water from one area to another may create a "cone of depression" and interfere with the water table. This is a particular problem for mines in muskeg, which are like mining a sponge in a bathtub.

If the area being drained is a peat swamp, it can also lead to releases of methyl mercury. Methyl mercury became a problem at the Victor diamond mine in northern Ontario. Research done by Wildlands League found that draining the water from the mine and placing it in the Attawapiskat River has resulted in a significant increase in methyl mercury, affecting the people downstream.[27] The rivers that have been affected are prime fishing areas for the residents of Attawapiskat, ninety kilometres from the mine site. In its environmental assessment, De Beers itself admitted that the levels of methyl mercury would be doubled by the mine.[28]

As we saw in chapter 1, the diamond mines in the Northwest Territories also require the dewatering of entire lakes or portions of them. At the Ekati Mine, each open pit has required the draining of at least part of the lake that sat atop each kimberlite pipe.

IMPACTS ON AIR

The chief sources of air pollution from the mineral sector are smelters and metal refineries, but air emissions throughout the mining sequence contribute to mining's reputation as one of Canada's top polluters.

Greenhouse Gases

Canada's national inventory of greenhouse gas (GHG) sources and carbon sinks reports about activities of the mineral sector in several different categories, making it difficult to ascertain the full extent of the sector's performance.[29] In 2015, three NAICS (North American Industry Classification System)-defined industry sectors accounted for the majority of GHG emissions: mining, quarrying, and oil and gas extraction. Together these sectors represented 33 percent of all GHG emissions (88 megatons), although of this total metal mining was only 4 percent, coal was 2 percent, and non-metallic minerals (e.g., potash and diamonds) accounted for 2 percent. Most GHGs were attributable to tar sands mining.

Smelting and refining were included in the manufacturing sector, which caused 29 percent of all GHGs (76 megatons). Iron, steel, and ferro-alloy manufacturing was 17 percent of this total, and aluminum production was 9 percent.[30]

Heavy Metals and Toxins

Base metal smelters are major emitters of sulphur dioxide, carbon monoxide, nitrogen oxides, particulate matter, and other toxins and metals. These pollutants are released into the atmosphere, where they can bio-accumulate and overwhelm natural balances.

Over the years, most smelters have reduced their emissions through the construction of sulphuric acid plants and the introduction of other technologies in order to comply with regulated limits. Despite this, the base metals sector remains the single largest industrial source of sulphur dioxide emissions, as well as emissions of a number of highly toxic metals—mercury, arsenic, cadmium, chromium, lead, beryllium, and nickel—in Canada.[31]

Flin Flon's Hudbay smelter, in operation from 1930 to 2012, was notorious for its emissions of mercury and lead, two of the most pervasive toxic substances known.[32] Emissions from this facility were in the order of twenty tons of mercury annually about twenty-five years ago; they remained inordinately high (over 1,400 kilograms annually) until closure, making this facility the largest point source of mercury emissions to air in North America.[33] There are untold amounts of mercury in the tailings ponds of this facility and in the community.[34]

Sulphur dioxide (SO_2), along with other pollutants, is a major cause of acid rain, which is linked to other environmental issues, such as climate change and the leaching of mercury (in its most toxic form, methyl mercury) into rivers, lakes, and streams. Likewise, toxic metals—arsenic, cadmium, and the like—settle and add toxins to water bodies and soil, affecting the health and diversity of the forests, wildlife, vegetation, and waters.

Exposure to sulphur dioxide can contribute to asthma, bronchitis, cardiovascular disease, and possibly lung cancer. Similarly, mercury and lead are a cause of developmental and neurological disorders, as

Mercury
LEVELS

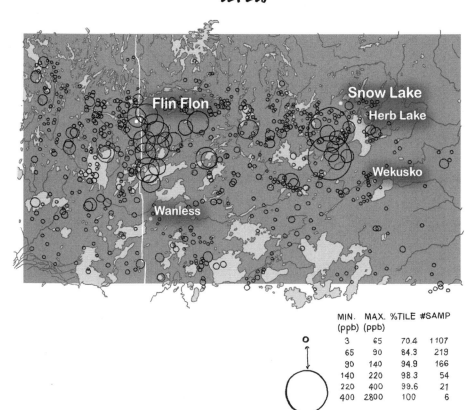

	MIN. (ppb)	MAX. (ppb)	%TILE	#SAMP
	3	65	70.4	1107
	65	90	84.3	219
	90	140	94.9	166
	140	220	98.3	54
	220	400	99.6	21
	400	2800	100	6

well as damage to organs. Arsenic, nickel, chromium, and cadmium can cause various cancers. For a number of these substances, there is no "safe" threshold below which adverse effects cannot be found.

Communities in Sudbury, Thompson, Port Colborne, Rouyn-Noranda, Flin Flon, Belledune, Trail, and other smelter towns bear the brunt of the pollutants most directly and are particularly at risk of having pollutant-related ailments. Because many of these pollutants, such as sulphur dioxide and mercury, are long-distance travellers, their influence on environmental and human health is felt hundreds and even thousands of kilometres from their source.

The legacy from these smelters will live on long after these facilities shut down. In economic terms, the costs for remediation, health care, and lost opportunities for other economic activities are significant.

Gold roasters are emitters of arsenic. The Yellowknife Giant Mine (discussed in chapter 17) gold-roasting process left a legacy of 237,000 tons of arsenic trioxide dust stored in the underground mine workings and 95 hectares of arsenic laden tailings on the surface, 10 to 15 metres deep. Arsenic trioxide is also stored underground at the mines in Red Lake, Ontario.

Aluminum smelters are emitters of fluorides and polycyclic aromatic hydrocarbons (PAHs), and they have been found to cause cancer in beluga whales in the Saguenay estuary of the St. Lawrence River. Perfluorocarbons are major contributors to global warming. Both fluorides and PAHs are carcinogenic.

Radon

Uranium minerals are always associated with radioactive elements, such as radium and radon. In addition to the radioactivity of the uranium itself, other elements of the ore are also radioactive.

Uranium mine tailings contain all the radium that was present in the original ore. When radium undergoes natural radioactive decay, one of the products is radon gas. Because radon and its decay products (daughters) are radioactive, and because the tailings are now on the surface, radon gas is a major release to air and a significant environmental concern.[35]

When radon-222 gas is released from a uranium mine, it deposits solid radioactive dust on the ground for hundreds of miles downwind from the mine site. The radon-222 and all of its radioactive decay chain products release twelve times as much radiation as is in the uranium-238 itself. The radioactivity will be measurable in the area for more than one hundred years after the mine is closed.[36]

Radon progeny is another name for radon decay products or radon daughters. It's the radon progeny, rather than radon gas itself, that delivers the actual radiation dose to lung tissues. The solid airborne radon progeny—particularly polonium 218 and polonium 214—are of particular health importance because they can be breathed into and retained in the lungs.[37]

Radon releases are a major hazard that will continue long after uranium mines are shut down. The US Environmental Protection Agency (EPA) estimates the lifetime excess lung cancer risk of residents living near a bare uranium tailings pile of eighty hectares at two cases per hundred.

Since radon spreads quickly with the wind, many people receive small additional radiation doses. Although the excess risk for the individual is small, it becomes significant given the large number of people concerned. The EPA estimates that the uranium tailings deposits existing in the United States in 1983 would cause five hundred lung cancer deaths per century if no countermeasures are taken.[38]

Tailings Dam Failures

Tailings dams always seep and can fail catastrophically due to weaknesses in construction or from overtopping (water flowing over the top of the dam).[39] In addition to extraordinary rainfall events, overtopping can occur because the spillway is inadequate or the dam is not high enough. Beavers frequently dam spillways, causing the tailings pond to overflow or increasing the water pressure on the dam, resulting in its collapse.

Seepage into groundwater (aquifers) underlying the tailings impoundment may also develop. The contaminants from the tailings impoundment are then carried with the water's flow, creating a "plume" of contaminants in the aquifer. Examples include an arsenic plume at the Goldcorp tailings near Balmertown in Ontario, the nickel plume under the Glencore tailings in Sudbury, and the zinc plume under the Faro tailings impoundment in Yukon. Generally, the plumes are managed with diversion ditches.

There are numerous examples of catastrophic tailings dam failures, both in Canada and abroad. There are increasingly serious tailings dam failures because open-pit mining of low-grade ore creates such huge impoundments, and because weather has become more unpredictable with climate change.

In November 2015, the Samarco tailings dam in Brazil let go, releasing 60 million cubic metres of iron waste tailings, destroying the River Doce ("Sweet River") downstream for six hundred kilometres, displacing thousands of people and killing nineteen outright. A 2017 report from the United Nations Environment Programme entitled *Mine Tailings Storage: Safety Is No Accident* highlights over forty mining waste failures worldwide in the last decade. These failures have killed some 341 people and have damaged hundreds of kilometres of waterways, affected drinking water sources, and jeopardized the livelihoods of dozens of communities.[40]

Canada is no exception. On November 30, 2004, Teck Cominco's tailings pond dam at Pinchi Lake failed, resulting in toxic, mercury-laden effluent spilling into a fish-bearing lake. The dam was one hundred metres long and twelve metres high. An ill-fated reclamation activity directed by the company resulted in its complete collapse. The dike itself was constructed with mercury-contaminated earthen material.[41]

MiningWatch Canada prepared a table of tailings dam failures in Canada from 2008 to 2017 (see page 52).

The worst tailings disaster in Canadian history took place at the Imperial Metals–owned Mount Polley Mine in British Columbia on August 4, 2014. The dam at the mine collapsed, spilling 25 million cubic metres of wastewater, tailings, and construction material into Hazeltine Creek, which empties into Quesnel Lake.

Writes former Chief Bev Sellars,

> The mine site is in the traditional territory of the Secwepemc Nation with the Xat'sull and Williams Lake Bands actively using and sharing custodial responsibilities over the area. . . . The timing of the spill was unfortunate as the sockeye salmon run was building in the Fraser River. The Quesnel watershed is critically important to the Fraser stocks as the streams feeding Quesnel Lake and the lake itself are important breeding and rearing areas. Quesnel Lake also provides drinking water for local residents and is a popular tourism and recreational destination.[42]

KNOWN MINING WASTE FAILURES AND SPILLS ABOVE 1 MILLION LITRES IN CANADA OVER THE LAST DECADE 2008-2017 (NOT EXHAUSTIVE)

Year	Mine (Corporation)	Location	Volume	Environmental Impacts	Fines or Sanction
2014	Mount Polley Mine (Imperial Metals, copper-gold)	BC	25,000 million litres	Polley Lake, Hazeltine Creek, Quesnel Lake; 10 km of terrestrial and aquatic habitat destroyed; drinking water and local fisheries affected; copper, selenium, arsenic, manganese, etc.; long-term impacts unknown.	None yet
2013	Obed Coal Mine (Coal Valley Resources & Sherritt International Corp.)	AB	670 million litres	Apetowun Creek, Plante Creek, Athabasca River; contaminated water and sediment made up of coal, clay, sand, various metals, and other substances; arsenic, mercury, and cadmium; affected waterways for tens of kilometres downstream; drinking water, fisheries, and farmers affected; long-term impacts unknown.	$4.4 million (guilty plea)[44]
2013	Quebec Lithium (now Jien International)	QC	50 million litres	Fiedmond River; spring fisheries; mostly liquid mine wastewater.	None known[45]
2013	Casa Berardi Gold Mine (Hecla Mining)	QC	62 million litres	Kaakakosig Creek; solid and liquid mine waste; undocumented, unreported impacts.	None known[46]
2011	Lac Bloom Iron Mine (Cliff Resources)	QC	Multiple spills, including one of 50 million litres	Affected waterways for tens of kilometres downstream (up to 14 lakes affected), but few details documented or reported on actual impacts.	$7.5 million (guilty plea)[47]
2008	Opemiska Mine (abandoned mine)	QC	11 million litres	50 m section of Hwy 113 destroyed and Obatogamau River impacted for tens of kilometres downstream.	None[48]

Source: MiningWatch Canada

PART II

WHAT IT COSTS

The chapters in this section discuss the many costs of mining that are not included in the company balance sheet. These include the displacement and dispossession of Indigenous people as well as social impacts on the people who live in mining communities and the people whose work depends on the mining industry. The impacts continue after the mine closes.

4

MINING AND COLONIALISM ON TURTLE ISLAND

Mining has always been on the front lines of colonial assault on Indigenous peoples, in Canada and elsewhere.[1] Indigenous peoples and their governments have tried to protect their people and homelands with everything they have. This chapter will look at a few key stories about those battles and catalogue the different ways Indigenous people engage with the industry.

HISTORY

Indigenous peoples mined and traded copper, silver, and gold on Turtle Island for thousands of years. Many Nations had a very different relationship to minerals than settlers, because they saw themselves as "striving to live in relationship with earth."[2] Noted Anishinabek legal historian John Borrows writes,

> [For the Anishinabek], the political relationship between humans and rocks creates mutual obligations and entitlements

that must be respected for this community to reproduce in a healthy manner.... Rocks are animate or living in verb-oriented Algonkian languages[;] ... the active nature of rocks means they have an agency of their own which must be respected when Anishinabek people use them. . . . Using rocks without their consent could be considered using another person against their will. Particular ceremonies and legal permissions are required.[3]

It was Indigenous mineral discoveries that drew early colonial explorers to the places that they turned into large-scale mines. There are many stories of people returning to their homes after a season of trapping or fishing to discover that they were burned to the ground to make way for mineral exploration.

Later, many Indigenous people worked for these colonial mining companies, forced by their impoverishment to take on the worst work, to live in shacks and tents, and to suffer the effects of injuries and industrial disease.[4]

Gerry McKay, CEO of the Independent First Nations Alliance and a former Chief of Kitchenuhmaykoosib Inninuwug (Big Trout Lake First Nation) in northern Ontario, says,

Big Trout Lake was always part of the mining industry. There were eight to ten mines in our area, including Sachigo, Pickle Crow, Pickle Lake, Dona Lake, [and] Golden Patricia. People walked and paddled to go to work in these mines. Even the women from the community worked at the mine site at one time, cutting timber and doing other jobs.

I am the son of a hard rock miner. My father's name was George McKay and he worked in the mines for about thirty years. He worked at Sachigo River Mine as a young man, and later at Pickle Crow Mine, and it eventually killed him because he could not breathe anymore.

I have a lot of friends whom I grew up with who are no longer with us. At one point there were about forty of us, and now there are only two of us alive. And I think maybe one or two have died a natural death; the others died of violence. The mining community in which we grew up was a very violent community.

While my dad worked for the mining company, we lived in Pickle Lake. In 1955, when Indian people were first allowed to go into the bars, we little kids used to stand outside and listen to all these different languages inside the bar—German, Italian—because after the war, these were the people who came to work in the mines.

These people were allowed to live in town. Us, we weren't allowed to live in town. We had to live across the slimes [tailings], and we built our shelters, our homes, from slabs from the mining sawmill. We weren't even allowed to take the lumber, so we built our homes from slabs and tarpaper.

Our wells were sometimes just two, three feet away from the river system, and the river system was full of slimes. The slime was dumped right into the river system. I sometimes think there is a connection between some of these deaths—people who died of heart failure, poisoned by the arsenic and other metals in the slimes. There were a lot of them—people who failed to wake up. You'd find them in their rooms, their beds, their cabins.

People lost their lives and were injured in the mines, but there was no real help for them from the companies. There were no roads out and a sparse population.[5]

In many regions, mining was the beginning of what John Borrows calls "the non-Aboriginal blockades and occupations of indigenous lands" in Canada.[6] In British Columbia, Yukon, Ontario, Quebec, and the Maritimes, gold rushes in the nineteenth century resulted in terrible epidemics of disease and the displacement of Indigenous peoples. They resisted with everything at their disposal. In 1864, six Tŝilhqot'in warriors were hanged for opposing the building of a road to gold fields at Barkerville.

The Robinson-Huron Treaty

In 1850, the government coerced the Anishinaabe into signing the Robinson-Huron Treaty.[7] The treaty was to enable settlers to stake mining claims and leases across the north shore of Lake Huron and north of the French River. By the time the treaty was signed, the people had already been decimated by epidemics of disease, such as the smallpox outbreaks in 1670 and 1763 that wiped out 70 to 90 percent of the people each time.

The Robinson-Huron Treaty is now the subject of an important lawsuit by the affected Nations against Ontario and Canada, for failing to increase the annual annuity stipulated in the treaty. The Royal Proclamation of 1763 had forbidden non-Indigenous people from purchasing or using unceded First Nations lands. When miners started to encroach on their territory, the chiefs and communities petitioned to stop them and blockaded a site at Mica Bay. A report about this incident said that a treaty should be signed that would "extinguish the Indian right . . . by granting the Aboriginals an equitable remuneration for the whole country" (in exchange for them ceding their rights and giving settlers access to their land and the minerals underneath).

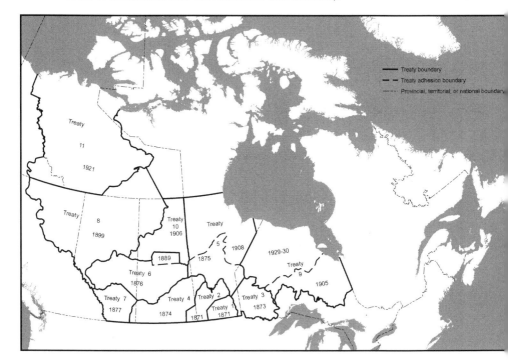

The Post-Confederation Numbered Treaties. *Source:* Natural Resources Canada, 2014. Mapping by HR GISolutions Inc. Reproduced with the permission of the Department of Natural Resources, 2019.

The treaty specified that the annuity would be increased as value taken from the lands increased. It was increased once, from two dollars a year to four dollars a year in the nineteenth century, but never again. Clearly, an increase based on the trillions of dollars of mining wealth taken from the territory, and the enormous consequences for Indigenous peoples, is overdue. The Robinson-Huron Statement of Claim says,

> In 1845, for the first time in the history of what is now Ontario, the Governor of the Province of Canada declared a region of the province to constitute public lands, without first making a treaty with the Nation of Indians then in possession of the land. . . . You will hear how this was done largely to facilitate the exploration and development associated with mining, an industry whose participants included many prominent and less prominent government officials. You will hear how this unauthorized development put the government and those running the mines into conflict with the Anishinaabe, who asserted their right to control and obtain wealth from the use of resources on their lands, and who repeatedly argued for the need for a fair treaty arrangement which would provide them with new sources of wealth, in the face of development that was driving away the animals on which the Anishinaabe had traditionally depended.[8]

In Sudbury, the largest and one of the oldest mining communities in Canada, the Atikameksheng Anishnawbek are the traditional occupants of the land, and parties to the Robinson-Huron Treaty. A mining company executive estimated in 2008 that $1 trillion of wealth has been extracted from the Sudbury mining camp in the over one hundred years it had been operating.[9]

In 2008, Chief Arthur Petahtegoose of the Atikameksheng Anishnawbek was interviewed for a radio documentary called *Path of Destruction*.[10] Chief Petahtegoose said,

> Knowledge of these deposits [gold and copper] had been obtained from Ojibway people, who had been using native copper for centuries before the Europeans arrived. In August

of 1834, for example, Kewekumegiscum—an Ojibway from the north shore of Lake Huron—sent the Lieutenant-Governor of Upper Canada samples of yellow metal (native copper) he had found on St. Joseph's Island, advising that there was a great deal more of it both there and on the mainland opposite.[11]

Chief Petahtegoose's position is that the area of the Sudbury mines belonged to the Nation and was stolen from it with the mines' creation. In 2008, the Nation launched a $550 billion lawsuit against the Canadian federal government and the Ontario government, on the basis that the area of the Sudbury mines belongs to the Nation, as does the wealth generated by their operations for the last century. He explains,

> We are bullied as a population. I think about the child in the schoolyard, where the bully comes and takes his money, pressures the victim to behave in a particular manner. That's how I've expressed our relationship in terms of how we sit with the Crown. . . . What we see today is that the boundary that was put into place has been moved from where we had intended that it be originally placed, and this is where we see the injustice on our part being suffered. The reserve has been made smaller, not by choice, but by design of the Crown's. . . . We were removed by the Crown so that the resources from the land would not have to be shared with us. . . .
>
> We're still going to be here, okay. We're not going to go anywhere. Other people may be mobile, able to move to other parts of the country or the world. But our people, we've always lived here and we intend to stay here. So the long-term impact of this accumulation of contaminants in and around our homes worries us.[12]

The lawsuit is currently on hold, pending the outcome of the Robinson-Huron case.

CURRENT DATA

According to the Mining Association of Canada's *Facts and Figures 2017*, "most Aboriginal communities are located within 200 kilometres of some 180 producing mines and more than 2,500 exploration properties. Also, many mines and projects are located on traditional lands. Aboriginal people across the country are, therefore, ideally situated to access employment opportunities (and other benefits) in the mining industry."[13]

Mining is now the most significant wage employer of Indigenous people in Canada, providing jobs to over eleven thousand individuals, mainly in exploration and quarrying. A number of impact benefit agreements (described later in this chapter) require that companies hire people from the affected communities,[14] and governments have targeted initiatives, including funding for videos and manuals, training, and "mining advisors" to increase Indigenous employment in the industry. However, Indigenous peoples are often in camp in service, clerical, and exploration jobs and remain underrepresented in certain occupational categories, particularly those related to jobs that actually engage in mining itself and in the most highly paid jobs, such as engineers, managers, and geologists.[15]

The colonial process of taking land and resources for the use of the settler population does not belong only to the past; it is happening now. Indigenous peoples still resist with everything they have. Some of their stories are heard throughout this book. How that resistance plays out depends on a number of factors: the power the community has to defend their interests; the cultural and spiritual leadership in the community; the strength of the peoples' attachment to the land and waters; the extent of the impoverishment and lack of economic alternatives affecting the community; the community's knowledge of mining impacts and company vulnerabilities; the kind of education the community leaders have received; the role of the Canadian state; the level of hope or despair in the community. The stages of the mine's life also affect what people are able to do.

The Serpent River First Nation in Ontario summed up the critical question of Indigenous peoples' lack of capacity to deal with all these issues following a 2016 workshop they hosted to develop their own mining policy:

> As a general rule capacity is a critical issue for most First Nations. When it comes to mining, the issue is having capacity to engage the government and the companies in consultations.

The message heard was that First Nations simply do not have the staff nor the time and other resources to develop the expertise required. The need for core capacity to respond and negotiate with government and individuals is critical. How can you consult equitably if on the one side you have government and industry at the table with a large, well-financed team of experts and lawyers backed by full research and on the other side just the Chief and a few councillors. . . .

An experience was shared by a First Nation with limited capacity, where a 400 page technical mining closure plan was delivered to them and they had 45 days to respond (that is the only consultation requirement in the present Mining Act). This was the first they had heard of this new mine to be built on their traditional territory. They had to scurry to hire an expert to review it and incur the cost to do so.[16]

DIFFERENT APPROACHES TO THE MINING INDUSTRY

In *The Reconciliation Manifesto*, Arthur Manuel and Grand Chief Ronald Derrickson write, "It is irresponsible of us to take a few dollars today to give access to a mine, and in doing so threaten the health of our land and our Aboriginal title, leaving our grandchildren politically weakened with an arsenic-laced tailings pond on their territory."[17]

However, many Indigenous communities are already forced to live with mining and its impacts. Almost 60 percent of Indigenous people now live in urban centres.[18] Some have little interaction with their homelands. Many Indigenous peoples feel that they have to find a way to benefit from the mining industry or end up with less than nothing. And some, like the rest of us, just want to make what they can from the system.

Like the settler population of Canada, Indigenous peoples in Canada deal with the mining industry in a range of ways, from complete rejection to sitting on corporate boards. Quite frequently, more than one of these approaches is being taken at the same time. These approaches are often at cross-purposes and are frequently the cause of heated conflict within Indigenous communities and governments. I have tried to summarize these approaches here.

Defensive Actions

Resistance to new mine and mine expansion proposals through asserting control by the Indigenous government over traditional lands and waters using title assertion, eviction orders, moratoria, and direct action such as blockades often leads to defensive action in the courts to deal with injunctions. Like many other Nations across the country, the Tŝilhqot'in have been trying to prevent a mine at Fish Lake in their traditional territory for almost thirty years now.[19]

Indigenous Organizing and Resistance

Indigenous organizations and networks in Canada that want to "put mining in its place" include First Nations Women Advocating Responsible Mining (British Columbia); Defenders of the Land, the Indigenous Caucus of the Western Mining Action Network; and the Indigenous Environmental Network.[20]

International Forums

Arthur Manuel argues that, since Indigenous peoples in Canada have not surrendered their lands, any trade agreements signed by Canada that affect their territories are invalid without their consent.[21] The Indigenous Network on Environment and Trade was founded to lead this fight.

Indigenous participation and leadership at international forums such as the United Nations Permanent Forum on Indigenous Issues and in trade and investment decisions have been expanding.

Indigenous Mining Policies

Some Indigenous peoples assert their governance responsibilities through Nation-specific mining policies for new and existing mines. Examples include the Taku River Tlingit First Nation Mining Policy, the Northern Secwepemc te Qelmucw Mining Policy, the Below the Surface: Anishinabek Mining Strategy, and the Kitchenuhmaykoosib Inninuwug Watershed Declaration.[22]

Environmental Monitoring Agreements

The Indigenous Leadership Initiative and the National Indigenous Guardians Network want to provide leadership to environmental groups and governments.[23] Modelled on programs in Haida Gwaii and the Innu Nation, the programs are advocating for federal funding to monitor the impacts of development on their territories. The Guardians Network has published a toolkit for communities.[24]

Wage Labour

Indigenous people often choose (or are forced by a lack of alternatives) to work in the mining industry. Indigenous people have worked for mining companies for generations. Labour shortages at mining camps have resulted in a number of targeted government and industry efforts to increase Indigenous employment. In British Columbia, there is even an Aboriginal Mine Training Association. Programs to help train Indigenous peoples for the mining industry can be found at all levels of government.

Modern Treaties

Where Indigenous peoples have signed "modern treaties"—comprehensive claims agreements—they have obtained title to a portion of their traditional territories and usually have subsurface rights on the title portion. The treaty territory is larger than the title area and usually reserves the subsurface rights to the Crown. They will also have relinquished any further claims to this territory as a condition of the treaty. The retained rights to the subsurface vary greatly. For example, the Tłįchǫ Land Claims and Self-Government Agreement allocates the Nation subsurface rights on 100 percent of the land; in Nunavut, only 1.4 percent of the land. The modern treaties usually also include revenue sharing with the Crown (getting a portion of the mining tax), participation in environmental assessment processes, and a requirement for resource companies to negotiate impact benefit agreements.

Consultation in Environmental Assessments and Permitting

Indigenous peoples participate in the Canadian, provincial, and territorial colonially shaped administrative processes for mine approval, operation, and closure, including environmental assessments (EAs) and the endless permitting and permit renewal processes. Whether to take part in these processes is a difficult decision for Indigenous peoples. Participation can be seen as "adequate consultation," but non-participation by the Indigenous government in these processes has been deemed by the courts to indicate a "lack of good faith" in the consultation and accommodation processes.[25] A number of Indigenous governments are now represented on environmental assessment panels. In 2017, Stk'emlúpsemc te Secwépemc conducted their own review of the proposed Ajax Mine in parallel with the federal/provincial process and said no to the mine.

Indigenous Representation at Policy Tables

A recent Supreme Court of Canada case found that the government was not required to consult Indigenous peoples before making laws.[26] However, governments actively seek the participation of "Indigenous representatives" at provincial/territorial, federal, and even international levels for consultation about law, regulation, and policy. The Canadian Aboriginal Minerals Association works to bring industry, government, and Indigenous leaders together at conferences and other events. It should also be noted that there are a number of Indigenous people working in mining-related departments of the federal and provincial governments.

Memorandums of Understanding and Letters of Agreement

Negotiation with companies and federal and provincial governments to try to get a Nation's rights and concerns respected sometimes results in Memorandums of Understanding (MOUs) or Letters of Agreement (LOAs) about how the parties agree to work together. Unfortunately, some of these documents include a provision that the communities will not speak publicly against the mine proposal.

Participation Agreements and Impact Benefit Agreements

The negotiation and implementation of participation agreements with mining companies, such as impact benefit agreements, determine how any revenues from the mine will be shared with the Indigenous government. They usually include commitments for jobs, locally awarded contracts, a royalty or share of profits (occasionally share ownership), training, and environmental monitoring. Companies usually insist that the terms of these agreements be kept confidential, often even from community members. Technically, they are contracts that can be enforced in the courts, but this is very difficult to do. There are a number of resources to help communities negotiating these agreements.[27]

Providing Supply and Services to Mining Companies

The development and operation of Indigenous-owned and -run businesses in the mining supply and services sector, including contracting for work in prospecting and exploration, closure, and remediation, are growing. Indigenous peoples also have equity ownership and joint ventures with mining companies and mining company contractors. Nuna Logistics is one example. It is a heavy construction and contract mining company owned by Kitikmeot Corporation (51 percent) and Nuna Management Group (49 percent). Kitikmeot Corporation is the business arm of the Kitikmeot Inuit Association.[28] Other examples include Lac Seul First Nation's mineral exploration company[29] and the Cree Mineral Exploration Board in Eeyou Istchee, which promotes and assists in Cree mineral exploration and prospecting.

Holding Shares in Mining Companies

Some First Nations hold shares in mining companies, a position that prevents them from being critical of the company in any public way. So, in the case of the Wolverine Mine in Yukon, Yukon Zinc agreed— as part of a participation agreement in 2005—to give the Kaska Dena $400,000, with which they were to purchase two million shares in the company.[30] In addition, the Kaska entered into a joint venture with Procon Mining to operate the mine.[31] The mine opened in March 2012 but never turned a profit, staggering along with serious flooding and industrial accidents.[32] Yukon Zinc was sold to Chinese investors, who closed the mine and applied for creditor protection in 2015.[33]

Sitting on Corporate Boards

A very few Indigenous leaders now sit on the boards of major mining companies. It should be noted that, unlike NGO directors, corporate directors are well paid for attending meetings and other services. Goldcorp, for example, pays its directors $100,000 a year, as well as payment in shares and options, just for attending meetings. Donald Deranger, Dene, a former vice-chair of the Athabasca Grand Council, is on the board of Cameco.[34] Matthew Coon Come, Cree, a former National Chief, is on the board of Goldcorp.[35] Phil Fontaine, Cree, another former National Chief, was on the board of Chieftain Metals during the company's negotiations with the Taku River Tlingit over reopening the disastrous Tulsequah Chief Mine.[36] Glenn Nolan, former Chief of the Missanabie Cree, is the Vice-President of Government Affairs at Noront Resources, leading the industry fight for government investment in the Ring of Fire in Ontario; he is also a past president of the Prospectors and Developers Association of Canada.[37]

5

SOCIAL IMPACTS

I lived for almost thirty years in Sudbury, the largest mining community in Canada, and still consider it home. The mining operations of Inco and Falconbridge (now CVRD and Glencore) dominated the landscape and the economy of the region. They also shaped our social and cultural lives in ways we did not always see. This chapter will look at some of the social impacts of mining, from exploration, development, and operations through to closure.[1]

Sudbury wastelands. Photo courtesy of Tanya Anne Bell.

For most of us, our family, neighbours, and friends are our primary supports. We create organizations and systems to help us take care of one another: medical services and hospitals; ways of getting around; schools, daycare, and youth services; emergency services like fire and ambulance; family violence programs, women's services, and drug and alcohol programs; and informal gathering places. Although they are often imperfect, and we know they are fragile, we depend on them to get us through. Altogether, these formal and informal systems create the social fabric of our community.

For many people—Indigenous people, refugees, and other Canadians forced to relocate from their homes—the almost total destruction of the social fabric upon which they depended has happened within their living memory through dispossession and displacement, and they are engaged in rebuilding it any way they can. Rebuilding and maintaining that social fabric is a skilled and exhausting process that goes on endlessly in mining towns.

How does mining affect the strength of the social fabric of a community? What is the fragility and strength of this fabric? Who does it serve and not serve? Where do the funding and staff for services come from? What is the capacity of these networks and services to adapt to changes?

The number of mining-reliant communities in Canada has not been reported since 2001, but at that time, Natural Resources Canada reported that there were 185, of which 88 had a reliance of 50 percent or greater and 97 had a reliance of 30 percent to 49 percent. The economies of these communities depended either on local mining activity or on metal-processing plants.[2] Since that time, many mines have been closed, and new ones that open tend not to develop new communities around them but use fly-in camps instead. The number of "mining towns" has shrunk, but mining dependence, as we shall see, is still an issue.

IMPACTS DURING EXPLORATION AND CONSTRUCTION

When there is only a hint that a mine may be built in an area, the industry hype about windfall profits creates anxiety and conflict over the project, and serious social divisions and violence can begin and tear communities apart.

Mining can displace whole communities from their land and homes, traumatizing them and affecting cultural identity, security, and subsistence.[3] Residents may end up in urban slums or even homeless.

Exploration and construction will see the influx of a mostly male workforce, often living in "man camps." The effect of these camps on women, particularly Indigenous women in the surrounding area, is well documented. A report from a workshop conducted by the Firelight Group of extraction-affected women at Lake Babine in British Columbia in 2016 sums it up:

> The addition of new pressures, from locating temporary and permanent industrial camps near these remote communities, introduces a new set of risks. In the literature, the effect for Indigenous women is known as the "risk pile up." Evidence suggests that Indigenous women and girls are subjected to the worst of the negative impacts of resource extraction at every phase. Increased domestic violence, sexual assault, substance abuse, and an increased incidence of sexually transmitted infections (STIs) and HIV/AIDS due to rape, prostitution, and sex trafficking are some of the recorded negative impacts of resource extraction projects, specifically as a result of the presence of industrial camps and transient work forces. . . .
>
> These industrial camps are male dominated, and the interactions with women in communities and at camps could have highly negative consequences. . . . There are impacts raised that cut the same way for men and women, such as increased traffic (leading to accidents or congestion) and the potential for traditional economies, resources, and lands to become a destination and hunting place for non-Aboriginal and off-time workers. . . .
>
> [There are] negative effects that could make already vulnerable women and children even more so. There is a "hyper-masculine" industrial camp culture at play at times, which leads to significant alcohol and drug consumption, and much higher access to these substances.[4]

IMPACTS DURING MINE OPERATIONS

At a workshop that MiningWatch organized in 2001, one of the Indigenous participants described the impact of a new mine proposal on his community roughly as follows: "It's like having a drunk break into your home after you have repeatedly told him to go away. He pisses on the furniture, throws up on the floor, attacks your wife, eats all your food and then says: 'Let's talk about the terms on which I get to stay.'"[5]

The extent of the social impacts of mining on the community will depend on how long the community has hosted a mine and the extent to which the settler population has displaced the original Indigenous population. Historically, once the mine is up and running, the Indigenous people have been almost entirely displaced or marginalized by the settlers, and the town's "culture" has come to be that of the people who displaced them.[6] So, cities like Yellowknife, Trail, Timmins, Sudbury, Rouyn-Noranda, and Schefferville coexist with the dispossessed Indigenous people who lived there in great numbers perhaps decades before. The "new" culture is very different from the old one.

The community will be made up of people who moved there to work at the mine or its supporting businesses. They may come from many different countries and places and will be eagerly engaged in forming relationships with each other, being good neighbours and friends, organizing a social fabric for themselves as quickly as they can. But in the process of doing this, the needs of the people upon whose land they are building will often be rendered invisible or turned into a romantic artifact. To recognize their right to the land and their existence as peoples gets in the way of "progress"—of building the new community.

People who live in these mining communities work hard to create a vibrant social and cultural life for themselves. Those who benefit from the mining activity are protective of the source of their income and of the company donations that determine which community projects— from hospital and college expansions to sports fields and art galleries— go ahead. There were many wonderful things about living in Sudbury: the people were generally warm and friendly; there was a vibrant arts and cultural scene across many cultures, including Indigenous; and the landscape was being reclaimed through the growing knowledge of scientists and the hard work of students and workfare participants. But these can be rough places with some serious social problems.

Social effects from mine activity, including increased alcohol consumption and drug use, have been well documented.[7] In 2017, Todd Godfrey published a paper confirming this increased alcohol consumption in people living within ten kilometres of a mine. He found that "individuals who live within 10 km of a mine consume, on average, an additional 2 alcoholic drinks a week. This effect decreases as mines get farther away. Additionally, we . . . find that the effect of proximity to mines is larger than, for example, proximity to casinos or bars."[8]

Because mining wages are so high, and jobs are few, mining projects inevitably create greater income disparity. Some populations will be much more vulnerable than others: women, youth, First Nations, immigrants. The mine will affect the services on which they depend, increasing the costs of housing and recreational activities, controlling the city council. Sudbury's Donovan/Flour-Mill neighbourhood, for example, is one of the lowest-income neighbourhoods in Ontario, despite the huge mining wealth created in the region.

In older mining and smelting communities, with their constantly growing mine footprint, any resource-based economic activities such as farming, fishing, and logging have been damaged by pollution from the mine and smelters, and communities become dependent on power grids, chain stores, and imported goods and services to supply their needs. Any other resource-based activities remaining have to take place a long distance from the town. Wild foods are a treat, not a regular source of food.

Mine operations are strongly tied to commodity prices set on the London Metals Exchange, and mining is heavily dependent on outside capital and external markets, with the head offices and decision-makers being both physically and socially removed from the local community. Towns with operating mines see their populations surge and shrink with mining booms and busts.[9] Even before an ore body is depleted, the mine may shut down due to low global metal prices or investment being drawn elsewhere. The result is suspended operations and laid-off workers.[10] Economic benefits related to mining can be relatively short term, given that minerals are nonrenewable resources and most new mines only last ten to fifteen years.

Mining projects are notorious for the creation of an "intrusive rentier syndrome" in the communities and regions where they are located. This term is used by Polèse and Shearmur[11] to describe an effect in regions dominated by a small number of highly capitalized (and high-wage) employers (such as a mine, smelter, or paper mill). The regions faced serious problems attracting people to fill lower-wage jobs and attracting investment in small- and medium-sized enterprises. Intrusive rentier syndrome is characterized by a heightened disparity in incomes and wealth between those who have and those who have not, a creation of dependency on a single employer, the destruction of alternative employments, the creation of a boom and bust economy, and increased domestic violence.[12]

Mining communities also suffer a number of health problems related to industry contaminants, including higher incidences of cancer, asthma, and other respiratory diseases in mine workers, their family members, and other local residents.[13] Mining is still dangerous and destructive work that carries with it a high incidence of industrial disease—cancers, white hand, silicosis—as well as on-the-job injuries and traffic accidents. Many former mine workers are unwell or disabled.

During operations, major power imbalances exist between communities and the mining companies they depend on. When communities try to organize to resist mine expansion, to fight company requests for water-taking, or to reduce pollution or to improve safety, they often cannot get the information and analysis they need. In order to effectively participate in any decisions around their community mines, people need access to a comprehensive understanding of all the impacts of mining. Yet this information, when it is available, is usually in a form and language that makes it inaccessible to the community.[14]

Because most of the wealth created by mines and smelters leaves the community, its municipal government will have trouble providing the day-to-day services that people need.[15] The municipality will also be dealing with increased heavy traffic on roads, more accidents, and potential competition with the mining company for land, energy, water, and sewage disposal.

IMPACTS AT CLOSURE

In communities acting as a base for mining operations, services and infrastructure (such as power lines, sewage, and housing) have often been expanded and developed to accommodate the larger population working at the mine. At closure, when jobs and contracts are lost, workers leave the community. Those left behind shoulder a greatly increased tax burden as a result of the community carrying the costs of over-sized and aging infrastructure.[16] In addition, health and environmental impacts from the mine may reduce a community's investment appeal to other sectors. These factors, singly or in combination, often leave mining communities—or formerly mine-dependent communities, as they may become—economically vulnerable, and perhaps even willing to consider economic development or activities that carry with them an additional environmental burden, such as hazardous waste disposal in the pits and shafts.

With closure, the social environment in the community where the mine was operating often gets worse. Violence, increased drug and alcohol use, depressed expectations, power struggles, more extreme social hierarchy, and paralysis of normal decision-making are common.

Different segments of the population respond to mine closure in different ways. Many miners and mining specialists may find work elsewhere and leave town. The young people leave, looking for opportunities and education. More likely to stay are those workers who mix their employment at the mine with marginal farming, hunting, fishing, trapping, and other activities, and thus have many other skills. Older workers (near retirement age) usually remain after closure because they are attached to the community, unable to sell their houses, or have a settlement package of some sort. Family employment after a closure tends to shift to the women, and to lower wages.[17]

Indigenous residents, being attached to the land base, respond differently than the settler community. One community, Lynn Lake, provides hospital and school services to the surrounding Marcel Colomb First Nation. Uranium City saw almost its entire white population relocate, while the Indigenous community stayed. The sudden availability of cheap housing has often resulted in a number of communities, like Elliot Lake, having an inflow of retirees and younger people. People drawn to rural communities by the inexpensive housing and closeness to nature are often involved in the informal economy and practice values like voluntary simplicity. Many of them are artists, craftspeople, and "jacks of all trades." They may be resilient, and bring education, creativity, and a real economic contribution to the existing population.[18]

6

WORKING IN THE MINING INDUSTRY

This chapter is about the workers: the people on whose back the industry is built. It discusses who is employed in the mining industry and the role of unions—how miners in Canada get respect and fair treatment from the mining companies—and ends with occupational health and safety issues.

Mining itself is a dangerous and physically demanding occupation that often takes place in remote areas with difficult climatic conditions. The safety clothing and protective gear miners are required to wear is cumbersome and heavy, ranging from safety glasses to respirators and steel-toed rubber boots to protective clothing. In an underground mine, working conditions will include darkness and gloom, heat and high humidity, diesel fumes, dust, and very loud noise. In an open-pit mine, workers can be exposed to cold that can reach down to -60 degrees Celsius in winter. Miners usually work long shifts of ten to fourteen hours and may work up to fourteen consecutive days without a break.[1]

Mines are often in places far away from friends and family. Miners frequently stay in mining camps with a no-alcohol and no-drugs regime. Although the camp itself may be quite comfortable, it is a walled environment, cut off from access to the outside world.

The dangers inherent in mining are from explosives, heavy equipment, and vehicles. There is the ever-present danger of rockslides and rock falls and of flooding in both underground and open-pit mines. Silicosis is still a concern in many underground mines, unless protective gear is worn at all times. In coal mines, there is always the danger of methane explosions. Methane is a highly explosive gas caught within coal layers that can be triggered by sparks of any kind. In uranium mines, there is the danger of radioactive contamination.

The fight for health and safety protection in mining is a never-ending struggle, as the Donkin coal mine story illustrates.

The Donkin coal mine in Nova Scotia began production in February 2017. The mine has two 3.5-kilometre tunnels stretching under the Atlantic Ocean. Coal will be extracted by mining the space between the two tunnels.[2] The mine's owner, American-based Kameron Collieries, has successfully fought off attempts to unionize the workers at the mine. The company has said they will close the mine down if it is unionized.[3]

Miners who worked on the construction of the mine say that the mine is a "disaster in the making, as employees are subjected to dangerous working conditions, including ceiling cave-ins, a lack of safety equipment and lax safety practices."[4] Miners interviewed in March 2017 about the mine told the CBC that there were frequent rock falls, that the ceilings had caved in several times, and that the roof supports for the galleries were inadequate.[5] Water regularly leaked into the mine. An employee said that one night he saw a five-metre-long roof bolt blow out. There were issues with safety harnesses and protection during the spraying of shotcrete, a fire-resistant material, on the mine walls. Despite methane explosion concerns, miners were being forced to cut steel underground.

Coal miners in Nova Scotia know only too well the dangers of coal mines. Nova Scotia has been home to mining accidents large and small since coal mining started there.[6] From 1838 to 1992 over twenty-five hundred workers died in Nova Scotia mines. The most recent large disaster was at the Westray Mine in 1992.

In July, Kameron Collieries was fined for paying temporary US workers almost twice what they offered to Canadian workers, after they laid off forty-five Canadian miners. The company said they had "trouble with productivity and equipment" and could not find local workers to take the jobs.[7]

MINING COMPANIES ARE NOT MINERS

Miners are the people who work in the actual mine, mill, smelter, or refinery, or at an exploration site, doing the physical work that pulls the desired minerals from the rock. These jobs include labourers; drillers and drillers' assistants; blast hole drillers and blasters; electricians; mechanics; crusher, grinder, and flotation operators; and warehouse persons. They include cooks, carpenters, machinists, plumbers, steamfitters, millwrights, and welders. They include the foremen for the mill, mine, smelter, electrical, maintenance, and safety; the mining technician; and the warehouse supervisor.

A mining company, on the other hand, is a business created to own and manage mines and mineral exploration in the interests of their shareholders. It will have a board of directors; an executive management team; an administrative, legal, and finance staff; a public relations staff, investors; and creditors. The mining company depends on the miners—those people who actually find and extract the minerals—to produce wealth for it. The relationship of the company to its miners and other employees is one of both dependency and conflict.

There are many other people working in the mining industry, some directly employed by mining companies and some indirectly—working at outsourced jobs, providing supply and services to the mining company. Increasingly, mining companies use contractors to do the work for them. There are also mining companies that do no real physical mining whatsoever and consist of just an office in Vancouver with a few promoters. These "junior mining companies" are discussed in chapter 8.

A lot of people who work to support the mining industry are in fact public servants in government departments and are usually in a union of some sort (the Public Service Alliance of Canada, the Canadian Union of Public Employees, or any one of a number of provincial unions). Many of these public servants use their knowledge of how government works in the interests of affected communities. It is important to remember that they have their own interests as workers vis-à-vis the mining industry; workers have a life outside the workplace that is often very different from their job. The values they are forced to live at work may be in conflict with their personal values—ecologists in the

Ministry of Natural Resources, for example. People deal with these conflicts in a variety of ways in order to maintain their self-respect: they become cynical; they blame the victim; they adopt corporate values; they look for ways to "get the system."

DATA ON WHO IS EMPLOYED IN THE MINING INDUSTRY

According to Natural Resources Canada, the mining and quarrying industry had 71,380 workers in 2016.[8] This figure included jobs in coal mining, the potash industry, stone mining and quarries, and diamond mining. The average total compensation per job of $115,174 in the mining and quarrying industry was nearly double the Canadian all-industry average ($59,903).

In 2016, employment in the mining support activities industry, which includes exploration activities, decreased 3.1 percent to 24,730, marking the fourth consecutive year of decline. Average total compensation per job in the mining support industry for 2016 was approximately $104,917.

The primary metal manufacturing industry, composed mostly of facilities engaged in the smelting and refining of ferrous and nonferrous metals, employed 64,740 workers in 2016; average total compensation per job in 2016 was $102,277.

People who work in the 3,700 companies in the mining supply and services sector are spread across these positions.[9] Mining companies are increasingly contracting work out, especially highly skilled work. For example, capital costing, mining plans, mine scheduling, building and repairing electrical equipment and machines, and artificial intelligence are generally contracted out now. In Sudbury, where the sector has really developed, less than five thousand people work for the two big mining companies, but sixteen thousand people work in the supply and services sector.[10]

Two-thirds of Canada's total mining sector employment is concentrated in Ontario and Quebec, which is largely attributable to the presence of a significant downstream manufacturing industry in these jurisdictions. Year over year, employment has fallen in all jurisdictions except Nunavut, which experienced increases in gold and silver ore mining, and New Brunswick, which saw an increase in employment levels in the support activities for the mining subsector.

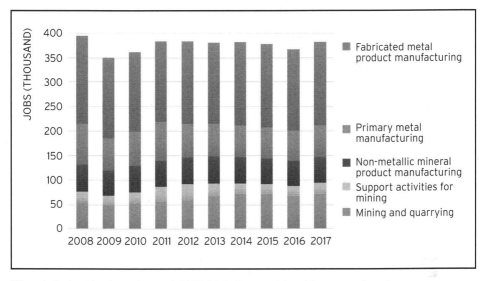

Minerals Sector Direct Employment, 2007–2016. *Source:* Natural Resources Canada.

The Mining Industry Human Resources Council forecasts that hiring requirements in the mining industry will escalate in the next ten years (to 2027) as older workers retire. Their predictions of the need range from 43,000 to 130,000 new workers.

The mining sector is an important employer of Indigenous peoples, providing jobs to over eleven thousand individuals, mainly in exploration and quarrying.

This is a male-dominated industry. Women comprise 48 percent of the Canadian workforce, but only 17 percent of the mining labour force. In mining-specific jobs, women represent only 12 percent of employment. "Mining-specific jobs" are those that are engaged in actual mine operations, as opposed to catering, camp services, and administration.

When new mines are being proposed, companies will always promote the number of jobs the new mine will create. Invariably, these numbers do not take into account the fact that most new workers at the mine project will have already been employed elsewhere. They are gross numbers, not net of previous employment. The companies will also use an inflated number of "indirect jobs" to promote their project, through a "multiplier." Actually, it has been found that the multiplier for mines

(1.5 percent) is considerably less than for arts and culture (over 3 percent).[11] (See the discussion of intrusive rentier syndrome in chapter 5.)

GETTING RESPECT AND FAIR TREATMENT FROM MINING COMPANIES

No one knows better than miners, millworkers, and smelter workers how difficult and dangerous the work can be, and how hard shift work and fly-in/fly-out schedules are on the worker, the family, and community life.

Mining companies in Canada know that unless they pay their workers well, deal with health and safety issues, and at least appear to be dealing with the social and environmental impacts of mining, they will not find anyone to do the work. Historically, companies have learned this the hard way, as a result of organized pushback from their workforce.

To push back, miners need unions.

A union is a formalized, democratic structure that enables employees in a workplace to make decisions collectively about what they need and want from their employer and through collective action address problems that arise on the job. The national (or international) union will have staff to carry out work that the membership wants done: research, organizing, and so on.

Miners' unions are set up so that members at one mining project usually belong to a "local" of a national or international union. The members of the local elect the executive of the union and choose their "stewards," the people who will handle specific job grievances with management for them.

The local union (with assistance from the national office) also handles negotiating a contract of work for all the workers with the employer when it is coming due. This is called *collective bargaining*. Since the company is so dependent on the work that miners do, the threat that they might strike for their demands is the chief bargaining tool. What will be asked for in the contract is determined by a vote of the local members and in strategy discussions with the national union. The national union will also have amassed a "strike fund" from union dues to pay workers a portion of their wages if they have to strike.

In Canada (and all provinces), the rules of the workplace and collective bargaining are set out in law. Because the laws governing the workplace have been worked out through power struggles between employers and workers, they reflect the outcome of these battles. Where the labour movement has been weak, the rules heavily favour the boss. For example, the rules require conciliation before a strike vote; they limit the number of people who can be on a picket line during a strike and for how long the picket can stop production. The rules require that the union is responsible for the costs incurred by the employer if the strike is not at a legally acceptable time and place ("wildcat"). If a workplace is considered an "essential service," workers may not be "allowed" to strike. On the other hand, the law enforces a compulsory dues check-off once a union is certified, and, when a union has been voted in by its members, requires the company to bargain with it.

As you can imagine, collective bargaining simplifies industrial relations for employers of large numbers of workers. However, it is in their interests to keep the union weak by pitting workers against each other and diminishing its ability to get public support. The company will also insist on its "management rights"—its power to determine how production is carried out, including questions like expansion and automation, pollution prevention, the way the workplace is set up, and what work might be contracted out.

Besides having protection against arbitrary discipline and firing, unionized workers have higher wages, and the wages are more equally distributed. Eduardo Regier writes,

> Unions also serve to raise social expectations for compensation and these effects "spillover" into non-unionized workplaces . . . . Of unions whose contracts were examined, most were found to include retirement or pension plans, paid time off, and healthcare coverage. They also show that union members are less likely to be exposed to hazardous or unsafe working conditions due to contracts that specifically outline [the] employer's responsibility to provide a safe working environment, as well as protections for employees who bring safety hazards to the attention of their supervisor.[12]

Given how important unions are to dealing with powerful mining companies, you would think everyone working in mining would belong to one. About 45 percent of the mining sector is organized.[13] However, in general, smaller mining companies, mining supply and services companies, and exploration companies are not unionized.

Employers are afraid that their workers will organize a union. They make sure this does not happen in a number of ways: providing wages and conditions of work that are comparable to unionized workplaces, vilifying the role of unions to their workers, encouraging intra-union battles, firing or intimidating anyone who tries to organize a union, and contracting work out to non-union shops.

The other way to deal with recalcitrant workers, of course, is to get rid of them, through automation or contracting out. When I moved to Sudbury in 1970, there were over 25,600 blue-collar workers at Inco and Falconbridge and a number of contractors.[14] Now there are less than five thousand, but the production has not diminished.[15] Open-pit mines, for example, use many fewer workers than underground mines. These workers spend the day in trucks and excavators with air-conditioned cabs. Unless they live in a mining camp, they are unlikely to meet other workers during the day, as even their lunch breaks are staggered. Many of the workers are being replaced by robots, controlled remotely from another place entirely.

Occasionally, companies will also offer shares to their employees to ensure their loyalty.

Social Unionism

When I moved to Sudbury with my husband, Don, in 1970, it was to apprentice myself to Weir Reid. Weir had been the director of recreation for the Mine Mill Union in Sudbury during the 1950s. He initiated award-winning dance and theatre groups, fostered cinema, reading, and sports, and developed a comprehensive summer camp program for children.

Don and I met him when we had travelled around the province organizing tenants to change the *Landlord and Tenant Act*, and we had been bowled over by the kindness of his wife, Ruth, and by the experience and knowledge Weir had about organizing. At that time, Weir was helping some Mine Mill Union members in public housing organize.

Mine Mill was a different kind of union than those that exist today. Writes John Lang,

> From its earliest days, Mine Mill emphasized political action, taking an active part in countless campaigns for legislative reforms and working to elect labour members to legislative office. It gave top priority to organizing campaigns, which in the heyday of Mine Mill ensured that virtually the entire hard-rock mining industry in Canada worked under union contracts. In the 1940s and 1950s its cultural and recreational programs quickly became models of their kind for the labour movement.[16]

Of course, the mining companies hated Mine Mill and attacked the union for being "communist." In the late 1950s, when the United Steelworkers of America sought to replace Mine Mill as the union at the nickel mines in Sudbury, Weir became a major target of the Steelworker organizers and their supporters. They accused him of recruiting communists through the cultural programs, a charge for which there was no evidence whatsoever. Weir sued his attackers for defamation and won on all counts, but not before his life and that of his family was brought to the brink of ruin.[17] Weir died at the age of fifty-three in 1971, worn out by the conflict.

Almost all the programs Weir brought to the city through the union were later taken up by community organizations. Mining unions today often support "cultural activities" such as the Mayworks Festival and community arts projects, including miner memorials and Workers' Memorial Day projects. Most also provide funds for international solidarity work through a one-cent-an-hour dues check off.

Unions Representing Miners and Smelter Workers Today

There are currently four unions and one quasi-union representing miners and smelter workers in Canada.

The United Steelworkers (USW) is North America's largest private-sector union, with a strong presence in the Canadian mining sector, representing workers in copper, nickel, iron ore, coal, potash, gold, silver, lead, cadmium, lime, and other ore-extraction operations. The union also represents mine-sector workers in smelting, refining, maintenance, and transportation, as well as office and technical employees.

Unifor represents over six thousand members working in mining and smelting. The sector includes potash, as well as aluminum and nonferrous smelting operations. Today, the largest number of Unifor members (1,850) in the sector work for Rio-Tinto-Alcan in Quebec and at Kitimat, British Columbia; 900 work for Mosaic Potash in Saskatchewan; 500 for Compass Minerals in Goderich, Ontario; and another 900 members work for Glencore in Sudbury. Workers in a number of smaller mines make up the rest of the membership.

The United Mine Workers of America represents active and retired coal workers in Nova Scotia, Alberta, and British Columbia. It was recently engaged in an unsuccessful attempt to organize workers at the Donkin coal mine in Nova Scotia.

The Union of Northern Workers (a component of the Public Service Alliance of Canada) represents workers at the Ekati Mine in the Northwest Territories (now owned by Dominion Diamonds).

Workers at the Diavik Mine are members of the Christian Labour Association of Canada (CLAC), which prides itself on its friendly management relations.[18]

OCCUPATIONAL HEALTH AND SAFETY

I worked at the Sudbury Community Legal Clinic for seven years, and much of my work had to do with representing injured workers who were trying to get their bad back, white hand, industrial deafness, chronic obstructive pulmonary disease, or some other awful disability recognized by the Workers' Compensation Board (WCB). The Mine Mill Union and the Steelworkers Unions handled claims for their members, but the unorganized workers, such as those working for contractors, ended up at the clinic.

One of the people I represented had seriously hurt his back spreading lime in 1984 to "reclaim" Sudbury's blackened hills as part of a welfare make-work project. The WCB claimed that it was a "pre-existing injury," the welfare office said he was "malingering," and the doctor found no bone damage on the X-ray. He never did get compensation, and his welfare was stopped for a few weeks in punishment. Nothing was done to the contractor that was in charge of the work.

In different provinces, the governments track workplace fatalities, critical injuries, and "lost-time claims" by sector. In the mining sector in Ontario alone, between 2012 and 2017 (five years) there were 17 fatalities, 169 critical injuries, and 54 refusals to carry out unsafe work. There were slips and falls, white hand and other vibration-related problems, back injuries from manual handling of materials, and repetitive strain. Worker fatigue was also identified as a serious problem.[19] The lost-time injury rate was 0.63 per hundred workers. Occupational diseases (like silicosis, chronic obstructive lung disease, and cancers) are a major concern, caused by toxins in smelters and mills, silica dust, diesel exhaust, and exposure to arsenic, lead, and asbestos. In Ontario alone, between 2011 and 2015, 106 mine workers died of occupational diseases.

Due to decades of organizing, lobbying, and advocacy by workers and their families, the federal government and all provinces and territories have workplace health and safety laws, workers' compensation regimes, and staff to enforce them. However, every one of them has come after many workers had been killed on the job, suffered a serious injury, or died of an industrial disease.

Most mines with unions have a joint health and safety committee between the union and management. If there is no union, then the workers have to rely on the government's *Occupational Health and Safety (OHS) Act* and regulations. The OHS laws apply to all workers. They include the right to refuse unsafe work and a means to make a complaint. The Canadian Centre for Occupational Health and Safety website provides a comprehensive list of legislation, hazards, and programs.[20]

There is also a Criminal Code provision called the Westray Bill, under which the company, its directors, and/or supervisors can be criminally charged for negligence if a violation of the health and safety laws result in serious injuries or death. The Act came into force on March 31, 2004, twelve years after a methane explosion at the Westray coal mine in Nova Scotia killed twenty-six miners. The mine—heavily subsidized by the federal and provincial governments—opened in 1991 and operated for only eight months before the disaster. Unions, the workers, and even government inspectors had been raising safety concerns since before it opened, but nothing had been done.

After the accident, a public inquiry was held, which found that "[Westray] is a story of incompetence, of mismanagement, of bureaucratic bungling, of deceit, of ruthlessness, of cover-up, of apathy, of expediency, and of cynical indifference."[21] Clifford Frame, the founder, principal shareholder, developer, and chairman and CEO of Curragh Resources, the company whose subsidiary operated the mine, refused to take the stand and testify. A criminal case against two mine managers (Gerald Phillips and Roger Parry) went to trial in the mid-1990s, but ultimately was dropped by the Crown in 1998, as it seemed unlikely that a conviction could be attained. Curragh Resources went bankrupt in 1993.[22]

Outrage at the lack of successful charges in the Westray disaster led the union movement to advocate for the Westray Bill, holding company directors and supervisors criminally liable for workplace crimes. It took twelve years before it passed.

Since 2004, there have been fewer than a dozen charges laid under the Westray Bill, and only one jail sentence. The only charge involving a mining company named two employees of Quebec-Cartier Mining for an accident on October 13, 2006. The court found that the employees were not guilty of criminal negligence and acquitted them. Justice Dionne held that the events of that day were attributable to an error of fact that arose from "a corporate culture of tolerance and deficient training, not wanton and reckless disregard for the lives and safety of a worker" on behalf of the two individuals.[23]

7

AFTER THE MINE: CLOSURE AND LONG-TERM CARE

If you are to fly over Pine Point Mines you would look down and you would think you were flying over the moon with the craters and open pits that are left open. The people have never been compensated for the hardships and heartaches induced by mineral development. While the company creamed the crop at $53 million during their peak years, we got very little jobs and what we did get were very low-paying jobs.

—Bernadette Unka, Chief of Fort Resolution's
Chipewayan Band[1]

Mine closure and rehabilitation is the last phase of the mineral development cycle. It is defined as the orderly, safe and environmentally sound conversion of an operating mine to a closed state. Upon closure, areas affected by the mining activity should become viable and self-sustaining ecosystems that are compatible with a healthy environment and with human activities.

— Natural Resources Canada, *Trainer's Manual: Exploration and Mining Guide for Aboriginal Communities*[2]

Orphaned or abandoned mines are those mines for which the owner cannot be found or for which the owner is financially unable or unwilling to carry out cleanup. They pose environmental, health, safety and economic problems to communities, the mining industry and governments in many countries, including Canada.

—National Orphaned/Abandoned Mines Initiative[3]

This chapter looks at the long-term legacy of mining projects and provides a case study from Yukon's Faro Mine to illustrate the key issues.[4]

There are more than ten thousand abandoned mines in Canada. Most have not been closed out properly. These sites are now the responsibility of taxpayers through their governments, as those who profited from them are long gone. Former mine sites are not only scars on the land, they are, as Scott Fields writes, "earth's open wounds":

Old mine workings may be partially caved in and timbers rotted, presenting physical hazards. Carelessly scaled openings are irresistible to children and thrill seekers. Workings that underlie streets and buildings can collapse. Tailings dams too, can collapse. Acid Mine Drainage (AMD) can contaminate streams, tinting them with the tell-tale orange sediment marking high concentrations of liberated iron. . . .

Other hazards are hidden. Along with the freed iron often come other, less visible elements, including potentially toxic cadmium, copper, lead, manganese, zinc, arsenic and mercury. High winds can carry dust contaminated with metals from tailings deposits and waste piles. Even ancient mining activities can release gases that make air unsafe to breathe—methane from coal mines, and carbon monoxide from so-called hard rock mines, where metals such as copper, silver, lead, cadmium and zinc are extracted. Waters from uranium and phosphate mines can carry radiation well above normal background levels.[5]

When MiningWatch started in 1999, a number of our board members were desperate for cleanup of the abandoned mine sites in their region and believed getting national attention for them was the only way anything would happen.

As a result, MiningWatch participated with the Mining Association of Canada in founding the National Orphaned/Abandoned Mines Initiative (NOAMI) in 2001. NOAMI became a vehicle to force government representatives to hear the horror stories from communities trying to deal with abandoned mines and to push governments to deal with these legacy issues through funding and changes to law and policy.

It took pressure from 2002 to 2017—fifteen years!—before NOAMI was able get the necessary information from governments and release a map and inventory of abandoned mine sites in Canada.[6] Maps from British Columbia, Yukon, and Quebec, all very significant mining jurisdictions, are still missing. British Columbia has its own map of "historic mines," as does Quebec, but these jurisdictions could not agree on how the scale of different threats posed by mines should be categorized.[7]

MiningWatch Canada estimates the total cost for cleaning up all these sites could be much more than $9.1 billion, including $3.1 billion for Ontario, $2.4 billion for British Columbia, $1.9 billion for Quebec, and $1.7 billion in the Northern territories.[8] It is costing over $1 billion just to contain the toxins at the Giant Mine in Yellowknife, where 237,000 tons of arsenic trioxide are stored in underground mine shafts. Giant Mine is discussed in much more detail in chapter 17.

The process of getting the problems from these mines under control can take decades. The Faro Mine is one example, not only of the huge impacts from the site, but also of the hurdles Indigenous peoples and communities affected by the site continue to face. The mine operated on and off for thirty years; the remediation planning process has already taken twenty. Actual remediation of the site is not expected to begin before 2022, and it will have to be monitored and managed forever.

THE FARO MINE

The Faro lead-zinc mine is one of Canada's largest abandoned mine sites. Located in Yukon, it operated sporadically from 1968 to 1998, with four different corporate owners: Cyprus-Anvil, Dome Resources, Curragh Resources, and Anvil Range. At its peak, the mine employed up to nine hundred people—15 percent of Yukon's workforce—and produced 40 percent of Yukon's annual GDP. When it went into receivership and closed for good, the reclamation bond held by the federal government was only $14 million, and over the mine's life, the company had received over $53 million in subsidies.[9] An entire town, Faro, had been built to house mine workers and their families, but it was decimated when the mine closed. Faro now has fewer than 350 residents. A lot of its housing has been torn down, and it is difficult for the town to support the sewer, water, and other infrastructure that was built for a lot more people.

About sixty-five kilometres east of the mine complex is the community of Ross River.

> Ross River is home to the Ross River Dena, members of the Kaska Nation. The mine complex is located in the traditional territory of the Kaska people and is an area of significant cultural importance. Before the mine was built, the Kaska considered the surrounding area as their "breadbasket." Here they fished and hunted for moose, caribou and sheep, collected wild berries and traditional plants and set up trap lines for lynx, mink and other animals.[10]

The Ross River Dena never benefitted from the mine. Currently they are facing a severe housing crisis, as one-half of their 130 houses are deemed too toxic to live in. They are contaminated with mould, radon, diesel, and sewage.[11]

Downstream from the mine site is the traditional territory of the Selkirk First Nation, centred on the community of Pelly Crossing. Waters draining from Faro flow into the Pelly River, which Selkirk First Nation uses for hunting, fishing, and cultural activities.

In the mine's on-again, off-again life, huge amounts of mine tailings were dumped in Rose Creek, which flows into the Pelly River. There are three open pits at the mine site, as well as 70 million tons of acid-generating tailings and 396 million tons of sulphide waste rock. There is urgency to the containment of these materials, as they have already been oxidizing (creating acid mine drainage) for almost forty years. The ability of the peat below the tailings to neutralize metals is also being depleted.[12] The gravest danger is further contamination of the groundwater and the poisoning of the Pelly River system.

The Faro Mine and tailings ponds. Photo courtesy of Gerry Whitely.

Concerns about the Faro Mine pollution issues were raised for many years by Ross River Dena, Selkirk First Nation, the Yukon Conservation Society (YCS), and even some line staff in government departments, but there was no political will to fund cleanup.

In 1999, the newly formed MiningWatch Canada, with YCS, began to lobby the federal government to remediate northern abandoned mines like Faro. In 2001, NOAMI held its first workshop in Winnipeg. In 2002, the federal auditor general's office released a damning report on abandoned mines under federal jurisdiction in the North. Faro was one of the case studies.

The federal government created the Contaminated Sites Management Working Group in 1995 but neglected to fund it for more than a few staff positions. In 2003, $175 million over two years was allocated to the program. At the end of 2003, the *Edmonton Journal* published a devastating series of articles on Northern abandoned mines (including Faro) written by Ed Struzik, which was syndicated nationally.

In 2004, brilliant work by member of Parliament Charles Caccia and some federal public servants changed federal accounting systems to an accrued liability model, so that contamination of federally owned sites became a liability on the public accounts—offsetting the "assets" that the government mine sites had previously represented. Since investing in site cleanup could then be counted as paying down the federal debt, the government committed $3.5 billion to the Federal Contaminated Sites Action Plan (FCSAP), an interdepartmental program headed by the Ministry of the Environment and Treasury Board.[13] It is this money that made creating an inventory of federal contaminated sites and a cleanup of some key mine sites in Yukon and Northwest Territories possible. In 2016, the FCSAP program was allocated another $1.5 billion over four years for the over twenty thousand sites identified.[14]

With the devolution of federal powers to Yukon, while the Faro Mine surface land was transferred to the Yukon territorial government, contaminated sites such as Faro remained the responsibility of the federal government, although water licences had to be obtained from the Yukon Water Board. The court-appointed interim receiver for the bankruptcy of the Faro Mine, Deloitte and Touche, was to oversee the care and maintenance program for the site until the receivership was wrapped up in early 2009. The Yukon government then took over management of the site through a five-year contract to Denison Environmental Services. Canada paid the bills. The contract was transferred to California-based Parsons Corporation in 2016.

Following negotiations with Ross River First Nation, Liard First Nation, Kaska Dena Council, and Selkirk First Nation, the federal government took back the care and maintenance of the site from Yukon on May 1, 2018. It costs more than $7.2 million per year just to maintain the site.

The federal government was planning to begin building a several -kilometres-long diversion system to collect and transport dirty water at the north fork of Rose Creek in August 2018. The work has been delayed until spring 2019. That project is supposed to last between two and two and a half years, and a contract for over $80 million has been given to Parsons for work in the next two years alone. It is expected that work to remediate the mine site itself will begin in 2022.[15]

Studies, Negotiations, and Delays

After the mine's closure in 1998, the possibilities of reopening the Faro Mine or reprocessing the tailings were considered for a few years, but in 2002, the remediation project office began a "multi-interest review" toward the development and implementation of a final closure plan. From 2003 to 2008, a number of workshops were held with the various groups involved in the site.

Over one hundred technical studies were undertaken to characterize the site and its hazards. Among these studies was a human health and ecological risk assessment undertaken by Senes Consultants, which concluded that "the current risks and impacts associated with the ARMC [Anvil Range Mining Complex] are low for resident aquatic life, terrestrial wildlife, and humans."[16] However, inside the risk assessment was disturbing data about excessively high levels of lead in berries, beaver, ptarmigan, and moose.[17]

In 2004, the federal and territorial governments entered into agreements with Selkirk First Nation and the Ross River Dena Council to work together on a closure plan. An oversight committee was created, made up of representatives from Indian and Northern Affairs Canada, the Yukon government, Selkirk First Nation, the Kaska Tribal Council (represented by Ross River Dena Council), and (after 2008) Liard First Nation.

The Faro Mine Oversight Committee did not actually oversee monitoring or provide any community communication. It was put in place to help select alternatives for actually closing the site and what sort of governance would be needed once remediation was underway.[18] A website, www.faromine.ca, was set up to communicate information about the project.

The final cleanup plan for Faro will require an environment assessment from the Yukon Environmental and Socio-Economic Assessment Board before it can proceed. Although a draft project closure proposal was prepared in early 2010, it has not yet been submitted.[19]

The Faro Independent Peer Review Panel[20]

In 2006, a team of independent experts was contracted through Deloitte and Touche to serve as an Independent Peer Review Panel.[21] They were asked to review and comment on the various alternatives for closure that were being considered and to report directly to the oversight committee. The panel submitted its report in April 2007.

The highly qualified Independent Peer Review Panel said some important things about Faro (which they referred to as the Anvil Range Mining Complex, or ARMC), which speak to our ability to manage these abandoned mines in the future. In thinking about the long-term implications in 2007, the panel found (in part) the following:

Soil covers at the Anvil Range Mine Complex should be planned to function for thousands of years. They are not "walk-away" solutions as ongoing care and proactive maintenance will be required to maintain their design function. If there were a significant degradation in the covers, there is the potential for a metal release rate from an accumulated reservoir of secondary mineral precipitates that could exceed that occurring in the absence of a cover placement. . . .

There are presently many unknowns and challenges. . . . Challenges include predicting repair costs, difficulty in detecting leaks, predicting future settlement of the underlying waste rock and monitoring changes in buried layers within the cover . . . .

It is inevitable that long term treatment of seepage, groundwater, and open pit waters will be required, possibly as long as 500–1000 years, a situation amounting to "perpetual care.". . .

Alternatives need to be assessed against the potential future physical and social conditions which they may face, . . . seismic and hydrologic conditions, . . . variations . . . . in the nature of society and . . . institutions including the capacity for knowledge transfer, the availability of needed human resource capacity, and the potential evolution of science and technology.[22]

The panel also warned about earthquakes, climate change, wildfires, and floods. They emphasized the need for:
- financial surety for site operation, for project regulation and oversight, and for dealing with full project lifecycle, predicted to be several hundred years
- ensuring the availability of trained and experienced workers for site operation through the unforeseen problems
- ensuring access—over centuries—to transportation systems, power supply, and supplies of needed materials and services[23]

DEALING WITH PERPETUAL CARE ISSUES

In the fall of 2010, Alternatives North engaged me to undertake a study (published as *The Theory and Practice of Perpetual Care of Contaminated Sites*[24]) as a part of the environmental assessment of the remediation plan for the Giant Mine in Yellowknife. The alternative being assessed by the EA was to create a block of permafrost to immobilize 237,000 tons of arsenic trioxide—the wastes from roasting arsenopyrite ores in order to extract gold over a fifty-year period—currently stored in underground drifts. Until an alternative plan is developed, the frozen block will have to be maintained "in perpetuity." (There is more about Giant in chapter 17.)

Perpetual care is also called "long-term stewardship" and "post-construction completion." Here are a few of the things I learned about perpetual care.

The writing on perpetual care of contaminated sites is multidisciplinary, ranging from psychology, ethnography, and community studies to nuclear physics, engineering, political science, and accounting. Many of these disciplines do not talk to one another.

In Canada, long-term contaminated sites are the legal responsibility of a number of different government bureaucracies with their own structures, cultures, and idiosyncrasies. The organizations that are charged with care of these sites tend to be complex and politically vulnerable. Information is managed in a secretive manner, handled selectively, and released slowly.

In places where mines are built, the ecosystem and people are treated as "sacrifice zones"—land and communities sacrificed for economic progress.[25] Most of these contaminated sites are situated in or near communities—often Indigenous—that opposed the mine in the first place and have advocated for the cleanup of the site for decades. The surrounding communities continue their advocacy, but face living with a toxic isolation facility forever. The efforts of the people who provide leadership for their communities often go unacknowledged, but they drive change on local and national levels.

The extent of the problem is also sobering. A 2003 US National Research Council Report estimated that there were 217,000 contaminated sites in the United States.[26]

The desire to build nuclear waste repositories has stimulated some thinking about ten thousand years into the future, although this has tended to focus on signs and markers for future generations. The problem of "long-term stewardship" of contaminated sites is a relatively modern problem, so there is no real experience to draw on. It is still an experiment. Our only experience is with built archaeological sites, like the Pyramids or the Acropolis.

To date, we have no examples of human-made structures that have lasted this long. Archaeological sites have been vandalized and destroyed by natural events and war, and have crumbled due to entropy. An enormous challenge in site planning is creating enduring monuments or markers that warn future generations of the existence of the hazard. Markers such as those envisaged for the Waste Isolation Pilot Project in New Mexico are extreme attempts to warn people to stay away over at least a ten-thousand-year time frame.

In many Indigenous cultures, there are places that are *tapu*—areas where the people are not supposed to go—but are trespassed upon by settler cultures. In some cases, their very existence is a challenge to the religious beliefs of others, which invites their despoiling. What kind of warning system ensures that people far in the future stay away from these sites and can understand the reasons they must do so?

PART III

PROFITS FROM LOSS: INDUSTRY STRUCTURE, FINANCING, AND INTERNATIONAL PRESENCE

This section looks at how the people who own mines and control the mining industry make profits from loss, even when a company may appear to be losing money. It starts with a description of how mining and exploration companies are structured and financed (including by the public). It then looks at the international presence of Canadian mining and how it is supported by the government. The last chapter in this section talks about the impacts of externalizing costs to other ledgers.

8

THE STRUCTURE AND FINANCING OF THE MINING INDUSTRY IN CANADA

Communities facing a mining issue find themselves dealing with a corporation that has very different interests and plays by different rules than they do. Understanding the rules by which the mining company operates can avoid needless conflicts within and among communities and can strengthen strategy. This chapter will attempt to demystify those rules.[1]

THE SISSON MINE

In New Brunswick, a small group of Wolastoq grandmothers have been occupying the site of a tungsten mine proposed by Northcliff Resources for more than three years. If the mine is built, it will deposit its wastes in the headwaters of their beloved Nashwaak River and displace entire communities from their land. The grandmothers have broad public support from the downstream local community of Stanley and from

Indigenous protectors at the Sisson Mine site. Photo courtesy of Tracy Glynn.

people in the nearby provincial capital of Fredericton, but they are worried that the mine will go ahead. The mine is on the traditional territory of the Wolastoq Nation. The people are also known as the Maliseet.

The mine proposal has divided the Maliseet, as some communities sign participation agreements with the company, afraid they will miss out on promised jobs and contracts if they do not. Northcliff Resources has been selling shares in the project to some local people and made small grants to community projects, creating more conflict. The lives of hundreds of people have been disrupted, as their time is taken up trying to prevent the mine from happening.

The company description of the mine and its project make it sound like its development is guaranteed to go ahead: "Northcliff Resources is a mineral development company focused on advancing the Sisson Tungsten-Molybdenum Project, located in New Brunswick. Northcliff is publicly traded on the Toronto Stock Exchange under the symbol NCF."[2]

The Sisson property hosts a large near-surface tungsten-molybdenum deposit amenable to open pit mining. Sisson has excellent potential to be a near-term metal producer, with the capability to meet increasing tungsten demand from North American, European and Asian markets. . . .

In January 2013, Northcliff announced positive feasibility results for the Sisson Project based on a 30,000 tonnes per day open pit mining and milling operation and an ammonium paratungstate (APT) plant. . . . The Sisson Project has received both provincial and federal approvals after progressing through a rigorous, four-year environmental assessment process. Current project activities are directed toward obtaining construction and operating permits, while the senior management team advances discussions to secure off-take agreements and project financing.[3]

In 2017, I was asked to research the company and help the community understand what was going on. Reading through what Northcliff had told investors (as opposed to the public), I discovered a number of interesting facts about the proposal that made it clear that the mine was very unlikely to go ahead in the near future and that the promised jobs, contracts, government revenues, and community benefits were not going to materialize. The grandmothers might be occupying the site for decades.

This is what a careful reading of their corporate filings revealed.

The Sisson Mine would be five to ten times bigger than most other tungsten mines in the world, but the ore grade (the percentage of tungsten and molybdenum in the ore) is three to seven times lower. The low ore grades appear to make the Sisson Mine the biggest tungsten waste management project in the world.

The mine was unlikely to be economically feasible, given low tungsten prices.[4] Prices in the feasibility study from January 2013 were based on $350/mtu (USD) for tungsten and $15/lb (USD) for molybdenum.[5] In December 2017, although the price of APT tungsten had risen, it was still only $315/mtu (USD).[6] Analysts did not expect the price to go higher.

There was little market for tungsten—it is very recyclable—and there were other, more profitable tungsten mines developing. In late 2015 the sole tungsten mine in Canada (Cantung) suspended operations because of low prices and was placed on care-and-mainte-nance status.

The company—Northcliff Resources—was one of many projects controlled by BC-based Hunter Dickinson Incorporated, which has only one successful operating mine and a history of hyping projects that later failed (see chapter 19). Although the Sisson Mine Project is a limited partnership with Todd Minerals of New Zealand, the company is set up so that its only asset is the mine itself, which would make it dif-ficult for governments to hold the company accountable for accidents or reclamation.[7] Until late 2018, Todd Minerals had one operating tung-sten mine in the UK: Wolf Minerals Drakelands Mine, which is 32.3 percent owned by Todd Corporation. However, deeply in debt and with serious technical problems, that mine is now in liquidation.

Northcliff is still seeking investors to make the Sisson project a reality.[8]

KINDS OF MINING COMPANIES

Mining is the most basic of wealth creation activities: it removes miner-als and crystals from the earth that have no value in currency and trans-forms them into mineral concentrates and gems, which can be sold for dollars and create revenues for the mining company and its owners.

Opening a mine is a very expensive proposition, costing as much as $4 to $5 billion. Each huge piece of earth-moving equipment that mining requires can cost millions of dollars; tires for mining trucks cost over fifty thousand dollars each. When mines are in remote areas, all necessary infrastructure has to be transported to the site, so a mine requires roads, power lines, diesel tank farms, a mill (to crush the ore), a camp, an explosives facility, pipelines, sewer lines, a tailings pond, and trucks, bulldozers, and mechanical shovels. Underground mines are more costly than open pits.

Operating a mine requires electrical power, water lines and pumps, steel balls and rods for the mill, transportation for equipment, concen-trates, labour and materials, catering services, administration, investor services, and banking. Mines also purchase services from consultants: mine planning, environmental consultants, government relations, law-yers, marketing and sales, and so on. Because a lot of money is required to open and operate a mine, a lot of investment is needed.

Canadian Junior Mining Companies

Junior mining companies are exploration companies that have no operating mines and that raise money through the sale of shares and government subsidies. Their balance sheets show nothing but operating losses, as the only cash they generate is from the shares they sell (which shows up in the assets-liabilities section of their financial statements). Geologist Michael Doggett calls them "spending machines."[9]

Many of these junior companies have no real expectation of developing a mine; "instead they are inspired by market trends and taking advantage of the madness of crowds when faced with an effective market hype program that permits these companies to raise millions in equity from naïve (or blindly greedy) public investors to keep their exploration programs going."[10]

As we will see, knowing what kind of mining company one is dealing with is extremely important in responding to a mining problem.

Corporations

Mining companies generally are corporations. A corporation is a separate legal entity distinct from its management and shareholders created under the laws of Canada or a province or territory. The corporate statute has specific rules about a corporation's rights, the governance of the corporation, and the responsibility of those that govern the corporation (generally the board of directors and officers) to the corporation and its shareholders and, in some statutes, other stakeholders. In Canada most corporate statutes generally follow the lead of the federal *Canada Business Corporations Act* (CBCA).

In general, the shareholders of a corporation elect the board of directors (who are paid to attend meetings and sit on committees) at the annual general meeting. The election of the directors usually takes place by proxy—that is, shareholders assign their votes to proxy-holders (other shareholders), who cast the votes for them at the annual meeting.

The board of directors is responsible for overseeing the management of the corporation. The board appoints the chief executive officer (CEO), who is responsible for carrying out the wishes of the board and supervising the day-to-day management of the corporation. There will likely be other officers, such as the chief finance officer (CFO) and various vice-presidents. These officers are usually referred to as *management*.

Corporations are considered in law to be a separate "person" or legal entity: they enjoy the same rights as people. However, corporations do not have a conscience, and their performance is largely driven by their financial performance—their bottom line. Issues like social, cultural, and environmental performance only matter if they affect the finances of the company. Most corporate statutes in Canada require the board of directors and officers to act in the best interests of the corporation. It has been held by Canadian courts that this duty permits the board and management to consider interests other than the shareholders and profit maximization.

The fact that a corporation is incorporated in Canada does not mean that it carries on business in Canada. Similarly, a corporation incorporated in a jurisdiction outside of Canada may carry on business in Canada. Today, under the CBCA, only 25 percent of the members of the board of directors must be resident Canadians. The business corporations acts of Ontario, Manitoba, Saskatchewan, Alberta, and Newfoundland all require 25 percent of directors to be resident Canadians, but the other provinces and territories have no residency requirements whatsoever.[11]

Yukon has the most permissive corporations act in Canada.[12] It allows meetings of directors to take place anywhere in the world and requires no filing of financial statements from "private" companies.

Regardless of where a corporation is incorporated, if it is doing business in Canada, it is subject to Canadian laws. However, if its operations are in another country, generally, Canadian law will not apply to those operations. Canadian courts can decide if the law of Canada or the law of a host country will apply. (More about this in chapter 9.)

Foreign corporations may also have additional rights under treaties such as the North American Free Trade Agreement (NAFTA). Chapter 11 of NAFTA protects US companies from an "expropriation of their value" caused by a change of law or regulation. Other rights are established through bilateral agreements and treaties with host countries. (There is more about this in chapter 9.)

Subsidiaries

Corporations often form and own other corporations, which are called *subsidiaries* (if the corporation owns over 50 percent of the voting shares) or *affiliates* or *related companies* (if it owns a lesser number). These subsidiary companies are considered to be corporate persons separate and distinct from the parent company.

Most mining companies incorporate a separate entity to manage each mine. Unless that separate company's agreements are guaranteed by the parent company, the only assets the subsidiary company owns will be the mine and its infrastructure. There can be an endless chain of subsidiaries, affiliates, and related companies, incorporated in many different jurisdictions. In many cases, the company has a number of holding companies, set up as tax shelters and administrative units in tax shelters like the Barbados, the Cayman Islands, and the British Virgin Islands.

Some mining company subsidiaries, affiliates, and related companies will be joint ventures with other mining companies, with some agreement to share profit or loss. The terms of the joint venture are spelled out in an agreement between the two (or more) companies. Indigenous governments and corporations may enter into joint ventures with mining companies on their territories.

Private and Public Companies

From the perspective of how they raise money, there are two basic kinds of mining companies: public companies (not to be confused with state-owned companies) and private companies.

A public company sells shares to the public and uses stock exchanges and similar public financial markets. Shareholders buy parts of the company, called *shares*, and are said to have *equity* in the company. People who buy shares of the company (whether private or public) are called *shareholders*.

A private company does not sell shares on financial markets or to the public generally. It raises its money from "private" sources (which under securities laws include founders, family, and sophisticated investors such as mutual funds, financial institutions, pension funds, and wealthy individuals). An example of a private mining company is De Beers

Canada, which owns the Victor diamond mine in northern Ontario. It is a subsidiary of De Beers plc, a holding company that controls the De Beers Group of Companies. De Beers plc is 85 percent controlled by Anglo American, one of the world's largest mining companies.[13]

Since private companies are not required to report to the securities commission, it is very difficult to get information about them.

Although some small prospecting/exploration companies are private companies, most mining companies are public companies, or private subsidiaries of public companies.

People who lend money to a company in the form of debt are called *creditors*. Creditors rank ahead of shareholders should the company go bankrupt. Consequently, although creditors are in a more secure position than shareholders, their return is generally limited to a set level of interest, while shareholders' return is limited only by the company's profitability (or lack thereof).

Shares and Securities

Shares form the basic raw material of mining industry financial markets. Mining companies can issue hundreds of millions of shares. The value of these shares goes up and down depending on a number of factors: the price they can sell their metals for, the level of speculation in the market, the number of shares they issue, the company's reputation. Some companies have penny stock: their shares are worth very little (for example, nine cents a share); others (and the same company at other times) may have shares worth fifty dollars or more. Speculating on share price is a key feature of the mining stock market. The *market capitalization* of a company is the number of shares multiplied by its share price.

Instruments used for investing are called *securities*, and the industry that buys and sells securities is called the *securities industry*. The securities industry is large and powerful in Canada and is now dominated by the banks. At the beginning of 2018, there were 166 securities firms operating in Canada. In 2016, the seven largest integrated securities firms, which include those owned by the six major domestic banks and one major US dealer, accounted for 71 percent of total securities industry revenues.[14]

Securities industry revenue is made up of commission revenues (including mutual fund transactions), investment banking revenues (underwriting fees and mergers and acquisitions), fixed-income and equity trading revenues, net interest revenues, and other revenues.

Regulation of the Canadian Securities Industry

Regulation of the Canadian securities industry is carried out by the provinces and territories, each of which has its own securities regulator. The thirteen provincial and territorial regulators collaborate through the Canadian Securities Administrators, whose goal is to harmonize and streamline securities regulation in Canada through enhanced interprovincial co-operation.

Since 2008, the Investment Industry Regulatory Organization of Canada (IIROC) has been the self-regulatory overseer for the securities industry. IIROC sets regulatory and investment industry standards and has quasi-judicial powers in that it holds enforcement hearings and has the power to suspend, fine, and expel members and registered representatives, such as advisors. In some provinces, it has the force of law. However, it has often been criticized by investor advocates as ineffective.

HOW THE FINANCIAL MARKETS WORK

Financial markets are where those who want money link up with those who have money and who are prepared to make it available—for a future profit.[15]

—Nick Hildyard and Mark Mansley, *The Campaigners' Guide to Financial Markets*

Companies buy and sell their shares through the financial markets. In Canada, the primary financial markets are the Toronto Stock Exchange (TSX) and the TSX Venture Exchange (TSXV) (responsible for junior equity, and owned by the TSX), and the Montreal Exchange (ME) (focused on derivatives such as stock index options, bond futures, and stock options). These stock exchanges are also public companies.

Stockbrokers and investment banks, through their securities departments, trade on a short-term basis, helping to establish the price of the shares. Their analysts research companies and provide commentary. They also sponsor companies when shares are first listed, market companies to investors, and buy shares with the intention of selling them.

In the short term, the share price depends on supply and demand. Because of the constantly changing price for shares, many investors (especially in exploration companies) are more interested in buying low and selling high in the short term than they are in the long-term performance of a company. A company can raise extra finance by issuing more shares, and they can also buy back shares from investors.

Most mining company shares are held by large financial institutions, including mutual funds, pension funds, bank investment houses, and insurance companies.

Mining companies also raise money by borrowing from banks or issuing bonds—a tradeable form of loan whereby the company agrees to give the buyer a certain amount of interest every year and then repays the bond after a specified number of years.

Companies with operating mines will usually be leveraging their assets—that is, using their existing mine(s) as security in order to build more mines or expand the one they have. It is not uncommon to see companies holding huge debts even when their mines are profitable.

Forms of Stock Instruments

The equity (ownership) in a public company is divided between common shares, preferred shares, options, and warrants:

1. Common shares: The basic shares of company equity held by investors. Shareholders have a vote in the election of the board of directors and carry the profit-loss risk. The value of the common shares is offset by the accumulated deficit and other liabilities, but shareholders are entitled to all that remains (if anything) after the creditors, preferred shares, and so on are paid.

2. Preferred shares: These are shares that are privileged over common shares in terms of the payment of dividends and the return on capital. They generally are non-voting, and their return is limited to a fixed dividend.

3. Options: A company may grant options to directors and officers totalling up to 10 percent of the number of common shares, and may grant more options to others, such as agents. An option is a contract that gives the buyer the right, but not the obligation, to buy or sell equity (shares) on or before a certain date for a specified

price. If, for example, the price of a share skyrockets, the person who holds the option can buy the share for the option price.

4. Warrants: Warrants are issued by the company, and each whole warrant gives the holder the right, but not the obligation, to buy a share at a certain price until a specified expiry date.

OTHER GAMBLING GAMES

There are a lot of other ways of gambling in shares that attract investors. In the mining market, the most significant are derivatives—contracts that gamble on the future prices of assets like shares, commodities, and bonds. The current price of an asset is determined by the market demand for and supply of the asset, but the future price of an asset is a gamble. A week or a month in the future, the price may increase, decrease, or remain the same. Derivatives buyers and sellers hedge their bets against this uncertainty about future price by making a contract for future trading at a specified price. The contract—a financial instrument—is called a derivative.[16]

Options, described in the previous section, are a form of derivative contract.

Hedging is a form of derivative contract that sets the sale price of a commodity (like gold or uranium) based on an anticipated future selling price. If the price goes up more than expected, the seller loses; if it goes down, the seller wins.

Forward selling (gold and/or silver streaming) is a financial transaction in which a company agrees to put money up front for the right to buy gold (or silver or copper, for example) at reduced prices in the future. There are companies that specialize in "streaming," such as Franco-Nevada, but so do pension funds, private equity groups, and hedge funds.

Investment Dealers and Brokers

When shares are offered on the financial markets, they are offered through investment dealers, also called brokers. There are basically two kinds of deals.

In an agency deal, the broker acts only as the agent for the share offering and charges a fee and a commission on sales. Shares that are unsold at the limitation date of the offering return to the mining company that issued the shares.

In an underwritten deal, the dealers effectively agree to buy the shares being offered and resell them to the public. There may be a number of conditions attached to the deal. If there are shares that remain unsold at the end of the offering period, then the dealer retains ownership of the shares (and of the company).

The first issuance of shares for a company is called an initial public offering, or IPO. Except for established mining companies, most share offerings are agency deals of one form or another. The fees charged by the brokers are described in the offering documents.

A NOTE ON DISCLOSURE AND "MATERIALITY"

In Canada, where the securities industry is regulated at the provincial level, the company must tell investors (disclose) information concerning a company's social and environmental affairs that could affect its bottom line in its published documents. The company is required to report "risk" to investors in its annual information return, presentations, and various share offerings. Generally, this is done is a very formulaic manner (and in very small print), which should give anyone pause before placing their money in a company. The fact that people invest anyway indicates the kind of risk-taking investors that are attracted to mineral exploration.

On the SEDAR website, investors and other authorized users can find and retrieve all SEDAR public securities filings and information.

> The System for Electronic Document Analysis and Retrieval (SEDAR) is an online filing system developed for the Canadian Securities Administrators to:
> - facilitate the electronic filing of securities information as required by Canadian Securities Administrator;
> - allow for the public dissemination of Canadian securities information collected in the securities filing process; and
> - provide electronic communication between electronic filers, agents and the Canadian Securities Administrator.[17]

The fundamental criterion for reporting specific risks is *financial materiality.* Social and environmental information has to be reported to the extent that it is deemed to be financially material. In Ontario, the *Securities Act* requires the timely disclosure of information about any "material change" in the affairs of a company. In addition, the TSX has established disclosure guidelines.

If an individual wants a company to disclose to investors information about environmental, social, or cultural impacts, they must couch their concerns in terms of "material costs" or "potential costs." Mining campaigners have complained to securities commissions about lack of disclosure and misrepresentation of material facts by mining companies, which appears to have resulted in changes to what and how companies report. Unlike in the US, in Canada the securities commissions do not publish their communications with companies nor otherwise publicly inform about any investigations undertaken in response to complaints, so it is difficult to know how effective these complaints actually are.

As an example, in May 2017, the Justice and Corporate Accountability Project (JCAP), based in Canada, submitted a thirty-seven-page report to the British Columbia Securities Commission (BCSC) on behalf of a number of Canadian NGOs about the failure of Tahoe Resources to report on opposition to its mining project in Guatemala:

> Tahoe claims strong community support for its Guatemala mine, but the JCAP report highlights Tahoe's annual report, which shows that opposition is so severe that the company was prevented from connecting to the main power grid. The BCSC is being asked to determine whether Tahoe failed to disclose known events or uncertainties that are likely to have an effect on Tahoe's business.[18]

One month after this was filed, the mine was suspended as result of an ongoing protest in which local residents prevented all mine-related traffic from accessing the mine. Mine operations were then further suspended by order of the Guatemalan Supreme Court for discrimination and lack of prior consultation with the Indigenous Xinka population in the area. Tahoe shareholders are also now suing the company for their failure to disclose.

PUBLIC FUNDING OF MINING PROJECTS

There are four basic ways the Canadian public at large helps to finance mining company projects: (1) direct investment (equity, loans, grants); (2) infrastructure support (building hydro lines and roads, providing free water and training of the workforce, negotiating with industry and communities, and permitting pollution without compensation); (3) unfunded liabilities—taking on the risk of catastrophic accidents and the costs of long-term care of the site; and (4) tax incentives and subsidies.

Direct Investment

Governments and public pension funds like the Canada Pension Plan and the Caisse de dépôt et placement du Québec are key sources of mining company investment in Canada. The pension funds of public servants and teachers are also major players. Funds like Fednor and their provincial equivalents provide training for Indigenous workers and heavily subsidize negotiations with communities.

For the international operations of Canadian mining companies, Export Development Canada, Global Affairs Canada, and World Bank institutions may be significant investors. Quebec is the only province that currently makes equity investments in mining companies.

A number of trade agreements—both multilateral and bilateral—also provide deals for mining companies, reducing withholding taxes, allowing tax shelters of various kinds, or, as in NAFTA, protecting companies against the toughening of environmental legislation in the partner country by disallowing the "expropriation of value of the investment" and allowing corporations to sue governments for millions (and even billions) of dollars.

Infrastructure Support

Support from public funds for infrastructure is a critical part of mine financing. Analysis is specific to and different for each mining project and requires careful digging through documents from different ministries in the jurisdiction affected. Subsidies and regulatory bypasses can often be found in forestry permits, fish habitat agreements, water permits, road construction and maintenance financing, port and airport cleanups and construction, railway construction and maintenance, and rates for energy, water, and transportation. Most mining projects benefit from worker training (and sometimes relocation), paid for by governments. Closure and reclamation costs are usually underestimated or not declared at all. Often the company makes assumptions about infrastructure support that has not been cleared with governments, and certainly not with taxpayers.

In Ontario, plans are underway to develop an enormous deposit of chromite and other ores in northern Ontario. The deposit is called the Ring of Fire. To date, the only feasibility studies for the deposit have been based on assuming an enormous contribution from the Ontario government—$1 billion (minimum) for an access road to the area. In addition, the project will not work without the construction of a ferrochrome smelter—the operation of which is not possible without substantially subsidized electricity from the Ontario government. Until a feasibility study is completed for the chromite deposit and ferrochrome smelter, the entire venture is little more than hype.

The Indigenous peoples in the area are demanding control over the Ring of Fire project, which has resulted in a considerable amount of conflict between different communities. "The development of our homelands is about more than any one mine or road, it's about the potential transformation of our lands and way of life—forever," said Eabametoong First Nation Chief Elizabeth Atlookan in a press release.[19] However, the Ontario government and the federal government have been doing everything they can to promote the Ring of Fire.

In 2016, the Ontario auditor general reported the following:

> Since it was established in 2010, the [Ring of Fire] Secretariat has incurred over $13.2 million in operating expenditures. It has also distributed $15.8 million in transfer payments to Aboriginal communities for capacity building (for example, operational support, and education and training initiatives to develop their ability to participate in the mining sector) and other funding support. This other support includes funding a local liaison position on the reserves, as well as funding the negotiation of the Regional Framework agreement between

the province and the nine Matawa First Nations impacted by resource development in the area.[20]

Unfunded Accident and Closure Liabilities

Although most mines in Canada now have to post a reclamation security with governments, these are frequently underestimated and are in a form that cannot be accessed when needed, or are only available for closure, not for accidents. The Mount Polley situation described in chapter 16 is an example—a $14.7 million cash surety for a cleanup that will cost over $176 million. At the heart of this issue is the use of discount rates to estimate the financial assurance that depends on constant economic growth.[21]

Tax Benefits and Subsidies

Given the importance (and complexity) of taxation to mining companies, this is discussed separately in chapter 13. It is important to recognize that most mining companies pay very little tax, even when their operation is apparently very profitable.

ESTIMATING MINERAL POTENTIAL: FEASIBILITY STUDIES

No mining project will go ahead without a credible ore body—enough of the desired mineral that is economic to mine. Generally speaking, all exploration companies hype the value of their findings to the extent they are allowed, in order to encourage investment and possibly sell the project to a big mining company. For affected communities, it is important to determine if the company's real intentions are to mine investors and the tax system, to mine minerals in the ground themselves, or to sell to another company. It is also important to know if the company will make enough money to meet its environmental, social, and worker health and safety commitments. Very marginal mines cannot do this.

The 1997 Bre-X scandal (where a Canadian company was found to be fraudulently providing mineral estimates from the Busang project in Indonesia) led to stricter rules about reporting about proposed mineral potential. The securities regulators have developed a policy, *National Instrument (NI) 43-101*, or the *CIM Definition Standards*, that describes the ways in which mineral potential must be described in public company documents.

NI 43-101

NI 43-101 provides standards for the classification of mineral resource and mineral reserve estimates into various categories, based on rules developed by the Canadian Institute of Mining, Metallurgy, and Petroleum. The definition standards can be found on securities commission websites.

The category to which a resource or reserve estimate is assigned depends on the level of confidence in the general geological information available about the mineral deposit, the quality and quantity of data available on the deposit, the level of detail of the technical and economic information that has been generated about the deposit, and the interpretation of the data and information. The NI 43-101 report may include a (usually overly optimistic) discussion of community and First Nations consultation.

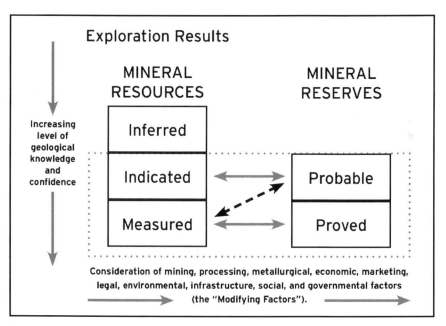

Resource Estimates Diagram. *Source:* CRIRSCO (Committee for Mineral Reserves International Reporting Standards)

Commodity Price

It is important to remember that mineral potential is closely tied to the price of the commodity and the extraction costs. The commodity price—the sale price of most minerals extracted in Canada and around the world—is set on the London Metals Exchange (LME), and is somewhat related to supply and demand for the mineral. Coal prices are set in April each year by major coal producers. Some commodities, like uranium, are also sold under supply contracts, with prices linked to the "spot" market price (or current market price).

Metal commodity prices are, like other products, vulnerable to speculative bubbles, which do not reflect real demand for a product. Future commodity prices used to predict mineral values over the long term (especially for speculative commodities) are often completely out of line with reality. Predicted and past metal prices can be found at www.infomine.com/investment/metalprices.

NI 43-101 requires that the estimates are verified by an "independent qualified person," or QP, in order to avoid a conflict of interest. In many of the cases we have looked at, the QP is not, in fact, independent, but is a geologist who is also an officer or director of the company, or a contractor. This conflict of interest can keep the estimate of mineral potential from being "NI 43-101 compliant."

Complaints

Complaints about resource hype are taken seriously by the securities commissions and most investors. In fact, investors have strong rights in law to sue:

> If a prospectus contains a misrepresentation, a person who purchases a security offered by the prospectus (a) is deemed to have relied on the misrepresentation if it was a misrepresentation at the time of purchase, and (b) has a right of action for damages against
> (i) the company
> (ii) the underwriter
> (iii) every director of the company at the time the prospectus was filed,

(iv) every person who signed the prospectus, and

(v) every person whose consent has been filed as prescribed.[22]

It is, however, extremely difficult to find a geologist in Canada who is willing to criticize a resource estimate and put their name on the criticism, as they fear being blacklisted by the industry. I am aware of at least two actual cases where this took place.

Scoping and Feasibility Studies

Companies that are serious about developing a project will usually undertake a scoping study (or pre-feasibility study) and then a feasibility study. These documents, which estimate all of the mine's costs and cash flow over time, are directed at potential investors and banks. They almost always contain information that contradicts what the company has been telling the community about the proposed mine.

The feasibility study provides an estimated internal rate of return (IRR) and a net present value (NPV). The IRR is based on the calculation of annual cash flows for a company. It is very sensitive to start-up dates, when the reclamation bond has to be paid, and the price of the metals over time.

MiningWatch Canada has undertaken a number of investor analyses of mining projects in Canada (see chapter 10). In almost every case it has reviewed, there were questionable assumptions and errors, which resulted in an overestimation of cash flow, NPV, and IRR.

Common errors in NPV and IRR calculation include:

- gross underestimation of the capital costs of the project
- a "cut-off grade" based on inflated metal prices
- errors in mine design (for example, how much waste rock needs to be removed to get at the ore)
- failing to provide for a reclamation bond up front
- assuming the project can get its permits earlier than it can
- crediting a sale of mine infrastructure at closure against remediation costs
- assuming government subsidy for power, rail, and roads
- overestimating the long-term commodity price
- underestimating the difficulty in getting equipment, materials, and labour when the demand for them is very high

- underestimating smelter penalties for contaminated concentrates
- underestimating climate change impacts

BANKRUPTCY

When companies get into serious financial trouble and cannot pay their debts, they have three possible remedies: they can sell the company to another company, they can seek to "restructure" under the *Companies' Creditors Arrangement Act* (CCAA), or they can go bankrupt under the *Bankruptcy and Insolvency Act* (BIA).[23]

Both of these acts are federal and apply in all provinces and territories. They are enforced through an application to the courts: the Supreme Court in Nova Scotia, British Columbia, Prince Edward Island, Yukon, and the Northwest Territories; the Superior Court of Justice in Ontario; the Superior Court in Quebec; the Court of Queen's Bench in New Brunswick, Manitoba, Saskatchewan, and Alberta; the Trial Division of the Supreme Court in Newfoundland and Labrador; and the Nunavut Court of Justice.

The purpose of the CCAA is "to facilitate compromises and arrangements between companies and their creditors." The Act provides a method for the company to "restructure" by way of a court-appointed "monitor" or trustee to satisfy at least two-thirds of those to whom the company owes money. Generally, all creditors receive a portion of what they are owed so that the company can continue to operate.

The BIA can be used at the same time as the CCAA, but is usually involved after the CCAA process has failed. The debtor company's assets are placed in the hands of a trustee appointed by the court. The assets and/or the company itself are sold (usually for very little) and the receipts distributed to those to whom the company owes money. This is called *liquidation*. This process can take a very long time to be resolved.

Those to whom the company owes money can be sorted into different groups that have different priority in terms of the money distributed during either the CCAA or BIA process. In order of priority, they are:
- the administrative costs of the bankruptcy or monitor
- workers and employees and employee pension plans
- government obligations (taxes, health tax, unremitted worker deductions, EI, some reclamation costs, etc.)
- secured creditors

- equity interest (shares, interest, etc.)
- unsecured creditors

Liability for Environmental Harms

Most mining companies will have been required by the regulator to post a financial assurance (FA) in some form in order to ensure that the government can access cleanup dollars in case of a bankruptcy. If this is done well, the FA will be outside the bankruptcy proceeding.

However, FAs vary widely. In Ontario, a company's FA might just be a line called an *asset retirement obligation* on a subsidiary balance sheet. The FA can be in the form of cash, a line of credit with a bank, a qualifying environmental trust, an insurance policy, and so on. Most jurisdictions do not require a full payment of the FA before a mine (or mining exploration) starts. It is almost always inadequate to cover the actual costs of cleanup. Government may also be unable to access it for accident cleanup, cost overruns, and other costs. If the mine operation is continued by the bankruptcy receiver, there may be other difficulties.

On January 31, 2019, in the *Redwater* case, the Supreme Court of Canada found that costly end-of-life environmental or other regulatory orders will effectively trump secured and other creditors in a bankruptcy. This is very good news.[24]

As to director and officer liability, the case *Baker v. Ministry of the Environment (Ontario)*, involving Northstar Aerospace, held directors and officers of a company individually responsible for environmental contamination caused by company operations, even after the company had gone bankrupt. An excellent analysis of this case and its implications can be found in a paper by Puri and Nichol.[25] The Supreme Court of Canada refused to hear the case in June 2016. As the authors point out, this liability decision creates a conflict of interest between directors trying to protect themselves and the company itself.

All Canadian provinces and territories and the federal government impose personal liability on directors for unpaid wages, accrued vacation pay, and termination and severance pay (in certain cases). Directors are also personally liable for payroll remittances for amounts deducted from employees' wages on account of income taxes, Canada Pension Plan (or Quebec Pension Plan) contributions, and employment insurance premiums. They are considered to be similar to trust funds.

Additionally, directors can be held personally liable in situations where a company defaults in payment of its GST or HST obligations. Canadian provinces that retain a separate retail sales tax (instead of HST) also impose personal liability on directors for failure to remit the required provincial sales tax. Directors can also be personally liable for failure to remit certain pension contributions, particularly for amounts that were deducted from the employees' pay.

Corporate directors can also be personally liable if the director acted improperly so as to cause loss to the company's creditors.

9

CANADA'S INTERNATIONAL MINING PRESENCE

Canada's mining industry has been an international industry since the first settlers staked their claims. The early explorers and mine developers were Europeans, mostly British. The financing for their mines came from European and American investors, and most of the profits were returned to them. Canadians thrived in the business, buoyed up by rich deposits of gold, copper, and silver, and became experts at identifying ore bodies, building mines, financing them, and managing workers, affected peoples, and sometimes intransigent governments.

As the world economy has increasingly globalized, Canada has been well positioned to extract resources and profits from other countries and sell its mining expertise.[1] In many cases, Canada is just a "flag of convenience" for companies that are essentially controlled by investors and creditors from all over the world.

This chapter turns to Canadian mining's international presence, the ways in which the federal government promotes Canadian mining companies abroad, and the violence that often ensues. It looks briefly at the role of trade agreements, public funding, and embassy support.

CANADA'S GLOBAL MINING PRESENCE, 2018

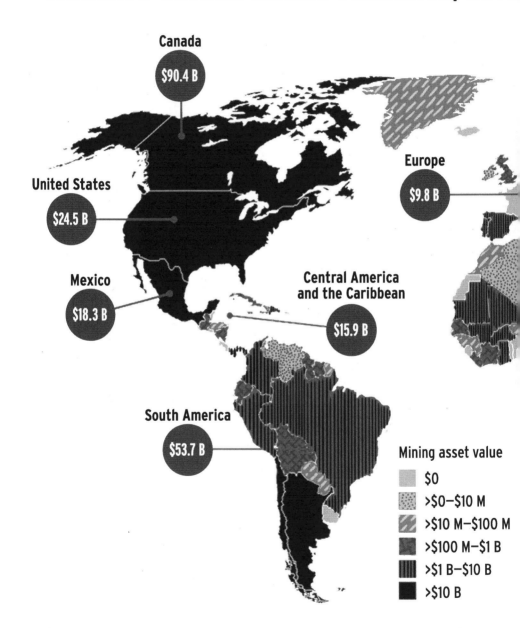

Canada
$90.4 B

United States
$24.5 B

Mexico
$18.3 B

Europe
$9.8 B

Central America and the Caribbean
$15.9 B

South America
$53.7 B

Mining asset value

$0

>$0–$10 M

>$10 M–$100 M

>$100 M–$1 B

>$1 B–$10 B

>$10 B

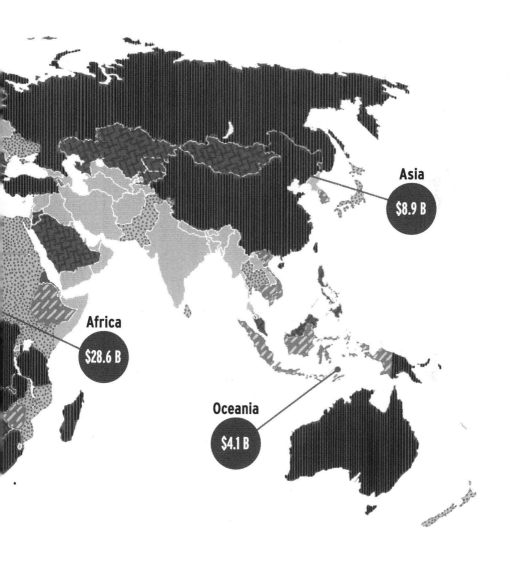

Asia

$8.9 B

Africa

$28.6 B

Oceania

$4.1 B

Source: Adapted from Natural Resources Canada, *Minerals and the Economy* (2018).

The impacts of corporate structures, our legal system, and corporate tax loopholes on the Global South are also briefly addressed.

Funds raised for the mineral industry from 2011–17 on Canada's two key stock exchanges, the TSX and TSX Venture (TSXV), accounted on average for 19 percent of the total mining equity raised globally.[2] In 2015, the TSX and TSXV listed 57 percent of the world's publicly traded mining companies, which together traded more than $148 billion of equity; 32 percent of the total number of mining and exploration companies in the world were headquartered in Canada.[3]

According to Natural Resources Canada, Canadian mining companies operate in more than one hundred countries around the world. In 2017, Canada had $62.6 billion worth of mining investment abroad. Its exports in minerals and metals reached $91.7 billion in 2015, 56 percent of this to the United States.[4]

INTERNATIONAL TREATIES AND AGREEMENTS

Canada has free-trade agreements with fifty-one countries and has signed bilateral foreign investment and protection agreements with thirty-seven countries. These agreements outline the conditions that countries have to meet to provide a "transparent and predictable" climate for investors.[5] In practice, this means that countries eager for foreign direct investment often enter into agreements that rob them of tax revenues and inadequately protect them from the social and environmental impacts of mining and smelting.

If a country legislates to stop a project, it is likely to be sued by the investor (the mining company) for millions and even billions of dollars for "expropriating the value of their investment." When disputes arise, decisions are made by the World Bank's International Court for the Settlement of Investment Disputes (ICSID), by unaccountable panels of commercial lawyers. Defending a country from such a suit can be extremely costly, and the cost award if it wins will not be adequate.[6] Trade agreements discipline countries that respond to the demands of their own people for justice and environmental protection.[7]

In June 2009, Canadian mining company Pacific Rim Cayman LLC sued the state of El Salvador under the Central American Free Trade Agreement (CAFTA) for $77 million (an amount that escalated to $250 million), after the company failed to meet requirements under El Salvador's mining law to get extraction permits for its El Dorado gold mine. When the Ministry of the Environment of that country refused to issue the permits, Pacific Rim pursued international arbitration against El Salvador using CAFTA provisions. Since Canada is not part of that free-trade agreement, Pacific Rim used its US subsidiary in Reno, Nevada, to try to gain access to CAFTA's investor-state dispute settlement mechanism.[8] The suit, which cost the government of El Salvador an estimated $12 million, was finally decided in October 2016. The ICSID tribunal ruled against the company, finding that it had not met mining law requirements and owed El Salvador $8 million. By the time the case was decided, Pacific Rim had been taken over by OceanaGold.

El Salvador has now banned open-pit mining (see chapter 18). This couldn't take place while the suits were in play, effectively putting a chill on such policy-making during the seven years it took to settle. Meanwhile, conflict continued at the local level, including violence and threats against people opposed to the mine.

In Canada, a similar clause under the North American Free Trade Agreement (NAFTA) was used by US-based Bilcon to challenge an environmental assessment panel decision to refuse to permit the Whites Point Quarry on the basis that it conflicted with "community core values" and demanded half a billion dollars in compensation. Bilcon won its case at the United Nations Commission for International Trade Law. In 2018, the federal court upheld the decision in Bilcon's favour.[9] The size of the arbitration award was decided separately. Bilcon had based its estimate of damages on the estimated profit if the quarry were to continue for fifty years. However, a court decision in 2019 found that the damages to the company caused by the environmental assessment panel decision were only $7 million. The quarry did not go ahead.[10]

VIOLENCE AND DEATH

Canadian mining companies operating in the Global South are often predatory in terms of local economies and resource rents, Indigenous and traditional rights, and the environment. They frequently dispossess Indigenous and traditional peoples from the land that sustains them, all the while touting the benefits the mine will later bring to them. When the people resist, they are called criminals and face jail time or worse.[11] As this resistance has grown, so have the attacks on land and water protectors.

In October 2016, the Justice and Corporate Accountability Project (JCAP) released a report consolidating the troubling reports of violence associated with Canadian mining companies in Latin America from 2000 to 2015.[12] All incidents were corroborated by two independent sources. JCAP found that:

- the incidents involved twenty-eight Canadian companies
- there were forty-four deaths, thirty of which were "targeted"
- there were 403 injuries, 363 of which occurred during protests or demonstrations
- there were 709 cases of "criminalization," including legal complaints, arrests, detentions, and charges
- the incidents were widespread: deaths in eleven countries, injuries in thirteen countries, and criminalization in twelve countries

JCAP research showed that TSX-listed companies did not usually report incidents of violence in their investor filings. Between 2000 and 2015, publicly listed companies only reported 24.2 percent of the deaths and 12.3 percent of the injuries listed in the JCAP report.

Five United Nations bodies and the Inter-American Commission on Human Rights have called on Canada to hold its mining companies accountable for multiple incidents of violence. A report commissioned by the Prospectors and Developers Association found that from 1999 to 2009, there were 171 reported incidents of Canadian companies operating internationally involved in community conflict, rights abuses, unlawful or unethical practices, or environmental degradation.[13] Canadian companies were responsible for 33 percent of all violations—more than four times that of India, Australia, the US, or the UK.

Yet Canada still has a no-strings-attached policy when it comes to regulations governing the behaviour of Canadian mining companies operating internationally.

Conflicts inevitably occur when a Canadian mining company in the Global South takes over the claims being worked by small-scale miners, also called "artisanal miners." In 2013, the World Bank estimated that there were one hundred million small-scale artisanal miners in the world,[14] who mine gold, copper, and cobalt in very unsafe conditions. They are driven to this work because it is the only income available to them.[15] Canadian mining companies frequently dispossess them of their claims, livelihoods, and homes in order to create open pits that are mined out in a few years.

As an example, in Tanzania, Acacia Mining, a Barrick Gold subsidiary, has been under increasing pressure about violence and deaths at the North Mara Mine gold property. Catherine Coumans of MiningWatch Canada visited the project every year from 2014 to 2018. In 2016, MiningWatch Canada and Rights and Accountability in Development (RAID) reported,

> There could have been more than 300 violent deaths at North Mara since 1999, including the deaths of women and children who were not trespassing on the mine site[;] . . . hospital records and postmortem reports have sometimes been falsified to conceal the extent of the mine-related deaths and injuries. . . . Their own investigation has found 22 cases of alleged unlawful killings by police or mine security personnel at the site, mostly since 2014.[16]

New cases documented by RAID and MiningWatch in June 2017 included

> loss of limbs, loss of eyesight, broken bones, internal injuries, children hit by flying blast rocks, and by teargas grenades thrown by mine security as they chase so-called intruders into the nearby villages. As in past years, villagers reported severe debilitating beatings, commonly with gun butts and wooden batons. Some are seriously wounded by teargas "bombs," or by so-called rubber bullets. Others are shot, including from behind. As in past years there were a number of deaths.[17]

FINANCING MISERY: EXPORT DEVELOPMENT CANADA AND THE WORLD BANK

Beginning in the 1990s, multilateral institutions led by the World Bank began rewriting over one hundred mining codes in developing countries. The goals included the removal of national control over capital movement, privatization, and the severance of mineral rights from surface rights. According to a Department of Foreign Affairs analysis document, Canada has been present on World Bank teams, contributing to "capacity building relating to various aspects of mining governance, particularly with respect to taxation and the distribution of the benefits from mining, Indigenous peoples' rights, and land ownership."[18]

Honest Accounts 2017, a report published by a coalition of groups concerned about African aid flows, describes the impacts these changes have had on African countries. Canadian mining companies are a significant contributor to the problem described in the report:

> Africa is rich—in potential mineral wealth, skilled workers, booming new businesses and biodiversity. Its people should thrive, its economies prosper. Yet many people living in Africa's 47 countries remain trapped in poverty, while much of the continent's wealth is being extracted by those outside it.
>
> Research for this report calculates the movement of financial resources into and out of Africa and some key costs imposed on Africa by the rest of the world. We find that the countries of Africa are collectively net creditors to the rest of the world, to the tune of $41.3 billion in 2015. Thus much more wealth is leaving the world's most impoverished continent than is entering it.
>
> African countries received $161.6 billion in 2015—mainly in loans, personal remittances and aid in the form of grants. Yet $203 billion was taken from Africa, either directly—mainly through corporations repatriating profits and by illegally moving money out of the continent—or by costs imposed by the rest of the world through climate change. . . .
>
> African countries receive around $19 billion in aid in the form of grants but over three times that much ($68 billion) is taken out in capital flight, mainly by multinational companies deliberately misreporting the value of their imports or exports to reduce tax.[19]

Export Development Canada (EDC) and the World Bank enable some of the most egregious Canadian mining projects to take place, and the screening of the projects they fund rarely takes their externalized costs into account.

EDC is a self-financing Crown corporation that supports Canadian businesses operating abroad with insurance and loans. Its credit is guaranteed by the government of Canada. EDC provides public money for mine development and political risk insurance.[20] Political risk insurance insures mining companies (and others) against the risk of rebellion, expropriation by governments, or other "political risks" to their projects, based on a guarantee from the host government to repay the costs to the EDC should the insurance be needed.

In boom year 2003 alone, EDC's Mining and Infrastructure team paid out more than $2.3 billion to support mining projects. EDC underwrote the development of the Antamina mine in Peru, the Alumbrera smelter in Argentina, the Mozal smelter in Mozambique, the Collahuasi mine in Chile, the North Mara and Bulyanhulu mines in Tanzania, and the Gros Rosebel gold mine in Suriname.

In February 2018, EDC's disclosure database revealed a loan of $1 billion to Turquoise Hill Mining. As reported in the *Toronto Star*,

Between 2010 and 2016, Turquoise Hill ran the finances for its massive Oyu Tolgoi mine in Mongolia through shell companies in Netherlands and Luxembourg, The arrangement allowed it to avoid paying $559 million (U.S.) in Canadian corporate income tax, worth $694 million Canadian at current exchange rates, according to a report put out by the Dutch NGO SOMO this week. According to the report, which was based on public financial declarations, Turquoise Hill declared $2.1 billion in profit in Luxembourg, where it employs only one part-time staff member. The company paid $89 million in tax in Luxembourg—a tax rate of 4.2 per cent. It paid no corporate income tax in Canada, the report states.

"Our job is to support and develop Canada's export trade," states EDC's website. "We are committed to the principles of corporate social responsibility. Our rigorous due diligence requirements ensure that all projects and transactions we support are financially, environmentally and socially responsible."[21]

In May 2018, a report issued by the auditor general of Canada found that EDC "lacks the systems needed to effectively manage risk .... EDC does not have a systemic process to gather risk information from its business units, and its directors are not being given the information they need to fully understand risks." The auditor general identified some of the same weaknesses a decade ago in a 2009 audit.[22]

AVOIDING RESPONSIBILITY: CORPORATE STRUCTURES

The corporate structure of mining companies allows them to avoid taxes and responsibility. Mines in other countries are held through a dizzying array of private subsidiaries, often incorporated in known tax havens such as the British Virgin Islands, the Cayman Islands, or Luxembourg. The Panama Papers (documents leaked from the office of a lawyer in that tax haven in 2015) confirm some of our worst suspicions about tax avoidance and other questionable mining company practices.

Transfer pricing—a business practice that consists of setting a price for the purchase of a good or service between two related companies— enables companies to distort prices to avoid taxation. "Many African tax authorities report corporate services, including procurement and management, as common causes of tax loss."[23]

Former Supreme Court Justice Ian Binnie is quoted in the JCAP report as follows:

> The way those [subsidiaries] are now being used is to have the profits taken from the bottom level of the corporations, sucked up to the top, then using the corporate veil to leave responsibility at the bottom, where there is no money left. It strikes me that, looking at the corporate structure as a whole, there is something wrong with that picture.[24]

EMBASSY PROMOTERS

Canada also promotes these companies through its embassies and trade commissions, representations to local and host governments, threats to withhold foreign aid, and arranging financing deals. As an example, on March 5, 2018,

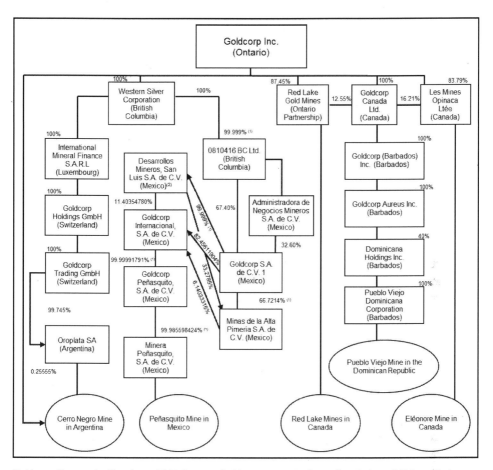

Goldcorp Corporate Structure, 2017. **Source:** *Goldcorp Annual Information Return, 2018*, pp. 5–6.

more than eight years after the murder of Mariano Abarca, a founding member of the Mexican Network of Mining Affected People (REMA in Spanish), in Chiapas, Mexico, the role of Canadian diplomats at the embassy in Mexico City—and their lobbying efforts on behalf of the Calgary-based mining company implicated in Abarca's death—is now being questioned.

Abarca was shot outside his home in 2009, allegedly over his opposition to a barite mine operated by Blackfire Exploration in Chicomuselo. Two Blackfire employees and a contractor for the company were arrested in connection with his murder, but never tried.

Last month, a delegation from Mexico, including Abarca's son José Luis Abarca, filed a complaint with the Office of the Public Sector Integrity Commissioner of Canada calling for an investigation into the actions—and omissions—of diplomats who intervened on behalf of Blackfire with Mexican officials, despite chronic pollution problems at its mine and accusations of human rights abuses against the company.

Only a few days after Abarca's murder, the mine was shut down by state authorities on environmental grounds. Documents filed as part of the complaint show the embassy continued to provide support to the company, advising how it could sue Mexican authorities under the terms of the North American Free Trade Agreement. "[Embassy staff] were getting direct information from the company about company concerns," says Charis Kamphuis, assistant professor of law at Thompson Rivers and co-founder of JCAP.[25]

STRUGGLES FOR JUSTICE IN THE COURTS

Transnational suits against Canadian mining companies face a number of legal challenges. First, foreign plaintiffs must establish that a Canadian court is the preferred place to hear their case. A plaintiff must establish that there is a connection between the case and Canada and the province or territory over which the court presides. In Canadian common-law jurisdictions (all but Quebec), the fact that a company is registered or operates in the jurisdiction is sufficient to establish a substantial connection. A court can still refuse to hear the case. The legal principle of *forum non conveniens* allows a court to dismiss a claim if it decides that another court is better positioned to adjudicate the case. A corporation may argue that the host state is a more appropriate venue due to its proximity to the parties, witnesses, and/or evidence. The burden is then on the plaintiffs to prove that the foreign court is unable to provide them with a fair trial.[26]

A further challenge for foreign plaintiffs concerns the legal structure of multinational corporations. The "corporate veil" is a legal construct that treats a parent company and its subsidiaries as separate entities, shielding the former from liability associated with the latter. In order to hold a parent company responsible for the wrongdoing of its subsidiary, plaintiffs may argue that the veil does not apply. Another approach is to seek to hold the parent company responsible for harms caused overseas. This basis of liability is currently being tested in five transnational cases that are before Canadian courts.[27]

In 2010 and 2011, three cases involving Guatemalan plaintiffs were launched in the Ontario Superior Court against Canadian mining company Hudbay Minerals Inc. One of the cases also names Hudbay's Guatemalan subsidiary as a defendant. The lawsuits allege that between 2007 and 2009, security personnel employed by Hudbay at its Fenix nickel mine killed a local community leader, seriously wounded another local resident, and gang-raped eleven women.

Hudbay initially sought to have the cases dismissed in Ontario on the grounds that it was an inappropriate forum. The company later withdrew this argument, a decision that allowed the cases to proceed but that prevented the development of a legal precedent in Ontario on the application of the forum non conveniens doctrine in this particular case.

Hudbay also brought a preliminary motion to strike the cases on the grounds that they disclosed no cause of action. Hudbay argued that the plaintiffs were attempting to assign it responsibility for the acts and omissions of its Guatemalan subsidiary, a legal argument that fails to respect the principle of separate legal personality (i.e. an attempt to lift the corporate veil).

In 2013, the Ontario Superior Court ruled in favour of the plaintiffs and denied the company's motion to strike. The judge determined "that the plaintiffs' claims are based on the direct negligence of the parent company. The plaintiffs do not seek to assign liability to Hudbay for the acts and omissions of its subsidiaries but rather, for the company's own acts and omissions. For this reason, the claims are consistent with the doctrine of separate legal personality and may proceed." The plaintiffs must now prove that Hudbay owed them a duty of care and that it failed to discharge that duty.[28]

THEFT

There are new demands being made against a number of Canadian companies alleging that the countries in which they are working have been robbed of royalties and taxation. In July 2017, Tanzania served Barrick Gold's Acacia Mining a $190 billion tax bill.[29] The dispute was still not settled two years later. At the time of writing, Barrick has a new CEO, Mark Bristow of Randgold Resources.

Cecilia Jamasmie wrote for Mining.com on July 24, 2018,

> Things are going from bad to worse for Acacia Mining (LON:ACA), one of the largest gold producers in Africa, as the government of Tanzania sent the company a $190-billion bill in fines and allegedly unpaid taxes from two of its mines.
>
> Together with disputing the astronomic bill, the company—Tanzania's No.1 gold producer—said it's evaluating all of its options and rights, adding it will provide a further update in due course. . . .
>
> Acacia, which spun off from Barrick Gold in 2010, but it's still majority-owned by the gold giant, first locked horns with the government of Tanzania last year, as it was accused of tax evasion in the ongoing case that triggered today's multi-billion bill. The dispute escalated in March, when the concentrates ban officially began.
>
> Less than four months later, Tanzania accused the company of operating illegally and said it had found evidence of the alleged tax evasion as a presidential team found the value of minerals within raw concentrate at the port of Dar es Salaam was 10 times higher than Acacia's declared amount.[30]

The Canadian government has clearly sided with Barrick. Writes Yves Engler,

> Amidst the violence at North Mara and an escalating battle over unpaid tax, Canada's High Commissioner set up a meeting between Barrick Executive Chairman John Thornton and President Magufuli. After accompanying Barrick's head to the

encounter in Dar es Salaam Ian Myles told the press, "Canada is very proud that it expects all its companies to respect the highest standards, fairness and respect for laws and corporate social responsibility. We know that Barrick is very much committed to those values."[31]

In February 2018, another Canadian company, First Quantum Minerals, was sued by the Zambian government for an alleged $8 billion in unpaid royalties and other benefits. Across the Global South there are increased demands for a fair share of royalties and taxes and revised mining codes, as well as a heightened resistance to any mining at all.

10

EXTERNALIZING MACHINES: ECOLOGICAL ECONOMICS

Corporations are externalizing machines; they seek to offload all the costs they can from their corporate account to the environment, individuals, and the public sector. The mining process requires the destruction of the natural environment, the transformation of rock and water into commodities, the reproduction of human labour, and the management of artificial mountains and lakes of toxins forever. Sometimes the very materials they mine do not answer real needs (such as gold and diamonds), or in themselves create more harm than good (coal).

This chapter will examine the "ecological economics" of the mining industry and (briefly) discuss some important questions. Can we recycle the metals we depend on? Do we need more coal and uranium? Do we need more gold and diamonds? How do government and industry measure the economic value of a mine? How do we ensure that the externalized costs are considered?

METALS RECYCLING

Natural Resources Canada reported in 2018 that mineral reserves had been seriously depleting since 1980. In the thirty-year period from 1980 to 2010, Canada's reserves of base metals declined continuously at annual average rates varying from 0.69 percent for molybdenum to 8.86 percent for lead. This period of prolonged decline resulted in some metal reserve levels of less than half of the known ore reserves reported at the end of 1980. Reserves in 2010 were 64 percent of 1980 reserves for copper, 37 percent for nickel, 46 percent for molybdenum, 15 percent for zinc, 4 percent for lead, and 20 percent for silver. Gold reserves saw an increase of 178 percent over that same period.[1]

The Canadian mining industry approaches the problem of declining mineral reserves by asking for more support for the exploration industry, so that more reserves will be discovered and, in turn, depleted. It also looks for and mines lower-grade deposits, creating more waste.

Without policies and incentives to protect any remaining reserves from immediate and total pillage, future generations are likely to find themselves with no metals left to mine at all. In a study published on January 17, 2006, in the *Proceedings of the National Academy of Sciences*, Yale University researchers said that their findings had determined that supplies of copper, zinc, and other metals cannot meet the needs of the global population forever, even with the full extraction of metals from the earth's crust and extensive recycling programs, and that depletion will be an immediate problem for some precious metals like platinum.[2]

The Carnoules Declaration in 1994 estimated that, to achieve sustainability worldwide, the material intensity of each unit of economic output will need to be reduced by 50 percent and, in industrial countries like Canada, it will have to fall by factors of between four and ten.[3]

EU Environment Commissioner Janez Potočnik said in 2014,

> It is essential for our future industrial competitiveness not only that we produce products using less raw materials, less energy and less water, but also that we are able to replace virgin materials and imports with supplies of secondary raw materials where they are available, and that we produce products that can be re-used, repaired, refurbished and recycled. . . . This is what we

mean by a circular economy. In essence we propose to make Europe a society without waste. To take the 600 million tonnes of materials contained in our waste and pump them back into productive use in the economy.[4]

In 2004, the Canary Research Institute for Mining, Environment, and Health commissioned Jay Fothergill to look at this issue in Canada. In *Scrap Mining: An Overview of Metal Recycling in Canada*,[5] he wrote,

Energy savings realized when metals are produced from secondary sources versus primary sources are: zinc, 60%; steel, 74%; lead, 76%; copper, 85%; aluminum, 95%. Additionally, the reduction in pollution realized from recycling can be immense. For aluminum, there is a 79% material conservation, a 95% reduction in emissions and a 97% reduction of effluents through recycling. For steel, one sees a 90% virgin materials savings, an 86% emissions reduction, a 40% effluent reduction, a 76% water pollution reduction and a 97% mining waste reduction through recycling.[6]

Most of the jobs in the mineral industry in Canada are actually in smelting, refining, manufacturing, and mining supply and services, not in extraction. Said Fothergill, "The Canadian metal recycling sector salvages an estimated 10 million tonnes of metal each year, valued at roughly $3 billion."[7] In 2017, out of almost 426,000 people that the industry claimed were directly employed by them, only 71,000 were working in actual mining and quarrying, while 40,000 were in scrap metal recycling.[8] Shifting from extraction to reusing and recycling would be unlikely to jeopardize the downstream jobs in smelters, refineries, or manufacturing.

In 2003, I presented on behalf of MiningWatch Canada to a Senate committee about a proposed tax bill, stating the following:

Society's demand for goods and services can be achieved through waste prevention and reduction in the design and delivery of goods, and the recycling and reuse of existing materials stocks, rather than disposing of used materials at one end of the materials cycle and inputting newly extracted ones at the other. Although the use of certain metals, such as mercury, should be phased out due to their extremely toxic properties, other metals are especially good candidates for these approaches. Metals do not lose their mechanical or metallurgical properties when recycled and moreover, retain their economic value. As a result metals can be re-used and cycled through the economy almost without limit.[9]

THE COSTS OF COAL

Coal is one of the most greenhouse gas–intensive means of generating electricity, and coal-fired power plants still account for almost 40 percent of the world's electricity today. This reality makes carbon pollution from coal electricity a leading contributor to climate change.[10]

In an important study published in the *Annals of the New York Academy of Sciences* in 2011, a number of scientists reported on the lifecycle costs of coal. They found that

> each stage of the life cycle of coal—extraction, transport, processing, and combustion—generates a waste stream and carries multiple hazards for health and the environment. These costs are external to the coal industry and thus are often considered externalities. We estimate that the life cycle effects of coal and the waste streams generated are costing the US public a third to over one-half a trillion dollars annually. Many of these externalities are, moreover, cumulative.[11]

The costs included in the study were to the economy (in the conventional sense), human health, and the environment. Even the scientists' careful analysis omitted many climate change impacts, the prolonged effects of acid rain and acid mine drainage, and mental health impacts.[12] The authors make it clear that the true ecological and health costs of coal are "far greater than the numbers suggest." They also say that using carbon-capture and sequestration technologies (CCS) is "costly and carries numerous health and environmental risks, which would be multiplied if CCS were employed on a wide scale."[13]

The Canadian government and at least some of the provinces agree that coal needs to be phased out. In fall 2017, Canada cofounded the Powering Past Coal Alliance to help accelerate clean growth and climate protection through the rapid phase-out of traditional coal-fired electricity. The sixty-member international alliance of city, state, and national governments is committed to phasing out coal power and providing a "just transition for coal workers."[14] Catherine McKenna, minister of Environment and Climate Change in Canada, said, "Phasing out coal power is good news for the climate, for our health, and for our kids. I'm thrilled to see so much global momentum for the transition to clean energy and the move away from coal power—and this is only the beginning."[15]

However, an International Monetary Fund report in 2014 found that "the coal industry in Canada receives $4.5 billion in annual subsidies—almost all of this is un-priced carbon and sulfur dioxide emissions."[16]

The issue is not just one of subsidies, but also of effective regulation and enforcement. In 2018, the International Joint Commission issued a report that said,

> the level of selenium in the Elk and Fording rivers is 70 times that in the Flathead River, which doesn't get runoff from five coal mines operated by Teck Resources. Back in June, however, the commission's two Canadian members refused to endorse a report on selenium in the Elk River watershed. Within this context, the U.S. commissioners wrote in their letter to the State Department that such negatives and the lack of immediate action could cause selenium to keep leaching into rivers and groundwater for centuries.[17]

Teck Resources, Canada's largest coal-mining company, has repeatedly been cited for environmental violations from its coal operations.[18] According to an article published on *DeSmogBlog* in April 2018,

> A 2016 report from B.C. Auditor-General Carol Bellringer found it concerning that permits were granted to Teck Resources to expand its Line Creek Mine after staff at the

Ministry of Environment found an expansion of the mine would exacerbate selenium pollution problems.

At the time, the BC Liberals granted a permit for the expansion invoking—for the first time in B.C. history—section 137 of the Environmental Management Act, which allows government to introduce waste into the environment if deemed in the public interest.[19]

DO WE NEED TO MINE MORE GOLD?

If you listen to the lobby for the gold mining industry, the World Gold Council, you will hear that

> [since gold mining started] around 187,200 tons of gold have already been mined, two-thirds of which were mined in the last 70 years or so. Pack this gold together and you've got a cube that measures about 21 meters on each side. A cube this size would fit comfortably in the middle of a baseball infield.[20]

The US Geological Survey estimates that there are about 57,000 tons of unmined gold remaining in the earth.[21] Most of the gold that has been mined throughout history is still in existence, as it does not degrade. Almost all of this gold is hoarded in reserves in central banks or kept as jewellery. A substantial amount can be found in our discarded electronic equipment. It takes more than a ton of ore to get one gram of gold. But you can get the same amount from recycling the materials in forty-one mobile phones.[22]

In 2018, researchers from Tsinghua University in Beijing and Macquarie University in Australia reported in the American Chemical Society's journal *Environmental Science and Technology* that "recovering gold, copper, and other metals from electronic waste isn't just sustainable, it's actually 13 times cheaper than extracting metals from mines."[23]

Given the enormous environmental and social costs of mining gold, why are we doing it at all?

DO WE NEED TO MINE MORE DIAMONDS?

In 1902, a massive diamond deposit was discovered in Kimberley, South Africa. This new source had the potential to flood the market with diamonds and bring down the cost for the stone. In order to prevent too many diamonds from hitting the market, De Beers intervened, bought up the mine, and maintained tight control over the global diamond supply. The company released only enough diamonds to meet annual demand and to displace interest in other gems (which were in fact more rare).[24]

In the mid-1930s, De Beers began an aggressive marketing campaign to promote diamond engagement rings. They wanted to replace the longstanding tradition of ruby and sapphire engagement rings to push up the price of diamonds.[25] The slogan "A Diamond Is Forever" is used to prevent people from reselling their rings, thus lowering the price. The resale value of diamonds is less than 50 percent of the price new.

Maintaining De Beers' control over the price of diamonds often meant some pretty ruthless behaviour. In 1957, a massive deposit of diamonds was discovered in Siberia. De Beers bought them all to prevent the supply being unleashed on the world market. When a large deposit was found in Australia, De Beers flooded the market to drive down their price.[26] In 2000, De Beers announced they were no longer maintaining their monopoly. But by that time, big diamond deposits were becoming increasingly rare.

Synthetic diamonds are a growing industry. They are about one-third the cost of natural diamonds and have been used industrially for many years. Their quality is improving rapidly, and even De Beers has a synthetic diamond unit.[27]

Although diamonds are beautiful, they are plentiful. We have built an entire economy in the Northwest Territories on this fragile foundation.

RECLAIMING ECONOMICS

The word *economy* comes from the Greek words *oikos* and *nomia* and means "to manage the household." If we managed our households based only on the money that comes in and the money that goes out, we would have a disaster on our hands. There would be no accounting for work we did for ourselves, like gardening, dishwashing, and waste recycling; no place for kindness and caring, for beauty and joy.

These days, Canadian communities are worried about retaining jobs and attracting money. Conventional economic practice seeks to use a variety of tax breaks and other incentives to lure investment and industry to a community. These incentives may include anti-union sentiment, low wages, overlooking environmental problems, and a pleasant natural environment for visiting executives or tourists.

Most communities are trying to chase a dream—a major employer—and they compete with one another to offer the most favourable climate. Even if they are successful, the employer is likely to be there only a few years, and will usurp the entire region's economy; the high wages paid by one employer will decimate minimum-wage jobs and small businesses in other sectors, and the remaining businesses will shift to meet the needs of the high-wage employer.

There is a generalized public suspicion that the way we keep accounts and run our financial system does not work. After the financial crash of 2008, many of us can clearly see that the economics of the global financial casino have almost nothing to do with the real economy—the production of the goods and services we need and the jobs that provide our livelihoods.

Even before the crash, there was a growing movement to enlarge the system of public accounts to keep track of the depletion of natural capital, and the health of the people, the cultures, and the social services of our communities.

Ecological (or social or Gaian) accounting is the development of ledgers for projects that measure the estimated real impacts of the activity on the individual, the household, the community, and the ecosystem. There is a serious risk to putting an economic value on nature, given how the dominant economy is capable of making everything a commodity. Any economic valuation of ecological services is going to be inaccurate. Such things are priceless and cannot be adequately compensated for once lost. The use of this kind of ecological economics has to be recognized as a strategic argument only.

Nevertheless, there is a thriving ecological economics movement that is exploring methods to take all these externalized costs and benefits into account. Pioneered by Kenneth Boulding, Hazel Henderson, Herman Daly, Bob Constanza, and Marilyn Waring, ecological economics and full-cost accounting have gained real public acceptance. In 1997, Costanza published a paper in *Nature* that set a value on "ecosystem services"—which he calculated at $33 trillion.[28] "Few economists speak of clean air and clean water as 'externalities' as they once did; the essential logic of accounting for costs is slowly spreading."[29]

One of the places where ecological economics becomes strategically important is in environmental assessment—the government process of looking at environmental effects before it licenses large projects to proceed. In evaluating a proposed mine, classical economics neglects to address a number of crucial questions. For example:

- What are the present uses of the land on and surrounding the site, and the benefits to the community from them (e.g., cultural and spiritual values of the land on the mine site downstream and within the watershed; informal recreation areas and tourism; wildlife and fish habitat and country food supply; trapping and agricultural production, including home gardens; oxygen production from the forest; trails and pathways from one area to another; waste absorption)?

- What are the costs in terms of: greenhouse effect; accidents; increased stress; changes in driving patterns for users; loss of arable land; air pollution and noise; disruption of the social and cultural fabric in the affected region; injury to wildlife; effect on house prices both near the mine site and in the area from which the workers are drawn; occupational hazards and costs of production; local retention of profits from production; future maintenance; training and manpower; potential contamination of aquifers and groundwater from leakages and spills?

- What is the actual economic viability of the mine? Chances are it will only be operating for ten to fifteen years maximum. Where will the waste be placed? How will it be managed? What will happen when the mine closes? Can the mess it leaves behind be fixed? What will it cost to close the mine and remediate the mess it leaves behind? How likely is the company to meet its commitments for cleanup years in the future? What price will be paid by future generations? (See chapter 7.)

- Are the gems or metals produced by the mine socially useful? Can they come from recycling instead? Could we conserve to avoid mining them? What will be produced with them? If a fuel such as uranium or coal is being produced, what is its long-term impact on the planet?

After intense struggles by affected communities, ecological economics has led to recognition of the externalized costs and the refusal of a number of different mine projects for the first time in the history of Canadian environmental assessment.

The Kemess North Mine was found to be "not in the public interest" in September 2007, because benefits to First Nations clearly did not justify building a mine with a twelve-year life and an environmental footprint that would last for centuries.[30] The mine would have used pristine Amazay Lake as a tailings dump. After lengthy hearings (including in the First Nations most affected) and thousands of submissions, the federal-provincial panel that reviewed the project developed a "sustainability framework" for evaluating the project:[31]

1. Environmental stewardship: Is the environment adequately protected through all phases of development, construction, and operation, as well as through the legacy post-closure phase?
2. Economic benefits and costs: Does the project provide net economic benefits to the people of British Columbia and Canada?
3. Social and cultural benefits and costs: Does the project contribute to community and social well-being of all potentially affected people? Is it compatible with their cultural interests and aspirations?
4. Fair distribution of benefits and costs: Are the benefits and costs of development fairly distributed among potentially affected people and interests?
5. Present versus future generations: Does the project succeed in providing economic and social benefits now without compromising the ability of future generations to benefit from the environment and natural resources in the area of the mine site?

The Whites Point Quarry on Digby Neck in Nova Scotia was turned down by a joint federal-provincial panel because the community was able to prove that the viable plan they had for their region's future would be ruined by the proposed quarry and marine terminal. The panel concluded that the project posed "unacceptable risk to the environment and the community" and did not fit with "community core values."[32] Bilcon, the company behind the proposal, has since used the dispute resolution process under NAFTA to sue the province and the federal government for "expropriating the value of their investment." The dispute resolution tribunal decided in Bilcon's favour, and in the end, Bilcon was awarded $7 million in damages.[33] The quarry and marine terminal have been stopped.

In the spring of 2005, the Athabasca Dënesuliné in the Northwest Territories were able to stop an advanced exploration project for uranium proposed by Ur-Energy, on the grounds that it would seriously affect traditional land use, wildlife habitat, and special ecological places and would not provide economic benefits to them. Faced with an EA they would lose, the company withdrew its application.[34]

The Prosperity Mine on Tŝilhqot'in territory in British Columbia was turned down twice by the Canadian Environmental Assessment Agency because (in part) "the Project would have adverse effects on the Tŝilhqot'in current use of lands and resources for traditional purposes, archaeological and historical sites, and cultural heritage and that these adverse effects could not be mitigated and therefore would be significant."[35] This project is discussed in greater detail in chapter 11.

More recently, the Ajax Mine near Kamloops, British Columbia, was refused a Certificate of Environmental Compliance by British Columbia, based largely on its likely impacts on the Indigenous community, but also its impacts on the City of Kamloops.

The Ajax Mine

The proposed Ajax Mine in Kamloops would have been a large, low-grade copper-gold mine with an ore grade of 0.3 percent copper, 0.19 grams per ton (gpt) gold, and 0.40 gpt silver. It would produce 2.65 tons of waste rock for every ton of ore it mined.[36] The company said the mine would have an eighteen-year mine life. The Ajax mill was expected to treat sixty-five thousand tons per day of a copper-gold ore, containing considerable amounts of mercury and arsenic.[37] Concentrates were to be trucked on BC roads and highways to the Port of Vancouver.[38]

The planned tailings impoundment would have been enormous— approximately six square kilometres, holding 440 million tons of tailings—and the mine would also generate over a billion tons of waste rock that would be piled up to 270 metres high. The open pit would eventually measure 2.7 by 1.3 kilometres and be as much as 550 metres deep.[39] The pit's highest wall was to be about fifty metres from Jacko

Honouring Our Sacred Connection to Pípsell:

Stk'emlúpsemc te Secwépemc says YES to healthy people and environment!

Stk'emlúpsemc te Secwépemc Nation formally expressed their opposition to the proposed Ajax Mine in 2017. Courtesy of Stk'emlúpsemc te Secwépemc Nation.

Lake, known as Pipsell, which is sacred to the Indigenous peoples in the region.

The entire project's fifteen-square-kilometre footprint would have been located on Secwepemc territory, and in places, it abutted the boundaries of the City of Kamloops. It was fiercely opposed by Indigenous peoples and by a significant proportion of residents in Kamloops.

The Secwepemc already have a number of mines on or bordering their territory, including Canada's largest copper mine, Highland Valley, the Gibraltar Mine, the Mount Polley Mine, and New Afton's New Gold Mine. They know about mining.

Jeannette Jules, a Secwepemc leader, speaking to a Western Mining Action Network conference,[40] said,

> We are situated on the Iron Mask fault, and for generations our family mined copper. We made plates that were traded with other First Nations along extensive trade routes. Our copper

can be found from Baffin Island to New Mexico. Then the province came along and gave our area to someone else to mine. . . . You cannot move a creation story from where it came from. You cannot move a song from where it was first sung.

When KGHM first proposed the Ajax Mine, Stk̓emlúpsemc te Secwépemc Nation (SSN) decided to conduct their own environmental assessment of the mine based on traditional cultural knowledge as well as Western science. They called the process "walking on two legs."

They set up a panel based on customary practices to examine the possible impacts of the mine on their culture, society, economics, and environment. Representatives were named to the panel from thirteen families in each of the two First Nations most affected as well as two youth representatives and two Elders. For most of a year, they heard and weighed testimony from scientists and experts, from community members and traditional knowledge keepers.

On March 4, 2017, SSN issued a press release:[41]

Stk̓emlúpsemc te Secwépemc Nation (SSN) does not give its free, prior and informed consent to the development of the lands and resources at Pípsell (Jacko Lake and Area) for the purposes of the Ajax Mine Project. The Ajax Mine Project in its proposed location at Pípsell is in opposition to the SSN land use objective for this profoundly sacred, culturally important, and historically significant keystone site which significance is fundamental and undiminished.[42]

The Kamloops City Council—which had also been dealing with the BC and federal environmental assessment processes—agreed and rejected the mine. Nine months after the SSN declaration, on December 14, 2017, the BC government rejected the mine's environmental assessment application. The federal government has now followed suit.

In 2016, the people opposing the mine in Kamloops had asked MiningWatch Canada and me to pull together a socio-economic risk assessment of this mine based on relevant research done by community experts.

Our report did two things: it attacked the credibility of the company's own estimates of costs to build and operate the mine, and it attempted to translate many of the externalized costs that local people had studied into dollars, so they could be recognized on a more holistic balance sheet. The report set out the main risks to investors, governments, and the public in regard to the financial viability of the mine. It became clear that the Statistics Canada and BC input-output models used by the company to estimate benefits from the mine and conventional economic models were not appropriate to evaluate the project.

After studying the cost estimates in the company's own feasibility study, we found there were many overly optimistic assumptions. The company appeared to have seriously overestimated long-term prices for copper and gold and used these figures to project the life of mine revenues. The company did not have confirmed markets for their concentrates, and contamination from arsenic and mercury would likely increase their smelter penalties. The feasibility study contained no allowance for changing, operating, or sustaining capital costs over the eighteen-year mine life.[43] There was an underestimation by at least $9 million for annual corporate overhead costs.[44] The feasibility study made no allowance for fluctuations in the exchange rate over the life of the mine. There was a $53 million (USD) discrepancy for the cost of reclamation and closure costs between the amount used for the feasibility study and that used for the environmental impact statement. There were no costs included for the perpetual care and maintenance post-closure of the pit, waste dumps, and tailings impoundment.

We also critiqued the company's tax revenue estimates. As all mine taxation is based on profitability, and the company was unlikely to be profitable for at least a decade, the marginal effective tax rate was likely to be less than zero. Payroll remittances were reported in the environmental impact statement as "revenues to government." The lack of transparency about the methodology used to model taxation was also an issue.

Energy economist Marvin Shaffer calculated an annual power cost subsidy to the mine of over $30 million (USD): British Columbia was charging $52 per megawatt for electricity when it cost the province at least $91.67 per megawatt to purchase new power.[45] This was a hidden cost to taxpayers of $39.67 (USD) per megawatt.

The company failed to tell investors that SSN had not consented to the mine.

We concluded that

the proposed mine presents a serious financial and economic risk to investors, to the public and to governments. If it manages to go into production, we believe the owners will have real difficulty meeting their commitments, that the mine will be only intermittently operating and will be at risk of early closure, leaving the public and taxpayers to clean up the mess, and shareholders potentially liable for millions in damages.[46]

When it came to the externalized costs of the project, our community partners were able to provide well-researched guesstimates of a number of missing and/or underestimated costs in the feasibility study.[47] These included gross underestimates (likely tens of millions) of the potential restitution costs if the First Nations did agree to the mine. (There was only $333,000 per year in the feasibility budget.) There was insufficient insurance against the consequences of potentially catastrophic accidents, such as a collapse of the barrier between the pit and Pipsell (Jacko Lake),[48] an accident that appeared very likely to happen. The company included no costs for delay and other costs associated with dealing with ongoing opposition from area residents. Neither did the feasibility study include compensation to the City of Kamloops or the Thompson-Nicola region for coping with a possible housing crisis; sunk costs for planning that was now moot; greater costs for roads, recreation, and health and social services; and adjustments when the mine closed. There was no allowance to compensate owners of residential development whose property would not be developable due to downwind proximity to the mine, and whose land might become contaminated from mine dust. Dust suppression costs were underestimated.

When our community partners attempted to monetize all these costs through extensive research, they estimated $30 million annually for air pollution, damage to grasslands of at least $3.4 million, impacts on tourism of $10 million annually, and losses in real estate values for properties near the mine of $155 million. There were myriad other costs that could not be translated into dollars.[49]

The mine made no sense, and—this time, at least—the governments agreed.

PART IV

JUSTICE OR JUST US? REGULATION AND ENFORCEMENT

This section addresses the role government plays in the mining industry. It starts by describing the powerful industry lobby, and then provides an overview of significant federal regulation, law, and policy, with an example from British Columbia to illustrate how the mining industry influence plays out. Taxation is an important public policy tool, and a chapter is devoted to outlining how it supports the mining industry. The section concludes with a chapter on uranium mining and its impacts, extent, and regulation.

11

THE MINING LOBBY

When I started with MiningWatch Canada, mining companies had a reputation almost everywhere for being thugs and bullies. Their public image in Canada has dramatically changed. Looking at industry websites, we now find all sorts of claims of sustainable development, responsible mining, community engagement, and environmental protection. Industry representatives are as likely to be Bay Street lawyers and investment dealers as they are to be mining engineers.

The industry lobby is ensuring that an initiative to develop a new "Canadian Minerals and Metals Plan" becomes the new "Mining Plan." The air is full of talk of new technologies, realizing community benefits, and advancing the participation of Indigenous people. The industry lobbyists have taken control of the conversation about how we get the minerals we really need, diverting our focus from the enormous and long-term physical and social footprint the mining industry leaves behind.

This chapter identifies the key industry lobbyists at the federal level and gives some examples of how the industry works at the federal and provincial levels to shape law and regulation to meet mining industry needs through promoting voluntary self-assurance measures, intensive lobbying, and strategic lawsuits and harassment of critics.

INDUSTRY ASSOCIATIONS

Federally, there are three main associations that advocate for the mining industry: the Mining Association of Canada, the Prospectors and Developers Association of Canada, and the Canadian Aboriginal Minerals Association. They are replicated in each province. Individual mining companies and moguls also have their own "community relations," "government relations," and "communications" departments. In addition, the myriad bankers, investment dealers, stockbrokers, and consultants who work with the industry have their own public relations strategies and staff.

Mining companies and the wealthy elites they create also frequently make tax-deductible donations to universities, colleges, and hospitals: think the Munk Centre, the Telfer School of Management, the Sprott School of Business, the Bharti School of Engineering, the Fielding Chapel. That their wealth comes from the costs they externalize, and the taxes they are not required to pay, is ignored.

Mining Association of Canada

The Mining Association of Canada (MAC) is headquartered in Ottawa and represents most of the major mining companies in Canada. The association describes itself as follows:

> Our members are involved in mineral exploration, mining, smelting, refining and semi-fabrication for a wide range of commodities. We also represent mining supplier companies that support the many facets of the mining business, such as finance, engineering and equipment companies.
>
> Working alongside our members and, often, in partnership with other mining-related organizations across Canada, MAC works to advance the interests of the sector. Together, we promote the mining industry nationally and internationally, work with governments on policies affecting the sector and educate the public on the value mining brings to the economy and in the daily life of Canadians.[1]

MAC's forty-three full-member organizations represent the major players not only in the metals and gems market, but also in the tar sands. MAC presents itself as the "progressive" voice of the industry. The association plays a facilitative role in some consultative processes, working with other stakeholders. For example, MAC has been actively involved in the National Orphaned/Abandoned Mines Initiative, and in recent reviews of the federal *Environmental Assessment Act* and *Fisheries Act*.

In 2004, MAC launched Towards Sustainable Mining (TSM). The association describes the initiative as being about the industry earning its social licence to operate, improving mining's reputation by improving performance, and aligning the industry's actions with the priorities and values of its communities of interest. There is a TSM Communities of Interest Advisory Panel with a multi-stakeholder membership (chosen by MAC) that meets twice a year. This panel enables MAC and its members to gauge where the biggest pushback to mining is coming from. Evidently the discussions at these meetings are "challenging and rich."[2]

In the TSM annual progress reports, MAC's member companies report on their annual self-assessments of company performance in seven areas: Aboriginal and community outreach, energy and GHG emissions management, tailings management, biodiversity management, safety and health, crisis management and communications planning, and preventing child and forced labour.[3] The reports are based on twenty-three indicators set out in the TSM; the indicators are entirely about the existence of management systems within the company, not about their actual effectiveness. TSM and E3, the Prospectors and Developers Association of Canada program to set guidelines for "sustainable" exploration practices, are examples of this kind of corporate social responsibility strategy. Although they set out guidelines for their members, there is no enforcement, no penalty, and no assessment of how the management systems they require work in practice.

Imperial Metals is a member of the Mining Association of Canada. At the time of the Mount Polley tailings dam failure on August 4, 2014, it had been part of the TSM program for two years. MAC had been publishing guides for tailings disposal practices since 1998. MAC did nothing to penalize Imperial Metals for the failure. (This is discussed in much more detail below.)

MAC also requires companies to have their TSM performance indicator assessments externally verified every three years using a trained Verification Service Provider (VSP).[4] The VSP only reviews the company reports and does not undertake its own audit. To answer the demand for "independent audits" of extractive projects, an entire international verification industry has sprung up. The client for these audits is invariably the mining company or mining association that employs the VSP. The objective of the audit is to "de-risk" mining projects for the company and its investors, not the public.

TSM is all about enhancing the industry's reputation with key federal decision-makers and with the public. MAC's campaign priorities are to streamline and reduce regulation, reduce taxes, and increase public subsidies to the mineral sector. MAC holds an annual lobby day in Ottawa, when mining executives go to Parliament Hill to meet with federal decision-makers, including several ministers and caucus chairs. It always includes an extravagant reception.

In 2017 alone, MAC logged 305 lobbying communications with the federal government; more were expected in 2018. MAC president Pierre Gratton complained to the *Hill Times* that "an unprecedented level of legislation and consultation (including changes to environmental assessment and the Fisheries Act) was creating a 'cumulative burden on all industry players. . . . We have trouble keeping up.'"[5]

Just imagine what this has meant for underfunded environmental and Indigenous groups.

Prospectors and Developers Association of Canada

We are proud to be the leading voice of Canada's mineral exploration and development community since 1932. With over 7,500 members around the world, our mission is to promote a globally responsible, vibrant and sustainable minerals industry.

The annual PDAC Convention is regarded as the premier international event for the mineral industry. It has attracted more than 25,000 people from 135 countries in recent years.[6]

The Prospectors and Developers Association of Canada (PDAC) states its goal as "supporting a competitive and responsible Canadian exploration industry." Its program includes getting access to land and capital, developing skills, "Aboriginal affairs," and "supporting Canadian companies abroad." Like MAC, the association is concerned with overcoming the thuggish reputation of the mining industry with communities and investors, and has E3 (Excellence in Environmental Exploration) and E3 Plus programs that set out rules for "a Framework for Responsible Exploration."[7] The program is voluntary. PDAC is a primary advocate for more subsidies and incentives for exploration, for "flow-through shares," for "certainty" when it comes to dealing with Indigenous peoples, and for "streamlined" (reduced) regulation.[8]

PDAC also promotes an initiative for schoolchildren called Mining Matters, which provides industry-focused curriculum resources, organizes student events, and trains teachers.[9] Mining Matters is a registered charity and receives substantial government support.

Canadian Aboriginal Minerals Association

The Canadian Aboriginal Minerals Association (CAMA) describes itself as follows:

> Since 1992, the Canadian Aboriginal Minerals Association (CAMA) has been instrumental in bringing both Aboriginal communities and the mineral sector together to help meet their objectives. Certainty of investment, a secured access to lands, resources and a healthy return for shareholders and members. It is through our vast network, our membership and our annual events, where we have had the most success. . . .[10]
>
> Our main objective is to bring Aboriginal communities, resource companies and suppliers together to collaborate and learn from each, work toward mutual benefits for the growth and health of Aboriginal communities and Industry.[11]

The names of its members are not publicly available, but its sponsorship comprises "interested Aboriginal communities," plus mining companies, governments, and suppliers. CAMA developed an "Aboriginal Toolkit" that was funded by industry and government. The kit's express purpose was to increase Indigenous participation in mining. The news release, dated March 17, 2004, announced: "For its part, the mining industry believes the tool kit will facilitate new mining development."[12] The toolkit is still used to explain mining across the country.

Although the toolkit provides a primer on activities at the stages of mine exploration, development, operation, and closure, it glosses over the serious environmental, social, and cultural impacts of mining on Indigenous governments and communities, omits any discussion of the relationship of mineral staking and exploration to questions of Indigenous rights and title, and provides no resources, links, or bibliography.[13]

CAMA annual conferences often include a number of thoughtful Indigenous leaders, but the events are primarily designed as opportunities for companies, consultants, and lawyers to make industry contacts and sell their "responsiveness" to the concerns of Indigenous communities.

Other Organizations and Provincial Lobbyists

Other national organizations that promote the interests of the mining industry include the Canadian Association of Mining Equipment and Services for Export, the Canadian Institute of Mining, Metallurgy and Petroleum, the Canadian Mining Industry Research Organization, the Mining Suppliers Trade Association, and a number of mineral-specific associations and institutes, such as the Coal Association.

Each province or territory has at least one and often several mineral-industry lobby associations, including groups like the Alberta Chamber of Resources, the Mining Association of British Columbia, the Association for Mineral Exploration British Columbia, the Québec Mining Association, and the Yukon Chamber of Mines. The provincial mines ministries regularly subsidize these organizations and their events and pay for key Indigenous leaders to attend conferences and tour mill and mine sites, as well as other industry events.

There are also international lobbyists, such as the International Council on Mining and Metals and the World Gold Council, that represent mining interests. Canada and Canadian companies play a large role in most of them. They also carry out pro-mining events and campaigns.

CORPORATE SOCIAL RESPONSIBILITY

When MiningWatch Canada was founded twenty years ago, peoples in the Global South (and Indigenous peoples in Canada) who were affected by Canadian mining companies were demanding that we get our government under control. The appetite of the industry for more and more ore bodies drove it into more remote regions. Our southern partners wanted us to change the laws, policies, and practices that were enabling this pillage of their lands. They wanted regulation and enforcement in Canada. They fought back effectively in their own countries and were able, through the growing use of the Internet and direct exchanges between affected communities, to communicate with one another. In response, mining companies began to talk about "getting a social licence to operate," and with it, "corporate social responsibility."

Corporate social responsibility (CSR) is the industry answer to demands for more regulation. CSR means that companies (or the industry associations) will develop standards for their behaviour, volunteer to meet these standards, and then police themselves. I think it is the fox guarding the henhouse. The history of the base metal smelter pollution prevention planning, described in chapter 12, is an example of how ineffective these initiatives can be.

It has always confounded me that the same companies that demand voluntary standards for issues of social justice and environmental protection want every *t* crossed when it comes to the international regulation of trade and investment. Agreements between mining companies are fine-tuned by expensive lawyers, and every word counts. Mining unions signing contracts with their bosses learned this long ago. When the Innu were negotiating with Inco over Voisey's Bay, they brought in Steelworkers Union negotiating experts to help them.

The CSR codes (like TSM and E3) have indicators and are based on international standards. One to which most international mining companies subscribe is the Global Compact: a voluntary agreement among mining CEOs on "best practices in sustainable development." At one point when I worked for MiningWatch, I was asked to look at what four major mining companies said in their annual CSR reports and what was happening on the ground. I found that the differences were staggering. Where there was progress, it was usually because the affected community or the union was fighting back—hard—or because it saved the company money if it improved its practice. It was difficult to get the information required to complete this investigation with the resources we had; effectively, I would have needed to tour the sites and undertake a forensic audit. Instead, I had to rely on what unions and communities were telling me or saying in the media.

Since the late 1990s, the mining industry has engaged in a massive offensive to sell the CSR solution to workers, the public, and governments as the alternative to regulation.

UNDERMINING THE LAW

In 2001, West Coast Environmental Law and the Environmental Mining Council of British Columbia released a report called *Undermining the Law: Addressing the Crisis in Compliance with Environmental Mining Laws in BC.* Their study found that monitoring in British Columbia was haphazard, record-keeping was poor, prosecution was not a real threat to industry (court fines rarely exceeded ten thousand dollars), and that citizens had very little recourse if they were wronged. "Perhaps the most important restriction on citizen involvement is the BC government's policy of staying private prosecutions. Under Canadian law, members of the public can initiate private prosecutions when an environmental violation has occurred. Under current provincial policy, the Crown takes over, and routinely stays (closes down) prosecutions."[14]

Almost two decades later, little has changed.

On August 4, 2014, one of the tailings dams at the Mount Polley Mine in British Columbia collapsed, releasing 25 million cubic metres of water-saturated tailings laden with selenium, lead, and other metals into Polley Lake, Hazeltine Creek, and Quesnel Lake. Polley Lake and Hazeltine Creek were destroyed. The company responsible, Imperial Metals, was allowed to reopen the mine, and it has a permit to discharge water from its mended tailings pond directly into Quesnel Lake. Even modest cleanup cost the province over $40 million. It was one of the largest environmental disasters in Canadian history. An independent panel formed to study the spill found that the initial dam design (built on very slippery glaciolacustrine clay) set the stage for the later collapse, a problem that was made worse by overfilling the tailings storage facility and by inadequately monitored increments to dam height. A number of other intervenors emphasized the lack of oversight and enforcement by government inspectors throughout the mine's life.

MiningWatch and others made the point that the problem was political: a result of the consistent choice of mining interests over safety and health in British Columbia.

Key to understanding what has gone wrong in an organization is to look at how power is exercised: the distribution of choice, prerogatives and resources. These are unfairly distributed within any organization. In organizations that are driven by schedules, place economic concerns over safety and environmental considerations, have insufficient resources to do a job properly, have ineffective communications, and are unresponsive to criticism, the ability to learn by trial and error is almost non-existent.[15]

By October 2018, no charges had been laid against Imperial Metals for the disaster by either the federal or provincial government, and a private prosecution by MiningWatch Canada and former Chief Bev Sellars of the affected Xat'sull First Nation had been taken over by the province and stayed.

TASEKO MINES AND BC REGULATORY CAPTURE

Taseko Mines Limited is a proud member of MAC and plays a key role in influencing mining law, regulation, and enforcement in British Columbia. In 2013 and 2017, it received an AAA rating under TSM for its Indigenous engagement.

For almost thirty years, Taseko Mines has been trying to construct an enormous open-pit porphyry copper-gold mine—Prosperity Mine—in the heart of the territory of the Tŝilhqot'in people. The Tŝilhqot'in title to 1,750 square kilometres of their territory was recognized in a very important Supreme Court of Canada decision on June 26, 2014.[16] This recognizes the Tŝilhqot'in right to control, benefit from, and choose how their land is developed. They are the first and only Indigenous group in Canadian history to have their Aboriginal title recognized by the Supreme Court of Canada.

The Tŝilhqot'in have fiercely and successfully opposed the Prosperity Mine proposal since 1991. (Imagine the public relations difficulties in trying to oppose "prosperity"!) The mine project has been turned down twice during the federal government's environmental review process: once in 2010, and then an altered plan—called "New Prosperity"—was turned down in 2014. The major reason given both times by the federal government was that it would "result in significant adverse effects on the Tŝilhqot'in cultural use of land and resources for traditional purposes, on cultural heritage . . . and on archaeological and historical resources." Says Chief Roger Williams,

> Unsound mining practices are not welcome in our territory. Our declaration of Aboriginal title in 2014 states that the land must be used in a manner that protects it for future generations. This is a principle that should be followed for all resource development in Canada.[17]

In its determination to develop the mine despite these decisions, Taseko continues to use every tool at its disposal to get its way, including using its power with the BC government.

Prior to and during the Prosperity and New Prosperity reviews, Taseko directors and key management were active participants in the Association for Mineral Exploration in British Columbia and the Mining Association of British Columbia, as well as lobbying on their own behalf to help shape the BC regulatory environment. Before he went to Taseko and while he was a senior manager at Teck Cominco's Highland Valley Mine, Russell Hallbauer, President and CEO of Taseko, chaired the Mining Association of British Columbia from 2002 to 2004, and was a director of that body from 1991.[18]

During the Prosperity and New Prosperity environmental assessment hearings, both BC industry associations made presentations repeating the key messages of jobs, GDP growth, and the benefits of the project to the BC economy.

The power of the mining industry in shaping regulation in British Columbia has been disastrous for people and the environment. In 2011 and again in 2016, the auditor general of British Columbia slammed the enforcement of mine regulation.[19] The May 3, 2016, audit looked at whether or not compliance and enforcement activities by the Ministry of Energy and Mines (MEM) and the Ministry of Environment (MoE) were protecting the province from significant environmental risks. The report was endorsed by the BC Government Employees Union.[20]

Auditor general Carol Bellringer wrote the following:

We found almost every one of our expectations for a robust compliance and enforcement program within the MEM and the MoE were not met. We found major gaps in resources, planning and tools. As a result, monitoring and inspections of mines were inadequate to ensure mine operators complied with requirements. The ministries have not publicly disclosed the limitations with their compliance and enforcement programs, increasing environmental risks, and government's ability to protect the environment. . . .

- Neither ministry ensures that permits are consistently written with enforceable language.
- Neither ministry uses a permitting approach that reduces the likelihood taxpayers will have to pay costs associated with the environmental impacts of mining activities (known as the polluter-pays principle). . . .
- Neither MEM nor MoE are conducting adequate monitoring and site inspections and neither have assessed how this is impacting risks.
- Both MEM's and MoE's enforcement responses have significant deficiencies and MEM's enforcement tools are in some cases, ineffectual. This is resulting in delayed or unsuccessful enforcement by the ministries and inaction by industry in several instances. . . .
- Neither MEM nor MoE have adequately evaluated the effectiveness of their regulatory programs.[21]

When the New Prosperity proposal was turned down by the federal government in 2016, Taseko applied to the government of British Columbia to amend the BC environmental assessment certificate for the project. Such an amendment "would allow Taseko to pursue the project through a narrow process that requires a review of proposed changes only, and not another full environmental assessment."[22]

In this context, the *Globe and Mail* reported that Taseko CEO Hallbauer had written a letter to BC premier Christy Clark on May 13, 2016, demanding the B.C. Environmental Assessment Office proceed with a request to amend the environmental certificate for the New Prosperity project despite Ottawa's repeated rejections ...[and] that if the province did not grant an amended environmental certificate, the government should buy the New Prosperity mineral tenures or Taseko would go to court seeking damages . . . based upon a claim of de facto expropriation, among other things.[23]

Not only did Taseko threaten British Columbia with court, it launched two judicial reviews (November 29, 2013, and March 26, 2014) against the federal government, and a civil claim (February 11, 2016).[24] On December 5, 2017, the federal court dismissed the applications with costs awarded against Taseko.[25]

Despite these victories, during the wildfires ravaging their territory in 2017 and again in 2018, the Tŝilhqot'in have had to engage repeatedly in the courts with Taseko's attempts to conduct new exploration drilling on the site of the New Prosperity Mine. The Tsilhqot'in are still fighting this incursion as this book goes to press.

In early 2012, Taseko Mines filed a lawsuit alleging that the Wilderness Committee, a non-profit preservation society, made defamatory statements about the company's New Prosperity Mine Project during the public comment period. Taseko argued that the articles published by the Wilderness Committee portrayed the company as having "callous disregard" for the environment. "What they're intended to do is silence critics by burdening them with the cost of legal defence," said Gwen Barlee, national policy director with the Wilderness Committee.[26] A Wilderness Committee press release describes the outcome of the initial case in January 2016: "Hon. Mr. Justice Funt dismissed Taseko's claims and awarded the Wilderness Committee court costs as well as extra costs incurred as a result of the lawsuit. . . . The court held that most of the criticisms of the project were not even defamatory, and all of them were fair comment."[27] Taseko appealed the decision; however, on December 13, 2017, the BC Court of Appeal dismissed the Taseko appeal.[28]

The costs to the Indigenous peoples and their allies to fight the Taseko bullying have been staggering in time, emotional energy, and legal expenditures.

12

CANADIAN MINING LAW AND REGULATION

As we saw in chapter 11, the mining industry works hard to ensure that politicians and government workers at all levels serve corporate needs before the public interest. The result is that mining law and regulation is almost exclusively about helping mines get built, and ensuring that they are operated profitably for the owners and protected from liability for the messes they create.

Any exceptions to this focus in mining law are a result of powerful, organized pushback from people affected by the industry. The land, water, and air; workers' health and safety; Indigenous rights; and other kinds of community-based economies are protected by other laws, regulations, and policy, like the *Fisheries Act* and the *Navigable Waters Act*; by provincial and federal environmental protection acts; by workers' health and safety acts; and by the precedents in common law regarding Indigenous sovereignty.

There is no single "Canadian mining law." Mining is largely provincial and territorial jurisdiction, so there are effectively fourteen different sets of laws (thirteen for the provinces/territories, one federal). Uranium is a federal responsibility, as are certain kinds of taxation and bankruptcy law. Provincially, coal, potash, and quarries all have separate and different laws from metal mining, and in all jurisdictions there are laws and regulations not only related to mining itself, but also for the protection of air and water, workers, and taxation.

In addition, there are a number of modern-day treaties, especially in the North, that transfer title to Indigenous governments for a portion of the lands in their traditional territories; these are variously referred to as *Inuit-owned lands, Category 1 lands*, and so on. In addition to these title lands, there is another category of lands where the Indigenous government has a substantial say over resource development, often with their own environmental assessment process. In British Columbia, the Tŝilhqot'in have federally recognized title over a substantial portion of their lands that does not have a treaty.

This chapter will first put Canadian law in the context of Indigenous law, and then provide a framework for understanding some current key mine permitting, monitoring, and enforcement provisions in federal, territorial, and provincial law.[1]

INDIGENOUS LAW

Indigenous legal traditions continue to exist. While they have been changed and constrained, they have not been widely extinguished. Though negatively affected by past Canadian actions, Indigenous peoples continue to experience the operation of their legal traditions in such diverse fields as, inter alia, family life, land ownership, resource relationships, trade and commerce, and political organization. Indigenous traditions are inextricably intertwined with the present-day Aboriginal customs, practices, and traditions that are now recognized and affirmed in section 35(1) of the *Constitution Act 1982*. In this respect they are also part of Canadian law.[2]

Indigenous jurisdiction and authority exist separate from Canadian law. Under Section 35 of the *Constitution Act* of 1982, the Canadian government affirms Aboriginal treaties and rights. Court cases expanding on Canadian responsibilities under this section include *Delgamuukw, Sparrow*, the *Haida/Taku, Tŝilhqot'in*, and others. These cases restrict the rights of the Crown and mining companies on traditional Indigenous lands, emphasize the "honour of the Crown" and reconciliation, and assign a "fiduciary responsibility" to the Crown to protect the rights and interests of Indigenous people. The difficulty is that, unless Indigenous governments have the resources to take a case to the Supreme Court and international courts, the Crown and resource companies tend to ignore their authority and rights.

In Canada, where Indigenous groups have negotiated modern treaties, surface and subsurface lands are treated separately. In several cases, Indigenous peoples have negotiated surface rights to land where the subsurface is still owned by the Crown. Generally, the portion of lands where the Indigenous peoples have control over mineral rights is very small.

The Nunavut Land Claim Agreement demonstrates this. While Inuit obtained surface rights to roughly 20 percent of the territory of Nunavut, they obtained full ownership, including mineral rights, to only 2 percent.[3] The Nunavut Impact Review Board reviews major resource projects for the territory and determines if they should go ahead, but because the Crown is considered to own the subsurface rights for most of the territory, the federal Minister of Crown-Indigenous Relations has the final decision for most of these lands.

The Tłįchǫ Land Claims and Self-Government Agreement, which came into effect on August 4, 2005, was the first combined land, resources, and self-government agreement in the Northwest Territories. The federal government, the government of the Northwest Territories, and the Tłįchǫ are parties to the agreement. It provides the Tłįchǫ with ownership of a single block of 39,000 square kilometres of land, including subsurface resources, centred on the four Tłįchǫ communities.[4]

Since 2006, Nunavik—the Inuit territory north of the 55th parallel in Quebec—has had a treaty with Quebec and Canada that sets out Inuit control over their lands, managed by the Inuit-controlled Makivik Corporation. The lands are divided into Category 1, 2, and 3 lands. Category 1 lands, over which Inuit communities have complete control, represent 1.4 percent of all the lands. On Category 2 and 3 lands, the subsurface rights are still owned by Quebec, but with considerable consultation requirements with Inuit.[5] The treaty includes a revenue-sharing agreement that awards Inuit 50 percent of the first $2 million of any mining revenues received by Quebec from their territory, and 5 percent of revenues above that amount.[6] Inuit do not, however, have the right to determine taxation policy for Quebec.

There are two mines and a number of mining exploration projects in Nunavik; one is the Raglan Mine, originally built by Falconbridge Nickel Mines, now owned by Glencore. The impact benefit agreement (IBA) for Raglan—the first full IBA to be signed in Canada—is publicly available. Makivik developed a mining policy as a result of its experience with Raglan that emphasizes environment, sustainability, and benefits to Inuit.

The price for these modern treaties is very high for Indigenous peoples, as to go ahead they always have to agree to an extinguishment of any other claims to title and/or to a "non-assertion" of any further Aboriginal rights and claims.[7]

A number of Indigenous Nations and organizations have established their own mining codes and policies; examples include the Taku River Tlingit First Nation Mining Policy, Northern Secwepemc te Qelmucw Mining Policy, Anishinabek Mining Strategy, and the Kitchenuhmaykoosib Inninuwug Watershed Declaration.[8] In these cases, where title or self-government has not been affirmed in a modern treaty, or where the federal government retains the right to reverse the Indigenous decision, Indigenous peoples have to fight to have their own protocols recognized and respected.

THE REGULATORY FRAMEWORK FOR MINING IN CANADA

Canada has a federal government, ten provinces, and three territories. Constitutionally, the provinces are not subordinate to the federal government. Provinces have full power over mineral exploration, development, conservation, and management. All provinces and territories have their own mining acts, and some related acts governing royalties and taxation.

At the time of writing, a new *Mineral Resources Act* is being developed in the Northwest Territories to replace regulations that were handed down from the federal government at the time of devolution in 2014. Other acts in the Northwest Territories govern environmental assessment and permitting of mines. For example, the *Mackenzie Valley Resource Management Act* regulates the environmental assessment of mines, and the federal government still can refuse to accept NWT decisions about mining projects on Crown lands.

In Yukon, the *Quartz Mining Act* and the *Placer Mining Act* govern the mining process, and the Yukon Environmental and Socio-Economic Assessment Board evaluates the impacts of mining. The board makes recommendations to a "decision body," which can be the affected Indigenous government, or, on occasion, Indigenous and Northern Affairs Canada.

The Nunavut Mining Regulations apply to Crown lands in Nunavut.[9] The Nunavut Land and Water Board undertakes environmental and social reviews of project proposals.[10]

The primary areas of responsibility and authority of the federal government with respect to mining can be summarized as follows:

- Crown-Indigenous Relations and Northern Affairs Canada is charged with implementing Section 91 (24) of the *Constitution Act* of 1867, which confers on Parliament jurisdiction over "Indians and Lands reserved for the Indians." This section has been held to authorize Parliament to pass laws directly in relation to Indigenous people. Most modern treaties do away with this section of the Constitution.
- The regulation of activities that may affect fish or waters where fish are found, in accordance with the federal *Fisheries Act*.
- Environmental assessment of projects listed under the *Canadian Environmental Assessment Act* (soon to be called the *Canadian Impact Assessment Act*).
- Natural Resources Canada has a relatively minor role as a regulator based on its authority over the explosives used in mining operations. However, it is the lead agency promoting mining; it calls the industry its "client."
- Through the *Nuclear Safety and Control Act*, the federal government's Canadian Nuclear Safety Commission has authority over uranium mines, mills, and refineries, including their development, operation, and closure.
- The federal government has responsibilities for transboundary waters, navigable waters, and import and export of hazardous wastes.
- The *Canadian Environmental Protection Act* provides the federal government with some regulatory control of toxic substances.
- The *National Parks Act*, the *Migratory Birds Act*, the *Oceans Act,* and the *Endangered Species Act* provide the federal government with

some responsibilities to protect lands, and endangered species and their habitats from mining damages.

The federal government also plays a promotion, facilitation, and research role in several key areas related to the mineral sector. For example, the development of a Canada Minerals and Metals Mining Plan, the annual meeting of Mines Ministers, and several intergovernmental working groups provide national venues for the discussion of the mineral sector. Important multi-stakeholder initiatives, such as Mine Environment Neutral Drainage (MEND) and the National Orphaned/Abandoned Mines Initiative (NOAMI), are supported by secretariats housed within Natural Resources Canada. Natural Resources Canada also does extensive research and analysis of both environmental and economic matters, and hosts the largest collection of national online mining-related information in the Geological Survey of Canada and the Canadian Minerals Yearbook.

Other federal and provincial legislation affecting taxation, securities, and corporate conduct are discussed in chapter 13.

ENVIRONMENTAL ASSESSMENT[11]

Usually, before permits for large mines can be issued, most federal, territorial, and provincial laws require that an environmental assessment (EA) be done; Ontario is the exception. The EA is used to determine if there are likely to be "significant adverse environmental effects" that cannot be limited ("mitigated"). Some provinces require a *certificate of environmental compliance* before project permits can be issued; most don't.

Federal EAs and most provincial EAs are an important step in exposing any problems with the mine proposal. In most cases, the research and extensive reports that the mine proponent has to produce for the EA will discuss many of the issues that concern all interested parties. However, under current law, the environmental impact statement and the highly technical studies on which the mine are judged are prepared by consultants for whom the mining company is the client. The studies can cost well over $1 million and are difficult for under-resourced opponents of the proposal to criticize. Most environmental assessment acts provide for public participation at different stages of the review,

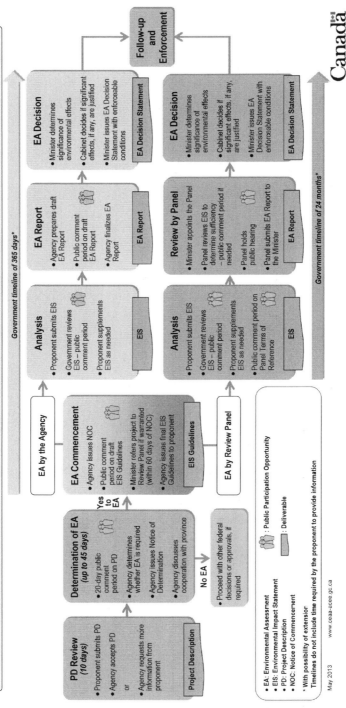

The Environmental Assessment Process under the 2012 *Canadian Environmental Assessment Act. Source:* Environment and Climate Change Canada.

but only the federal government has a provision for intervenor funding. Even that funding is usually too little and can come too late to be useful.

As this book goes to press, the federal EA regime is in flux. A bill to substantially amend the *Environmental Assessment Act* legislation is before Parliament. Even if the amendments are passed, it is likely that any projects initiated before the new Act and regulations become law will be assessed based on the old Act.

The following discussion about federal EA is based on 2012 legislation (*Canadian Environmental Assessment Act* [CEAA 2012]). Under CEAA 2012, the Act is brought into force—"triggered"—by the need of the mine proponent for a permit or authorization of some kind from the federal government, or for federal funding. CEAA 2012 applies to projects described in the Regulations Designating Physical Activities and to projects designated by the Minister of the Environment and Climate Change. Mines and mine expansions of a certain size are designated in Sections 15 to 17 of the regulations.[12] The Canadian Environmental Assessment Agency is the responsible authority for most designated projects. Upon acceptance of a project description, the agency undertakes an analysis to decide if a federal EA is required.

This step does not apply to uranium. Designated uranium projects are regulated by the National Energy Board and the Canadian Nuclear Safety Commission and EAs of these are mandatory.[13] (The regulation of uranium is discussed in chapter 14.)

Most provinces and territories also have their own environmental assessment regimes. Some provinces only apply EA to mine projects over a certain size. As noted, Ontario is the only jurisdiction that does not automatically assess mines and mine projects. In Ontario, an environmental assessment review of privately owned projects is required only if the project is designated by the Environment Minister. In recent years, some mining projects have voluntarily agreed to an Ontario EA, conducted at the same time as the federal one.

Some projects may also require a provincial/territorial EA, as provinces have additional and more stringent environmental protections than the federal government. "CEAA 2012 includes provisions for cooperation and coordinated action between the two orders of government. As such, CEAA 2012 aims to achieve the goal of 'one project–one review.'"[14]

Under the 2012 legislation, federal EA looks at the following factors:

- environmental effects, including environmental effects caused by accidents and malfunctions, and cumulative environmental effects
- significance of those environmental effects
- public comments
- mitigation measures and follow-up program requirements
- purpose of the designated project
- alternative means of carrying out the designated project
- changes to the project caused by the environment
- results of any relevant regional study
- any other relevant matter

There are two types of environmental assessment conducted under CEAA 2012: environmental assessment by a responsible authority, or by a review panel.

A responsible authority is the federal government, which has to issue the major permits required. For example, the need for a permit for a mining company to destroy fish habitat makes the Department of Fisheries and Oceans a responsible party in the EA process.

An environmental assessment *by a responsible authority* is conducted by the Canadian Environmental Assessment Agency, the National Energy Board, or the Canadian Nuclear Safety Commission (CNSC). Information on the process for environmental assessments conducted by the agency is provided below. Environmental assessment by the CNSC is discussed in chapter 14.

The review by the responsible authority has resulted in a substantial drop in the number of full environmental assessments done by the federal government. Prior to CEAA 2012, thousands of projects were assessed annually; since its implementation, only twenty-five to fifty each year.[15]

An environmental assessment by review panel is conducted by a panel of individuals appointed by the Minister of the Environment and Climate Change and is supported by the agency. Often a review panel will be done in harmonization with a provincial authority, and—occasionally—with an Indigenous government, with each party appointing one member. Generally speaking, the quality of the experts appointed to these panels is good.

The CEAA decision against a project can be overturned by the minister if they believe the project is "justified under the circumstances" or "in the national interest." Both of these reasons are politically loaded. Decisions in favour of projects can also be overturned by the minister.

There are tight timelines for each step in the EA process for government, Indigenous, and public input, but no deadlines or penalties for delays caused by the mine proponent. These deadlines create anxiety, stretch resources, and also result in improper consultation. The minister can extend the deadlines, but this rarely happens, unless the proponent requests it. The deadlines are overseen and enforced by the Major Project Management Office.

Although most provincial EA acts have provisions for monitoring and follow-up to mitigation measures, there have been substantial cuts to the government departments that monitor and enforce compliance, making it difficult to evaluate how effective the mitigation measures have been. I have talked to provincial regulators who tell me there is no follow-up to mitigation measures at all.

CEAA 2012 does allow for "strategic environmental assessment"— the review of government programs and policies—but it has rarely been implemented in an effective way. Nunavut and other modern treaty organizations do sometimes conduct strategic EA when trying to decide on policy. Environmentalists and Indigenous governments have also advocated for "regional environmental assessment"—an overall review of major project effects across a bioregion or watershed. There is nothing in CEAA 2012 to prevent this taking place, as the minister has discretion to initiate an EA, but it has never happened. In the new Act, both strategic and regional EA are mentioned but not made mandatory.

The process of federal EA under CEAA 2012 includes a number of steps, which are set out on the Canadian Environmental Assessment Agency website. If the process proceeds by review panel, there are some opportunities for public participation, and opportunities to get some funding to hire technical expertise to help with submissions.

The trade agreements Canada has signed also present a threat to the Environmental Assessment Agency's ability to say "no" to projects based on environmental, social, and cultural values. (See the Bilcon case described in chapter 10.)

POLLUTION CONTROL

There are a number of acts and regulations in all jurisdictions that set limits for pollution from mines, mills, and smelters. The key federal laws are the *Fisheries Act* and the *Canadian Environmental Protection Act.*

Fisheries Act and the Metal and Diamond Mining Effluent Regulation

Substantial changes to strengthen the effectiveness of the federal *Fisheries Act* are being debated as this book goes to press.

The Department of Fisheries and Oceans administers Section 35, the key habitat protection provision, prohibiting any work or undertaking that would cause the harmful alteration, disruption, or destruction of fish habitat. Environment and Climate Change Canada administers Section 36, the key pollution prevention provision, prohibiting the deposit of deleterious substances into waters frequented by fish, unless authorized by regulations under the *Fisheries Act* or other federal legislation.

For years, these two sections provided some protection for fish against polluters. As usual, the devil was in the details, and in 2012, the Harper government gutted their effectiveness.

The regulation that allows exemption from Sections 35 and 36 is the Metal and Diamond Mining Effluent Regulation (MDMER). The current *Fisheries Act*'s MDMER sets limits for eight pollutants (arsenic, copper, cyanide, lead, nickel, zinc, suspended solids, and radium 226) in effluent water from mines. Although a significant part of effluent from some mines, mercury is not included in the mining exceptions, and so—technically—is still banned. The *Canadian Environmental Protection Act* sets limits for emissions of toxins such as mercury, and most provinces do have regulatory limits for mercury.

The MDMER was amended in 2018 (the Metal Mining Effluent Regulations became MDMER), but most provisions will not be in force until 2021. The other changes gazetted in 2017 included adding a criteria for un-ionized ammonia, and expanding the *acute lethality test* to *daphnia magna* (water fleas). The MDMER requires this acute lethality test: if more than 50 percent of fish die when exposed to the undiluted mine effluent for 96 hours, it is deemed to be *acutely lethal.*

Schedule 2

The other part of the MDMER is a provision whereby a mining company can apply to have a fish-bearing water (like a lake, river, or stream) declared a *tailing impoundment* and added to Schedule 2 of the regulation. Magic. This is attractive to metal mining companies because it allows them to avoid the *Fisheries Act* prohibition of putting "deleterious substances into waters frequented by fish" and place tailings in an existing body of water. This is considerably cheaper than engineering a new wet cover to prevent acid mine drainage.

When this plan was first floated to the public in 2002, there was a huge outcry from local and Indigenous communities, environmental organizations, and the general public. As a result, adding a fish-bearing lake, river, or stream to Schedule 2 requires a decision at the federal Cabinet level, and an actual amendment to the regulation for each body of water taken. How effective this is depends entirely on who sits at the Cabinet table. There are now more than forty-five water bodies that have been redefined as tailings impoundments.[16] Since doing so requires a Fisheries authorization, the request to designate a water body as a tailings impoundment triggers a federal environmental assessment under the *Canadian Environmental Assessment Act*. A habitat compensation plan must also be in place before any federal permits are issued for the mine, and it must be approved by Fisheries and Oceans Canada and any First Nation involved.

Environmental Effects Monitoring

Another MDMER requirement is that companies conduct environmental effects monitoring (EEM) of their effluents and undertake some environmental scans and report the results annually to Environment and Climate Change Canada. There is limited auditing of their performance by government regulators. The results are publicly available.[17]

Responsibility for the administration and enforcement provisions of the *Fisheries Act* is shared by Fisheries and Oceans Canada and Environment Canada. Environment Canada is the lead for the administration and enforcement of the MDMER.

Canadian Environmental Protection Act

The *Canadian Environmental Protection Act* 1999 (amended in 2000) is an "Act respecting pollution prevention and the protection of the environment and human health in order to contribute to sustainable development." Essentially, the Act requires that the government study substances, determine if they are "toxic," and then assess tolerable limits for their use. The government is also charged with "managing" the use of these substances.

Base Metal Smelters and Refineries

As we saw in chapter 3, smelters are a major source of pollution, particularly to air (and to land and waters as their toxins settle on the surface). Until 2017, Canada was home to eleven base metal smelters and ten aluminum smelters.

In September 2002, the releases from primary and secondary copper and zinc smelters and refineries were declared toxic under the *Canadian Environmental Protection Act* (CEPA). CEPA toxic substances include sulphur dioxide, lead, mercury, arsenic, cadmium, and nickel. The recommended levels of these substances are called BLIERs (Base Level Industrial Emission Requirements). Once a substance is declared to be a "toxin," CEPA requires the company releasing it to develop a risk management strategy and an instrument to address the BLIER. This must be finalized within two years of the substance being declared toxic.

The "instrument" selected through a decades-long negotiation with the mining companies and the government was "pollution prevention planning." This meant that pollution prevention plans had to be negotiated for each smelter in Canada's base metals smelting sector, including producers of zinc, copper, lead, nickel, and cobalt. Smelter owners were required to develop plans voluntarily to meet the Environmental Code of Practice for Base Metals Smelters and Refineries[18] and to reduce their output of sulphur dioxide and particulate matter. In 2002, they were given until 2020 to meet the standards. Until they were threatened with regulation in 2015 if they did not act, the companies refused to budge.

In February 2018, Environment Canada reported that they had reached agreements with Glencore, Vale Canada Limited, Teck

Metals Limited, and Hudbay. But the scene had shifted dramatically since 2002. By this time, the only copper smelter left in Canada was the Horne smelter (now owned by Glencore) in Rouyn-Noranda, which was also accepting recycled materials. Vale's Thompson operations were closing; the Kidd Metallurgical Smelter in Timmins had closed, as had the Hudbay smelter in Flin Flon. The companies claimed that they could not afford to meet the base metals standards.

As of February 2018, BLIERs have been negotiated for smelters owned by the following companies for sulphur dioxide emissions and particulate matter.[19] They had also agreed to implement the applicable recommendations in the Environmental Code of Practice for Base Metals Smelters and Refineries.[20] The status of Canadian base metal smelters, as of 2018, is as follows:

- Teck Metals Limited: zinc-lead Trail Operations
- Glencore-Horne copper smelter (Rouyn-Noranda, Quebec)
- Glencore lead/zinc smelter (Belledune, New Brunswick)
- Glencore-Noranda Income Fund: CEZinc Refinery (Salaberry-de-Valleyfield, Quebec; the second largest zinc refinery in North America)
- Glencore CCR copper (anodes) refinery (Montreal, Quebec)
- Hudson Bay Mining and Smelting (Hudbay's) copper smelter (Flin Flon, Manitoba); closed in 2013
- Vale Inco Ltd. (now Vale Canada Ltd.) (Thompson, Manitoba); closed in 2018
- Vale Inco Ltd. (now Vale Canada Ltd.) nickel smelter (Copper Cliff, Ontario); recently got extension on emissions
- Vale Inco Ltd. (now Vale Canada Ltd.) refinery (Port Colborne, Ontario);
- Vale Inco Ltd. (now Vale Canada Ltd.) nickel-hydrometallurgical plant (Long Harbour, Newfoundland and Labrador)
- Xstrata Nickel (now Glencore-Sudbury Integrated Nickel Operations) (Sudbury, Ontario)
- Xstrata Copper-Kidd/Timmins Glencore; closed in 2010

Aluminum Smelters and Processing

Aluminum comes from bauxite ore, which is not mined anywhere in Canada. It is imported from tropical countries in the Global South.

However, Canada is host to a number of aluminum smelters and refineries. Because the process is so electricity intensive, the cheap electricity available in Quebec from the province's many hydro-electric dams on Cree territory attracts the companies.

In 2012, a new code to guide aluminium smelter operations was introduced by the federal government, as well as the governments of British Columbia and Quebec. Like the base metals smelter agreements, the Code of Practice to Reduce Emissions of Fine Particulate Matter (PM2.5) from the Aluminium Sector is voluntary and effectively unenforceable.[21]

National Pollutant Release Inventory

Under CEPA there is also a public-right-to-know instrument called the National Pollutant Release Inventory (NPRI), which reports on pollutant releases in Canada.[22] Until 2009, the NPRI did not require reporting of CEPA toxins disposed of in waste rock and tailings. That year, MiningWatch Canada took the federal government to court to force it to include these major sources of toxins, and now companies have to report annually.[23] The Commission for Environmental Cooperation reported in 2018 that mining leads all pollutant releases and transfers in North America.[24]

NATIONAL PARKS AND MARINE PROTECTED AREAS

The federal government has the responsibility to protect natural environments that are representative of Canada's natural heritage. Parks Canada is responsible for managing national parks to maintain their ecological integrity while providing opportunities for public understanding, appreciation, and enjoyment. The Fisheries Department plays a similar role for marine protected areas established under the *Oceans Act*.[25]

The *Canada National Parks Act* states that public lands within the parks shall not be disposed of and no person shall occupy them except under the authority of the Act. Ecological integrity is the first consideration in management planning. Human activities that threaten the integrity of a park's ecosystem are not permitted. Generally this includes mining claims and activity.[26] (It should be noted that parks governed by Indigenous, territorial, and provincial governments often do not have these restrictions, and mining exploration and development is often allowed.)

MINE CLOSURE REGULATION
(FEDERAL AND PROVINCIAL)

Most jurisdictions in Canada now require that some kind of closure planning be in place before a mine goes into operation, accompanied by a financial assurance. At some mines, estimated closure costs and associated financial securities posted by the mining companies in conjunction with the mine closure plans are much lower than real costs are likely to be. The financial assurances against mine closure are unlikely to include assurance against catastrophic accidents during operations such as a tailings dam rupture. In Ontario, mining companies with a credit rating of BBB- or higher are allowed to self-assure. A credit rating lower than BBB- is considered "junk status."[27] The financial assurance can amount to nothing more than a line on a subsidiary's balance sheet.

Closure plans for mines may not include appropriate disposal or treatment of massive piles of acid-generating/leachate toxic waste rock, and may not appropriately evaluate the risk of groundwater contamination to the area through seepage from the tailings areas and underground workings.[28] There is great variety in terms of closure regulation in Canada. British Columbia appears to be the least stringent, and Quebec, the most.

In Ontario, there is a requirement for a public notice and an information centre in the local area to view the closure plan prior to mine development. A notice is also posted on a provincial electronic registry advising members of the public of a thirty-day comment period during which they can visit the Ministry of Northern Development and Mines offices in Sudbury and review a mine closure plan. After considerable pressure from MiningWatch Canada, the form and amount of financial assurance for mineral properties held by the province is available on the ministry's website.

In British Columbia, there have been a number of important studies of the closure regime.

On May 16, 2016, the Union of B.C. Indian Chiefs released an in-depth study by economist Robyn Allan, only days after a scathing report by Auditor General Carol Bellringer detailed a damning failure of the province's environment monitoring of mines and failure to ensure companies are liable for the cost of accidents and remediation. "This failure to hold companies responsible rewards risky behavior because when companies know they can escape being held financially responsible for reclamation, they are more likely to cut corners on safety measures, leading to more accidents and more severe consequences when they happen," stated Grand Chief [Stewart] Phillip.

Ms. Allan's analysis shows the Ministry of Energy and Mines had $1.3 billion in site reclamation costs that hadn't been funded by mine operators as of March 31, 2014, and notes that amount could be higher today because of a spate of recent mine closures. However, the province no longer makes the figures publicly available. The province has also assumed responsibility for reclaiming abandoned mines, putting taxpayers on the hook for a further $275 million.[29]

A Model for Effective Mine Closure Regulation: The Quebec Example

Quebec now has the most effective mine closure system in the country, after strong advocacy from Coalition pour que le Québec ait meilleure mine for improvements. The Quebec closure regime is as follows.[30]

Before a mining lease is issued, the company has to submit a closure plan to the Ministry of Energy and Mines (MERN), which consults the Ministry of Sustainable Development, Environment, and Fight against Climate Change (MDDELCC) before approving the plan and the amount of the financial guarantee that must accompany the plan. It may require additional study before approving the plan.

It has to include a full, scheduled plan for the site reclamation, including a study of the feasibility of backfilling any open pits. The closure plan must be revised every five years. However, the MERN may fix a shorter period for revision when it approves the plan. It may require that the plan be revised if there is a change in the mining operations.

The financial guarantee—in a form that can be easily accessed by the government—has to cover the full costs of the expected reclamation work. It is paid in three instalments, in the two years following the date on which the plan is approved, with an initial instalment covering 50 percent of the total amount of the guarantee due 90 days after approval. The MERN can also ask for full payment upfront.

The company can get a release from responsibility for the site if all the reclamation has been done, if no money is owed the government, and if "the site does not pose a risk for the environment or for human health and safety, and in particular, poses no risk of acid mine drainage."

Long-Term Stewardship Regulation (Provincial and Federal)

Where mines have been abandoned or "orphaned" by their owners, the government (federal, if the mine is on federal lands; provincial, if it is on provincial lands) becomes responsible for the proper closure, care, and maintenance of the mining property. The federal Department of Indian and Northern Affairs (now Indigenous and Northern Affairs Canada) became responsible for the Giant, Colomac, and Faro mines—some of the largest toxic waste sites in Canada—following the bankruptcy of their owners in 1998 and 1999. When the federal government devolved governance to the territories, the federal government remained responsible for these sites.

Provincial governments have found themselves in a similar position. Provincial auditors general now require governments to declare these sites as liabilities on their public accounts, and to ensure that the costs of managing them shows up in government financial statements. In Ontario, when the First Nickel company walked away from its Lockerby Mine, the Ministry of Northern Development and Mines was forced to operate the underground mine until the province could properly close it.

PROVINCIAL AND TERRITORIAL REGULATION: A SUMMARY

Since the provinces are responsible for the management of mineral resources, they are also responsible for most mine permitting, monitoring, and enforcement. Different provinces have different requirements. Since most provinces bend over backwards to encourage mining, most provincial mining ministry websites set out the rules quite clearly and can be found easily online. Links to the relevant department in each jurisdiction (as of February 2016) can be found in Natural Resources Canada's *Exploration and Mining in Canada: An Investor's Brief.*[31]

Historically, provincial mining laws have been quite similar to one another. Most mining laws set out the manner in which the Crown may dispose of its minerals and others may obtain rights to them.[32] Provincial regulatory controls over the environmental and social impacts of mining are done through laws governing environmental assessment, water acts, waste management acts, planning acts, and so on. Almost all provincial land use planning acts exempt mining from most land use plans and treat it as the highest and best use of land. In Ontario, in areas of significant mineral potential, ideas for other kinds of economic activity or development have to get special approval to proceed.

In many provinces, there has to be some kind of public notice that a mining permit is going to be considered. For example, in Yukon and the Northwest Territories, permits for advanced exploration are subject to public consultation, as are water permits and land use permits. In Ontario, applications for permits with environmental impacts have to be posted under the *Environmental Bill of Rights.*

There are many types of provincial and federal permits that may be required to develop a mine, and the reader will have to investigate the individual websites of each jurisdiction. The following federal permits will likely be required:

- for exploration work
- to destroy fish habitat
- under the *Migratory Birds Act*
- under the *Endangered Species Act*
- for amendment to federal regulation to use fish-bearing waters for tailings disposal
- for works in navigable waters
- for uranium: construction and operation permits from the Canadian Nuclear Safety Commission
- for storage and use of explosives

- for transboundary shipment of hazardous waste
- to discharge toxins into water
- for approval for air emissions

And provincial permits are likely to be required:
- for archaeological disturbances
- for timber cutting
- to burn materials, including brush
- to take water
- for a mine closure plan
- for approval for roads and transmission lines
- for work permits
- for approval of fuel handling
- for taking aggregates
- to discharge toxins into water
- for industrial/private sewage works
- for approval of waste management systems
- for registration of generators
- for approval for air emissions
- for approval of drinking water systems
- for land use
- for approval from agricultural commission in Quebec
- for approval under a municipal official plan

13

WHY TAXATION MATTERS[1]

The policies and laws through which our governments collect money from individuals and companies determine how much government can spend on public goods like health care, roads, public transit, education, environmental protection, recreational services, and so on. Taxation is possibly the government's most important policy tool.

The shocking cost of the minerals we take for granted must be respected in government policy and industry practice. This means conserving and recycling the minerals that have already been extracted and reducing the need for mining wherever possible. When government provides tax incentives to mineral exploration and mining instead of to recycling, conservation, and rehabilitation measures, it is making a policy decision.

Analysis by the Organisation for Economic Co-operation and Development (OECD) in 2017 recommended that "the preferential tax treatment of conventional resource sectors, such as oil and gas, and minerals and metals should be eliminated on both environmental and economic grounds."[2]

The mining industry recognizes the power of taxation to shape mineral policy: "The taxes imposed by any particular government are crucial to the viability of a mining project. Too high a tax burden can make a project uneconomic even though the project may have excellent mining fundamentals."[3]

The level to which the mining industry has shaped taxation policy federally and provincially is disturbing. For most of us, tax policy is an intimidating and bizarre process. We don't pay attention to it, except when we are filing our own tax returns. It is rife with myths that are promoted by the corporations and those who benefit most from the system.

In 2004, I was making a presentation about metal mining issues to a Senate committee on finance. In response to what I was saying, one of the senators burst out, "But the industry pays billions in taxes!" I had no response, but went back to the office and started researching. Even I found it difficult to believe how little tax mining companies actually paid to any level of government. Statistics Canada reported that for 1997, federal taxes paid were $251 million and provincial taxes were $147 million—less than half a billion dollars.[4] These figures included income tax and capital tax.

THE LACK OF DATA TO ANALYZE TAXATION

In 2012, the Pembina Institute and MiningWatch Canada released a study assessing the value of government support for the metal mining industry in Canada, entitled *Looking Beneath the Surface.* The research for this study took more than a year and involved poring over public accounts, and industry and Statistics Canada reports, analyzing and digesting what was found. The work was hampered by the lack of data available from government. Governments generally were unable to provide estimates of the value of a number of important tax measures introduced to support the industry. Other information was considered confidential for commercial or privacy reasons. In many cases, closure and long-term care costs were underestimated or not estimated at all.

In addition, mining data is frequently aggregated with data from industries like smelting, refining, and metals manufacturing—industries that would still exist if the inputs were recycled materials. It is also often aggregated with tar sands, oil and gas, and quarrying.

Corporate income taxes paid are confidential, except as they are aggregated from all their projects and subsidiaries and reported in their financial statements. Mining companies are not required to be transparent about their accounting practices that shrink the base on which tax is assessed.

Two corporate practices reduce taxable profits and shift profits between subsidiaries. They are called *base erosion* and *profit-shifting* by tax experts, as they have a major impact on taxes assessed against companies with operating mines in Canada. They are explained clearly in the *Hidden Cost of Tax Incentives* (2018), a toolkit prepared by IGF-OECD.[5] Although the report and the BEPS toolkit program were developed for African countries, most of the findings are applicable to provinces, territories, and Indigenous governments in Canada.

Two practices are especially problematic. The first is "transfer mispricing," as it is called in a 2017 report for the African Tax Administration Forum. It is an effective tax avoidance scheme for many mining companies. It is extremely difficult to trace. It involves the sale of goods and services between the subsidiaries of a parent company, often with the intent of hiding actual costs and profits. Writes report author Alexandra Readhead,

> While transfer mispricing is no more prevalent in mining than it is in other sectors dominated by MNEs [multinational enterprises], tax avoidance by mining companies has an outsized impact on domestic resource mobilization in countries heavily reliant on mining revenues. The problem is particularly acute for resource-rich developing countries, given the importance of corporate income tax to total tax revenue. Whether mineral prices go up or down, existing and future mining operations should contribute their full share to government budgets. Minerals are a non-renewable resource: any abusive erosion of the tax base by mining companies is a net loss for the country and its population.[6]

The second practice that lowers the base to be taxed is "thin capitalization," which happens when a company is financed through a high level of debt compared to equity, resulting in excessive interest deductions. This appears to be a major reason why the operating mining companies in Canada (Barrick Gold, Teck Cominco, Goldcorp, Agnico-Eagle, Imperial Metals, Taseko, and so on) pay so little tax; they constantly leverage their operating properties to fund the expansion of an existing mine or the purchase of new ones.

THE EXTRACTIVE INDUSTRIES TRANSPARENCY INITIATIVE

Twenty years ago, the Extractive Industries Transparency Initiative (EITI) was developed by the UK government to limit corruption of governments by transnational companies. It was a response to the demands of the Publish What You Pay coalition,[7] supported by George Soros among others, which sought the mandatory disclosure of payments made by oil, gas, and mining companies to governments for the extraction of natural resources. The coalition also called on governments to publish full details on revenues as a necessary first step towards a more accountable system for the management of natural resource revenues.

The Canadian mining industry was strongly opposed to implementing the EITI requirements in Canada, although it supported their use in the Global South.[8] However, at the 2013 G8 leaders' summit in Northern Ireland, Canada announced that it would take action to enhance the transparency of payments to governments made by Canadian extractive companies by introducing mandatory reporting. The resulting legislation, the *Extractive Sector Transparency Measures Act* (ESTMA), came into force on June 1, 2015. The first reporting happened in 2017 and does provide important information about company revenues to all three levels of government.

James Wilt, writing in *The Narwhal*, July 16, 2018, says,

> Mining companies are extracting billions of dollars worth of gold from Canada every year but are paying only a tiny fraction in taxes and royalties compared to operations in other countries, an analysis by The Narwhal has found.
>
> Experts say Canadian governments are collecting a smaller percentage of mineral value than almost any other jurisdiction on earth, ranging from Burkina Faso to Chile to Finland.
>
> For example, Barrick Gold, the second-largest mining company in Canada, extracted close to $250 million in gold from its Hemlo mine in northwest Ontario in 2017, the most recent year for which data is publicly available. In return, the

company paid $14.4 million in taxes and fees—or only 5.8 per cent of the gold's worth.

That same year, Barrick extracted roughly $817 million in gold at its Pueblo Viejo mine in the Dominican Republic. There, the company paid $327 million in taxes, royalties, fees and infrastructure improvements—a full 40 per cent of the gold's total value.

Meanwhile in Peru, the government received $45.5 million in compensation for the company's Lagunas Norte mine—or 9.4 per cent of the recovered gold's worth. When broken down, the disparity between fees paid is stark: Barrick paid the Dominican Republic roughly $503 per ounce of gold, paid Peru $117 per ounce of gold and paid Canada $73 per ounce.[9]

THE ONTARIO VALUE FOR MONEY AUDIT

In 2016, at the urging of MiningWatch Canada, the auditor general of Ontario undertook a "value for money audit" of the Ministry of Mines. She found that (in 2014) industry production was worth almost $11 billion:

Over the last 20 years, from 1995 to 2014, mining revenue [as reported to the provincial government] fluctuated considerably and dropped to its lowest point in 20 years in 2014 (to $18.6 million, from a high of $236.7 million in 2008). Mining revenue [to the provincial government] is impacted by fluctuations in the global demand and commodity prices for the minerals, and in the last few years, lower commodity prices and global demand have resulted in lower mining revenue for the province. . . .

Ontario ranked ninth among Canadian provinces and territories in investment attractiveness in mineral exploration, even though it has one of the lowest mining tax rates on income from mining operations in Canada. Ontario has a marginal effective mining tax rate of 5.6%, compared to a national average of 8.6%.[10] Exploration spending in Ontario peaked in 2011, and has since dropped by over 50%.[11]

In effect, all of these tax subsidies and incentives are doing little or nothing to attract new mining dollars to the province. In 2019, Ontario launched a new program to further incentivize mining exploration and development and to "cut red tape."

LAYERS OF TAXATION PAID BY MINING COMPANIES[12]

The federal government imposes a number of taxes on the mining industry, including corporate income taxes, GST, payroll levies, and excise taxes and customs duties.

Corporate income taxes for mining under the *Income Tax Act* were at 28 percent (of net income) until November 7, 2003, when Bill C-48 lowered corporate tax rates for the mining industry and brought them in line with other industrial sectors. The rate has been reduced year by year and is now 15 percent. Corporate income tax is based on "net income," and mining companies are able to claim substantial expenses and deductions with carry-forward provisions, so many of them pay very little federal income tax at all. The federal and provincial governments, in fact, are often in the position of owing tax refunds to mining companies. Mining companies are able to convert their losses into credits against future mining taxes and show these credits on their books as "tax assets." Provincial and territorial governments impose income taxes varying from 10 percent to 16 percent, based on the value of production. There is also a mining tax or royalty imposed by provinces and territories, supposedly to pay a rent for the use of mineral resources that belong to the people.

Provincial governments have different approaches to mine revenue for mining tax purposes. British Columbia considers the valuation of the resource to be the ultimate selling price by the mining company. Other provinces tax mineral wealth at "mine mouth," meaning that they tax the unrefined product and deduct estimated costs for processing it. This allowance for processing is set arbitrarily based on a percentage of the cost of the assets (buildings, equipment, etc.) used for the processing, subject to a maximum, usually 65 percent. The rate varies from a low of 8 percent (no processing, applied in Quebec, New Brunswick, and Newfoundland and Labrador) to the maximum of 65 percent (for a smelter/refinery in the province) in Ontario.

For the purposes of the mining tax, companies can also deduct mining and processing asset depreciation—often at 100 percent in the year of purchase. Deductions are also made for pre-production development expenses, exploration expenses, and mine reclamation fund contributions. Ontario exempts the first $500,000 of mining income annually; New Brunswick exempts the first $100,000.

Generally, the mining tax is a percentage of net profits, that is gross revenues minus most of the mine's costs. There are a few exceptions: Alberta, British Columbia, New Brunswick, and Nova Scotia each have a two-tier mining tax. In Alberta, the first tier is 1 percent of mine mouth (gross) revenue, and the second tier is 12 percent of net profits. In British Columbia, the first tier is 2 percent of operating revenues, and the second tier is 13 percent of net profits.[13] Many provinces provide an exemption from mining taxes for new mines in the first years of production. Natural Resources Canada provides a table comparing federal and all provincial tax regimes.[14]

Tax Holidays

Some provinces also provide mining tax holidays for new mines. Ontario provides a $10 million tax exemption for new mines, as well as a three-year tax holiday (ten years for mines in remote locations north of North Bay), and a lower tax rate for remote mines. Quebec has tax credits for new mines in northern Quebec. British Columbia exempts new mines from the net profits portion of mining tax until all costs have been recovered. Saskatchewan exempts new mines from mining tax until accumulated profits exceed the investment in the mine. The definition of a "new mine" for tax purposes can often be stretched to include new shafts on the same ore body.

When calculating income tax payable, all provinces, with the exception of Quebec, allow a 100 percent deduction for Cumulative Canadian Development Expenses (described in the next section). Quebec allows up to a 125 percent deduction for exploration expenses and a 150 percent deduction for development expenses.

Quebec is currently the only province that invests directly in mining companies, through SOQUEM, the provincially owned and funded exploration company.

It is noteworthy that since July 2001, British Columbia provides an exemption for the purchase, lease, or use of mining machinery and equipment for coal and mineral exploration and the development of coal and mineral mine sites.[15]

As with other industrial sectors, mining companies are required to pay health tax, sales tax, workers compensation, and so on. Companies also, of course, remit taxes and pay the employer's portion of some benefits. When they tell the public about the "government revenues" they generate, these amounts are invariably included.

FEDERAL EXPENSES AND DEDUCTIONS SPECIFIC TO THE MINING INDUSTRY IN CANADA

The mining industry enjoys a number of deductions and expenses in the computation of income for tax purposes. Many of these are unique to the mining industry.

Cumulative Canadian Exploration Expenses[16]

Cumulative Canadian Exploration Expenses (CCEE) are expenses incurred for the purpose of determining the existence, location, extent, or quantity of a mineral resource, including prospecting, geochemical and geophysical surveys, drilling, trenching and preliminary sampling, removing overburden, and sinking a mine shaft; these are pre-production development costs. They include expenses for environmental assessment and Indigenous consultation. Any portion not used in the year the expenditure was incurred can be carried forward indefinitely.[17] This creates a pool of expenditures that can be transferred to subsidiaries and upon sale of the company, which is often a reason to keep a floundering mining company alive rather than close it down.[18]

Cumulative Canadian Development Expenses[19]

Cumulative Canadian Development Expenses (CCDE) are expenses incurred in excavating a mine shaft, acquiring new resource properties, and building underground workings "prior to the commencement of production of the resource in reasonable commercial quantities."[20] Excavating a mine shaft or similar underground work *after* the mine has come into production is also included. CCDE is accumulated in a tax pool. Up to 30 percent of the unclaimed balance in the pool may be claimed each year. The pool is transferable and can be carried forward indefinitely.[21]

Flow-Through Shares

Flow-through share (FTS) programs "provide tax incentives to promote the exploration and development of mineral resources in Canada, particularly by encouraging new equity investment in junior mining companies."[22] Companies are allowed to renounce or flow-through CCE and CCD expenses to shareholders so that an investor can use them as a tax loss. Investors get a 100 percent tax deduction for the money they invested in the shares, and they are allowed to speculate on the value of the share over time. The federal government also provides a 15 percent tax credit to investors under the "super flow-through share program,"[23] which has been extended annually since it was introduced in 2006. The graph on page 198 shows the great savings to investors by jurisdiction from FTS programs in 2017. A $1,000 investment in an FTS share only costs $295 in Manitoba, $307 in Quebec, and $356 in British Columbia.

Mineral Tax Credits for Exploration

Mineral Tax Credits for Exploration (METCs) are available federally (15 percent) and in many provinces for exploration, in addition to the credits for super flow-through shares. The credit can be carried back three years and forward for twenty years. There are also other investment tax credits for scientific research for investments in some regions of Canada.

Deduction of Mine Reclamation Trust Contributions

Mining is a waste management industry; it leaves behind tailings, waste rock piles, and other environmental hazards that often have to be managed in perpetuity. The federal government and most provinces require a reclamation bond to be posted in some realizable security before a mine can be developed, or—at the least—while it is in operation. The federal government now allows a deduction for contributions to the reclamation trust. However, where the trust rests with the company, income earned from the trust is subject to tax, as are withdrawals from the trust.

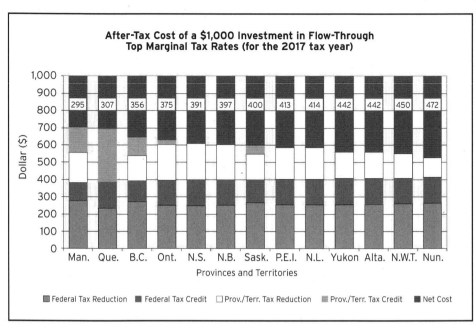

Flow-Through Shares: What They Cost Investors. *Source:* Natural Resources Canada.

When reclamation is taking place (either during mine life or after), reclamation costs are fully deductible at the time they are incurred.

TAX PLANNING CONSIDERATIONS: THE VALUATION ALLOWANCE

The valuation allowance is a method of raising or lowering the current value of a company by adjusting the value of its assets to reflect market value. The valuation adjustments may be accumulated and released to the operating account as required to affect taxation. For example, in 2003, because of higher gold prices, Barrick Gold was faced with paying an accumulated income tax expense of $44 million. It was able to offset the potential tax expense by releasing valuation allowances of $39 million. The tax valuation allowance had been created by a construction start-up at the Veladero Mine in Argentina and by a corporate reorganization that enabled the company to take advantage of certain tax assets.[24]

Valuation allowances can also be accumulated by changes in tax law and regulation, by currency exchange rates, by re-evaluation of the extent and quality of ore bodies, by changes to "good will and reputation"—in effect, by anything that affects the realizable value of the company assets.

IMPLICATIONS FOR REVENUE SHARING WITH INDIGENOUS PEOPLES

Most of the comprehensive claims treaties include revenue-sharing provisions that grant the Indigenous government a share of the mining tax, or of the mining revenue collected by the federal government or the province. In Quebec, British Columbia, and some parts of Ontario, there are provisions for revenue-sharing agreements with individual Indigenous governments. These revenue-sharing agreements usually provide for a percentage of the mining tax (or royalty) on an operating mine collected by the province or territory to be paid out to the Indigenous government.

There are a number of concerns about this process. First, as previously discussed, governments actually collect nothing from exploration and, even when a company is in production, deductions and allowances mean that governments still receive very little relative to the profits generated by the company. Most corporate structures are designed to minimize tax for companies. As a result, the First Nation gets very little, and can even owe money to the province if the tax owing is a negative figure.

Second, in the comprehensive claim areas, eligible royalties may only apply to mining in Category 1 lands (the lands where the Indigenous government owns the mineral rights).

Third, this provision usually substitutes for the mining company itself paying a royalty to the Indigenous government for the use of their territory and resources, and effectively lets the mining company off the hook.

Aboriginal development corporations are not tax exempt, but Band Councils and individual Band members are. In a partnership, the partner's ownership interest may be regarded as a capital property for tax purposes and give rise to a capital gain or loss when it is sold. Each partner pays its own tax, and holds its own legal liability. Joint venture operations have more flexibility because the joint venture partners can determine their own treatment of costs and benefits through the agreement they write.

TAXING INTERNATIONAL OPERATIONS OF CANADIAN COMPANIES

There are special provisions for tax for Canadian companies operating internationally.

If exploration is carried out through a "branch" controlled by the company, then expenses can be deducted from income in Canada, and tax paid to a foreign government is creditable against Canadian taxes. If a "foreign subsidiary" is set up, then the income is only included when it comes back to Canada as dividends.

If the foreign affiliate carries on business in a country with which Canada has a tax treaty, the *active business income* is exempt from taxation and is considered *exempt surplus*. Active business income is anything other than income from rents, investments, leases, and so on. The determination of business income is complex. It is known to accountants as *foreign accrual property income.*

Canadian Foreign Resource Expense (CFRE) is another benefit. The parent company is allowed to deduct between 10 percent and 30 percent of expenses incurred in acquiring, exploring, and developing a foreign resource property. The CFRE can be held in a tax pool, but a separate pool is required for each country in which the company operates.[25]

Companies operating internationally are usually taxed by the host country on the dividends and capital gains from a mine that they export back to Canadian subsidiaries (and vice versa). This tax is called a *withholding tax.* Canada signs treaties with other countries that limit the rate of withholding tax.[26] However, international holding companies are used to minimize withholding taxes on dividend flows and capital gains taxes when companies and/or properties are bought and sold. Withholding tax varies from 0 to 35 percent.

Capital gains tax will only be levied when the gain is distributed in Canada, but the tax can be deferred if it is invested outside Canada.

Although there are rules against "treaty shopping," most mining companies can avoid these by setting up foreign investment entities in countries that are tax havens like the Cayman Islands, the British Virgin Islands, Barbados, and the Netherlands. It is almost impossible to trace the movement of this money.

The practices that shrink the base on which tax is assessed (transfer pricing and profit shifting, described above) also apply to assessing taxation on Canadian mining companies operating internationally. For more on this, see *The Hidden Cost of Tax Incentives in Mining*, published in 2018.[27]

PROTECTING RESOURCES FOR FUTURE GENERATIONS

There is an obvious need to rethink the system of taxation that has evolved for mining in Canada. The subsidies, incentives, and tax planning rules result in most companies paying little or no tax and do not serve the Canadian public well.

Everyone needs to be concerned about the depletion of natural capital. Even the OECD has called for a reduction in all material inputs, including metals. Mining is a heavy user of water and energy—and our mineral deposits are running out. In addition, as we have seen, the long-term management of mining wastes is a huge problem. Tax policies must de-emphasize mining and exploration and offer incentives for tailings re-mining, mineral conservation, recycling, and reuse.

To address these issues will require a major shift in how society thinks about minerals and mineral extraction.

14

NOTES ON URANIUM

For many years, Canada was the world's largest uranium producer. For national security reasons, the regulation of uranium mining is a federal responsibility. This chapter looks at the history of uranium mining and its impacts on the communities where it is mined, starting with the story of the Port Radium mine and the Sahtu Dene. It then looks at the extent of uranium mining in Canada and how it is regulated both federally and in Saskatchewan, where most of the country's uranium mining takes place.

George Blondin recorded an ancient story prophesying the grim legacy of Port Radium, which the Dene called Sobak'e (literally "The Money Place"):

In the old days, the Sahtu Dene used to travel across the lake towards the Barrenlands every summer, to hunt caribou. Some of these Dene hunters were paddling near the shore on the east side of Sahtu (where Port Radium is today) and they came to a place where rocky cliffs rise high over the water. Like all Dene, they believed it was bad medicine to pass in front of this rock: it was said that loud noises came from within it. These particular hunters pulled their canoes out of the water, but decided not to portage. . . . Instead they camped near the cliff. During the night everybody was awakened by the singing of the medicine man. . . . In the morning, when the medicine man stopped singing the people at last spoke to him. . . "Why did you sing all night. . . ?" "I foresaw many things and I was disturbed," replied the medicine man. . . . The medicine man told them of his strange vision. "I saw people going into a big hole in the ground—strange people, not Dene. Their skin was white . . . [and] they were going into a hole with all kinds of . . . tools and machines. . . . On the surface where they lived, there were strange houses with smoke coming out of them . . . I saw . . . big boats with smoke coming out of them, going back and forth on the river. And I saw a flying bird—a big one. They were loading it with things . . . "I watched them and finally saw what they were making with whatever they were digging out of the hole— it was something long, like a stick. I wanted to know what it was for—I saw what harm it would do when the big bird dropped this thing on people—they all died from this long stick, which burned everyone. . . . But it isn't for now; it's a long time in the future. It will come after we are all dead."[1]

There are stories from Elliot Lake, Ontario, and from Denendeh (Land of the Dene)[2] in the Northwest Territories that indicate that the people were able to smell pitchblende/uranium ore. In Lorraine Rekmans' book about Elliot Lake, *This Is My Homeland*,[3] she writes: "It was said that Anishnabe people could actually smell the veins of uranium underground. They said it stunk, smelt bad and would not live on the ground above the veins. They scouted with geologists to help locate sites for mine development."

THE PORT RADIUM MINE

The radium and uranium mining industry began in Canada in 1930 with the discovery of the Port Radium deposit in the Northwest Territories, when a Dene man named Beyonnie found the black rock east of Great Bear Lake. Beyonnie gave the rock to a white trapper, who rewarded him with bags of flour, baking powder, and lard.[4]

A radium mine called Eldorado was established at Port Radium in 1932. The first concentration plant was erected at the site in 1933, with a radium refinery built at Port Hope, Ontario. Concentrates were shipped by barge and airplane to Fort McMurray, Alberta, then by train to Port Hope.

The mine was secretly expropriated by the Canadian government in 1943–44 to provide material for the Manhattan Project, which manufactured the atomic bombs that were dropped on Hiroshima and Nagasaki.[5] Uranium mining at Port Radium ceased in 1962. The mine reopened as a silver mine in the late 1960s, and operated until 1982. In all, about seven thousand tons of radioactive material was shipped from the mine at Port Radium. Canadian documents reveal that another 1.7 million tons of uranium waste was either left exposed at the mine site or simply dumped into Great Bear Lake.

While the mine operated, Déline Dene men were hired for unskilled labour around the mine site and to carry sacks of ore to barges and over portages for three dollars a day. Recounting twelve-hour days of grinding work, eighty-four-year-old Dene former ore carrier Paul Baton said, "The dust coated you like flour, it covered our clothes, our heads, our hands. We would sleep on the sacks. No one told us anything about it being dangerous. No one told us about cancer."[6]

Although white miners at Eldorado Mine wore protective clothing and were required to shower off the uranium dust after every shift, Dene labourers, referred to as "coolies," did not have the same privilege. Neither the white workers nor the Dene were told of the dangers.

Cindy Kenny-Gilday told a parliamentary committee the following in 1998:

It was not just the men who came into contact with the radioactive dust. . . . This is a tribe that takes the family wherever they go. In the '70s, the men began to die of all kinds of cancers. It was the first time the people of Great Bear Lake ever heard of cancer. . . . We now have a village of widows. . . . Dene in the village no longer have grandfathers to pass down the spiritual practices, nor uncles to slap their wrists when they do something wrong. Now, Dene fear that their fish, caribou and moose at Great Bear Lake are contaminated by radioactive waste and tailings.[7]

The Dene started raising questions in the 1970s when the men started to die, but written documentation of their fears doesn't start until 1982. In 1989, a motion was passed at a Dene leadership meeting to engage the Minister of Health to "investigate the circumstances of the old Port Radium Mine."[8]

As Van Wyck says in *Highway of the Atom*, "An imperceptible tide of suspicion washed over the past. In a stroke, lives lived around the mine, on the river and the portage, on the lake, were transformed into something quite different. . . . Domestic life, the very intimacy of the home... was also and retroactively contaminated."[9]

In 1997, the people took their questions and a couple of government studies they had found to Cindy Kenny-Gilday, a community member who knew her way around the outside world. She was appalled. And she started organizing. The community formed the Délįnę Uranium Committee, and Kenny-Gilday "started running around Canada"[10] trying to get support, information, and analysis. Lawyers Andrew Orkin and Murray Klippenstein volunteered their help as did a number of academics and medical doctors.

In 1997–98, environmental reporter Andrew Nikiforuk went through recently declassified documents on the nuclear industry in the United States and came to the conclusion that federal officials on both sides of the border were aware of the health risks involved in uranium mining, yet did not warn the workers.[11]

The Délįnę Uranium Committee wrote a 106-page report documenting their story, entitled "They Never Told Us These Things."[12] In March 1998, the committee held a community meeting to share what they had found out and to approve an action plan. The news release from the meeting stated: "We the Dene have been subjected to over 60 years of horrible injustice because of apparent national interests. Our people have paid for this with our lives and the health of our community, lands and waters. We have set out a 'Plan for Essential Response and Redress.'"[13]

The media were engaged. Peter Blow produced a documentary called *Village of Widows*.[14] Journalists from the CBC undertook an investigative report. *Maclean's*, the *Toronto Star*, and other outlets took up the story.

By June 1998, the Délįnę Dene had meetings in Ottawa and appeared before a sympathetic Parliamentary Committee on Environ-

ment and Sustainable Development. They asked for immediate crisis assistance, environmental and social assistance, full public disclosure of government actions, cleanup of Great Bear Lake and the surrounding area, acknowledgement that the government was responsible for the situation, and funding and assistance for community healing and cultural regeneration.

The Dene of Great Bear Lake had never been told that they were transporting a secret weapon—uranium—that the United States would use to produce the first atomic bomb. Appealing for world peace, Dene Elders visited Hiroshima in August 1998—the fifty-third anniversary of the atomic attack—and expressed their sorrow. They said the Dene were a peaceful people and would never have been involved in production of a weapon of mass destruction had they been told.

The June 1998 meetings in Ottawa led eventually to the formation of the Canada-Délı̨nę Uranium Table (CDUT), with the federal Department of Indian Affairs and Northern Development (DIAND) and Délı̨nę representation.[15] Over $6 million was set aside by DIAND for the consultation process, in addition to ongoing remediation costs and regulatory costs.[16]

The CDUT held a number of workshops and an expert review in Délı̨nę. The Dene attempted to make their need for healing a significant part of the CDUT mandate:

> The community of Délı̨nę is severely affected by the issues addressed during the workshop. Not only is the presence of the Port Radium mine in their traditional territory a threat to them, but their past experiences as mine workers, ore carriers or families living near or at the mine site had important repercussions on the entire community. . . . If the land, the water, the fish, the caribou are healthy, us Dene people will be healthy.[17]

Even though an official promise to "heal the land" was made, the community remained sceptical. More than twenty years after the mine closure, little had been done to address their concerns.

The CDUT chose Intertec Management Limited as the fact-finder to look at the archival record. When the fact-finder's request for access to the record was formally denied by Library and Archives Canada, the company history was limited to two corporate biographies written by Robert Bothwell under contract to the Eldorado Mine and then to Atomic Energy of Canada Limited.[18]

As Van Wyck writes, "To read the final report of the CDUT is to remark how little the authors were able to discover about the mine and its operation. Even after engaging a fact-finding consultant, so little was known to them. And yet the report is cloaked in a language of adequacy. . . . The poverty of the facts become the facts nonetheless."[19]

The lead fact-finder, Walter Keyes of Intertec Management, was "vocally pro-nuclear and anti-regulatory, a former deputy minister in the pro-uranium Saskatchewan government (with Indian and Native Affairs and Northern Affairs) and an active member of the lobby group the Canadian Nuclear Association, and the editor of a pro-nuclear press."[20]

There was an enormous disconnect between the oral history of the community and the Intertec findings. The oral history volume released in 2005 was entitled "If Only We Had Known: The History of Port Radium as told by the Sahtuot'ine." It carried the memories and stories of the ore carriers and their families.

In the end, the fact-finder and the federal health study (described below) concluded that there was no evidence that the Dene were treated differently than other workers with respect to health and safety standards; there were no employment records for the Dene and therefore no evidence that they actually worked as ore carriers.

Federal health and ecological risk assessments were also undertaken at the same time. The health study concluded that "it is not possible to know for certain if the illness or death of any individual ore carrier was directly caused by radiation exposure, due to the small number of predicted excess cancers and the presence of other risk factors. The risk of radiation-related cancer to family members is small compared to the increased risk to ore carriers, and for both groups the risk of radiation-related cancers is not much greater than 'normal' cancer risk."[21]

By the end of February 2003, sixty years after the Dene had been unknowingly exposed to the radioactivity, the community of Délįnę signed a three-year, $6.7 million agreement for the Remediation Action Plan, which included the cleanup, monitoring requirements, and future community health needs.[22]

Two years later, the federal government gave the Délįnę community members the findings of the five-year effort to examine the health and environmental impacts of the mine. The studies showed that the mine had an effect on water quality at the site and in the immediate vicinity of Great Bear Lake. Elevated metal levels were found in soil at the site. But the report said studies showed the water and fish in Great Bear Lake were "safe for people to consume."[23]

In January 2007, a further $6.8 million contract for remediation work at the former Port Radium mine was awarded by the federal Department of Public Works and Government Services to Aboriginal Engineering of Yellowknife.[24]

No apology was ever made.

CANADIAN URANIUM MINING TODAY

The World Nuclear Association reports that Canada was the world's largest uranium producer for many years, accounting for about 22 percent of world output, but in 2009 was overtaken by Kazakhstan.[25] To 2014, more uranium had been mined in Canada than any other country, about one-fifth of the world total. Over 85 percent of production is exported.[26]

Canadian production comes mainly from the McArthur River and Cigar Lake mines in northern Saskatchewan, the largest and highest-grade uranium mines in the world. The quality of these high-grade deposits is one hundred times the world average.[27] Most uranium is used for fuel in nuclear power plants (where the highly radioactive waste products have to be stored in perpetuity) and for military purposes. It also has a limited use in medical diagnosis and treatment.

In the early 1950s, uranium deposits were discovered around Bancroft and Elliot Lake in Ontario and at Beaverlodge, Saskatchewan. By 1959, twenty-three mines with nineteen treatment plants were in operation. Most were in Elliot Lake and were operated by Rio Algom and Denison Mines. Uranium production in the Bancroft area and at Beaverlodge ceased in 1982 and the last of the Elliot Lake mines closed in 1996.

In the 1970s, discovery of the world's richest uranium deposits in the Athabasca Basin in northern Saskatchewan created huge excitement. Mines at Rabbit Lake, Cluff Lake, and Key Lake started up in 1975, 1980, and 1983, respectively. Cluff Lake, Key Lake, and the original open pit at Rabbit Lake have now been mined out. (Underground mining continued at Rabbit Lake to 2016 and is now mined out.)

In the late 1970s the Saskatchewan Mining Development Corporation (SMDC), a provincial Crown corporation, had a 20 percent interest in the Cluff Lake development and a 50 percent interest in Key Lake. In 1988, SMDC merged with the federal Crown corporation Eldorado Nuclear Limited to form Cameco Corporation, a joint federal-provincial Crown corporation. In the same year, Cameco announced the discovery of the massive McArthur River deposit. It was after this discovery that Cameco began to be privatized. It sold its first public shares in 1991 and was fully privatized by 2002. The company has gone on to become a transnational mining giant.

In 2016, the Canada Revenue Agency (CRA) took Cameco to court, alleging that it owed over $2.2 billion in unpaid taxes, due to illegal transfer pricing.[28] The CRA says that Cameco set up a subsidiary in Switzerland specifically to evade taxes in Canada. A similar suit in the United States was settled out of court. At the time of writing the Canadian suit continues.

The main uranium producers in Canada are Cameco and Areva Resources (a French multinational). Their mines currently are McArthur River and Cigar Lake, which mill their ores at the Key Lake mill and McClean Lake mill.

The McArthur River uranium mine is the world's largest in terms of annual production and has enormous reserves of high-grade ore (16.5 percent U_3O_8 [triuranium oxtoxide]) located six hundred metres underground. Remote-control methods are used to mine the ore, which is then trucked eighty kilometres south to be milled at Key Lake, site of the closed mine that once produced 15 percent of the world's uranium. At the Key Lake mill, the ore is blended with "special waste rock" and processed to produce U_3O_8. Tailings are deposited in the mined-out pit. In November 2017, Cameco announced the temporary suspension of production from the McArthur River mining and Key Lake milling operations due to low uranium prices and high operating costs.

Mining began at Cigar Lake in 2014, after underground floods in 2006 and 2008 set the start date back and increased the overall capital cost of the project from $660 million to about $2.6 billion. The ore reserves at Cigar Lake are extremely large and very high grade. The ore body of the 480-metre-deep underground mine is set in the soft Athabasca sandstone. Hence, ground freezing and remote-controlled high-pressure water jets are used to excavate the ore. Ore slurry from remote mining is trucked to Areva's expanded McClean Lake mill, seventy kilometres northeast.

At McClean Lake there is a high-quality new mill and infrastructure. The operation uses the mined-out pit for tailings disposal and waste rock dumping; this is known as the JEB Tailings Management Facility. The facility has a licence from the Canadian Nuclear Safety Commission to 2027.

Recent Mine Proposals

- Saskatchewan: There are a number of uranium mines proposed for Saskatchewan, but their opening has been put off because of a dramatic fall in uranium prices.
- Nunavut: The Kiggavik uranium project was a joint venture headed by Areva. The company had been conducting a feasibility study on a deposit in the Thelon River Basin, eighty kilometres west of Baker Lake. The project involves the development of three open-pit mines at Kiggavik and both an open-pit and an underground mine at Sissons. In May 2015, the Nunavut Impact Review Board declined to approve the project, and the project was then turned down by the four government ministers responsible. Areva is keeping the project on care and maintenance.[29]
- Northwest Territories: The Boomerang project in the iconic upper Thelon Basin was proposed by Cameco. On September 11, 2008, the project was turned down after an environmental assessment by the Mackenzie Valley Environmental Impact Review Board, which heard strong objections to the project from the Lutsel Kue Dene. The decision stated: "In combination with the combined impacts of all other past, present and reasonably foreseeable industrial developments in the area [the operations of the mine] are likely to have significant adverse cultural impacts on the Aboriginal peoples who value the Upper Thelon River Basin. It is the opinion of the Review Board, informed by the evidence on the public record, that the likely adverse cultural impacts are so significant that the development cannot be justified."[30]
- Labrador: The Michelin project, which includes six uranium deposits, was proposed by Aurora Energy Resources. Five of the deposits are within Labrador Inuit lands. A Nunatsiavut government three-year moratorium on uranium exploration was in place until March 2011, but was lifted by unanimous agreement of the Nunatsiavut Assembly. However, in 2015 the Michelin project was suspended due to low uranium prices and sold to Paladin Energy of Australia.[31]

Current Moratoriums on Uranium Mining

Exploration for uranium is considered to be a provincial responsibility, and there are moratoriums or bans on uranium mining in three provinces in Canada.

- Nova Scotia: There has been a ban on uranium mining in the province since 1981.
- Quebec: Strateco began exploring the Matoush project in Quebec in 2006, and in 2012 applied for a licence from the Canadian Nuclear Safety Commission for advanced underground exploration.[32] Despite strong objections from the Cree (whose land it was on) and environmental groups, the CNSC granted the licence in October 2012. There was outrage, and in April 2013, the Quebec government placed a moratorium on uranium mining in the province, and refused to authorize the Matoush underground exploration phase.[33] In December 2014, Strateco launched a $183 million claim against the provincial government for the loss of its investments. In February 2016, it added $10 million in punitive damages to the claim. In June 2017, the claim was rejected by the court. Strateco filed for bankruptcy protection in the Superior Court of Quebec.
- In British Columbia, the Blizzard prospect south of Kelowna, which was first explored in the 1980s, was revived by Boss Power. The company challenged a provincial government moratorium on exploration and mining imposed in April 2008, and, after a massive public outcry, the British Columbia government settled the issue by paying the company $30.36 million in 2014. The moratorium remains.

HOW THE URANIUM INDUSTRY IS REGULATED IN CANADA[34]

The governing federal legislation for the uranium industry is the *Nuclear Safety and Control Act* (NSCA) and the lead department for oversight of the Act and regulations is Natural Resources Canada. Health Canada also has a Radiation Protection Bureau, which is "responsible for promoting and protecting Canadians' health with respect to the risks posed by exposure to natural and man-made sources of ionizing radiation in living, working and recreational environments."[35]

The Canadian Nuclear Safety Commission (CNSC) is the federal regulator. The CNSC describes itself as an "independent, quasi-judicial administrative tribunal and court of record." The commission's seven members are appointed by Cabinet for terms not exceeding five years and may be reappointed. The president of the CNSC is a full-time commission member, while other members generally serve on a part-time basis. In 2008, CNSC president Linda Keen was fired by the federal government after she refused to re-license the Chalk River nuclear refinery due to safety concerns. The firing certainly called the independence of the CNSC into question.[36]

The Commission's key roles are to

- establish regulatory policy on matters relating to health, safety, security, and the environment
- make legally binding regulations
- make independent decisions on the licensing of nuclear-related activities in Canada

The CNSC administers the NSCA and its associated regulations. Among these regulations are the CNSC Rules of Procedure, which outline the public hearing process, and the CNSC Bylaws, which outline the commission's meeting process. There are four major branches of CNSC staff: regulatory operations, technical support, regulatory affairs, and corporate services.

CNSC's Research and Support Program provides staff with access to independent advice, expertise, experience, information, and other resources, via contracts or contribution agreements made with private sector companies, as well as other agencies and organizations in Canada and internationally. The CNSC Research and Support Program claims to be independent of research and development programs conducted by industry.

Key regulations under the NSCA, enforced by the CNSC, are the Uranium Mines and Mills Regulations.[37] These regulations are implemented by a special division of the CNSC located in Saskatoon, close to Canada's major uranium mining operations.

The regulations apply to all uranium mines and mills, including mill tailings. Each stage—including mandated annual or five-year reviews—requires licensing by the CNSC. The regulations explicitly include the information needed to apply for different types of licences for uranium mines and mills, which match the life cycle of a facility, including site preparation and construction, operation, decommissioning, and abandonment. These regulations also include requirements for a code of practice, the obligations of licensees, and records to be kept and made available. They contain information on decommissioning licensing requirements.

The 1996 National Framework for the Management and Regulation of Radioactive Waste and Decommissioning in Canada sets out federal responsibilities and provides a set of principles "to ensure that the management of radioactive waste is carried out in a safe, environmentally sound, comprehensive, cost-effective and integrated manner."[38]

In keeping with the 1996 framework, Canadian uranium mining companies are responsible for the funding, organization, management, and operation of facilities required for their wastes—unless, of course, they are abandoned. Different arrangements are established for different categories of radioactive waste: nuclear fuel waste, low- and intermediate-level radioactive waste, and uranium mine and mill tailings.

The activities covered by the financial assurance under the NSCA include not only dismantling, decontamination, and closure, but also any post-decommissioning monitoring or institutional control measures that may be required, as well as subsequent long-term management of all wastes.

Exploration for Uranium

Exploration for uranium does not fall under the NSCA, and, as noted, is considered to be a provincial responsibility. However, sinking an exploratory underground shaft does require a CNSC licence. There is considerable controversy over whether the province or CNSC is responsible, which often comes to a head when a province attempts to enforce a moratorium on uranium exploration. As a result, a company may claim that it is actually looking for "rare earth metals," rather than uranium, as uranium removed during exploration for other metals, as a "naturally occurring nuclear substance," is exempt from the NSCA.

SASKATCHEWAN ASSUMES RESPONSIBILITY FOR PERPETUAL CARE OF ALL MINE SITES

In 2006, Eric Cline, then minister of Industry and Resources for the Government of Saskatchewan, presented a new provincial initiative at the World Nuclear Association meeting in London.[39]

The Saskatchewan Institutional Control Plan (ICP) was the product of three years of interdepartmental discussions about how to satisfy industry demands to be rid of the responsibility for the long-term management of their decommissioned uranium mines, while quelling public concerns about the safety of these sites.[40]

According to Cline, the ICP was developed because "if companies were to be responsible for perpetual care and maintenance at former uranium mines, this would be a significant barrier to investment in new uranium developments."[41]

In order for Saskatchewan to undertake the task of perpetually managing some of the most dangerous uranium wastes in the world, it had to develop an arrangement with the CNSC and the federal government that would meet the requirements of the International Atomic Energy Agency's Joint Convention on the Safety of Spent Fuel Management and on the Safety of Radioactive Waste Management (2001).[42]

The ICP was established in 2007 to manage and monitor mine sites (mostly uranium) once decommissioning has been completed. The ICP applies to decommissioned mine and mill sites on provincial Crown land. The owner of the site can transfer custodial responsibility to the province "upon which the site will be monitored and maintained in perpetuity."

There are two primary components to the ICP: the Institutional Control Registry and two Institutional Control Funds—the Monitoring and Maintenance Fund and the Unforeseen Events Fund, which are held separately from the province's revenues. Both funds are handled by the Saskatchewan Ministry of Finance.

The Institutional Control Registry maintains a formal record of closed sites, manages funding, and performs any monitoring and maintenance work. Registry records include the location and former operator; site description; historic records; site maintenance, monitoring, and inspection documentation; and future allowable land use at the site. It also references CNSC documentation and decisions.

The Monitoring and Maintenance Fund pays for long-term monitoring and maintenance. The fund has dedicated site-specific funding established by the previous mine owner. Both it and the Unforeseen Events Fund are established based on net present value calculations "in perpetuity."[43]

The Unforeseen Events Fund pays for events such as damage from tornadoes, fire, floods, and earthquakes. The money in this fund is not tracked by individual site contributions and can be drawn on for contingencies at any of the registered sites. It is established through mine operator contributions of 10 to 20 percent of their total contribution to the Monitoring and Maintenance Fund. The Unforeseen Events Fund monies are invested in bonds to target a specific return.

This is very early days for the ICP, and it is impossible to assess its effectiveness at this stage. The first site accepted into the program was the former Contact Lake gold mine in May 2009. In October 2009, five former uranium mines (without tailings and previously exempted from CNSC licensing requirements) at the Beaverlodge operation were accepted.[44] Most Saskatchewan sites are likely to remain under CNSC licensing for the foreseeable future. A five-year review is mandated by the legislation.

Abandoned uranium mine and mill sites including Gunnar mine (operated from 1955 to 1963) and Lorado mill, as well as thirty-five satellite mine sites near Lake Athabasca are awaiting some kind of reclamation under Project CLEANS (Cleanup of Abandoned Northern Sites) —a multi-year, multi-million dollar project funded by the federal and Saskatchewan governments.[45]

There has been pressure from governments and the industry to bury nuclear waste from other parts of the country in the existing pits and waste dumps in northern Saskatchewan. This, and any expansion of nuclear power, has been strongly opposed by groups such as the Committee for Future Generations, which was formed in 2011 by people in northern Saskatchewan concerned about the targeting of local Indigenous communities for a repository to store millions of highly radioactive fuel rods.[46]

HOW TO PUT MINING IN ITS PLACE

This section describes how communities and their allies work to resist and transform the mining industry to put mining in its place. It recognizes that the strategies we use differ with the stages of mining (exploration, operations, closure). They also differ according to what people want to achieve for themselves, their communities, and the broader public, and who is undertaking the work: a community group, an Indigenous government, or a provincial or national organization.

I am a community organizer, and—as described in the introduction—have spent most of my adult life dealing with impacts from the mining industry. As a result, much of the information and analysis in this part will be presented as advice, with many first-hand stories and anecdotes sprinkled in.

This section begins by describing lessons learned by communities that are trying to stop a mine at the exploration stage, before discussing the successes and difficulties in organizing in mining-dependent communities. It then focuses on lessons learned from mine sites requiring perpetual care. It moves on to look at some of the ways communities and civil society organizations help limit the predatory practices of Canadian companies in other countries. It describes the research needed and campaign strategies to influence mining investors, and the often frustrating strategies for trying to get our governments to hold mining companies accountable. The final chapter pulls together the learnings from the book and offers some conclusions about effective demands and strategies to make change.

15

STOPPING A MINE BEFORE IT STARTS

Very few people choose to spend the precious hours of their lives trying to stop a mine; they are thrust into it because they care about their community and their environment.

People usually find out that there is the possibility of a mine in their area when they come across prospectors or exploration activity. In most provinces, Indigenous governments and municipalities should receive formal notification of exploration. In some provinces, like Ontario and Quebec, the law requires that individual homeowners must be notified that exploration is going to occur.

However, Marilyn Crawford found out her cottage lands near Green Lake in Ontario were staked when she saw the claim posts on a walk in the bush. Barriere Lake Algonquin First Nation in Quebec heard about Copper One mining exploration on their lands from a tourist camp owner. Although provincial and territorial websites provide information about which lands are being claimed and by whom, most people don't know it.

For Indigenous governments, there may actually be a staking rush going on, and more than one exploration company wanting to "consult." There is often no one in the Indigenous government office who really knows about mining. At Wolf Lake First Nation, it was the forestry expert who had to deal with mining demands for permits. Learning how mining works can be a "nose-bleed" learning curve.

It is important to remember that most claims do not become mines. There is usually a "fatal flaw," which can include any of the following:

- the ore body itself turns out not have enough of the desired metals, or the price of the metals is too low or the cost of extracting them too high to justify the mine.
- the mining company cannot get access to the deposit either for physical reasons (lack of water, power, transportation routes, etc.), or because those who control the land will not let them have it or they cannot get a social licence or government permits (for example, the proposed mine is on or near a sacred site or on a family trapline).
- the company cannot get the labour needed to work the mine. The industry sees this as an increasing problem; it is one of the reasons it so badly wants Indigenous peoples to work in mining.
- the company cannot raise the money it needs to build and operate a mine. Chapter 19 explains the questions that investors will ask.
- the site itself is prone to earthquakes, severe flooding, or some other natural impediment.
- in international cases, the metal claimed is considered "strategic" by a foreign government.

Communities that don't want the mine to proceed need to organize to make sure that at least one of these issues becomes a showstopper.

From the very outset, communities and governments should take the position that a mine in their location will externalize so many costs and cause so much damage to fragile ecosystems that it should not be built. They must put the onus on the mining company to prove that it is economically viable, will have minimal environmental impact, and will contribute positively to the local area both now and in the future. The mining company is an intruder in the community's space, and the community owes it nothing. It is important to remember that the free-entry concept means that if the company's exploration discovers a metal of interest, it basically has the right to continue until the mine is built. The staking of the claim can be the first step in an escalating process and the earlier the community starts organizing, the better.

This chapter provides some lessons learned about how to keep a mine from happening. We begin with the story of a fight to end free entry in Ontario.

THE FIGHT TO END FREE ENTRY IN ONTARIO[1]

In July 2008, the Ontario government agreed to reform the province's *Mining Act*. This announcement followed years of intense resistance by First Nations to the occupation of their traditional territories by mining exploration companies, and by surface rights holders to the staking of mineral rights on their properties. In the four years prior to the government decision, ending the free-entry system had become a campaign, with many environmental, social justice, and faith-based organizations joining in. When seven Indigenous leaders were jailed for protecting their traditional territories in February 2008, the Ontario public was outraged.

In the end, the reforms did not end free entry nor did they recognize the right of Indigenous people to free prior informed consent (FPIC) before claims are staked, although they did increase consultation requirements at the exploration stage. Following the reforms, the lands of Kitchenuhmaykoosib Inninuwug First Nation and the Ardoch Algonquins were withdrawn from staking by the province, and the mining companies involved went away.

However, the battle continues. Here is what happened.

Almost twenty years ago, a number of residents and cottagers in the Rideau Lakes area of eastern Ontario noticed that trees had been cut down, trenches had been dug, and stakes were up all over their properties. That's when they found out that they did not own the subsurface rights to their properties. They also found out that the prospectors who had laid claim to the minerals underneath had a right to use the surface lands to access their mining claims.

The neighbours formed Bedford Mining Alert (BMA) to deal with these claims. Its first meeting took place at the home of Mary and Don Loucks in 2000, and "from that point on, the outrage they each felt turned into iron resolve. Everyone played their own role, and they did not always agree on tactics or even goals, but each . . . was part of the change that took place."[2]

Marilyn Crawford was one of the BMA members. She and her husband, Buddy, had moved to their cottage on Green Lake when they retired from teaching in Toronto, hoping for some peace and quiet. One day, Marilyn found claim stakes on the property. It changed her life. She became an expert on the *Ontario Mining Act*; in fact, "she became so well versed in the act that when ministry officials came to meetings in Bedford and elsewhere in Eastern Ontario, they found themselves being instructed on some of the details of the act as they defended ministry practices."[3]

At the same time, in northern Ontario, the staking frenzy that marked the early 2000s forced a number of First Nations to place development moratoriums on their lands, although these were respected by neither government nor industry. By 2005, many of them were very concerned about the long-term impacts of this invasion on their land and people. The following is a timeline of the events that joined communities in these two locations, northern Ontario and the Rideau Lakes area of eastern Ontario, in a battle against mining on their lands:

October 27, 2005: Four First Nations in northern Ontario reaffirmed a moratorium on mining exploration and forestry in the Far North. In a news release entitled "No Means No," chiefs and representatives from Kitchenuhmaykoosib Inninuwug (KI), Muskrat Dam, Wapekeka, and Wawakapewin First Nations declared a development moratorium on their traditional territories. Other First Nations later joined.

November 2005: In response to a proposed Ontario Mineral Development Strategy, Nishnawbe Aski Nation (NAN) (representing forty-nine communities in the Far North) wrote,

> We are facing a multitude of First Nation grievances triggered by mining exploration that could at any time lead to an explosive conflict. A number of NAN First Nations have declared moratoriums on mining exploration and development. The immovable object of mining company shareholders and mining act assessment requirements will one day meet the irresistible force of Treaty rights with predictable consequences. At issue is the so-called free entry system. The ownership of the land itself is in dispute.[4]

February 2006: Platinex, a junior mining company that had purchased mining leases and staked claims in the Big Trout Lake area, the traditional territory of the KI First Nation, was prevented from accessing its claims by a blockade of the winter road. The KI First Nation asserted that their inherent rights were violated by the Ontario government when it granted the mining company a permit under the *Mining Act.*

Platinex withdrew from the area and filed a $10 billion lawsuit and injunction application against the First Nation. Countering this, KI brought its own injunction application against the mining company and counterclaimed for $10 million in damages. In addition, KI filed a third-party claim against the Province of Ontario for, among other things, a declaration from the Superior Court of Ontario that the *Mining Act* was unconstitutional, as it did not meet the requirements of Section 35 of the Constitution, which affirms Indigenous treaties and rights. KI First Nation organized a rally and press conference in Toronto, and walkers made the trek from the community to the rally.

"We want our children and grandchildren to continue to use the lands and resources to pursue their usual vocations of hunting, trapping, and fishing," said Kitchenuhmaykoosib Inninuwug elder Mark T. Anderson who led a group of KI protesters on a 2,100 km walk from northern Ontario to Toronto in 2006. "We want to protect the environment at the potential drilling/mining site plus the surrounding area which includes our Kitchenuhmaykoosib Lake."[5]

The general public was outraged by Platinex's actions and the lack of action by the Ontario government. A number of civil society organizations wrote letters, fundraised, and held public meetings in support of KI. The list of organizations involved soon exceeded twenty, and included Amnesty International, the Christian Peacemakers, CPAWS Wildlands League, MiningWatch Canada, and Ontario Nature.

July 2006: Ontario's Superior Court issued a decision in favour of KI First Nation, ordering Platinex to halt drilling operations in KI traditional territory, and ordered the parties to go back to the table and engage in a proper consultation process.

After the province and Platinex engaged in "reasonable" consultation with KI, the court permitted Platinex to resume some drilling while requiring ongoing consultation to occur. But because access was by winter road, the company could not resume until winter. The community said they would not allow the company back on their land, no matter what the court said. The consultation talks dragged on into December 2006 with no resolution in sight.

November 2006: In eastern Ontario, BMA and some of their neighbours discovered that there was renewed staking in the area, this time for uranium. Gloria Morrison told Chief Paula Sherman of the Ardoch Algonquin First Nation about it.[6] The alarm spread. The Ardoch Algonquin discussed strategy with their neighbours, the Shabot Obaadjiwon, and agreed on a four-point strategy: education, direct action, legal action, and political lobbying.

January 2007: The Province of Ontario was added to the Platinex legal proceedings as a party to their injunction motion. Back in KI First Nation, under the pressure of mounting legal costs and Ontario's position that consultation must lead to drilling, KI leadership began to consider how to get out of the litigation. Leaving the court would likely mean that KI would be found in criminal contempt.

April 2007: Justice Smith of the Ontario Superior Court gave the parties two weeks to come to an agreement on a consultation protocol and a memorandum of understanding with Platinex.

May 2007: Justice Smith unilaterally imposed the consultation protocol and memorandum of understanding agreements on KI and ordered that Platinex could access its "property" beginning on June 1, 2007. The KI leadership returned to their community and began a door-to-door canvass to seek direction from the membership, taking the position that "from this point forward, the KI community has to look to each other rather than the law to find the solutions to their struggle with Ontario and Platinex."[7]

July 13, 2007: In eastern Ontario, the Ardoch Algonquin and Shabot Obaadjiwan and their supporters took over the closed Robertsville

Mill site near Kingston, which Frontenac Ventures Corporation (FVC) was using to stage its uranium mineral exploration in eastern Ontario. FVC had begun aggressively exploring for uranium on land in Frontenac County in eastern Ontario in 2006. By July 2007, FVC had staked approximately four hundred mineral claims covering more than eight thousand hectares of land. The company now wanted to move to drilling for core samples to determine how much uranium was under the land they had staked. They were on Ardoch Algonquin First Nation land. A statement from the community at the time of the occupation stated,

> Our people have occupied, used and protected this land since time immemorial and we have never signed any treaty or land claim agreement with Canada. We have never ceded Aboriginal title to any of our lands and resources in our traditional territory, including the lands within Frontenac County. AAFN [Ardoch Algonquin First Nation] members, together with our neighbours, the Shabot Obaadjiwan Algonquin First Nation, have now occupied the site of the proposed uranium mine and we have informed Frontenac Ventures that no further mineral staking or exploration activity will be allowed within our territory.[8]

July 2007: The Citizens Committee Against Mining Uranium (CCAMU) was formed in the Rideau Lakes area to stop FVC from staking there. CCAMU set out to get support from every conceivable organization and public body. In a few months, the committee had received written support from five politicians, ten municipal councils, seven landowner associations, and eight environmental groups—all requested a moratorium on uranium mining. A petition that included 107 signatures from twelve counties demanded changes to the *Mining Act*. One of CCAMU's members went on a three-month fast. A number of artists and musicians who had property in the area begin to mobilize to oppose the mine. The protest of the Ardoch Algonquin and Shabot Obaadjiwan First Nations at the Robertsville Mill continued in the ditch across from the mine site (with land defenders often huddled under blue tarps in pouring rain).

August 29, 2007: KI First Nation advised the Ontario government that they were pulling out of the consultation talks. Platinex was undeterred.

September 24, 2007: Platinex CEO James Trusler and his archaeological consultants ignored KI's letters and notices saying that they were not welcome and instead flew into the community. They were met at the gravel airstrip by more than one hundred KI community members who told them to go home or face trespassing charges if they set foot on the reserve. They were forced to leave.

October 25, 2007: KI First Nation replaced its legal counsel, Olthius, Kleer, and Townshend. KI, according to their spokesperson John Cutfeet, had spent almost $700,000 on their battle with Platinex and Ontario; they were out of money and in serious debt to their lawyers. At this point, "from KI's perspective, the community was a victim of a legal strategy adopted by the Company in collaboration with the government of Ontario that had effectively bankrupted an already impoverished community."[9] For Platinex, this was the opportunity to proceed with a contempt-of-court hearing against KI. The First Nation said that they would not cease their blockade nor engage in any further negotiations with Platinex.

December 12, 2007: The Environmental Commissioner of Ontario released his annual report, addressing complaints filed by First Nations organizations, and found the following:

> The Ontario government should amend the Mining Act to include specific criteria that reflect MNDM's [Ministry of Northern Development and Mines'] constitutional duty to consult with First Nations when granting mining claims and leases that may impact their rights. This case also provides strong direction for the government to re-evaluate the existing regulatory structure that treats public land as freely open to mineral exploration.[10]

February 15, 2008: Co-chiefs Robert Lovelace and Paula Sherman of the Ardoch Algonquin First Nation were convicted of contempt of court for failing to obey two injunctions against the occupation of lands that FVC wanted to explore for uranium. Lovelace was issued a six-month jail sentence and a $25,000 fine; Sherman was fined $15,000. The Ardoch community was also fined $10,000. The contempt charges against the settlers were dismissed. The day before the sentencing hearing, the Shabot Obaadjiwon had agreed to cease protesting and enter into negotiations with the province.[11]

March 17, 2008: Seven KI members including Chief Donny Morris and some Band councillors were charged with contempt. Six pled guilty and received six-month jail sentences. The seventh, John Cutfeet, was outside the community when the leaders decided to plead guilty and he fought the charge, hiring his own lawyer. The charge was later dismissed. The community said it had to obey its own laws and continued to refuse to allow the company on their land, in contravention of the court's order. The community had run out of money and could no longer pay their lawyers. The six jailed KI leaders—Chief Morris, deputy chief Jack McKay, spokesperson Sam McKay, councillors Cecilia Begg, Daryl Sainnawap, and Bruce Sakakeep—became known as the "KI Six."[12]

February to May 2008: There was an outpouring of support for KI and Ardoch Algonquin First Nations and calls from Indigenous gov-

Five members of the KI Six, jailed in 2008 for trying to stop mining on their lands. Photo courtesy of KI Lands.

ernments and organizations, environmental groups, unions, churches, and community activists to reform the outdated *Mining Act* in order to allow communities to say no to mining. KI Elder Mark Anderson walked from KI to Toronto in support of the KI Six. Almost all provincial government consultation processes with Indigenous governments and organizations were disrupted. Twenty municipalities in Ontario passed resolutions demanding changes to the *Mining Act*. A number of celebrities joined in the outcry, including Bruce Cockburn, Margaret Atwood, and Michael Ondaatje.

May 22, 2008: Six days before the appeal of the contempt charges was to be heard, Platinex launched a lawsuit against the government of Ontario for $70 million in damages resulting from Ontario's failure to adequately consult with KI.

May 26, 2008: Hundreds of people converged at a gathering of Mother Earth protectors for "four days of ceremony, speakers, workshops, music, and a three night sovereignty sleep-over," in an unprecedented tent-in on the front lawn of the legislature at Queen's Park.

May 28, 2008: The Ontario Court of Appeal ordered the release of Robert Lovelace and the KI Six for "time served" and the public was delighted.

July 7, 2008: The Court of Appeal handed down its reasons for the decision to release Lovelace and the KI Six. The judges said that the outdated *Mining Act* "lies at the heart of this case."

The Court called the Act "a remarkably sweeping law" that allowed prospectors to stake claims on any Crown land, and allowed no role for communities in deciding whether mineral exploration could occur in their territories, even when they had unsettled land claims to those areas.

Although costs for the appeal on sentencing were awarded to the First Nations, for the Ardoch the injunction still stood. For defending their lands against Frontenac Ventures, the Ardoch Algonquin First Nation was left facing a default judgment on the FVC lawsuit of $77 million, and costs for the injunction hearing of over $100,000. FVC had also requested leave to appeal the Appeal Court sentencing decision to the Supreme Court. (These cases were later dropped.)

July 14, 2008: Faced with the Court of Appeal's decision and an outcry across the province, the Ontario Premier promised to modernize and reform the *Mining Act*. But he also announced the *Far North Act*—a planning process seeking to shift First Nations demands for control over resource use on their lands into a process of consultation, leading to "yes to mining." He also agreed to withdraw the contested lands in eastern Ontario from staking, and to buy out the Platinex claims and leases and withdraw them from staking. Although this protected the lands in both eastern and northern Ontario for now, neither withdrawal was permanent.

July 2011: KI First Nation held a community referendum and passed into law a Watershed Declaration that in effect "nationalized" all of the resources on their homelands and protected all of the waters flowing in and out of Big Trout Lake watershed.

ADVICE FOR THOSE TAKING ACTION TO STOP A MINE

From the beginning of your battle against a mining company, you will be dealing with the mythology that the mining industry has developed for itself and endlessly promoted. These myths include the following:

- Exploration has a tiny footprint.
- This is possibly the biggest deposit (in the area, the province, the world)!
- The mine will create hundreds of jobs and enrich governments.
- The mine can make community members rich and solve all of their social and economic problems.
- Modern engineering will ensure that the mine doesn't damage the water, air, or the wildlife.

Some people in your own community or in the government will believe them and become company advocates. They will say, "Let them explore and see what they find, and then the environmental assessment (EA) process will reveal whether we let the mine go ahead or not." It is important to remember that the environmental impact statement and the highly technical studies used to judge the mine are written by consultants for whom the mining company is the client. If there has not been vocal, sustained community opposition demanding proof that the mine is a good idea from the beginning, you can be sure that the environmental assessment process will permit the mine, whether it is a good idea or not.

If your government (or you) really want exploration to go ahead, fight for an agreement with the company that pays you to hire your own technical experts to review the company's results and do your own studies from the beginning. Make sure the company cannot use this agreement to tell investors that they have "agreement with the Indigenous/municipal government" for the mine proposal.

Make sure the agreement is airtight and that as many people as possible in your community have seen it negotiated and have a copy of it. The company will demand a confidentiality clause, but it is usually a big mistake for the community to agree to this. It only creates suspicion and divides people.

If the initial exploration looks promising, the company will want to do more exploration and is likely to hire someone as their community/Indigenous liaison officer. This might be a local person, who is then "trained" by the company to sell the project, identify people in opposition, and distribute small grants to local groups to win them over. In the Ring of Fire in Ontario, the community "mining advisors" are paid by the province.

At this point, there will be other exploration companies in the area who want a piece of the action. Even if there is a mining camp, other workers for the exploration site will stay at tourist lodges and hotels and will rent apartments. I remember visiting Timmins, Ontario, in the midst of a mining boom and there was not a room available. It was late September, and I slept in a provincial park, where workers were also staying in their pickups.

You need to organize. Rally your friends. Do your research about the company and the permits they need to go ahead. Tell people about what is going on. Do anything you can to slow the company down, to get in their way; the minerals aren't going anywhere. Work to get formal resolutions from local governments, Band Councils, and other representative bodies. Send letters to politicians.

In 2017, at Grenville-sur-la-Rouge in Quebec, the opposition to a proposed graphite mine managed to get control of the municipal council and overturn support for the mine. The mining company, Canada

Carbon, launched a $96 million lawsuit against the municipal council. The lawsuit contained a John Doe defendant, so that anyone who opposed the mine could be added to the suit. It is clearly a SLAPP, or strategic lawsuit against public participation. As this book goes to press, the suit is still pending.

Reach out to other groups for help, like MiningWatch Canada or the Coalition pour que le Québec ait meilleure mine. Set up tours to visit existing mines (or do virtual tours on the Internet). Bring in people from other communities who have lived through similar experiences to talk to your community. Celebrate and strengthen the cultural and economic alternatives to mining for a living, such as the traditional food economy. Make lots of noise; let governments and the world know that you are saying "no."

At the same time, unless the company goes away, you will have to intervene in government-driven permitting processes (which include exploration permits, EAs, *Fisheries Act* [Schedule 2] and others) to make your case about the damage a mine will cause. Encourage people to speak out. You will need to find legal and other expertise to do this, so apply for participant funding, write grant proposals, and bring in experts (again, ask for help); make sure people understand what they are talking about.

Some Indigenous peoples in Canada have successfully conducted their own EAs in parallel with federal and provincial ones (see the Ajax Mine in chapter 10). This is likely to be a very costly undertaking, and although you may be able to get participant funding from the federal government, it will probably not be enough.

Make sure any hearings and negotiations happen in your own community and are transparent. Where mines have been defeated at the permitting stage, the EA panels have travelled to local communities to hear testimony from Elders, children, and everyone affected.

Make sure that any social or economic impact studies are based on the World Health Organization's social determinants of health, not just a company-serving health risk assessment. The social determinants of health address questions of impact on the community social fabric and how the distribution of power and privilege will be affected. There are some useful tools for carrying out a community-led health impact assessment process on the PATH (People Assessing Their Health) webpage.[13]

At some point, you and your community will probably have to physically block the company from accessing the land. The company may be having trouble raising money for further exploration and may ignore you, hoping that boredom will put an end to the protest. However, you may also face an application for an injunction to authorize the police to physically remove you from the place.

Arthur Manuel writes that for Indigenous communities, "the injunction should be viewed in terms of colonial law versus the recognition and affirmation of aboriginal title and rights. We believe that governments must not use injunctions to bulldoze away our rights or as a cover for inadequate laws and policies toward Indigenous peoples and their legal and political rights."[14]

Some Comments on Strategy and Tactics

Strategy and tactics are not the same thing. Strategy is the long-term plan to reach a goal. Tactics are tools that can be used to get there. In choosing tools, you cannot forget to think holistically; to work with ideas like theatre, music, and relationship building, as well as political tools like demonstrations. Demonstrations can be festivals of art and drama. We can work on community economic development alternatives while we stop the mine. We can begin our protest with a circle of prayers. We can hold a potluck supper and sleepover on the steps of city hall. We can create murals about our dreams.

In choosing tactics, it is extremely important to remember *what* you want to achieve. Generally, you want to win lots of people over to your way of thinking. You want to expose the hypocrisy and lies of the mining industry and their allies in a way that enables people to hear you. In Canada, ensuring that your protests are non-violent is crucial to building the public support you will need.

You will want to encourage the people working within institutions to join you and agree with you. And you want people to believe that "another world is possible." Tactics that they perceive as hostile or crazy will only alienate them. Remember, people are afraid, and frightened people protect themselves and their families first; they don't join social change organizations.

Sometimes, however, direct action—the assertion of our responsibility to protect the earth and one another—is necessary. It is necessary to protect endangered spaces and resist destruction of land, water, and community.

Blockades and Occupations: A Few Points

Blockades are one of the most necessary and effective tools for land and water protectors. John Borrows makes the point that it is non-Indigenous governments that actually blockade lands in Canada, and that Indigenous people are defending their rights to be there.[15] However, under Canadian laws, most blockades and occupations are usually illegal, and charges can range from a summary charge of mischief or trespass to heavier indictable offences. There is also the possibility that the organization to which the defenders belong will be sued for damages including loss of income to the target group (the mining company) and policing costs.

In Canada, many land defence occupations take place in remote areas or in soulless industrial parks. When organizing this type of action, it is important to make sure that participants and supporters know exactly how to get there, and that there is sufficient shelter, toilets, parking, food, and warmth for everyone who comes. The magnitude of arranging for transportation and meeting everyday needs can be overwhelming for some groups. You also need to ensure that a good communications system with the outside is in place.

You should gear the extent of the land/water defence to a realistic assessment of support. People may be arrested and removed almost as soon as they arrive. Most people have to work at regular jobs, or have kids to look after, or have other struggles they are deeply engaged in; civil disobedience will take them away from this. Quite often the very people who need to engage in this kind of action have criminal records or are on probation or parole (often because of the class and race biases of the court system) and will face more severe repercussions than others if arrested.

It is also important to humanize the opposition. The Teme-Augama Anishnabai people opened their second occupation against the Red Squirrel logging road with a Remembrance Day service and invited the provincial police officers at the site to join in. One of the Elders then spoke about the role of the police, who had to do the "dirty work for the people who make the policies." He made an appeal to them to support the blockade. By the end of the blockade, even the construction workers were beginning to sabotage their own equipment.

You need to be clear that decisions about continuing the action or what to do during the action can be made by the people on the front line.

You need to be prepared to work through the court system after the action, because people are bound to be arrested; you will need to have good legal advice lined up.

Those in power learned a long time ago that boredom can be as effective as fear in disorganizing groups. To resist this, the time during the action can be used for educational, cultural, and social group building and to show the public how things could be done if profit were not the sole focus.

In the Global South, and increasingly in Canada, land and water protectors are criminalized and face jail terms, violence, and even death.

HAVING AN ALTERNATIVE VISION

The importance of an alternative vision for the economic, social, and cultural future of the community cannot be overemphasized. Mining triumphs because people are convinced that it is the only way to get cash and jobs for the community.

I have had the privilege of working with many communities that are trying to counter propaganda from mining companies that want to sell their projects to governments and local people. The company claims invariably have the same faulty premises and make the same flawed arguments: lots of jobs and economic growth measured in GDP and contributions to governments.

Communities that are successful in stopping these mines are always able to prove two things: (1) that there is already an economic plan in place for the affected area that provides substantial economic benefits locally, and (2) the mine would irrevocably damage that plan. Effects on the Indigenous landholders and their assertion of authority and rights are often a key part of that argument.

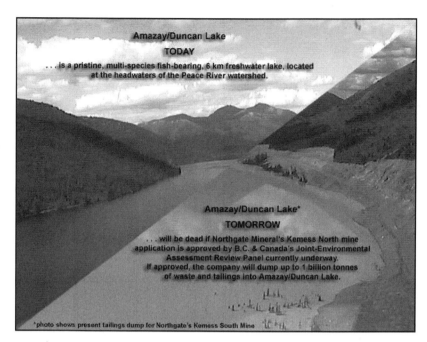

Sekani First Nation poster about protecting Amazay Lake from the Kemess North Mine. Courtesy of Carrier Sekani Tribal Council (cstc.bc.ca).

16

DEALING WITH AN OPERATING MINE

Organizing once a mine is in place is a very different story from trying to stop a mine before it starts. It is about holding the mining company and government accountable and dealing with crises caused by the company. This chapter looks at some ways people organize to do just that.

THE CONTEXT: CULTURES OF CONTAMINATION

The mining industry knows full well that once a mine is operating (and expanding daily), few people will want it to close, for many reasons.

The local economy will now be almost totally dependent on the jobs and contracts that the mine provides, and other economic alternatives will have been damaged for the reasons described in chapter 10.

No local government wants the responsibility of managing the growing and multiplying open pits, tunnels, waste dumps, and tailings storage facilities from the mine or the air, water, and soil pollution created by smelters and refineries. We depend on laws, regulation, and enforcement at higher government levels that are almost always inadequate to protect us, and changing this situation is a long-term process.

Depending on the length of time the mine (or mines, in many cases) have been there, the culture and social fabric of the community will be different that they were pre-mine. The original inhabitants of the area will have been displaced, income and gender inequality are likely to be greater, and many local businesses and activities will have been replaced by franchises. There may be roads and airports that weren't there before. The "hyper-masculinized" culture described by the Firelight Group Report will have become the norm.[1] If the community is an old mining camp, long-time residents will have become accustomed to the environmental damage that the mines and smelters have caused. In effect, the community will now have what Edelstein calls "a culture of contamination."[2]

Organizing to effect change in mining practices in a mining dependent community is not easy. For one thing, it is very difficult to find out what is actually going on, unless a relative works at the mine or smelter or in a related government department. The local media is generally intimidated by the mining company's communications people and threats of lawsuits. Local organizations are dependent on company grants to function. The university and college (if the community has these) receive donations from the company and its executives. The union, which is likely focused on bread and butter issues like contracting out, health and safety, and pensions, will not want to be involved.

Although they are often out of sight of the public, mines constantly expand: the underground tunnels snake further and are often replaced with huge open pits. The waste rock dumps get bigger and the tailings impoundments—usually hidden behind huge dikes—get larger and deeper and release more water from them. Roads are full of trucks and/ or rail cars loaded with chemicals, supplies, and materials going to the mine and smelter, and carrying concentrates, slurries and other products out. Those who live in mining towns have no idea what is on the roads and rails, or what risks this traffic poses.

It is a daily struggle for the Indigenous peoples and land-based settlers downstream or downwind from the projects to protect their livelihoods from the effects of mining. However, given the other pressures on their lives and governments, finding the time and resources to deal with the bureaucratic permitting processes is difficult.

INDEPENDENT ENVIRONMENTAL MONITORING AND TECHNICAL SUPPORT[3]

An independent environmental monitoring agency or oversight body with enough resources to hire its own technical experts and do its own sampling is crucial for a community dealing with an operating mine. At the diamond mines in the Northwest Territories, independent monitoring agencies, paid for by the mining companies and governments, but held in a trust and controlled by the First Nations, can do just that. These independent monitoring bodies exist because people knew their importance and fought for them during the environmental assessment process.

At Ekati mine, the Independent Environmental Monitoring Agency is set up as a non-profit society under an environmental agreement with the Indigenous governments.[4] It is paid for by the mine owner, Dominion Diamond Ekati Corporation. At Diavik mine, the Environmental Monitoring Advisory Board plays the same role, although much of its funding comes from governments.[5] At the closed Giant Mine, an Oversight Board keeps tabs on the remediation process, studies technical reports, and pushes governments for change to the regulatory controls.

Communities find themselves overwhelmed by requests to participate in "consultations" about permit renewals and government plans to change regulatory limits on water releases from tailings impoundments, air quality, mine expansion, and so on. When the company asks for a 50 percent increase in the effluent it releases to a river,[6] the community will be up against company lawyers and scientists in trying to protect its waters, land, and people. The language and form of the request and discussion that follows is usually specialized and requires finding (and hiring) experts to deal with the company demands. Most people have no idea where to find this expertise or how to pay for it. In response, a few technical support organizations have been established. In British Columbia, the Fair Mining Collaborative helps communities with these requests.[7] The Centre for Indigenous Environmental Resources is located in Winnipeg.[8] In northern Ontario, Mushkegowuk Environmental Research Centre was established to do this.[9] However, it still costs money to find and hire experts, and grants are hard to come by. When the Mount Polley disaster happened, the Indigenous community demanded (and got) money from government to hire their own technical experts to help them.

THE IMPORTANCE OF INSIDER INFORMATION

Because mining companies and governments operate with considerable secrecy, it is very important to be able to find out what the company is planning or doing. Having insider knowledge from people who work at the mine and smelter is crucial to protecting the land and water.

Another source of information is people working for the contractors or consultants that advise the company about the environment. Whistle-blowers in government and at the mine workings take considerable risks when they decide to tell the community what is happening.[10] Canadian whistle-blower protection is weak, which is another reason to ensure the workers are unionized and have access to a good grievance procedure.

GETTING A SHARE OF THE WEALTH

As we saw in chapter 10, the mining industry is structured to concentrate profits in the hands of a few and to externalize costs to communities and the environment. As mines continue to grow and expand, Indigenous peoples and local governments invariably discover that they are being cheated; for example, the impact benefit agreement (IBA) did not provide for enough compensation, or the municipal taxes paid by the company are not enough to cover the damage to roads and the local economy caused by mining activity. The damages are often much greater than anyone predicted.

When communities organize to demand more, the mining company usually says it cannot afford it, and that it will have to close the mine/smelter, taking jobs with it. Certainly, this is not an idle threat. After they could no longer avoid meeting the base metal smelter air quality limits set out by the federal government, a number of companies closed their Canadian smelters and moved processing to other countries (see chapter 12). This threat of closure is usually enough to make governments back away from their demands.

A community's effort to get more money from mining activities can take a number of forms. The Robinson-Huron Treaty of 1850 and the

Atikameksheng Anishnawbek court cases discussed in chapter 4 provide excellent examples of treaty-based actions.[11]

Most communities and groups reduce their demands to requests for charitable donations to help defray hospital and educational capital costs, and pay for scholarships, sports teams, creek and land remediation, and arts activities. The company is usually very willing to engage in "philanthro-capitalism"[12] in order to avoid demands that they pay more taxes or make higher IBA payments. It also increases the power of the company to influence who is a leader in the community and what kinds of activities are promoted.

MINES EATING THE CITIES THAT FEED THEM

Throughout the geological gold belt that runs from Timmins, Ontario, to Malartic, Quebec, new open-pit gold mines are being established under the rubric of "dealing with old mining legacies." Building a gigantic new open pit to get at the remaining low grade ore is presented as a solution to collapsing underground mine shafts and inadequately built tailings impoundments from previous mines. Despite the debt owed to the workers and families that built these mines, new expansions in places like the Abitibi gold belt in northern Ontario and Quebec are displacing local communities, creating even more enormous waste rock dumps and tailings impoundments, and endangering future generations.

Malarctic is a town that was built in 1939 to house workers for underground gold mines in the Abitibi Region of Quebec. The gold mines in the area were all closed by 1980. In 2008–09, exploration by Osisko Mining revealed an untapped new gold deposit, estimated at approximately nine million ounces, beneath the town. At the time, there was little effective opposition from townspeople to the project and the company received approval from the government of Quebec to launch what would become Canada's largest ever open-pit gold mine. It opened in 2011. Over two hundred homes were relocated to the north side of town and their owners compensated.[13] In September 2016, the owner, Canadian Malartic put a voluntary compensation process in place. The "Good Neighbour Guide" outlined the terms and conditions under which residents could be compensated for "annoyances caused by dust, vibrations, overpressure, and noise." However, for most residents, as the pit grew, the situation became untenable, and, in October 2017, they launched a lawsuit demanding that they be relocated elsewhere.[14]

SUPPORTING THE WORKERS

In the absence of other economic opportunities, communities become dependent on the mine/smelter and the people who work there for their survival. Unless a community can develop another way of supporting itself, it needs to protect the jobs with the mining company and the health and safety of the people who work there.

The people working for the mine and smelter usually live in the surrounding community and have families and friends that experience the negative impacts of the mine as much as they do. As discussed in chapter 6, their income is likely quite high relative to other jobs in the community and their spending is crucial to the local economy and the area around it.

Their work is often dangerous and industrial disease is common. Studies have shown that people who live in mining/smelting towns are less healthy than people who do not. The culture of mining work shapes the culture of the community. The boom and bust nature of the mineral industry results in frequent layoffs and shutdowns, which affect everyone who lives in the area. If the workers are unionized, the community will frequently be faced with labour disruptions: strikes and lockouts. Unless the community supports the strikers, the workers will lose the strike and everyone is poorer for it. There are some useful resources for building this support, including McAlevey's *No Shortcuts* and Loreto's *From Demonized to Organized.*[15]

CATASTROPHIC ACCIDENTS

It is often only when something catastrophic happens that people in the community find the social energy to get involved. A mining disaster may be something like the explosion at Westray described in chapter 6, or the collapse of a tailings dam.

When Imperial Metals' Mount Polley tailings dam collapsed in British Columbia on August 4, 2014, the impact was horrific and dramatic for the Secwepemc peoples and the residents in Likely. They quickly mobilized. The Secwepemc Women's Warrior Society quickly established a camp and sacred fire at the site.[16] The affected First Nations demanded—and got—money to hire their own experts; emergency shelters were created; social media buzzed. The local people, First Nations Women Advocating Responsible Mining (FNWARM), and a number of supporting NGOs, university groups, and environmental organizations got involved. Forty thousand people signed their petition. In 2018, FNWARM undertook a project called Stand for Water,[17] which included a tour of key cities and towns in British Columbia to publicize issues

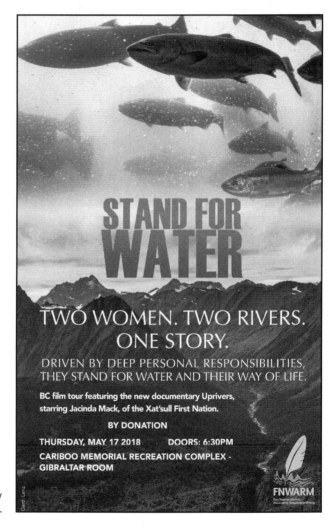

Image courtesy of FNWARM.

around mining and water in the province and transboundary areas of the United States. They made a film about the issue.

For the company (Imperial Metals), the mining industry, and the BC government, the immediate issue was managing the public relations fallout. For the workers at Mount Polley and the community that depended on their wages, the issue was reopening the mine. The Steelworkers union local and some residents in nearby Williams Lake actually lobbied to get the mine reopened as soon as possible. A few months after the Mount Polley disaster, Imperial Metals opened another mine, Red Chris, near Iskut in northern British Columbia; it is an enormous mine with a tailings containment similar to that of Mount Polley.

A huge power struggle played out, with numerous attempts to get Imperial Metals to pay for the damage and properly remediate the Mount Polley site. The lives of people in Xat'sull First Nation and the town of Likely were dramatically changed. Citizens' charges were laid under the federal *Fisheries Act*, but then taken up and stayed by the province and federal government.[18] Despite three years of organizing by local First Nations, Likely residents, and their allies across British Columbia and Canada, in the end no charges were laid against Imperial Metals. The mine reopened and received a permit from the provincial government to discharge directly into Quesnel Lake.[19]

However, as this book goes to press, Imperial Metals is on the brink of bankruptcy and is selling off the Red Chris Mine. Lower-than-expected production from the Red Chris Mine, a recent two-month strike at Mount Polley, and the impacts from the tailings disaster mean that the company is paying $75 million annually in interest on its debts. The reclamation bond for the company's mines is only secured by $14.3 million in cash—and even Imperial Metals estimates the "full undiscounted cost" of its environmental liabilities at $173.6 million.[20]

RISK ASSESSMENTS: THE SUDBURY SOILS STUDY

Communities that are concerned about health effects from a proposed or existing mine are likely to have to deal with a proposal from government or the mining company for a health risk assessment or an ecological risk assessment.[21] These are extremely complex and costly "scientific" undertakings based on "acceptable level of risk."

As a friend once said, the assessors estimate how many people (and which ones) are going to get sick and/or die, and then decide how many is okay. In fact, the "acceptable level of risk" is a political decision, not a scientific one.

In November 2008, the National Orphaned/Abandoned Mines Initiative held a workshop to look at risk assessment of abandoned mines.[22] Approximately one hundred participants from Indigenous organizations, non-governmental and academic organizations, the mining industry, private consultancies, and federal, provincial, and territorial governments attended.

There was quite a fight. People from communities and NGOs said they were unable to trust the risk assessment process in their communities. They challenged how the criteria—the acceptable level of risk—were set. They had serious concerns about the impartiality of risk assessors. They felt that power to interpret results was overwhelmingly with governments and mining companies. In Indigenous communities, translation was almost impossible.

At any mining or smelter site where risk assessment had been undertaken, the results said that there was "no immediate danger" or "no discernible health risk," even though the water, soil, and air sampling indicated high levels of contaminants, and the number of people with cancers and asthma was elevated. This is because "the standard of proof for causality is set at such a high level that even if a near perfect correlation exists between local health problems and proximal levels of pollution or contamination, many communities still cannot prove causality."[23]

In Sudbury, the unions and community groups had been raising questions about pollution in the city for years. In the late 1960s and 1970s, the mine unions made the impacts of acid rain a major issue and were a key reason why pollution from base metal smelters was eventually regulated. Pressure from the community, the unions, and other concerned allies had resulted in substantial "re-greening" efforts in the city, spreading lime and seeds on the barren, black hills. This work had resulted in a real change to the appearance of the city and to the companies' reputations. How much this really changed the health impacts is another story.

SOAR (the Steelworkers Organization of Active Retirees) described the situation in Sudbury:

We wanted to make sure that contamination from mines and smelters in the Sudbury region is properly identified, remediated and (where it cannot be remediated) contained, and wanted to ensure that those people whose health is at risk are provided with diagnosis, treatment and (where this is not possible) with compensation.

Sudbury has some of the worst health indicators in the country. Statistics Canada reports that, in 2000, Greater Sudbury had the lowest life expectancy for all metropolitan areas in Canada, at 76.7 years. We were second only to Saint John in terms of people with high blood pressure, at 16.2%.

The Sudbury and District Health Unit reports that cancer rates in their district were 442.3 per 100,000, as opposed to 400 per 100,000 in all of Ontario. We exceed provincial cancer rates for prostate, lung, colorectal, kidney, pancreatic, lymphoma and cervical cancers. Although our smoking and drinking rates are also remarkably high compared to other cities, it is too easy to only blame these lifestyle choices.[24]

Largely as a result of concerns raised by workers and their allies, in 2001, the Ontario Ministry of the Environment undertook an extensive soil sampling program in the region. Almost ten thousand samples were taken. However, this was still not enough: only 10 percent of residential properties were sampled in the Copper Cliff and Coniston areas and an even smaller percentage of residential properties were sampled in the remainder of the City of Greater Sudbury. Only six "chemicals of concern" (arsenic, cobalt, copper, nickel, lead, and selenium) were chosen for the risk analysis study out of twenty inorganic chemicals sampled. This meant that aluminum, barium, cadmium, and molybdenum were all excluded.[25] Radon was not even considered, as it was not deemed to be a result of the smelting process; however, it was known that radon was a serious problem in Sudbury, due to uranium in the rocks.[26] The highest chemical concentrations (those in the ninety-fifth percentile range) were excluded from the discussion of concentrations, as they were considered to be "outliers" for statistical purposes.[27]

When the results were released in 2005, they were alarming. High concentrations of nickel, lead, and other contaminants were found in many yards, schools, and parks.

The results also alarmed the mining companies, and they rushed to get control over how the study's findings would be interpreted. The companies volunteered to pay for a further study, the Sudbury Soils Study, and partnered with three other major stakeholders in Sudbury to oversee it: the Sudbury and District Health Unit, the City of Greater Sudbury, and Health Canada First Nations and Inuit Health Branch. These partners appointed a technical committee to oversee the study, which met in secret.

The partnership also established a public advisory committee to help address questions and concerns about the potential impact of elevated metal levels on the local environment and human health. Its role focused on providing advice to the technical committee on the "process," and on how to communicate with the public; it did not provide scientific or technical advice. There were two union representatives in the group, who confessed that they had trouble understanding what was being discussed.

The Sudbury Area Risk Assessment (SARA) Group was hired to prepare a human health risk assessment (HHRA), which was released in May 2008. It seriously underestimated risk to people living in and around Sudbury. The study took a single-chemical approach, and did not address cumulative, synergistic, or additive effects among the six chemicals of concern and radon, lifestyle choices, and other (missing) chemicals like aluminum and cadmium.

The HHRA was concerned only with toxins from the smelters. People are, of course, exposed to pollutants from many other sources, and it is the cumulative effect of all of these toxins that threatens our health. Whether the lead comes from the smelters or from paint is not what matters to individuals who just want it identified and cleaned up.

The HHRA provided risk estimates based on the *average* resident of a community—it did not address concerns about the most vulnerable and most exposed individuals. For example, although one in five children probably eat dirt, this behaviour was not considered in the study.

It excluded occupational exposure as a source of additional body burden. The workers at CVRD Inco and Xstrata are a significant percentage of the population in the affected communities and are exposed both at work and at home.

The study's lead findings were bizarre. Lead is a potent neurotoxicant affecting both the central and peripheral nervous systems. Even low levels of blood lead are associated with problems in children's behavioural development, with no evidence of a threshold. Lead is also associated with kidney damage.

The HHRA set the soil risk management level for lead at 400 ppm (parts per million), when it is well known that there is no safe level for lead exposure, and the federal government level is 140 ppm. The 400-ppm level is double the provincial standard. The HHRA showed that approximately 129 samples had lead levels at or above 200 ppm. However, one of the key findings was that of the 553 properties sampled in the communities of concern, on only 9 sampled properties did lead exceed the soil risk management level of 400 ppm. When considering these findings, it is also important to remember that only 10 percent of residential properties were sampled, and it was not known if they were representative. No further soil sampling was done to see if other locations near the 9 sites were also contaminated.

There were problems with the study's nickel findings. The HHRA said that there was only a "minimal risk" of respiratory inflammation from lifetime exposure to airborne nickel in two areas of Sudbury and that the health risks related to nickel inhalation were negligible in the other communities. However, Environment Canada says that nickel compounds are "carcinogenic to humans," a label applied to "substances for which there is believed to be some chance of adverse health effects at any level of exposure."[28]

The study's arsenic findings were also a problem. The 2001 study conducted by the Ministry of the Environment showed that both soil and inhaled arsenic levels were significantly increased throughout most of the Greater Sudbury Area. The SARA study did undertake some urinary arsenic testing, but found that levels were high in both the study area and the control group. The control group was in Hanmer, Ontario, where decades of pesticide-laced potato production have taken place. The HHRA concluded that purchased food was the main source of arsenic exposure. Since the arsenic levels could not be blamed exclusively on smelter emissions, they were dismissed.

Angry and concerned by the study's findings, a group of individuals (including me) from the unions, the university, and the community organized the Community Committee on the Sudbury Soils Study. The Mine Mill and Steelworkers unions commissioned a review of the HHRA by Environmental Defence Canada, which was conducted by Dr. Khapil Khatter. The community committee and Dr. Khatter's report were launched on October 22, 2008.

> In response to the report, a number of community residents and organizations have banded together to form the Community Committee on the Sudbury Soil Study. The Community Committee is urging the Ontario Ministries of Environment and of Labour to step up and assume their responsibility for the health of Sudburians. . . . We want to see the Government ensure that the public decides what level of risk it can accept, what will be done to clean-up affected properties, and what will be done to treat those whose health is at risk. The process to date has been dominated by the companies who are responsible for the mess.

The Environmental Defence report set out a number of serious findings:

- Lead contamination is above safe levels in Greater Sudbury, and children may be harmed at these levels.
- Air levels of nickel are higher than recommended exposure in three communities.
- There are concerns that inhaled arsenic and specific types of ingested arsenic may put Sudbury residents at risk.
- Higher levels of lead, arsenic, and nickel in Sudbury-grown foods are a concern for those eating them.
- The HHRA assumes it is acceptable to expose workers, who receive greater doses of nickel and other contaminants during their employment, to greater levels of risk.

The committee demanded that effective remediation be undertaken at sites where contamination was unacceptable, and to have the community decide where those sites were. We worked on this in one way or another for three years. It felt like we got nowhere. In the end, if anyone acted on the report, it was without acknowledging that they were doing so.

Our committee had increasing problems getting anyone to take up the issues. Very few people wanted to know if they and their children were being contaminated. Eat Local Sudbury refused to support us, as they were trying to stimulate a local food movement. Even friends found the issue too big; they didn't understand the technical stuff. Media increasingly were uninterested, and we couldn't raise the money needed for further studies.

The public did not want people talking about contamination as it would affect property values, and might mean that soils at schools and other public buildings would have to be decontaminated. When I talked with a few remediation scientists who did understand the study, I was told that they felt "panic would be unproductive." A lot of their funding came from the mining companies.

The Sudbury and District Health Unit also refused to undertake any blood testing for metals or even to criticize the study; they too worried about "panic."

The Ontario government held a number of public participation events around changes to the air quality regulations for the smelters in town, for which they duly notified the committee. Preparing to intervene in these exercises required a level of technical expertise that the members of the committee did not have, and they quickly exhausted the group.

When an ecological risk assessment was later released by the SARA Group, it set out in meticulous detail the poisoning of the environment by smelter emissions of eighty thousand hectares around the smelter. The committee hired an expert, Glen Fox, to review the assessment, who said that this report was credible. However, when we tried to bring attention to the report results, the response in the community was thunderous silence. When Homer Sequin, the labour activist who led the committee, died (prematurely, as a result of industrial disease) the people in the committee moved on to other issues.[29]

STRENGTHENING THE SOCIAL AND CULTURAL FABRIC OF THE COMMUNITY

When we live in cultures of contamination—those communities that have become dependent on the mining industry—countering the powerlessness that we feel in the face of the companies' environmental and political footprint is done indirectly. It is accomplished by strengthening the community's cultural and social fabric and making the vision of a more holistic and democratic way of life feel possible.

Before I went to work for MiningWatch Canada, I was the program coordinator for an innovative community project called Better Beginnings, Better Futures in my own neighbourhood in Sudbury. Led by the N'Swakamok Native Friendship Centre and funded by a provincial government longitudinal research program, Better Beginnings was set up to provide parent-driven programs for children in the low-income Donovan and Flour Mill neighbourhoods of the city, two of the most disadvantaged neighbourhoods in the province.[30]

The project bridged artists and educators from these programs to the children and their families in our neighbourhood. Since the days of the social unionism of Mine Mill (see chapter 6), Sudbury has seen a lot of cultural innovation, for Indigenous theatre, music, and community programming, for franco-ontarien theatre and the arts, and for one of the most original community arts programs in the country: Myths and Mirrors.

Since 1995, Myths and Mirrors (the brainchild of Laurie McGauley, a community member) has used collectively developed arts to build community, challenge cultural assumptions, and inspire hope. At the heart of their work is the genuine respect they always show for the people they organize with, whether they are punks, skaters, or seniors. Myths and Mirrors drew its inspiration from groups like Bread and Puppet Theatre in Toronto, and from the popular theatre work of Augusto Boal. They worked with the neighbourhood through "performance art, murals, mosaics, music and drumming, gardens, celebrations, rituals, stilting, face painting, costuming, visual arts, installations, video, film, games and popular education."[31]

Myths and Mirrors played an important role in helping Better Beginnings work out neighbourhood tensions and differences by creating a culture particular to the neighbourhood that was playful, consensus based, and respectful of needs and responsibilities. Myths and Mirrors organized all sorts of collective projects in the neighbourhood: giant puppet shows, celebrations of seasons, decorating all the buildings with collective murals and art, undertaking murals with the roughest teens in the neighbourhood, and creating community gardens. Myths and Mirrors is still in existence and now works all over Sudbury.

This kind of community-based cultural work is essential to stimulating our imaginations and providing an antidote to the kind of diminished community created by the mining industry.

Myths and Mirrors community arts. Photo courtesy of Tanya Anne Ball.

17

ORGANIZING WHEN THE MINE IS GONE

In chapter 7, I discussed the literature review and case studies I undertook for the environmental assessment of the Giant Mine remediation plan.[1] The cases taught me a lot about effective organizing by communities when they have to get governments to invest in the cleanup of an enormous toxic mine waste site. This chapter shares this knowledge and starts with the story of the Giant Mine.

GIANT MINE

The Giant Mine is located on the shores of Great Slave Lake in the city of Yellowknife.[2] The mine (one of a number in the area) operated from 1948 to 1999, when its owner, Royal Oak Mines, went into receivership. The mine then operated intermittently for a few more years under Miramar ownership, closing for good in 2004. The area where the mine was built had been the breadbasket for the Yellowknives Dene. The Dene and their ancestors had lived in the area to the north of Great Slave Lake for over seven thousand years, before prospectors seized on the gold they found there in 1890. Gold mining started in earnest in the 1930s.

The gold was found in arsenopyrite ore, which had to be "roasted" to separate the sulphur and arsenic from the gold. The released hot arsenic initially went up the smokestack and was dispersed in the air and, when it cooled, it settled in a fine dust on the ground and waters. After a Dene child died from eating snow in 1951 and some community members got sick from arsenic poisoning, Royal Oak began collecting the arsenic trioxide from the smelter fumes. It decided to blow the stuff into the mined-out chambers of the underground mine. The company thought that permafrost would keep it contained.

There are now over 237,000 tons of arsenic trioxide stored underground in Yellowknife. On the surface there were ninety-five hectares of contaminated mine tailings, "the equivalent of about three hundred football fields, ten to fifteen metres deep. Eight open pits and a roaster complex on the surface contain another 4,900 cubic metres of arsenic trioxide and other waste."[3] This is enough arsenic to kill everyone on the planet, and would wipe out the Mackenzie River system if there were a major leak.

Without the work of Kevin O'Reilly, I am pretty sure that the various Canadian government policy-makers would still just be pretending that the Giant Mine mess did not exist.

A member of the Legislative Assembly in the Northwest Territories since 2015, Kevin has spent most of his adult life living by his principles. A graduate of geography at the University of Waterloo, in 1985 he moved to Yellowknife to work for the Dene Nation. He was a researcher for the Canadian Arctic Resources Committee and executive director of the Independent Environmental Monitoring Agency for the Ekati mine. From 1997 to 2006, he sat on Yellowknife City Council. Alternatives North, the volunteer organization he helped create, was once described to me as "the official opposition in the NWT." Kevin was on the MiningWatch board from its beginning until 2015. Kevin says that when he moved to Yellowknife in 1985,

> You would get that sour taste at the back of your mouth and know it was the sulphur from the roaster. The main recreation area for Yellowknifers is the Ingraham Trail, lots of little lakes, cabin subdivisions and so on. To get to it, you would drive right by the Giant Mine, past the smoke stack belching out stuff, and you would see all the scars on the land, junky old buildings, piles of debris and crap, the bare, burnt rocks.

Working with the Dene Nation, I travelled to a lot of the smaller communities to meet with the five regional coordinators I worked with. . . . People would come into the office and I would get invited to Ndilo and Dettah, and heard the stories about the Giant Mine and the damage it had done to their traditional territories, and how they had to truck in water to drink because the bay was contaminated. I heard the stories of children dying and people getting sick. How do you reconcile that stuff? The injustice of it struck me. Part of my culture and my background had helped create that and at the time the stack was still belching the stuff out. It made me very angry; something had to be done.

Then the strike came along.[4] Peggy Witte had run the company into the ground. But government had allowed this to happen and perpetuated it.[5]

In April 1991, Kevin and Chris O'Brien began to push the federal government for an environmental and human health risk assessment of the Giant Mine. Two years later, an NWT report admitted that there had been damage to trees from sulphur dioxide, and the federal government concluded that the sulphur dioxide was causing only mild irritation to some people but that "there were no safe levels for arsenic."[6] Nothing was done.

Over the next fifteen years, Kevin and his friends and allies found themselves in a Kafkaesque battle to get Yellowknife City Council, and the Northwest Territories and federal governments to act on the arsenic issue. They wrote briefs and letters, attended and organized workshops, and tried to find technical experts to help them understand what they were being told, all with no financial resources. He tells the story in chronological and depressing detail in the book *Mining and Communities in Northern Canada*.[7]

In 2004, mining ceased for good at the Giant Mine. The toxic mess was now completely the responsibility of the Department of Indian Affairs and Northern Development (DIAND). DIAND began a process of trying to figure out what to do, and Kevin, the Yellowknives Dene, and Yellowknife City Council pushed for a full environmental assessment of DIAND plans for cleanup and long-term care of the site. In the end, it was Kevin's contacts from his days on city council that led to Yellowknife City Council forcing the EA to happen. Kevin describes this as "an extraordinary convergence of interests and resistance from individuals and organizations that had not worked together effectively in the past."[8]

The environmental assessment process, which began in 2009, was fraught, with the Yellowknives Dene and Alternatives North leading the opposition to the federal government's plan. There were a number of concerns. The plan selected by the government was to leave the arsenic in the ground and create a freeze wall around it through the use of thermosyphons. Alternatives North and the Yellowknives Dene argued that this could only be "phase one" and that phase two would have to set up funding and a process to seek out alternatives that would permanently immobilize the arsenic. They wanted a financial trust established for perpetual care. They wanted an independent oversight body to monitor

Giant Mine environmental assessment hearing in Dettah First Nation, Northwest Territories. Photo courtesy of Kevin O'Reilly.

the process. And they wanted an apology and compensation for the Yellowknives Dene.

The environmental assessment took over five years. In the end the Mackenzie Valley Impact Review Board agreed with Alternatives North and the Dene. The federal government agreed with their recommendations on August 11, 2014. The independent environmental monitoring agency that Alternatives North and the Yellowknives Dene had demanded—the Oversight Board—is now functioning, the remediation of the surface has begun, and the containment of the underground arsenic is in process. It is costing the federal government more than $1 billion.

Despite strong urging from the Oversight Board, there has yet to be an apology or compensation for the Yellowknives Dene.

When asked what he wanted people to know about this struggle, Kevin offered the following advice:

> It took me a long time to get over the anger and outrage. How do you transform that into something constructive? Giant is a very technical problem; there is no magic button you can press to make it go away. You need to be very strategic and look for pressure points. We never have the resources available that government and mining companies do.
>
> Some of it is serendipitous. The work and connections you make come back to help you in ways you never anticipate. Never underestimate the power of what one person can do. That one person can get other voices. Change requires collaboration with others.
>
> I am a total and complete packrat. It is very important to keep records and keep documents organized. If you are committed to an issue, you will outlast the people working on it in government. Make sure you get everything in writing. Institutional memory is a huge problem. If they haven't lived up to their promises, and you have the records, you can hold them accountable. I want to see a centre that stores all these records and interprets them. It is so important to know what happened here.[9]

LESSONS LEARNED FROM THE RESEARCH

In all the cases I studied, the affected citizens had been consistently lied to about the severity of the pollution they were facing and risks had been downplayed and minimized until their advocacy forced the truth to surface.[10] It takes enormous vigilance and mobilization by citizens to draw attention to the problems of contamination. There is no reason to assume this will change in the near or far future. Response to slow leakage or catastrophic failure of containment will still require decisions and action by politicians—and they won't move without a mobilized public.

Local communities have to be involved in planning for long-term care; in particular, the Indigenous communities who have strong attachment to the very land upon which the waste repository sits. There is likely to be resentment and resistance to getting involved, since these affected communities have come to this point through a long history of trespass and pillage by the very structures of colonialism that now want their help in dealing with the consequences. It is also difficult for the people who have settled in the region and have come to call it home.

As Van Wyck says in *The Highway of the Atom*, "Where communities discover—after the fact—that their land and people have been irretrievably contaminated, it alters their perceptions of themselves, their cultural memory. The need for understanding how the site came to be; for healing, telling the history, for lament, for commemoration, is essential."[11] The opportunity for people to heal themselves culturally, spiritually, politically, and socio-economically has to be part of any long-term stewardship plan.

The affected community also has to be formally involved in monitoring and governing the site, but should be free of financial responsibility for this. However, this is likely to create conflict for government agencies and officials who may see community interests as challenging their institutional roles or jeopardizing their work plans.

Unfortunately, these tensions may be made worse by political and industry interests that want to keep the matter quiet or downplay it. Effective advocacy for remediation and effective long-term stewardship will likely result in increased cleanup costs, which government and industry certainly will try to avoid. For example, in Quebec, the government allocated $600 million to the cleanup of abandoned mines in 2016. However, the awarding of the tender was bound by a provision that the lowest tender had to be accepted. This has created serious problems with the quality of the work done. Internal disputes in governments over the level of cleanup at sites are common.

As we saw in chapter 5, in most communities there is a history of tension between those who want to get on with "economic development" and/or don't want to acknowledge the pollution problems in the community, and those who advocate to get it remediated. This tension won't go away once it is recognized that the toxics have to be stored on site. Some community members will be more concerned about the economic and social implications of "environmental stigma,"—the shunning of local people, property, and crops as a result of public knowledge of contamination—than they are about long-term health and ecological effects of the contamination.

Even before the actual containment and remediation can take place, decision making about how the containment is to be done is likely to go on for decades (see the discussion of the Faro Mine in chapter 7). These abandoned sites are loaded with technical unknowns and surprising booby traps. It is frustrating, complex, difficult work for government workers and communities that demands a great deal of time and attention.

In the cases studied, the risk assessments undertaken to estimate costs for long-term health problems all used a cost-benefit "insurance" model. In all the communities I studied, risk assessments concluded that there was no provable relationship between the contaminants of concern and the shockingly poor health of the local people, except for psychological reactions like "radiophobia."[12] Chapter 16 includes an example of a community trying to deal with risk assessment. The entire process of health risk assessment needs to be rethought and harnessed by the affected communities themselves.

Managing the Site

The current laws and regulations needed for perpetual care of toxic waste isolation structures are inadequate. Laws and regulations need to be in place to govern long-term stewardship requirements, that set out emergency response, record-keeping, the need for periodic environmental assessment, and how inter-jurisdictional conflicts are to be dealt with (especially in an emergency).

The first efforts to manage the toxic site over the long term are simply to keep people away from the site. This means a reliance on various institutional and administrative controls, such as fencing, signs, restricted access, registering contaminants on the property deed, and zoning. However, over the long term, most of these controls can be expected to fail for one reason or another. Most organizations attempt redundancy of controls (duplicate them) so that there are always backups when one fails.

All of the research said that the choice of organization charged with long-term stewardship of the site is very important. It needs to be a "high reliability organization (HRO)" with access to appropriate resources in the event of catastrophic failure. It has to have an "unwavering commitment to safety and reliability . . . Other organizational goals, such as efficiency, organizational prestige or profit-making must be continuously subordinated to avoiding serious organizational failures."[13] It needs to be able to operate flexibly in a crisis, with many redundant features. Long-term stewardship requires humility about our errors and ignorance, as well as the flexibility to change direction.

Eugene Rosa, a researcher who looks at long-term stewardship and risk management, says that the responsible organization's particular challenges will include the following:

- "the atrophy of vigilance in an environment where the need to act is intermittent" (maybe spanning decades)
- "the splintering of responsibility amongst different actors" (through organizational silos, jurisdictional differences, and contractor relationships)
- "structural secrecy" (the need to protect the institutional reputation, national security issues, and fear of producing panic)[14]

Unless there is sustained and effective advocacy for such an HRO by the local community, it is not likely to be put in place. After all, our governments cannot even keep potholes out of our roads for a year.

Questions Communities Need to Ask

There are several areas that need to be addressed in relation to the long-term stewardship plan for these sites, including records, the physical works, response to crisis, funding for long-term care, and the ability to develop and use new technologies. Issues and questions for communities to consider for each are provided below:

1. Records: Because of the plethora of laws, regulations, and institutions responsible for long-term waste sites in the United States and Canada, it is difficult for the public to access to records about these sites. How are records to be kept so everything is not lost when/if there is an environmental or social catastrophe, or a major change in computer software, or a failure of the electrical systems? Are the records publicly available? Over time, who will have access to them and how simple is that access? Even those waste sites with websites generally have very selective public access to documents.

2. Monitoring and response: Monitoring of the site must be done extensively and on a regular basis so that even early problems with leakage can be identified. What is sampled? By whom? How often? Five-year monitoring by contractors appears to be the norm, but cost-cutting always trumps effectiveness over time.[15] Is an endowed independent monitoring agency with responsibility to the affected community possible?[16] The responsibility to analyze the monitoring data in depth on a regular basis has to be clearly established especially when/if the work is contracted out. How is this to be sustained over centuries? Who is responsible for translating monitoring results into real action?

3. The physical works: How are the physical works (dams, diversion ditches, roads, water treatment plants, power supply) maintained? By whom? What is the process for community consultation on engineering matters over the long term? Does the public have resources for technical advice? It is important to ensure the long-term availability of materials, skills, and technology to fix unfolding problems.

4. Response to crisis: Catastrophic failure can result from neglect over time, earthquakes, fires, floods, or civil unrest, or all of these together. Or it can result from a series of minor, unrelated failures. Long-term stewardship has to clearly identify, and have the means to continue to identify, which organization is responsible for acting in a crisis and where the resources will come from to respond.

5. Funding for long-term care: Difficulties maintaining adequate funding for long-term stewardship are legion. Most programs

renew their funding through annual appropriations in government budgets that have to compete with projects that are politically more attractive.[17] A number of authors recommend the use of trust funds or endowments to protect resources for long-term stewardship. How is the bond set? Renewed? Is the model dependent on continued economic growth? How is losing the bond to corruption avoided?[18] All of these funds are based on net present value and discounting calculations that assume endless long-term economic growth, take no account of growing ecological degradation, and unfairly minimize the costs to future generations of today's pollution.[19]

6. Ability to develop and use new technologies: If there are new remediation technologies discovered in the future, or if resources are found to make remediation cost-effective, does the cleanup plan allow them to be implemented? Or does the plan obviate them? How does the long-term stewardship plan drive innovation so that the site may eventually be neutralized?

Intergenerational Equity

The importance of creating opportunities for local peoples to carry on the story of the site and build the capacity of youth to be effective guardians comes up repeatedly in the literature about perpetual care.[20] This task invariably falls to the land's original inhabitants, as the settlers are likely to leave once the mine is gone.

The long-term containment of toxic wastes passes the externalized costs and responsibilities of modern industrial production on to future generations of Indigenous peoples. Even if the financial assurance were adequate to cover the costs when the isolation facility fails centuries or millennia in the future, it will not make up for the enormous sacrifice zones—land and communities sacrificed for economic progress—that its failure will create.

Intergenerational guardianship is important to perpetual care sites. In July 2006, representatives of several Native American tribes issued the Bemidji Statement on Seventh Generation Guardianship. This statement assigns "responsibility to the current generations to protect and restore the intricate web of life that sustains us all, for the Seventh Generation to come."[21]

18

INTERNATIONAL SOLIDARITY WORK

As we saw in chapter 9, Canada is a major predator on mining's world stage: arranging finance, setting up companies, and trading around the globe. Canada's export development corporation (Export Development Canada), treaties, pension plans, and banks invest in environmentally and economically risky projects that are often opposed by local people and exploit host governments. This chapter looks at some of the ways Canadians can act in solidarity with them. It starts with the story of a mining ban in El Salvador.

EL SALVADOR BANS MINING

In March 2017, El Salvador made history and became the first country to ban metal mining outright. MiningWatch Canada reported,

> In a startling development driven by a groundswell of opposition to the social and environmental risks that mining poses to this Central American nation, El Salvador's Legislative Assembly voted Wednesday to become the first country to ban mining for gold and other metals, in effect canceling any projects now in the pipeline.

Banner of activist organization La Mesa reads, "We demand a law prohibiting metal mining in El Salvador; National Roundtable against Metal Mining." Photo courtesy of Robin Broad.

The vote, in which 69 of the country's 84 legislators cast ballots to prohibit the mining of metals, makes tiny El Salvador the unlikely hero in a global movement to put the brakes on a modern day "gold rush"; for much of the past few decades, companies have been scouring the earth for every last deposit of gold and other metals. A run of mining projects in El Salvador and other Latin American countries, and a legacy of contamination from old ones, has made the region and its highlands, farms, forests and waterways a focal point in the fight. . . .

Dozens of lawmakers and advocates inside and outside the chamber cheered enthusiastically after the vote in the chamber, where desks were decked in yellow signs emblazoned "No to Mining, Yes to Life."

The vote is the culmination of more than a decade of intense protest over projects that foreign mining companies have sought to exploit in El Salvador's highly vulnerable environment.[1]

There is much to learn from the work of peoples in the Global South, who bring about changes such as this with their fearless organizing. The win in El Salvador took place despite a campaign of brutal repression, including four unresolved murders. Not only did the people of El Salvador organize effectively in their own country, but support from the international community was also significant in the win. The people of El Salvador were able to get the support of hundreds of organizations around the world.

When MiningWatch Canada works with communities in the Global South (and Canadian Indigenous peoples), the local people will beg the organization to work to change the behaviour of the "developed" countries that are disorganizing them and pillaging their resources. They don't think that Canadians have much to offer them in terms of advice or community practice. In their view, it is the power structures in Europe and North America that need to change.

LESSONS LEARNED ABOUT SOLIDARITY WORK

I asked Jen Moore, the former Latin American program coordinator for MiningWatch Canada, what she saw as effective organizing in Canada for solidarity work with other countries:[2]

The strongest campaigns [in support of international partners] are rooted in solidarity organizations, those groups that were organized around the dirty wars in Latin America in the 1970s. During that time and since, those people have been getting information out, then demonstrating the atrocities to the public. A lot of that energy has been transferred to mining now, for example, in the Breaking the Silence Network, CISPES (Committee in Solidarity with the People of El Salvador), and others responding to what their partners are asking for. They do a lot of bringing delegates to Canada and have good two-way communications. The communities want to know about Canadian mining, how it is governed (or not). Breaking the Silence has a history with Guatemala; they are people who really care about Guatemalans and have been with them through thick and thin.

Often these groups have to fight through their own structures—like the church or the union—to get support for their partners. Breaking the Silence and their United Church members spent ten years trying to get the United Church to divest their shares in Goldcorp as a protest against the Marlin Mine and the company's other activities in Latin America. The [United Church's] General Council [GC] only meets every three years, and the shareholder activists went before it twice before they got a decision to divest. And then the Church Board of Trustees overruled the GC decision. The trustees were worried about pensions, even though they held a tiny number of Goldcorp shares.

There is a kind of Canadian logic that says we can only influence the company if we are engaged with them. There are times when that engagement is harmful to the demands from communities and can be very divisive in terms of their strategy.

These groups set up demos, do educational events, respond to urgent actions with letters, etc. We need to put more energy into nurturing these groups; they are just clusters of people. What do we need to do to support them more?

Effective solidarity is about education, building community relationships, standing with the people on what they are actually asking for. The mining model of development is unjust, and we have to learn to think/work beyond it. The funding big NGOs get from mining companies affects the discourse.

Salvadoreans were clearly anti-mining and managed to get this message out. Although they had plenty of difference between them, they could agree on the mining ban for the whole country. There is a *huge* resistance in Latin America to mining, but Canadian NGOs are afraid to say it. We have been able, however, to build support for local struggles by focusing on the water or land that communities are defending.

Connecting the dots between struggles here and overseas is important. Our networks send people from Latin America to affected communities in Canada and vice versa. This is using the Canadian government strategy backwards. Our government sends people like Gerry Asp and Glenn Nolan to talk about how wonderful mining is for Indigenous people in Canada. We make sure the people hear the other story, through media and through one-on-one conversations; debunking the myths/lies about Canadian mining companies, how we are exporting our colonial model. It is also good to share strategic thinking. We need to counter government/industry arguments and messaging.

CONFRONTING THE CORPORATE SOCIAL RESPONSIBILITY OFFENSIVE[3]

About twenty years ago, in response to the rising fury of mining-affected communities around the world, Rio Tinto led an initiative of twenty-three major mining companies called Mining, Minerals, and Sustainable Development.[4] The initiative produced an enormous report that set out most of the problems with the minerals industry quite well.[5] The International Council on Mining and Metals,[6] a minerals indus-try–based organization, was established to provide follow-up based in corporate social responsibility programs.

The pressure on the mining industry from communities and NGOs supporting them continued and resulted in the World Bank Extractive Industries Review (2004), the Initiative for Responsible Mining Assur-ance (IRMA), the Global Compact, the International Cyanide Code, and the Extractive Industries Transparency Initiative (described in chapter 13).[7]

Activists from all over the world found themselves sitting with industry and governments at a number of national and global events and on committees to develop standards and programs by which indus-try would agree to abide. How effective these industry- and govern-ment-driven initiatives could be in actually stopping the pillage by, and pollution from, mining companies was a huge question.

The resources of activist groups and their NGO supporters were stretched to the limit while building the base for mine-by-mine fights, resisting increasing violence from the state and mining companies, and carefully documenting community struggles and company lies to a standard that could stand up in courts of law. Participating in the initia-tives required huge inputs of time and resources. Were these initiatives real and would they actually change things? Or were they just more industry spin? Activists and supporters found themselves confused and divided about how to use the limited resources at their disposal.

The Mines and Communities network was organized out of London, England, to provide an opportunity for mining activist community-based groups to figure out how to respond together.[8] In 2001 and again in 2007, community-based activists and their in-country organizations were assembled to talk about what the industry offensive was doing to work on the ground and to figure out how to respond. MiningWatch Canada was a proud member of this group, which included networks from Latin America, Africa, Asia, Australia, and the United States. MiningWatch Canada was dealing with its own process—the Roundtables on Corporate Responsibility and the Extractives Sector in Developing Countries (described in chapter 20).

The Mines and Communities network came up with the London Declaration 2008, which stated (in part),

> In recent years the mining industry, abetted by some state authorities, has become more aggressive and sophisticated in manipulating national and international legislation to suit its interests, through mechanisms such as free trade agreements.
>
> The mining laws of over a hundred countries have already been drastically changed (liberalised) to suit the interests of mining capital. Protocols protecting Indigenous Peoples and the environment continue to be diluted or undermined, as mining expansion reaches unprecedented levels and even more mining-dependent states turn away from being responsible for the well-being of their citizens to becoming servants of the global corporations.
>
> At the same time, we have seen at first hand community resistance significantly increasing, and new partnerships forming between local people and workers, themselves suffering from the insecurity of imposed short-term contracts or corporate encroachment on traditional small-scale mining areas.[9]

The London Declaration went on to describe what had to be done to bring the predatory international mining industry under control. The analysis is as true today as it was in 2008:

1) Rejection of any official development assistance or multilateral development aid—from the likes of the World Bank IFC [International Finance Corporation] and IDA [International Development Association], European Investment Bank or Asian Development Bank—aimed primarily at promoting mineral extraction or infrastructure for the minerals industry, promoting further dilution of protective legislation, royalty and taxation regimes, and designed to favour the interests of the private minerals industry and its investors.

2) Cancellation or renegotiation of existing mining and mineral processing contracts and licenses which effectively rob peoples of their resources, squander their rights to the commons, result in exportation of the true value of minerals extracted, or sacrifice in any way citizens' rights to sustainable livelihoods. In addition we call for repeal of all mining codes and cancellation of free trade, bilateral investment and multilateral aid agreements, which provide or allow for such contracts and licenses.

3) Abandonment of all corporate codes of conduct, or promises of enhanced corporate social responsibility which are dependent solely on voluntary observance, without transparent and independent monitoring of their implementation.

4) Assurance that Indigenous Peoples are guaranteed their rights, using as a minimum standard the September 2007 UN Declaration of the Rights of Indigenous Peoples. Central to these is the right of self-determination, one important instrument of which is FPIC (Free, Prior and Informed Consent). Indigenous Peoples should be entitled to grant or withhold FPIC before any mineral exploration or extraction is undertaken within their territories. If an indigenous community chooses to withhold FPIC from any mining company, the company must respect this by removing itself from the community's territory.

5) Respect for the right of all communities to say no to mining and mineral-related projects they consider will impact adversely on their environment and deprive them of resources on which they depend.

6) Repeal of anti-terrorism laws and other policies that threaten the lives and curtail the rights of communities and activists protesting mining projects.

7) Halting of the violence used by state forces or those employed by mining companies, against opponents of mining, including extra-judicial killings.

The London Declaration also had strong recommendations for NGOs that purport to help mining-affected communities in the Global South. The participants asked them to ensure that mining-affected communities were fully informed and spoke for themselves in response to mineral projects, to refuse to participate in initiatives spearheaded by the industry to serve its own purposes, and to advocate for politically and legally enforceable measures that would hold the mining industry accountable to affected communities.

WORKING TO CHANGE LAW AND POLICY IN CANADA

There are a number of coalitions and organizations that specialize in understanding how international institutions, international trade, and bilateral agreements work, and in translating what these bodies are up to into language and forms everyone can understand.

Internationally, these groups include the Transnational Institute in France, Inter Press Service (IPS) and the Center for International Environmental Law (CIEL) in the United States, Rights and Accountability in Development (RAID) in the United Kingdom, and the Center for Research on Multinational Corporations (SOMO) in the Netherlands.[10] They have staff and members who gather intelligence for activists and community members working on the ground. These organizations put them in touch with other communities all over the world that are fighting similar battles. They play a crucial role in shifting power. They track how national and international governments are supporting transnational corporations, and mount campaigns and lobby for changes.

In Canada, there are also organizations that do this kind of work. A coalition called the Canadian Network on Corporate Accountability (CNCA), of which MiningWatch Canada is a founding and active member, has been playing the coordinating role.

Uniting almost thirty civil society organizations, the CNCA provides an effective forum for collaborative research, advocacy and public education work regarding the overseas activities of Canadian companies. The network's Open for Justice campaign seeks to improve access to remedy in Canada for the foreign victims of corporate abuse. The CNCA was the civil society focal point to the National Roundtable process on the Canadian extractive industry and led civil society efforts in support of Bill C-300.[11]

The CNCA members include a number of labour unions that represent mining industry workers, church groups, and development organizations. A key member is Above Ground,[12] which provides legal and policy expertise, strategic orientation, and important links to international allies and processes. Above Ground is linked to ECA Watch,[13] an international network of NGOs that campaigns for export credit agency (ECA) reform, and to ESCR-Net (initials stand for economic, social, and cultural rights), an international network that works worldwide to facilitate learning and strategy sharing, develop new tools and resources, engage in advocacy, and provide networking. It has a Corporate Accountability Working Group (CAWG) and is a member of the Corporate Capture Project Advisory Group.

Other groups involved in this kind of work in Canada include the Canadian Coalition for Tax Fairness, which researches and advocates for tax policy and opposes tax havens.[14] Another is Kairos Canada, "a joint venture ecumenical program administered by the United Church of Canada. Ten participating member denominations and religious organizations are involved in the development and delivery of [its] shared work."[15]

Understanding that we are part of a global movement for change is essential to building our strength. However, the power of a movement lies in the capacity of the communities and groups that compose it. Although work on the national and international level is important, it will go nowhere unless we build the base at home. It is a question of where we put our energy: some people will have to do the networking and travel, but a lot more need to do the hard slogging where they live.

We need to be aware of the networks and activists that work on the global issues that touch our communities. Communities need to learn from them, find ways to explain why these issues matter at home, and participate in exchanges, gatherings, and demonstrations where we can afford the time and money to do it. If local groups participate through a larger issue-based organization, we need to ensure that affected communities are in control of the agenda, and that this is a partnership, not a client relationship. We need to be careful about dependency.

Getting the Word Out, Telling the Stories, Changing Public Opinion

There are a number of locally based solidarity networks across Canada that provide support to communities in the Global South and work to educate about mining issues and shift public opinion.

The Mining Injustice Solidarity Network (MISN) is one of them:

[MISN is a] Toronto-based activist group that organizes to draw attention to and resist the negligent and abusive practices of Canadian mining companies. In solidarity with affected communities and in response to their calls for support, MISN: educates the Canadian public on mining injustices in Canada and around the world; advocates for stronger community control of mining practices and in support of self-determination in mining-affected areas; and agitates against corporate impunity and in support of substantive regulatory change.[16]

MISN is particularly effective in carrying out public education and awareness activities in Toronto. Working as a collective, it undertakes "public acts of protest and popular education, [and] work[s] to bring the stories, experiences, and strategies of mining affected communities and their advocates to be heard in Canada."

Since 2015, MISN has intervened at the Prospectors and Developers Association of Canada convention, an enormous industry gathering and trade show. Its objective is to make people at the event pay attention to the externalized costs of the industry, and to make people outside the industry aware of its power and impacts. The first year, right on the PDAC trade show floor, members of MISN hosted a vigil paying respects to those the industry had killed. They were immediately kicked out. In 2017, they brought two buses full of over a hundred people (who read about it in *NOW* magazine and on social media) for a "toxic tour" of the convention. Many made it inside the investors' exchange where they read out the names of land and water defenders killed in mining areas in the last three years. They were removed by the police.

In 2018, MISN carried out a "treasure hunt" at the venue, where participants unearthed the real costs of mining, and talked to exhibitors about the impacts. They wore t-shirts with a hashtag for a thunderclap: "#PDAC2017, we see through your lies and shiny PR. No mining without community consent! #DisruptMining #DisruptPDAC http://thndr. me/RbF9pK."

Merle Davis of MISN told me that bringing affected peoples to company annual meetings is another important focus of the organization's work: "We get the information about the company we need, and it shows our partners in the Global South that we care about them."[17] The targeting of particular companies and their annual meetings—bringing people from affected communities together to confront investors—has been a successful tactic used by other groups like Protest Barrick for decades now.[18] MISN has also started a project to track mining-related violence around the world, based on the Justice and Corporate Accountability Project (JCAP) methodology.

"We look for actions that are humorous and for street theatre that is inspired by the communities we work with," says Merle. In 2015 in

Source: Mining Injustice Solidarity Network.

Montreal, members of MISN dressed in Santa suits and handed out coal to protest a court verdict. "It is easier for people to approach you when you are being a bit silly."

After the Barrick Gold annual general meeting in 2018, MISN organized a vigil to protest violence against women in Papua New Guinea and handed out flyers about what they were doing. MISN does a lot of workshops with youth, helping them to see the structural causes of mining problems. In the summer of 2018, they brought a giant puppet of the legendary sea monster the Kraken to parks to do workshops and teach-ins about the impacts of mining. Said Merle,

> It feels hard sometimes. The consequences for land and water protectors in the Global South include violence, death, sexual violence. It is important to honour them, but it feels like Canadian civil society does not take this seriously enough. Getting people to imagine the magnitude of this problem is the challenge of this time. We can't ethically consume our way out of this.[19]

Countering Company Misinformation and Lies

One of the things local communities often need from their supporters is documentation about their lived reality that can stand up to legal scrutiny. If I have learned anything in my years of experience, it is that mining companies lie if they think they can get away with it. They will lie about the pollution they cause, about social impacts, about injuries from violence, about the monies they pay to governments.

This kind of on-the-ground documentation is meticulous work. It often requires specialized scientific expertise in anthropology, geology, hydrology, toxicology, and engineering. For a community's story to be recognized in courts and tribunals in the Global North, the research often needs to be validated by a report from a recognized North American or European expert and it has to be 100 percent accurate. Experts will hesitate to do this work as the mining industry has been known to blacklist experts who help debunk company claims.

Working for the industry is much more lucrative than working for an NGO. The level of documentation required to counter company lies is intimidating. For small, under-resourced groups, it can be overwhelming. Most of the experts that work for mining-affected communities do it out of commitment.

In 2001, when lawyer Tundu Lissu, now a Tanzanian member of Parliament, came to Canada to confront Barrick Gold with claims of deaths at the Bulyanhulu Gold Mine, his affidavits from affected small-scale miners and the video evidence he had were dismissed by media in Canada on the word of a Barrick Gold lawyer. When MiningWatch Canada assembled a delegation—headed by the Dean of Law at the University of Calgary—to go to Tanzania to talk with the miners and their families, they were denied access to the mining area.[20] The miners had to travel out by bus to meet the delegation in the city of Mwanza. Barrick was believed over even the affidavits, first-person accounts, and video evidence.

Legal Hammers: Supporting Court Cases and Intervention at Administrative Tribunals

Until recently Canadian courts refused to hear lawsuits brought by foreign plaintiffs who said they had been injured by a Canadian mining company (see chapter 9). Klippensteins, a Toronto-based law firm,[21] working with Rights Action in Guatemala, and the Canadian Centre for International Justice, working with the law firm Camp Fiorante Matthews Mogerman LLP, have been at the forefront of some lawsuits that are changing this paradigm. The Canadian Centre for International Justice is a charitable organization that works with survivors of genocide, torture, and other atrocities to seek redress and bring perpetrators to justice.

Two of the lawsuits, *Garcia v. Tahoe Resources* and *Araya v. Nevsun Resources Ltd.*, were filed in 2014 and are still wending their way through the courts. In June 2017, the Supreme Court of Canada denied Tahoe leave to appeal an earlier BC Court of Appeals decision that determined that British Columbia is the best place for the case to be heard.[22] Three others, *Choc v. Hudbay*, *Chub v. Hudbay*, and *Caal v. Hudbay*, are about wrongs that happened over ten years ago. They have been and will be in court in Toronto for a long time.

The network of Canadian solidarity groups and NGOs ensures that these cases are brought to the attention of the Canadian public.

They make sure that the plaintiffs speak in or outside corporate annual general meetings. They document the stories and make sure they are reported in online and regular media. They provide friendship and places to stay when community members have to appear in court. In almost all cases, the lawyers representing the communities are working pro bono or for a very reduced fee.

These cases challenge company impunity on a profound level.

19

TAKING ON THE COMPANY AND ITS INVESTORS

This chapter discusses strategies that help communities by making investors and companies responsive to the risks and costs of the capital casino that drives mining. These can be used at any point in the mining sequence, but are usually most effective when the company is seeking to develop a new mine or when communities are trying to force a company to act on its environmental and social liabilities for an existing project.

All markets involve an element of gambling.[1] The riskier the venture, the more an investor expects to gain if he "wins." There are few stocks as risky as mineral exploration companies, and investment houses have to do risk assessment and due diligence in relation to these. If they do not, they can be liable in lawsuits. When communities are able to expose hidden costs of or risks related to these investments, it might shift the balance of risk and reward.

Beyond a few ethical funds, it is safe to assume that most investors do not care about impacts on the environment. They do, however, care about potential delays or reduced returns on their money, as well as the financial effects of increased liability and poor management decisions that may harm the company.

A key objective of *follow the money* strategies is to get greater direct or indirect access to investors to make them think twice about keeping money flowing to "high-risk" projects. Affecting the availability of capital may be the most direct way to affect mineral activities themselves.

In 2003, UK corporate watchdog Corner House suggested using the following checklist before deciding to embark on a campaign to influence investors:[2]

- Is the company publicly listed? If it is private, it will not have investors that can be identified.
- Is its finance from mainstream institutions such as banks and pension funds, which might be influenced?
- Is the project (and the ore body) marginal on financial grounds?
- Is this the best option for influencing the project: are other avenues closed or difficult?
- What is the level and type of financial institution involved? Will they be responsive to a campaign?
- What are the synergies with other kinds of campaigning?
- Can the organization's resources be more effectively used elsewhere?

When undertaking any kind of investor campaigning, it is important for organizations to ensure that they are consistently accountable to the local communities they work with. There is always a risk of an NGO substituting its own agenda for the community's. The rule is "first, do no harm." Organizations must make sure that affected people retain the initiative, and maintain long-term engagement with the community and issue.

Finance strategies also pose serious risks for both the company and its opponents. They can result in SLAPP suits (strategic lawsuits against public participation) and severe political reactions. Our research must be 100 percent accurate and our communications carefully worded. Company lawyers will be reading what we publish.

Communities, Indigenous peoples, and NGOs are often strongest where financial institutions are most vulnerable. We may have "privileged local knowledge" about Indigenous communities' opposition to a mine, or the environmental setting or land ownership history, which are significant to a mine's ability to go ahead. The company's reputation is of major concern to investors. There are many examples of times when well-documented case studies have affected investors. This is where our power lies—in our specialized knowledge about mining impacts and about communities.

There are a number of ways to make points to investors powerfully. Where there is evidence of environmental damage, link it to corporate governance failures, a lack in the environmental impact statement, or a failure to cite material risk. Tell investors about protests that have been under-reported by the company, and about the instances where the company has bungled its handling of environmental, cultural, and social issues. Investors will be interested in damage done to a company's reputation by scandals affecting its directors and management, including conflict of interest. Show the ways in which the company's attempts to manage its reputation will backfire if it is not committed to really changing its behaviour.

As important as the research is our strategy for rolling it out and getting investors to pay attention. Communities will at least have to pay for posting it on a newswire that investors look at, and it will be worthwhile to try to find an expert in corporate communications to help.

FRAMING AN INVESTOR CAMPAIGN

A campaign to influence mining company investors proceeds roughly as follows:

1. Undertake basic research about the corporation: This will include finding information about its subsidiaries and other projects, its investors and its creditors by reading through its website, company presentations, and corporate filings on SEDAR (see chapter 8). What are its vulnerabilities?

2. Decide what you want to achieve: Do you want to stop mineral exploration on your lands? Do you want the government to buy out the claims? Are you negotiating an impact benefit agreement? Are you trying to prevent a major company from investing in an exploration project? Are you trying to get concessions from an existing mine? Win a strike? Are you worried that the financial assurance is not accurate?

3. Decide who can make decisions in your favour: Do you have the ability to influence these decision-makers? For example, regulators, investors, the company itself.
4. Work with your allies and local community to decide on a strategy to get what you need.

If the company responds to our campaign, it's because it wants or needs something from us. We need to ask: Are we in a legitimate political position, with sufficient technical expertise, to enter into discussions with a company or other stakeholders? To whom are we accountable and how?

Understanding Corporate Culture

If you are considering a campaign to influence investors, either those speculating on junior stocks or those looking at the development of a real mine, it is important to have an understanding of the corporate culture of mining companies—but, it is equally, or even more important, to understand the culture and psychology of the financial institutions you are seeking to influence. Corner House writes:

> Financial institutions do not have a single culture . . . Their modes of operation are local and evolving.[3]

> Their culture is different if they are a limited partnership set up to sell and promote flow-through shares, a chartered bank or an investment firm specializing in mining stocks. . . . Investors are motivated by greed and fear: any campaign has to feed these motivations.[4]

We need to clearly understand the audience for our information and analysis. Once financiers have pronounced on a company, they are not usually receptive to outsider opinions. Since the securities industry is overwhelmingly conservative, it is important for campaigners to appear professional and knowledgeable about their case. Approaches should be in the form of crisp briefing notes, not lengthy tracts. Analysts—who are deluged with mail every day—are, as Corner House says, "competitive and keen, have a short-term focus, and will distrust reports from campaigners, so it is necessary to use an independent analysis."[5]

Researching Ownership

A great deal of information about company ownership can be found through company websites, filings with securities commissions, and Google searches. Securities commission filings in Canada are all posted to an electronic registry known as SEDAR. The most fruitful documents to research on the SEDAR website are a company's annual information form, management information circular, financial reports (in particular the notes), management discussion and analysis, prospectus (if filed), share offerings, and technical reports (in the case of mining companies). The annual information form and information circular in particular provide a company history, a list of directors, and name any insider with shareholdings over 10 percent.

If the company is registered in the United States, it is required to file an annual Form 10-K (or equivalent), which is a public document, with the Securities and Exchange Commission (SEC). US disclosure rules generally require more disclosure than Canada's. To access SEC filings, visit www.sec.gov/edgar.

Finding the Shareholders

Shareholders of a corporation are permitted under most corporate statutes to request a shareholders list or to inspect the shareholders list if it is for a legitimate purpose (which is defined mainly in terms of what is best for the corporation and its shareholders as a whole). The *Canada Business Corporations Act* allows inspection of the list at the corporate head office or annual meeting. The BC *Corporations Act* requires companies to send the shareholders list to any person who wants it for a restricted set of purposes, most related to influencing shareholder decision-making.

However, there are three practical problems for those who want to access this information:

1. Most shares are now held in nominee form (e.g., CDS—the Canadian Depository for Securities—and broker accounts) so you will not get the beneficial holders' names.

2. The request must strictly comply with the requirements of the corporate statute (which sometimes requires a relatively high minimum shareholding).
3. There may be a financial cost.

Each jurisdiction has different rules about what has to be made available to the public. As an example, in Ontario, the only persons who are required to disclose their investment in an Ontario public company (any company listed on the TSX or TSXV) are insiders (directors, officers, and those who own over 10 percent or, in certain limited circumstances during a takeover bid, over 5 percent). The insider report that companies are required to file should disclose all shares, options, warrants, and any other security held. The Ontario *Securities Act* requires these reports to be updated within ten days of any change in their holdings. The system is electronic and can be found at www.sedi.ca (System for Electronic Disclosure by Insiders); it is maintained by the Ontario Securities Commission. The rules for disclosure are available on different securities commissions' websites.

The key mutual funds and other investors that own shares of the company may be found at Stockwatch.com and Targeted.com, but a subscription is required to view these sites. Targeted Inc., the Canadian Institutional Holders Database, provides the most complete comprehensive and timely business intelligence data on listed companies, portfolio managers, and global institutional and insider ownership of securities. The current database consists of Canadian institutional holdings of over forty thousand listed securities. It does not provide data for US holders.

The name and affiliations of the directors and officers of a public company (but not its private subsidiaries) will be found in the company's filings: the annual information returns and management information circulars. More information about their affiliations is likely to be in the Bloomberg executive profile database. Most jurisdictions now require political donations to be listed on an online database. The Northern Miner and other industry media (like Mining.com) are often good sources of information about key mining people and company history.

WHAT QUESTIONS DO INVESTORS ASK: A TEMPLATE FOR EVALUATING A MINE PROPOSAL

When investors are contemplating a large investment in a new mining project, they ask a number of questions about it and about the company that is proposing the project. The kinds of questions they ask will be determined by the kind of company and by the project's stage of exploration or operation.

These same questions can help a community or Indigenous government figure out what they need to know in negotiating with a mining company. It is the right of the community to seek answers to any and all of these questions.

When commodity prices are high, a lot of mining exploration is only a market play. The company is "mining investors" and not seriously interested in mining ore. It is looking to buy low and sell high, or to profit from flow-through shares. This part of the industry is dominated by "junior mining companies," which only do exploration. They are effectively spending machines and have no income except investor dollars and debt. An example of this kind of company is Hunter Dickinson Incorporated, described later in the chapter. Junior mining companies attract very risk-averse investors.

Even mining investors create problems for the communities and municipal and Indigenous governments that have to deal with them. It takes time to review applications and monitor their activities, which is taken from other work. A staking rush can cause serious and uncontrolled damage to the land (because even speculators have to show drill results to attract investors). Anxiety and hype create divisions in communities that are already fragile. In addition, the longer the project is tolerated, the more likely it is that the company will claim "an expropriation of its value" under some trade agreement or other pretext and sue (see chapter 8).

More damaging and long-term impacts on the land and water will come from serious mining exploration leading to development. Mining companies engaging in this activity need sustained investor interest and lots of money—often billions of dollars—to develop their projects. At the point where a project is moving from exploration to mine development, the company will start looking for a very different kind of investor—and investors will ask a very different set of questions. To sustain investor interest in a project that a company wants to develop, the company needs to demonstrate its feasibility to investors.

The following is a template that I developed to look at the questions that investors (and communities) need to explore before deciding to invest in a mine development.

1. Does the project have a credible ore body?
   a) Are drill results and estimates reliable? (grade, how the cut-off grade was set, how extensively the area was explored, recovery rates, dilution, waste rock to ore ratio.)
   b) What is the story of exploration on the deposit: Did a large mining company walk away from it in the past? Does a credible company have an option on the project?
   c) Do the results meet all securities commission criteria—are they resources or measured reserves? Was the "independent qualified person" who verified the estimates truly independent? Are there any problems with their previous work?
   d) If this is a polymetallic mine, what will be the relationship between product streams in terms of costs, smelters, etc.? (For example, if this is a zinc mine with lots of selenium, is there a market for selenium?)
   e) Does the ore contain considerable contaminants (e.g., arsenic, antimony, and mercury) that will result in serious smelter penalties or even refusals?

2. Does the company have access to the ore body and the land to develop it?
   a) Is there community and First Nations willingness to support the project and its supporting infrastructure? What is the company history of relationship with First Nations? With local communities and governments?
   b) Does the company have clarity of title to the mineral rights? Is there Indigenous title or claims on the land? (In older settled areas, the mineral rights may still belong to the surface rights holder and the government may not have the right to lease them to the mining company.)
   c) What are the significant spiritual and cultural uses of the area?

d) What are the geographic barriers to access? Are there difficulties that the company might face in terms of land for roads/rail, obtaining power for the project, etc.?

e) What are other political/legal barriers to access? (For example, planned protected areas or parks, a conflicting land use.)

3. Is the company management trustworthy?
   a) Who are the principals in the company and what is their history?
   b) What is the history of other projects the principals have been involved with?
   c) Who are the major investors and are they committed?
   d) Are their regulatory filings transparent, clearly reflecting all liabilities and risks?
   e) Have there been many management changes?
   f) What other projects is the company committed to? What, if any, impact could they have on this mining project?

4. Where will the project get its energy?
   a) How much power will the project require? What are its GHG emissions?
   b) What is the source of that power? How much will it cost? Are prices likely to remain affordable?
   c) Are there huge infrastructure costs to develop the power source? Who will pay?
   d) Will they need separate regulatory approvals?

5. What transportation issues could the project face?
   a) What are the plans for transportation infrastructure (rail, roads, port development, etc.)?
   b) Does the company expect government to pay a portion of these costs?
   c) Will it be transporting dangerous chemicals?
   d) Will it need separate regulatory approvals?
   e) Are prices realistic and affordable? Are they volatile?
   f) What are the potentials for costly accidents and disruptions (avalanches, earthquakes, hurricanes, flooding, etc.)?

6. What are water-related issues associated with the project?
   a) How much water does the company need? Where will it come from?

b) Is the water source reliable? Is it contested?

c) What (if anything) will it cost?

d) Will water be contaminated? How will the costs of treatment be covered?

e) What hydrological impacts will the project have? How will it affect groundwater/aquifers?

f) Will the project affect fish habitat? Aquatic ecosystems?

7. What are labour-related considerations for the project?

a) What are the company's labour needs: skilled and unskilled? At construction? Are the workers likely to already be employed elsewhere?

b) What are the likely health and safety issues?

c) Where will the labour supply come from? Is this realistic given other mining developments around the country?

d) What is Indigenous interest in the jobs/contracts? What about training, timing, etc.?

e) Where will workers from outside the area stay? Are the costs of transporting them properly estimated?

f) What is the labour history in the area (strikes, dissatisfaction, laws, etc.)?

8. How will markets affect the project?

a) Where will the ore be processed? Is there a need to transport ore to different smelters and refineries (e.g., zinc, copper, gold)?

b) Is the anticipated market price correct/likely to go up or down (FOB [freight on board] or "mine mouth," etc.)? What is the market price history for the commodity?

c) What competition can the company expect for its product? Nationally? Internationally?

d) What penalties will there be for contaminants?

e) Can the company get the product to market? (See transportation questions above.)

9. What are the issues related to regulatory approvals and permits?

a) What provincial and federal permits are required?

b) Is the project transboundary? What are the implications of this?

c) What are the requirements for closure and reclamation approvals and bonding?

d) Are there anticipated delays and blockages to getting permits? (For example, valued wilderness area; area of Indigenous heritage interest; competition with commercial fishery, hunters, etc.; endangered species; public opposition?)

e) Where are there areas of regulatory uncertainty: changes to federal or provincial legislation or governments, political uncertainty (e.g., Metal and Diamond Mining Effluent Regulation [MDMER])?

10. What are the issues related to unfunded liabilities?

a) What is the project's accident potential: earthquakes, avalanches, flood events, experimental technologies, etc.?

b) Are there adequate provisions for climate change impacts?

c) What kind of emergency plans do they have? Are they realistic?

d) What are the government closure and reclamation bonding requirements, including state of regulatory enforcement, political environment, long-term liability, and discount rates?

11. What issues are related to competitive rate of return?

a) Given the above, what is the reliability of the company's net present value (NPV) and internal rate of return (IRR) predictions?

b) What prices are the NPV and IRR based on? What is the discount rate used for the NPV? For the reclamation bond?

c) What is the rate of currency exchange/fluctuation used for the feasibility study?

d) How does the company expect to finance development?

AN EXAMPLE: UNDERSTANDING HUNTER DICKINSON INCORPORATED

As an example of how junior mining companies operate, let's look at Hunter Dickinson Incorporated (HDI). In 2017, MiningWatch Canada and I were asked by Musicians United for Bristol Bay to look at the company behind the Pebble Mine, a huge copper-gold mine proposal in Bristol Bay, Alaska. If it goes ahead, the mine is very likely to destroy one of the most profitable wild sockeye salmon fisheries in the world. At the time we were doing the research, HDI was trying to interest a large mining company in bankrolling the mine's development to the tune of billions of dollars. Our friends in Alaska wanted to know where the company's vulnerabilities lay.

Like so many of these projects, Pebble Mine is owned by a Canadian public company, Northern Dynasty Minerals, headquartered in Vancouver and registered on the TSX. We knew that Northern Dynasty was controlled by HDI and we had worked with communities facing their projects before. The final investor report can be found on the MiningWatch website.[6]

Since HDI was a private company, it was difficult to get information about it. However, it had been affiliated with over fifteen public companies in the past twenty-five years, and at least nineteen mine projects. I plowed through the corporate filings and websites of all these companies and read newspaper articles and corporate presentations. This is what I found.

Since the mid-1980s, HDI has set up public companies like Northern Dynasty to advance exploration projects, then installed and compensated its own directors and key management in these companies, and entered into contracts with its own companies to supply services to these public companies.

HDI companies then report to investors through consolidated financial statements, which means that any transfer pricing and other financial strategies (that may or may not exist) among the subsidiaries are not visible to investors. HDI, its directors, subsidiaries, and affiliates also make loans to these companies, and purchase shares, options, and warrants in each other.

Key management personnel and directors of many HDI companies overlap and are also employees of HDI or one of its subsidiaries. Robert Dickinson, Ronald Thiessen, and Russell Hallbauer, together with their families, own 50 percent or more of HDI.[7] HDI directors and managers are well remunerated for their involvement, even when the company involved is, in fact, producing little for shareholders, no revenues for governments,[8] and catastrophic challenges for the communities it affects.

HDI hypes a successful track record for all its affiliated companies, bragging about the "shareholder value" created. Our research found that this was not really the case. Among our findings was the following information.

HDI is currently associated with only one operating mine: the Gibraltar Mine near Williams Lake, British Columbia, a huge marginal porphyry copper-molybdenum mine operated by Taseko Mines Limited.[9] It was purchased from Boliden in 2001 and reopened in 2004 with substantial government support; it continues to operate, although burdened with debt, with an underfunded reclamation bond and ongoing government help.[10]

Any other mines HDI affiliates have attempted to operate have not succeeded in the long run. In South Africa, the Bokoni Mine, Tirisano Mine, Rockwell Diamonds alluvial mines, and Burnstone Mine were all eventually bankrupt, leaving creditors responsible.[11] The Campo Morado Mine in Mexico was closed and the Hollister Mine in Nevada also went bankrupt.[12] When Great Basin Gold went bankrupt in 2013 (the affiliated company that owned the Hollister and Burnstone mines), Credit Suisse sued for fraud, saying that the resource estimate had been misrepresented. The case was settled out of court.

Of the nineteen mine projects we examined for which HDI claims affiliation and success, five current projects are being fought—and will continue to be fought— ferociously by the communities affected: the Ike mining exploration project in British Columbia, the Sisson tungsten mine in New Brunswick, Florence Copper in-situ leach copper mine in Arizona, the Pebble Mine, and the New Prosperity Mine on Tŝilhqot'in land in British Columbia (see chapter 11).[13] An advanced exploration project in Tibet owned by subsidiary Continental Gold from 2004 to 2011 was opposed by local villagers and monks and by the Free Tibet Committee; it was sold for $447 million to a Chinese company.[14]

Of HDI projects underway in 2018, four appeared to be uneconomic at current commodity prices (Sisson, Ni-Black in Alaska, Olza in Poland, and Ike).[15]

The Pebble Mine has not yet produced a feasibility study and major company Anglo American walked away after spending $595 million (USD) on the feasibility study. The project was also abandoned by Rio Tinto, and earlier by Mitsubishi. After our report was published, First Quantum Minerals also decided not to invest.[16]

There are large underfunded liabilities for potential catastrophic failures of tailings technology at Taseko's Gibraltar Mine and Florence Copper.[17]

In four other instances, the company that bought the HDI project took serious losses on it a few years after its purchase (Golden Bear and Mt. Milligan in British Columbia, Bokoni, and Campo Morado).[18]

The accumulated ratio of corporate earnings to deficit of HDI-affiliated companies was concerning. Even for a junior mining company built on negative earnings, HDI-affiliated firms had taken on extraordinary accumulated losses. Most of that loss was attributable to Northern Dynasty. When we did our report, the Northern Dynasty deficit at the end of the third quarter of 2017 was $459 million, leaving total equity at $144 million with over 304 million shares issued.[19]

As this book goes to print, no major company has invested in the Pebble Mine, and the sockeye are still safe.

20

SCALING UP: WORK TO CHANGE LAW, REGULATION, AND POLICY

In all the community struggles discussed throughout this book, people organizing with their neighbours on the ground needed to address structural issues created by our governments and industry lobbyists. To make changes to law, regulation, and policy, they needed to go beyond their community and involve many more organizations and individuals. Even if they did not make the sweeping changes they wanted, their efforts often resulted in protecting their own communities and bringing public attention to the bigger issues with mining.

This chapter pulls together the lessons learned from trying to scale up from community struggles to work changing law and regulation at the provincial or federal level. It starts by looking at how MiningWatch Canada came to be and then recounts a frustrating story of "bureaucratic management"—a twenty-year-long low-intensity conflict to try to force the federal government to hold Canadian mining companies accountable for their international crimes.

MININGWATCH CANADA

Three different mining confrontations came together to create Mining-Watch Canada in April 1999.

The first was a battle in the early 1990s to stop the Windy Craggy Mine in the St. Elias Mountains of northern British Columbia. Geddes Resources had the claims at Windy Craggy, a copper-gold project on the wild Tatshenshini River on the BC–Alaska border; the largest earthquake in North America occurred just north of the river's mouth in 1899. Ric Careless describes it as "one of the most dangerous mining projects ever proposed in North America."[1] It was fiercely opposed by environmentalists in both Canada and the United States. To help them in this battle, the environmentalists hired Alan Young to organize the Environmental Mining Council of British Columbia (EMCBC), which Alan did, very well.[2]

In the mid-1990s, environmental groups in Canada such as Northwatch, the Yukon Conservation Society, the Canadian Environmental Law Association, the Canadian Parks and Wilderness Society, and the Canadian Nature Federation had been trying to deal with many different kinds of mining impacts. Although each organization was accumulating experience and strategic knowledge, they needed a place to share it, and they had organized a mining caucus within the Canadian Environmental Network.

The EMCBC was the first mining-specific watchdog in Canada, and Alan became the only paid mining activist in the country. Inundated by pleas for help from communities and organizations all over the country, EMCBC undertook literature reviews and research on an urgent basis to explain to the general public the need to deal with mining-related issues: acid mine drainage, abandoned mines, free entry, and inadequate regulation. Industry and its government allies also took notice and wanted to "consult" Alan at every opportunity. He was exhausted.

The second confrontation was the battle of the Innu Nation to deal with the proposed Voisey's Bay Mine in Labrador. In 1993, prospectors looking for diamonds instead found a huge nickel deposit on Innu and Inuit territory. The deposit was quickly bought up by Diamond Fields Resources; the company touted it as "one of the greatest deposits of nickel in the world." In 1995, Diamond Fields sold the deposit to Inco,

Sudbury's mining giant, for $4.3 billion.[3] However, neither company had paid any attention to the Innu or Inuit, who said that the companies had no rights to stake claims or explore on their land. The two Indigenous peoples mounted a sophisticated and committed campaign to stop the mine, and when they were unable to do that, to try to keep its environmental and social impacts under control, and to get everything they could from it. The first public activity that the fledgling MiningWatch undertook was organizing a consultation with Indigenous people in Canada on behalf of the Innu Nation.

The third stream came from some development-focused NGOs— Inter Pares and the Primate's World Relief and Development Fund of the Anglican Church—that had long-time community-based partners in Ghana, Nicaragua, and the Philippines. In the latter country in 1996, the collapse of the drainage tunnel in the Taipan open pit, owned by Canadian mining company Placer Dome, destroyed the Boac River, killed two children, and displaced many villagers. In Africa, Third World Network was pushing its Canadian partners to take on the mining industry and change mining laws. The NGOs realized that they had to ramp up their work on international mining issues and "do something" about these companies in Canada.

In 1997, the regular meeting of the Asia-Pacific Environmental Cooperation summit was held in Vancouver. Some international NGOs were involved in organizing a "people's summit" to take place at the same time and decided that—given the urgency of the mining issues—it should include a mining caucus.[4] A secretariat was established, housed at Rights and Democracy, an NGO in Montreal.

A call went out through the Canadian Environmental Network and the Canadian Council for International Co-operation for people and groups who were interested to participate in the mining caucus.[5] From that caucus, goals were agreed on and a group was selected to work on a "national environmental mining strategy."

A number of people who had been dealing with mining issues in their communities and regions were key to the strategy: Jamie Kneen, who had been working for the Inuit Tapirisat of Canada and had also worked for the Dene who were trying to challenge uranium mining in Saskatchewan; Kevin O'Reilly from Yellowknife, who had serious concerns about the Giant Mine; Brennain Lloyd of Northwatch in northern Ontario, where mining at all stages was a huge issue; Sue Moodie, a toxicologist in Whitehorse with the Yukon Conservation Society; Ken Traynor from the Canadian Environmental Law Association; as well as representatives from Inter Pares.[6] Two labour-sponsored funds were represented (the Steelworkers Humanity Fund and the Canadian Auto Workers Social Justice Fund), two national environmental organizations (the Canadian Nature Federation and the Canadian Parks and Wilderness Society) and the ecumenical church group that became Kairos.[7] This was a diverse, committed, and knowledgeable group.

It took two years for this group to find the resources to set up a national mining watchdog organization. In April 1999, MiningWatch Canada was launched, with one full-time staff person (me) and two half-time, Jamie Kneen and Catherine Coumans. The board of directors that was established included many of the founders, but it was decided that directors would sit as individuals, not as organizational representatives, in order to avoid coalition gridlock. The tiny staff worked as a collective.

During the early years of MiningWatch Canada, we held two conferences. The first, only five months after we opened, was the Innu Nation consultation to share what they had learned to that point from their experience with Voisey's Bay. Called "Between a Rock and a Hard Place," the conference enabled Indigenous peoples to share the issues facing their communities in Canada.[8] Many of the people who attended (including the Innu) were willing to have mining on their lands, and some already did. Others were adamantly opposed. They told us this was the first time they had been able to meet with each other without government or mining company representatives present.

The second, less than a year later, was a consultation with representatives of communities affected by Canadian mining around the world, and a few Indigenous communities in Canada.[9]

In both cases, we asked the participants what they thought the new MiningWatch should be doing. Since at least 60 percent of mining in Canada was taking place on lands that were still in Indigenous control, we felt we needed their direction and permission before we could really go forward.

The findings of the two conferences were remarkably similar. The communities insisted on being in control of any solidarity work. They wanted us to provide research on mining companies and how the industry worked and where its vulnerabilities lay. They wanted us to help get the story of their struggle out to the world in a way that built support for their cause. They wanted us to change Canadian laws to get companies under control and to protect the lands, waters, and people where their mines were.

What we learned from them was that leadership for a vision of real change would come from the Global South, from the Indigenous peoples who were taking responsibility for the protection of their traditional lands and resisting the predations of Canadian mining companies with creativity and courage.

After these conferences, it was agreed by MiningWatch directors and staff that, as most mining in Canada was taking place on Indigenous lands, at least 50 percent of the board should be Indigenous, and at least 50 percent should be women. There were co-chairs, and at least one had to be Indigenous. This decision has helped to make Mining-Watch's work relevant and respected across the country and the world. The board members are, or have been, engaged in mining battles on the ground, or in providing support to communities that are.

In our early days, we learned a lot from a number of other experienced mining watchdogs in other countries, such as Mines and Communities, the Australian Mineral Policy Institute, the African Initiative on Mining, Environment and Society, JATAM, CooperAcción, and Project Underground.

One of the things MiningWatch did, because it was so small, was to always work in coalition with our member organizations and with others to get NGOs, academics, and labour groups to take up mining issues. This meant putting in the work and "paying our dues" with other groups. It worked. There are now a number of academic initiatives that focus on mining communities and the kind of research they need. Other NGOs, like Amnesty International and Development and Peace, began to focus on supporting mining communities and addressing mining issues. Now there are substantially more research and educational materials out there than before.

In 2008, the Coalition pour que le Québec ait meilleure mine was established to carry out similar work in Quebec.[10] Ugo Lapointe is the spokesperson for this successful coalition as well as the Canada program coordinator for MiningWatch Canada.

We have also been part of a network of mining-affected communities in the United States and Canada, the Western Mining Action Network (WMAN), since its inception, within which we can share information and analysis about mining struggles across North America. Every two years WMAN holds a gathering of these grassroots members to share stories and learnings from our work.

Bureaucratic Management: The Canadian Way

In Canada, anyone trying to change law, regulation, and policy is faced with *bureaucratic management*, the tedious and seemingly never-ending process of government meetings, consultations, studies, reports, and intimidation that can go on for years. It wears everyone down, and slowly erodes the vision they are fighting for. It can reduce a community's demands to "acceptable asks."

These processes use the skills of highly educated people and leave those who cannot read legalese behind. They are deliberately structured by government and industry to use up organizers' and activists' valuable time, finances, and energy, and to divert them from on-the-ground organizing needed to build power. An illustration of how this works can be found in the fight to hold Canadian companies operating internationally accountable for their predatory behaviour.

Since its founding in 1999, MiningWatch Canada and other groups have advocated for action to hold Canadian mining companies accountable in law, instead of having the companies police themselves through voluntary measures like corporate social responsibility (CSR) (see chapter 11). Time after time, MiningWatch and our partners brought community representatives from the Philippines, Latin America, Ghana, and other places to Canada to tell their stories and make the public and the federal government aware of what Canadian companies were doing overseas. Hearings were held before the Standing Committee on Foreign Affairs. Workshops with churches, NGOs, and solidarity groups were organized. Politicians and senior bureaucrats were lobbied. Petitions were signed. Finally, in June 2005, the Standing Committee on Foreign Affairs passed a unanimous resolution asking Parliament to support programs to enhance the corporate responsibility of Canadian mining companies operating internationally with clear legal norms.

Open for Justice rally on Parliament Hill, May 2014, where protestors called on the Canadian government to hold mining companies accountable for their international activities. Photo courtesy of Jamie Kneen.

It took months before the government responded. It established four government-sponsored forums—the Roundtables on Corporate Responsibility and the Extractives Sector in Developing Countries—with industry and civil society to review the Standing Committee report and make recommendations. The forums required a huge investment of time and resources from all of us, but we felt we had no choice but to participate. Again, Canadian NGOs brought partners from the Global South to testify; hours were spent poring over, debating, and negotiating position papers.

It appeared that the mining industry agreed with the activists on at least some of the demands and a joint roundtables report from the industry and civil society participants was submitted to government in March 2007. It called for a code of conduct for Canadian companies operating internationally, an ombudsperson to hear complaints, and tying public support of the extractives sector (like Export Development Canada dollars) to good corporate behaviour. The report called on the government to stop using taxpayer dollars to support destructive Canadian mining projects abroad. It argued that Canadian mining companies should be legally accountable for environmental and human rights violations in other countries.

This was much less than the demands that the London Declaration had formulated (see chapter 18), but the Canadian groups felt it was all they could ask for.

Starting in 2006, Development and Peace, Kairos, and some other church-based groups made holding Canadian companies accountable a focus of their work, educating, signing petitions, and participating in lobbying and demonstrations. By 2008, almost 500,000 postcards demanding that the government accept the roundtable recommendations had been sent to the federal government.[11]

After the Conservatives were elected in 2006, the industry enjoyed more impunity. In 2009—two years after the roundtables process produced their consensus report—the Harper government released a policy report. *Building the Canadian Advantage: A Corporate Social Responsibility Strategy for the Canadian International Extractive Sector* laid out the corporate agenda, ignored the roundtable recommendations, and reaffirmed weak voluntary measures while calling for more resources to promote mining companies' CSR programs. The report went so far as to suggest that Canada needed to help other countries enhance their capacities to "manage the development of minerals and oil and gas."[12]

Building the Canadian Advantage enabled our foreign relations institutions to support unaccountable mining abroad. International aid funding was cut from human rights advocacy groups in mining-affected communities and diverted to development NGOs willing to partner with mining companies. Some NGOs like Save the Children and World Vision took the bait and accepted money from the mining companies.

The facilitator of this velvet-gloved attack was a new NGO called the Devonshire Initiative,[13] founded the very same month that the roundtables process first published their consensus report. Made up of mining companies and some development NGOs, it was seen as a "parallel institution" to undermine the work of the roundtables process.

In February 2009, John McKay, a Liberal MP, introduced Bill C-300, the *Corporate Accountability of Mining, Oil, and Gas Corporations in Developing Countries Act*.[14] The campaign to hold mining companies accountable rallied to support the bill and there was a massive outcry across the country. When it came to the floor of the House of Commons in November 2010, it failed to pass in a close vote, 140 to 134. All of the Conservatives voted against it. Fourteen Liberals and four NDP members did not attend when the vote on this private member's bill was taken. The four NDP members were from mining ridings.

Industry was greatly relieved. The *Canadian Mining Journal* wrote,

> A weight was lifted from the shoulders of many in the Canadian mining industry recently when Bill C-300 was defeated in the House of Commons. . . . Most importantly, the implementation of Bill C-300 would negatively impact Canada's competitiveness as a world leader in mining. No other country is contemplating legislating activities of its domestic mining industry in such a manner, and the enactment of Bill C-300 would have created a strong incentive for Canadian companies operating in the developing world to relocate outside Canada or avoid financing and investment from EDC [Export Development Canada] and CPP [Canada Pension Plan]. Since the credit crisis, export credit agencies such as EDC have been important sources of financing and capital for Canadian mining companies operating in the developing world.[15]

Before the vote on Bill C-300, in an attempt to make the demands to hold the industry accountable go away, the government of Canada created the Office of the Extractive Sector Corporate Social Responsibility Counsellor, who was charged with advancing CSR performance of Canadian mining companies. The post was given to industry insider Marketa Evans, the founding executive director of the Devonshire Initiative.[16] A voluntary dispute resolution process was adopted in which the office would act as "an impartial advisor and facilitator" to bring parties together for the purposes of "fostering dialogue and problem-solving."

The office was an abject failure. According to a Justice and Corporate Accountability Project (JCAP) report written in 2016,[17]

> The CSR Counsellor was established in 2009 with no power to investigate, no power to require meetings, and no power to report. Parties could voluntarily participate in mediation.

However, no mediations have taken place: three that were initiated were ultimately terminated when the companies withdrew. In 2014, the government of Canada supplemented the policy by saying that companies that ignore CSR best practices, and that fail to participate in a voluntary resolution process, may lose the support of the Canadian embassy and funding from Export Development Canada. Two years after the introduction of the new policy, the website of the CSR Counsellor does not show much activity. As of October 2016, there is no annual report and the only "publications" listed on the web pages are news reports of six speeches given by the current CSR Counsellor. The website does not disclose a single case taken on by the office of the CSR Counsellor since 2013. In fact, the CSR Counsellor has not even developed a process for withdrawing support or withdrawing funding. If sanctions are the destination, the government has not built a path to get there.

During a keynote address at the Devonshire Initiative CEO Summit in 2011, then minister of International Co-operation Bev Oda announced a $26.7 million contribution by the Canadian International Development Agency (CIDA) to four new CSR projects at Canadian mines around the world.[18]

Advocacy continued, with most lobbying taking place through the Canadian Network on Corporate Accountability's Open for Justice campaign, which was mostly led by staffed NGOs, not by grassroots members. The energy had gone out of the grassroots movement in Canada. The "ask" was reduced to an ombudsperson.

In Latin America, Africa, and the Pacific, communities continued their mine-by-mine fights and national organizing often with some success. State and corporate violence and criminalization against water and land protectors increased. Despite the nice words in Canada, things were definitely getting worse for people on the ground, even as some mine-by-mine fights were won.

In January 2018, after years of lobbying and mobilizations by human rights and environmental NGOs, the government announced

the creation of an independent Canadian Ombudsperson for Responsible Enterprise (CORE), the first of its kind in the world. The CORE will be mandated to investigate allegations of human rights abuses linked to Canadian corporate activity abroad. The CORE will seek to assist wherever possible in collaboratively resolving disputes or conflicts between impacted communities and Canadian companies. It will be empowered to independently investigate, report, recommend remedy and monitor its implementation.[19]

The ombudsperson *still* has no authority to enforce any of its recommendations. Such tiny steps for almost twenty years of work. In fact, more than a year after creating the position, the government had not yet appointed anyone to fill it.

Says Jen Moore, the former Latin American coordinator of Mining-Watch Canada,

The recent decision by the federal government to have an ombudsperson risks doing more to bolster government and company public relations, while communities and their partners will still have to fight with everything they have to get any recommendations implemented.[20]

What we cannot know is what would have happened had all this organizing work *not* taken place. Trying to change law, regulation, and policy when we are pushing against an industry lobby that is so much better resourced than we are is like Sisyphus and the proverbial rock. The story shared here is replicated in almost every policy battle Mining-Watch has engaged in, from amendments to the *Environmental Assessment* and *Fisheries Acts* at the federal level to mining regulations in the provinces.

For me, our experience raises more questions than it provides answers for organizations working in solidarity with mining-affected communities: How might we resist getting caught in the bureaucratic management wheel, and have more control over the process? How can organizations like MiningWatch best use their scarce resources? How do we reconcile the demands from communities that want us to rein in Canadian mining companies, with demands from movements—like that in El Salvador—to stop all large-scale mining? Should we resist reducing the "ask" and instead make the demands of our government more profound and inspiring?

These are key strategic questions not only for international solidarity work, but also for our work in Canada supporting mining affected communities.

Movements are made up of many different organizations and, by their nature, struggle on different levels and in different ways. At least some of the organizations in the movement need to engage with governments on regulation and face the power of the industry lobby. But we can do nothing without a sustained, audible outcry from communities and people on the ground. We can do nothing without a movement.

21

CREATING A NEW STORY: PUTTING MINING IN ITS PLACE

Throughout this book you have heard about all the different ways people are fighting back to limit the impacts of the mining industry. The battles include work at the community level, challenges to investors, and efforts to change law, regulation, and policy at all levels of government (including Indigenous). You have a pretty good idea of how mining works, and the extent of the industry's power and how that power is maintained and extended. It is easy to be overwhelmed.

But you have also seen the industry's vulnerabilities. The places where community resistance has stopped unwelcome mines from being built; a country that banned mining altogether; communities that have been able to force the government to invest over $1 billion in cleaning up an abandoned mine site; court cases to hold the activities of Canadian companies operating internationally accountable; and places where investors have refused to put money into dangerous mines. You have seen how the huge industry lobby has had to mobilize to counter our efforts and to keep control of the discourse about minerals and metals. We are more powerful than we think we are, and the industry knows it.

This chapter looks at alternatives to our dependency on the mining industry and at the sources of our power to change it.

A NEW MINERAL STRATEGY

Throughout Canada, if you are called "anti-mining" or "anti-development," anything else you have to say about the industry is immediately discounted by governments. *Sustainable mining, responsible minerals industry*, and *green mining* are terms that have been captured by mining companies and their associations. Generally, their first concern is to ensure that the mining regime as they know it is sustained. The industry controls the discourse; we need to reclaim it.

In the spring of 2015, the province of Ontario released a draft new Mineral Development Strategy and asked the public to comment on it. The entire document was written from the perspective of mining companies and the businesses that depend upon them.

In the few years prior to its release, there were sustained protests across the country about the overwhelming power of the mining industry to trump treaty obligations to First Nations, the protection of water and land, non-extractive forms of economic development, and the ability of communities to determine their own future.

Ontario's Mineral Development Strategy was all about increasing mining industry profits, expanding mineral investment in the province, increasing government investment in research and development, ensuring that regulations were "efficient and cost-effective," and developing northern infrastructure (especially transportation) and subsidizing electrical rates. At the same time, it bragged about new tax cuts of almost $20 billion to benefit business in Ontario. It talked about how it would ensure more Indigenous people could get jobs and contracts from the mining industry. It talked about "green mining," or providing metals for new "green" technologies. It said nothing about free prior informed consent. There was not a single mention of recycling, conservation, or reuse of metals.

A few of us got mad. We got together and organized Ontarians for a Just Accountable Mineral Strategy. This is what we said:

> We want to see a world where there is respect for the awesome cost of the minerals, gems and metals we take for granted. We

all want stable economies that heal the environment and do not pollute the waters, land and air. We want long-term work for their children and their grandchildren. We want livelihoods that sustain the planet and communities. We want to put mining in its place.

We can no longer think that more mining can build a decent future for our grandchildren. It is a short-term, waste management industry with long-term consequences. It is not sustainable; it depletes the very resources upon which it depends. We need to reduce our consumption of metals, conserve, reuse and recycle them. We do not need more gold, silver, uranium, coal or diamonds. Only as a last resort, should we contemplate new mines. And those mines should be created in the most cautious way possible.[1]

HOW WE CAN PUT MINING IN ITS PLACE

A movement to put mining in its place has many different targets and campaigns. Our power is that of the blackfly. Alone we may be squashed, but in large numbers we can drive mining companies out of the forest.

In the following section, I summarize the key levers we have to transform the minerals industry: forcing companies to internalize the full costs of mining and withholding government subsidies and tax incentives, preventing companies from accessing the deposit or the infrastructure (water, power, roads, ports) for a new mine or for expansion, creating "no-go" zones for mines, withholding the labour companies need to operate, making it impossible for companies to get the financing they need, regulating and enforcing best practices, and holding mining company owners responsible for the damage their companies do.

Internalize the Full Costs

The secret to putting mining in its place is to find ways to make those who really benefit from the extraction of metals and gems—the major shareholders and management of mining companies—pay the full costs of what they do, costs that have been described in detail in this book. Forcing companies to internalize even some of their costs will make most mines uneconomic.

A mine will not be built and cannot continue if it turns out that the ore body itself does not have enough of the desired metals, the price of the metals is too low, or the cost of extracting them at that location is too high to justify the mine; if government does not subsidize the mine through infrastructure, tax incentives, direct subsidies, training, and inadequate closure and perpetual care financial insurance, political risk insurance, and export credits; or if communities and Indigenous peoples demand fair reparations for damages.

Perhaps the most important cost to internalize is that of insurance against catastrophic failures, reclamation, and perpetual care of the site. Companies should post up front full bonding in realizable securities with governments before any mining can take place. To the extent that these costs are adequately predicted, this would effectively stop mines that cannot bear the environmental costs of their operations and would ensure that the polluter pays. Note the cautions in chapter 13 about the use of discount rates by mining companies to reduce the amount paid up front.

Taxation is possibly the government's most important policy tool. Statistics Canada and the Department of Finance should facilitate an ecological analysis of tax measures for the mineral industry. Strategic environmental assessment and "value for money" audits could enable informed and ecologically sound decision-making. Not renewing the "flow-through share" programs would go a long way to reducing the speculative nature of mining investment in exploration. For similar reasons, provisions for the pooling and transfer of Cumulative Canadian Exploration and Development Expenses (CCEE and CCDE) should be withdrawn.

Restrict Access to Land

A mine will not be built and cannot continue to expand if the company cannot get access to the deposit either for physical reasons (lack of water, power, transportation routes, etc.), or because those who control the land (or water) will not let them have it. Indigenous peoples and communities need free prior informed consent before a mine goes ahead or expands. If a company doesn't have a "social licence" or government permits and community resistance is strong, a new mine will be unable to go ahead and an existing mine unable to expand.

Demanding "no-go" zones for mining exploration and development in critical watersheds, habitats, and cultural sites would be helpful. In Nova Scotia, when the province issued a request for proposals for gold mineral exploration on a seventy-thousand-hectare area, Sustainable Northern Nova Scotia responded with its own sustainable development plan for the area and said "no" to mining.

Encourage the Agency of Industry Workers

All corporations are made up of human labour and mining companies are no exception. If the employees in a company or the government departments that support the company refuse to do work that goes against their moral fibre, the company will be unable to function. The employees could be in investment houses, banks, and offices, as well as at mine sites and in transportation services. Mining companies are having increasing difficulty finding people to work for them and they predict huge labour shortages in the future. If mining industry employees have whistle-blower protection and some job protection through a union, they could be our biggest allies in the fight for truly responsible mining. However, we need to help them understand the externalized costs of the industry, and support their right to safe, well-paid work and to "just transition" strategies when the industry shrinks. In Alberta, an association of energy workers called Iron and Earth does just that.[2]

Research and Tell Investors the Truth

A mine cannot go ahead or expand if the company cannot raise the money it needs. Investor campaigns and complaints to securities regulators can have a significant effect.

We need changes to international financial accounting rules that require companies to disclose potential liabilities for environmental damage, catastrophic accidents, and perpetual care, or for restitution that may be due to First Nations or landowners. In a 2004 report written for the Yale School of Forestry and Environmental Studies, Robert Repetto investigated the adequacy of Canadian and US mining companies' disclosures of material environmental information. Disclosures were found to be deficient, especially those made to investors of known material environmental risks and liabilities. Community resistance and Repetto's work fueled demands for stricter enforcement by securities regulators of existing environmental disclosure requirements and better compliance by publicly listed companies with current environmental disclosure rules.[3] Recent massive tailings dam failures at Vale operations in Brazil have brought public attention to the issue.

Insist on the Regulation and Enforcement of Best Practices

Laws and regulation must be written and enforced so that they truly protect the lands, waters, and air before they consider the mining industry's need for "efficient and streamlined processes." We need to remember that the rules we do have—even though they are limited and poorly enforced—have been won through the advocacy of people like us. Companies will argue that they cannot afford to follow them. Sometimes the only victory is keeping those rules in place. Occasionally governments change and we can make some headway if our movement is strong enough. We need to continue to push to get best practices in legislation and expose corrupt practices.

There are a few "responsible mining" frameworks that do set out best practices for the entire mining sequence, for relationships with Indigenous peoples and communities, and for returns to governments. The Fair Mining Collaborative in British Columbia has published two documents available online: *Fair Mining Practices: A New Mining Code for British Columbia* by Maya Stano and Emma Lehrer (March 2013) and *The Mine Medicine Manual: A Community Resource* by Glenn M. Grande (2015).[4]

Another resource is the Framework for Responsible Mining, which is being developed by the Initiative for Responsible Mining Assurance (IRMA) in a prolonged consultation with a variety of mostly North American players. IRMA is an alliance of mining companies; jewellery and electronics producers and other downstream users of mining products; some environmental and human rights non-profits/NGOs; some organizations representing affected communities; and labour unions. For more than a decade, IRMA has been working on this detailed framework of best practices. The published drafts of the work-in-progress are available online.[5]

Hold Directors and Officers of Companies Accountable

Current corporate legislation enables the people who actually make decisions and profit from mining companies to "hide behind the corporate veil." The legal fiction that a company (and its subsidiaries) exists separate from these persons is a serious problem. There need to be changes to laws to create personal civil and criminal liability for directors and officers for the actions of the corporation for which they are individually and—in some circumstances—collectively responsible. An example of such a change is the Westray Bill described in chapter 6. This amendment to the Criminal Code expanded the duty of care in occupational health and safety to directors, officers, and anyone associated with directing the work of others, and made them liable to criminal prosecution.

Another place to look to hold directors personally responsible for the full costs of mining is in the bankruptcy process, described in chapter 8. Many mining projects at both the exploration and operating stages end in bankruptcy, leaving contaminated land and waters behind with inadequate financial assurance. The short- and long-term containment and remediation costs fall to governments. The case law is clear that mining company directors can be held personally accountable for these costs, and they should be.

AFFECTING CANADIAN COMPANIES OPERATING INTERNATIONALLY

As we saw in chapter 13, the Canadian government provides many incentives that enable mining's predatory role in other countries. The remedies to this situation are also outlined in that chapter. To summarize, Canada should not be party to trade and investment agreements that make governments subservient to corporate interests. We must continue to pay attention to Canada's tax policies. The work to stop promoting mining interests through Canadian embassies must continue and the work to hold companies accountable in Canada for their misdeeds abroad—although frustrating—must also continue.

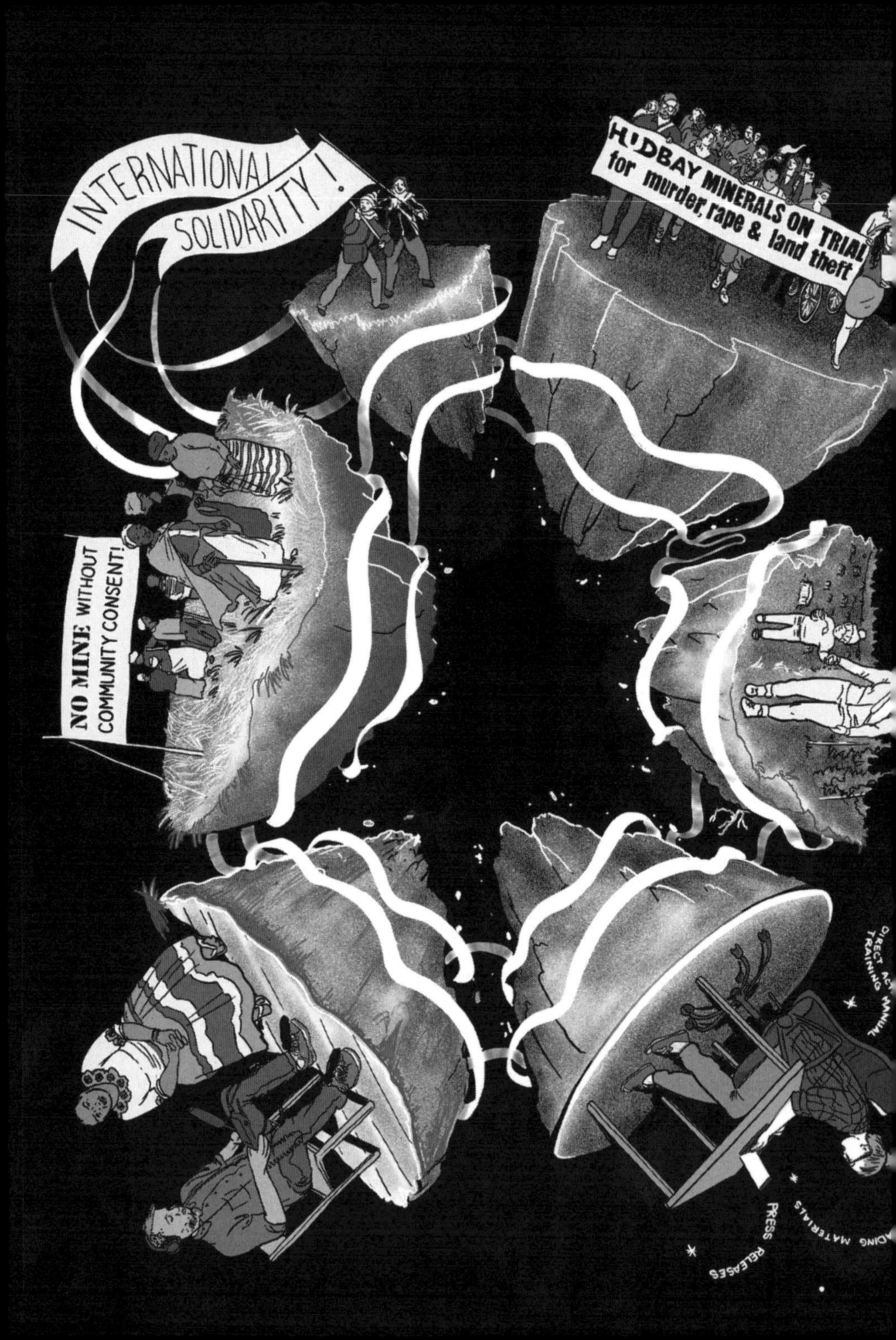
INTERNATIONAL SOLIDARITY!
HUDBAY MINERALS ON TRIAL for murder, rape & land theft
NO MINE WITHOUT COMMUNITY CONSENT!
PRESS RELEASES

BUILDING THE ALTERNATIVE

The alternative to a mining-centric economy recognizes that although we depend on metals and minerals, we must always ask what the real need and purpose of a mining project is, who bears its risks, and who reaps its benefits.

From 2000 to 2002, the International Institute for Environment and Development housed a project driven by the world's biggest mining companies to address the difficulties the mining industry was having getting access to ore deposits and a "social licence." The North American division report stated:

> If there is a fundamental question underneath all others, it is the question of whether society—or the world—"needs" any given project or operation.... The question arises because of growing concern that current human activity is undermining the capacity of future generations to meet its needs. This concern is a central driver of the sustainability/sustainable development set of concepts and the issue is very simple: why do something that is undermining the capacity of future generations?[6]

A new story about minerals means that we put the preservation of land and water and the health of future generations, the rights of Indigenous peoples and traditional landholders, food, shelter, and community before the need to extract more minerals and gems. We phase out mining gold, diamonds, coal, or uranium. We turn to solutions already found in the social economy movement to figure out how to live.[7] This new story promotes metals conservation and recycling (as described in chapter 10), helps employees move from the extraction economy to a sustainable one, and finds ways to heal the earth, waters, and cultures we have already damaged.

We are doing this through a global movement anchored in the struggles of thousands of communities facing the greed of mining companies here and abroad.

I end with the inspiring story of the defeat of the Raven Coal Mine.

THE RAVEN COAL MINE[8]

From 2011 to 2014, I worked with some brave folks on Vancouver Island who were trying to stop the proposed Raven Coal Mine.

In 2009, Compliance Energy announced a plan for a coal mine in the mountains above Fanny Bay. The mine itself would be in the territory of the K'ómoks First Nation and the Pentlatch people, part of the Coast Salish Nation. They had already had their lives turned upside down by "King Coal" as the mines near Cumberland were developed after 1850 and they were dispossessed and died of disease. They were negotiating with the federal government for the lands between the proposed Compliance Energy mine site and the sea. Many of their members were seafood growers with significant agricultural interests. In central Vancouver Island and in Barclay Sound, the lands and waters of the Hupacasath and the Tseshaht—members of the Nuu-chah-nulth Nation—would face mining impacts from the roads, port, and shipping.

The coal was going to be trucked to a new coal port at Port Alberni on a twisting two-lane highway that was the only link in the middle of the island between a corridor of busy cities: Nanaimo, Comox, and Courtenay on the eastern side of the island and Port Alberni, Ucluelet, and Tofino on the West. This is also one of the most popular tourist areas in British Columbia.

The Comox Valley, Barclay Sound, and Baynes Sound were already home to a thriving shellfish aquaculture industry, sports fishery, arts community, tourist industry, specialty food processors, wineries and distillers, artisan cheese producers, specialty meats and game producers, and organic fresh produce growers and farm markets.[9] One study estimated the annual value of agri-food production and processing (including shellfish aquaculture) in the Comox Valley alone at almost $61 million.[10] Years of consultations following the collapse of the forestry industry in the area had led to a vision for the Comox Valley as a "New Provence." Similar work had been done for Barclay Sound and Port Alberni on the west side of the Island. The Raven project was likely to put the clean air and water on which these visions depended at risk through its effluents, dust generation, subsidence under creeks and rivers, increased traffic on the roads, and accidents.

Compliance Energy promised that the mine would provide 200 construction jobs for one to two years and 325 mining, port, and transportation jobs for sixteen years with an average salary (with benefits) of $100,000. Compliance said it would contribute $1.1 billion (in GDP) to the local economy over the life of the mine. The company also asserted that new coal mines were desperately needed, a very questionable assumption given global warming.

A more stupid project is difficult to imagine. Very few would benefit from it—few who would gain from the mine live in the affected area— and many would lose a great deal.

From 2009, the people organized and CoalWatch was formed. As early as June 2011, the K'ómoks First Nations declared their opposition to the mine. From 2009 to 2015, the people lived and breathed the Raven Coal Mine. Led almost entirely by people like John Snyder, who had retired to this gorgeous place expecting to relax, CoalWatch leadership worked tirelessly to contact other community leaders, organizations, and experts, to promote a different story about how this part of Vancouver Island was developing its local economy. The organization's website, CoalWatch.ca, kept supporters informed. The group developed a loose network of shellfish producers and their organizations, Indigenous peoples, farmers and vintners, tourist operators and artists, academic supports from the University of Victoria, environmental groups, and retired government employees. With great skill, CoalWatch wove the expertise of all these people together to effectively counter the mining company with huge crowds at every environmental hearing and thousands of submissions. And they won.

In March 2015, the company withdrew its application, citing "public misunderstanding" and in April 2016, Raven became the first mining proposal ever terminated by the BC Environmental Assessment Office. On February 26, 2016, Compliance Energy filed for bankruptcy.[11]

We do know how to create a world where the awesome cost of the minerals we take for granted is recognized; where the treasures the earth gives to us are treated with respect and conserved for future generations; where we concentrate on healing the damage already done. I hope this book provides some tools to make this new story a reality, so that we can put mining in its proper place.

NOTES

INTRODUCTION: MINING AND COMMUNITY RESISTANCE IN CANADA

1   Jacinda Mack, presentation at the Western Mining Action Network conference (Kamloops, British Columbia, September 29, 2018). Jacinda Mack is a Xat'sull leader and the spokesperson for Stand for Water, which was formed after the Mount Polley Mine tailings dam collapsed on August 4, 2014, sending 25 million cubic metres of waste into Polley Lake, Hazeltine Creek, and Quesnel Lake just before the wild salmon run. The Mount Polley disaster is discussed in other parts of this book (see, in particular, chapter 3).

2   The Voisey's Bay Mine in Labrador is a huge nickel project initially owned by Inco (now Vale), which has deeply affected Innu peoples and Inuit in the region. Daniel Ashini, an activist and negotiator who worked all his life to protect his land and people from the impacts of industrial development, gave the keynote address at a foundational conference for MiningWatch Canada in Ottawa, Ontario, in September 1999. The entire speech can be found in *Conference Results: Between a Rock and a Hard Place; Aboriginal Communities and Mining* (Ottawa: Innu Nation and MiningWatch Canada, 1999). Daniel died in 2009 at the age of forty-nine.

1: THE PHYSICAL FOOTPRINT OF A MINE

1   "Footprint of Mining," Resource Works, resourceworks.com.

2   "Closure and Land Rehabilitation," Ontario Mining Association, oma. on.ca.

3   Paraphrased from James E. Shigley et al., "Mining Diamonds in the Canadian Arctic: The Diavik Mine," *Gems and Gemology* 52, no. 2 (Summer 2016).

4   For a more detailed explanation of pit wall design, see W. Scott Dunbar, *How Mining Works* (Englewood, CO: Society for Mining, Metallurgy, and Exploration, 2016), 40.

5   Shigley et al., "Mining Diamonds."

6   "Tibbitt to Contwoyto Winter Road," Dangerous Roads, dangerousroads. org.

7   Shigley et al., "Mining Diamonds."

8   Northwatch and MiningWatch Canada, *The Boreal Below: Mining Issues and Activities in Canada's Boreal Forest* (Ottawa: Northwatch and MiningWatch Canada, 2008). This excellent resource was developed by a team of people, led by Brennain Lloyd and Catherine Daniel of Northwatch. Some of the material is now out of date, but it provides an overview of mining in the Boreal across Canada, including history, legislation (broken down by province and territory), and environmental effects.

2: THE MINING SEQUENCE

1   For a much more detailed (and industry-focused) discussion of the mining sequence, see W. Scott Dunbar, *How Mining Works* (Englewood, CO: Society for Mining, Metallurgy, and Exploration, 2016) and Northwatch and MiningWatch Canada, *The Boreal Below: Mining Issues and Activities in Canada's Boreal Forest* (Ottawa: Northwatch and MiningWatch Canada, 2008). Some of the material in the latter is now out of date, but it provides an overview of mining in the Boreal across Canada, including history, legislation (broken down by province and territory), and environmental effects. There is also a description of mine life cycle activities in Environment and Climate Change Canada's Environmental Code of Practice for Metal Mines, "Chapter 2: Mine Life Cycle Activities," canada.ca.

2   Ministry of Northern Development and Mines, "Backgrounder: Ontario's Mining Act" (January 2002), ontla.on.ca.

3   "Latest Report on Nak'azdli and Shus Nadloh (Mt. Milligan) Mine," First Nations Women Advocating Responsible Mining, October 21, 2010, fnwarm.com.

4   Janis Shandro et al., *Ten Steps Ahead: Community Health and Safety in the Nak'al Bun/Stuart Lake Region during the Construction Phase of the Mount Milligan Mine* (December 2014).

5   Gordon Hoekstra, "First Nations Series: Nak'azdli Getting Cut of Resource Wealth in Traditional Territory," *Vancouver Sun*, June 5, 2015.

6   Indian Mining Regulations (C.R.C., c. 956).

7   Karen Campbell, "Undermining Our Future: How Mining's Privileged Access to Land Harms People and the Environment," West Coast Environmental Law Association (January 2004).

8   Campbell, "Undermining Our Future."

9   Ross River Dena Council v. Government of Yukon, 2012 YKCA 14 (CanLII).

10   Jorge Barrera, "Ontario Court Quashes Gold Mining Permit over Lack of Meaningful Consultation with First Nation," CBC News, July 17, 2018.

11   Joan Baxter, "Fool's Gold: Nova Scotia's Myopic Pursuit of Metals and Minerals (Part III)," *Cape Breton Spectator*, May 30, 2018.

12   Campbell, "Undermining Our Future."

13   Peggy Witte (also known as Margaret Kent) was the operator behind a number of projects discussed later in the book, including Kemess South, Giant Mine, and Pine Point. Robert Friedland is a mining developer known for a tailings collapse at Summitville, Colorado, in 1993, with investments in Burma, the Congo, and Mongolia. Clifford Frame was the CEO of Curragh Resources, owner of the Westray Mine, when a methane gas explosion in 1992 killed twenty-six miners. Curragh was also an owner of the Faro Mine (discussed in chapter 7).

14   Quebec, Land Use Planning and Development Act, Section 246: "No provision of this Act, or of a metropolitan plan, an RCM plan, an interim control by-law or resolution or a zoning, subdivision or building by-law has the effect of preventing the staking or designation on a map of a claim, or exploration or search for or the development or exploration of mineral substances or underground reservoirs, carried on in accordance with the Mining Act (chapter M-13.1). The first paragraph does not apply to the extraction of sand, gravel or building stone on private lands where, under the Mining Act, the right to those mineral substances belongs to the owner of the soil."

15   "Windy Craggy Settlement Prompts Kemess Development," Northern Miner, northernminer.com.

16   MiningWatch Canada and Environmental Mining Council of British Columbia, *Mining in Remote Areas: Issues and Impacts* (Ottawa: MiningWatch Canada, 2001).

17   Environmental Mining Council of British Columbia, *Environmental Mining Primer: A Citizen's Guide to Issues, Impacts and Options in Mineral Development* (2001).

18   Dunbar, *How Mining Works*, 33–34.

19   MiningWatch Canada and Environmental Mining Council of British Columbia, *Mining in Remote Areas.*

20 For good information on radiation and health, see Dale Dewar and Florian Oelck, *From Hiroshima to Fukushima to You: A Primer on Radiation and Health* (Toronto: Between the Lines, 2014).

21 See Dunbar, *How Mining Works*.

22 See Ontario's Mining Act, Section 3 (1): "For the purposes of Part VII of the Act and this Regulation, 'advanced exploration. . .'"

23 Cemented paste backfill is discussed in detail in Morteza Sheshpari, "A Review of Underground Backfilling Methods with Emphasis on Cemented Paste Backfill," *Electronic Journal of Geotechnical Engineering* 20, no. 13 (2015), ejge.com.

24 Dunbar, *How Mining Works*, 129–150.

25 British Columbia Ministry of Energy and Mines, "Design and Operation of Large Waste Dumps," edumine.com.

26 Pembina Institute, *Uranium Mining: Nuclear Power's Dirty Secret*, Fact Sheet no. 2 (May 2007), 1.

27 "Gold Cyanidation," Ground Truth Trekking, May 27, 2013, groundtruthtrekking.org.

28 Natural Resources Canada, *Tailings Management at NRCan* (2013).

29 Environment Canada, "Table 6: Summary of Data Reported in the Mining Sourcebook on Ore Mined and Rock Removed to Access Ore by Mining Operations in Canada, Reported in Metric Tons Per Day," *Mining Environmental Scan Working Document* (2007).

30 Mining Association of Canada, *Facts and Figures 2017: Facts and Figures of the Canadian Mining Industry* (2017).

31 "Aluminum Facts," Natural Resources Canada, nrcan.gc.ca.

3: KEY ENVIRONMENTAL IMPACTS

1 Jacinda Mack, quoted in Carol Linnitt, "Jacinda Mack Wants to Get Real about What That Mine Is Actually Going to Do to Your Community," *The Narwhal*, June 21, 2018, thenarwhal.ca.

2 This chapter is a summary of environmental impacts from mining. There are a number of online and print resources that describe the issues in much more detail. In 2013, Hatch (a mining engineering consultancy) produced a report for the Canadian Mining Innovation Council on mining environmental effects: *Environmental Analysis of the Mining Industry in Canada*. The report catalogues the effects and talks about "tools" to deal with them. Although it is a good scan of available coping technologies, it is light on data about the issues. See also Environment

and Climate Change Canada's Environmental Code of Practice for Metal Mines, "Chapter 3: Environmental Concerns through the Mine Life Cycle," canada.ca. MiningWatch Canada and Environmental Mining Council of British Columbia, *Mining in Remote Areas: Issues and Impacts* (Ottawa: MiningWatch Canada, 2001); and Northwatch and MiningWatch Canada, *The Boreal Below: Mining Issues and Activities in Canada's Boreal Forest* (Ottawa: Northwatch and MiningWatch Canada, 2008) also provide well-referenced information about environmental pollution from mining, although they are slightly out of date. Both are available on the MiningWatch Canada website.

3   Northwatch and MiningWatch Canada, *The Boreal Below.*

4   For further detailed reading, see International Network for Acid Prevention, "Chapter 2: The Acid Rock Drainage Process," *Global Acid Rock Drainage Guide* (2014), gardguide.com; see also Charles Roche, Kristina Thygesen, and Elaine Baker, eds., *Mine Tailings Storage: Safety Is No Accident. A UNEP Rapid Response Assessment* (Arendal, Norway: United Nations Environment Programme and GRID-Arendal, 2017).

5   Stephen Hume, "Alaskans Gear Up to Fight B.C. Company's Mine Plans," *Vancouver Sun*, January 18, 2017.

6   Federal/Provincial/Industry SubCommittee on Mine Waste, *Report on the Economic and Policy Aspects of Acid Discharge* (Ottawa: Intergovernmental Working Group on the Mineral Industry, 1988).

7   William A. Price and John C. Errington, *Guidelines for Metal Leaching and Acid Rock Drainage at Minesites in British Columbia* (Victoria: Ministry of Energy and Mines, August 1998).

8   "pH Scale," Business Dictionary, businessdictionary.com.

9   W. G. Kimmel, "The Impact of Acid Mine Drainage on the Stream Ecosystem," in *Pennsylvania Coal: Resources, Technology and Utilization*, eds. S. K. Majumdar and E. W. Miller (Easton, PA: Pennsylvania Academy of Science, 1983): 424–37.

10   Environmental Mining Council of British Columbia, *More Precious than Gold* (Victoria: Environmental Mining Council of British Columbia, May 1998).

11   For excellent analysis of impacts on wildlife, including fish and other water life, see Jane Earle and Thomas Callaghan, *Impacts of Mine Drainage on Aquatic Life, Water Uses, and ManMade Structures* (Harrisburg, PA: Department of Environmental Protection, n.d.), ei.lehigh.edu.

12   Earle and Callaghan, *Impacts of Mine Drainage.*

13   *Still Standing*, episode 4X05, "Cobalt, Ontario," aired October 16, 2018. CBC Television.

14 Lisa Sumi, "Table 6," in *Environmental Mining Primer: A Citizen's Guide to Issues, Impacts and Options in Mineral Development*, Environmental Mining Council of British Columbia (2001), 124.

15 Senes Consultants Ltd., "Appendix B," in *Report on Technologies Applicable to the Management of Canadian Mine Effluents* (March 1999).

16 Lisa Sumi, in *Environmental Mining Primer: A Citizen's Guide to Issues, Impacts and Options in Mineral Development*, Environmental Mining Council of British Columbia (2001), 150.

17 Sunny Freeman, "Barrick's Bad Day: Shares Fall 10% as Investor Confidence Shaken by Third Cyanide Spill at Argentine Mine," *Financial Post*, April 25, 2017.

18 "Goldcorp Moving Ahead with Coffee Gold Mine Project near Dawson City," CBC News, May 23, 2017; "Eagle Gold," Yukon Government: Energy, Mines and Resources, www.emr.gov.yk.ca.

19 "Carmacks," Copper North Mining Corp., coppernorthmining.com; Chuck Tobin, "Plans for Yukon's Biggest Mine Delayed," *Whitehorse Daily Star*, September 25, 2017.

20 Alisha Hiyate, "10 Development Projects with Momentum," *Canadian Mining Journal*, August 1, 2017.

21 Canadian Council of Ministers of the Environment, *Canada Water Quality Guidelines for the Protection of Aquatic Life: Ammonia* (2010).

22 Canadian Council of Ministers of the Environment, *Canada Water Quality*.

23 Greenpeace Canada, *Chlorine Fact Sheet* (2000).

24 US Environmental Protection Agency, "Hydrochloric Acid: Toxic Chemical Release Reporting," *Federal Register* 60, no. 220 (November 15, 1995): 57382–86.

25 "Threats to Water Availability in Canada," *NWRI Scientific Assessment Series*, no. 3 (Environment Canada, 2004), nwri.ca.

26 Environment and Climate Change Canada, *Canadian Environmental Sustainability Indicators: Water Withdrawal and Consumption by Sector* (Gatineau, QC: Environment and Climate Change Canada, 2016), 11.

27 "Environmental Group Takes Diamond Giant De Beers to Court," Ecojustice, December 6, 2016, ecojustice.ca.

28 Lenny Carpenter, "Proposed De Beers Activity Would Contaminate Fish, Prof Says," *Wawatay News*, November 1, 2007.

29 Environment and Climate Change Canada, *Environmental Sustainability Indicators: Greenhouse Gas Emissions* (Gatineau, QC: Environment and Climate Change Canada, 2018).

30   Environment and Climate Change Canada, *Overview of 2015 Reported Emissions* (Gatineau, QC: Environment and Climate Change Canada, 2017).

31   "Air Pollutant Emissions: Sulphur Oxide Emissions by Source," Environment and Climate Change Canada, canada.ca/en/environment-climate-change.

32   Jen Skerritt, "Flin Flon Smelter: Pollution Blamed on Feds, Province," *Winnipeg Free Press*, June, 19, 2010.

33   Helen Fallding, "Manitoba Smelter Is No. 1 in North America in Lead, Mercury Air Pollution," *Resource Investor,* May 24, 2005.

34   Fallding, "Manitoba Smelter."

35   "Environmental Aspects of Uranium Mining," UIC Briefing Paper 10 (February 2006).

36   Community Coalition against Mining Uranium, "Fact Sheet on Uranium Radioactivity and Human Health," 1, no. 1 (November 2007).

37   R. William Field, "Radon Occurrence and Health Risk," College of Public Health, University of Iowa (1999), cheec.uiowa.edu.

38   Peter Diehl, "Uranium Mining and Milling Wastes: An Introduction," World Information Service on Energy (August 2004), wise-uranium. org.

39   The best up-to-date resources on tailings dam failures can be found at Worldminetailingsfailures.org and in (loaded with excellent images and explanatory infographics) Roche, Thygesen, and Baker, *Mine Tailings Storage*. For information on seepage, see Earle Klohn, "Seepage Control for Tailings Dams," in *Mine Drainage: Proceedings of the First International Mine Drainage Symposium*, eds. G. Argall and C. O. Brawner (San Francisco, CA: M. Freeman Publications, 1979).

40   Roche, Thygesen, and Baker, *Mine Tailings Storage.*

41   Tlazten First Nation, "We Want to Make Teck Cominco Responsible," news release, February 21, 2005.

42   Chief Bev Sellars, Xat'sull First Nation, and Ramsey Hart, MiningWatch Canada, "The Mount Polley Mine Spill: Impacts on Aboriginal Rights, the Environment and Fisheries: Briefing Note for MPs," November 6, 2014.

43   Environment and Climate Change Canada, "Company Sentenced to Pay $3,500,000 for Obed Mountain Mine Spill," June 12, 2017; Alberta Energy Regulator, "Guilty Plea Leads to $925,000 Penalty for Obed Mountain Coal Mine Spill," news release, June 9, 2017; Canadian Press, "Companies Charged over 2013 Coal Tailings Pond Spill: Alberta

Energy Regulator," October 17, 2015; Alberta Wilderness Association, "Obed Spill Charges," December 1, 2015.

44 Environment and Climate Change Canada, "Company Sentenced to Pay $3,500,000 for Obed Mountain Mine Spill," June 12, 2017; Alberta Energy Regulator, "Guilty Plea Leads to $925,000 Penalty for Obed Mountain Coal Mine Spill," news release, June 9, 2017; Canadian Press, "Companies Charged over 2013 Coal Tailings Pond Spill: Alberta Energy Regulator," October 17, 2015; Alberta Wilderness Association, "Obed Spill Charges," December 1, 2015.

45 Ministry of Sustainable Development, Environment, and Fight Against Climate Change, "Déversement de résidus miniers: Municipalité de La Corne (Abitibi-Témiscamingue)," news release, March 19, 2013; La Presse, "Déversement à la mine Québec Lithium," March 19, 2013; Gaia Presse, "Important déversement de résidus miniers à la mine Québec Lithium," March 20, 2013.

46 Ministry of Sustainable Development, Environment, and Fight Against Climate Change, "Déversement de résidus miniers: Baie James (Nord-du-Québec)," news release, May 2, 2013.

47 Ministry of Sustainable Development, Environment, and Fight Against Climate Change, "Déversement d'eau chargée en matières en suspension à l'entreprise Consolidated Thompson de Fermont," news release, May 24, 2011; Philippe Teisceira-Lessard, "Mine de fer du lac Bloom: déversements à repetition," La Presse, September 22, 2012; Radio-Canada, "Côte-Nord: Cliffs ressources naturelles sous enquête pénale," September 24, 2012; Ugo Lapointe, "Pour que le Québec ait meilleure mine," presentation, Lakehead University, December 5, 2013, www.lakeheadu.ca.

48 Ministry of Sustainable Development, Environment, and Fight Against Climate Change, "Chapais: Bris d'une digue du parc á résidus miniers restauré de l'ancienne mine Opémisca," news release, June 23, 2008; Lapointe, "Pour que le Québec"; Charles Côté, "Bombe environnementale à retardement," La Presse, July 5, 2008; Radio-Canada, "Importantes consequences environnementales," July 2, 2008.

4: MINING AND COLONIALISM ON TURTLE ISLAND

1 For background reading on colonialism in Canada, the following are a few of a number of good books: Arthur Manuel and Grand Chief Ronald M. Derrickson, *Unsettling Canada* (Toronto: Between the Lines, 2017); John Borrows, *Canada's Indigenous Constitution* (Toronto: University of Toronto Press, 2010); Thomas King, *The Inconvenient Indian* (Toronto: Doubleday, 2012). For more on mining impacts on Indig-

enous communities in Northern Canada, see Arn Keeling and John Sandlos, eds., *Mining and Northern Communities in Canada: History, Politics and Memory* (Calgary: University of Calgary Press, 2015). Raven Trust provides resources for understanding Indigenous cases (raventrust.ca).

2   Borrows, *Canada's Indigenous Constitution*, 243.

3   Borrows, *Canada's Indigenous Constitution*, 243–46.

4   See Keeling and Sandlos, *Mining and Northern Communities*, as well as later examples in this book.

5   Gerry McKay interview, October 17, 2018.

6   John Borrows, "Crown and Aboriginal Occupations of Land: A History and Comparison," research paper commissioned by the Ipperwash Inquiry (October 15, 2005): 1, attorneygeneral.jus.gov.on.ca.

7   The website to follow the Robinson-Huron Treaty 1850 case is rht1850.ca.

8   Robinson-Huron Statement of Claim, court file no. C-3512-14.

9   Bill Bradley, "FNX Chief: Sudbury Ore Body a Trillion Dollar Treasure," Sudbury.com, May 9, 2008.

10   Asad Ismi, "Path of Destruction," Canadian Centre for Policy Alternatives, February 1, 2009, policyalternatives.ca.

11   Asad Ismi, "Path of Destruction: Canadian Mining Companies around the World," radio documentary, http://www.asadismi.info/path-of-destruction-canadian-mining-companies-around-the-world/.

12   Ismi, "Path of Destruction: Canadian Mining."

13   Mining Association of Canada, *Facts and Figures 2017: Facts and Figures of the Canadian Mining Industry* (2017).

14   An interactive map of impact benefit agreements can be found at "Indigenous Mining Agreements Lands and Minerals Sector," Natural Resources Canada, atlas.gc.ca.

15   "Minerals Sector Employment," information bulletin, Natural Resources Canada (January 2019), nrcan.gc.ca.

16   Anishinabek Nation, *Below the Surface: Anishinabek Mining Strategy Final Report* (January 15, 2009), 10.

17   Arthur Manuel and Grand Chief Ronald Derrickson, *The Reconciliation Manifesto* (Toronto: Lorimer, 2017), 123–24.

18   Statistics Canada, "Aboriginal Peoples in Canada: Key Results from the 2016 Census" (October 25, 2017), 150.statcan.gc.ca.

19   The Tŝilhqot'in struggle is discussed in chapter 11.

20   The organizations' websites are as follows: fnwarm.com, wman-info.org, and ienearth.org.

21   Manuel and Derrickson, *Reconciliation Manifesto.*

22   Taku River Tlingit First Nation, *Taku River Tlingit First Nation Mining Policy* (March 2007); Northern Secwepemc te Qelmucw Leadership Council, *Northern Secwepemc te Qelmucw Mining Policy* (November 19, 2014); Anishinabek Nation, *Below the Surface*; Kitchenuhmaykoosib Inninuwug, *A Set of Protocols for the Kitchenuhmaykoosib Inninuwug* (July 5, 2011), scribd.com.

23   "Indigenous Guardians: Moccasins on the Ground and in the Boardroom," *Northern Public Affairs*, August 3, 2018.

24   The Indigenous Guardians Toolkit, indigenousguardianstoolkit.ca.

25   Taku River Tlingit First Nation v. British Columbia (Project Assessment Director), 2004 SCC 74, [2004] 3 SCR 550. The Supreme Court found that the Taku River Tlingit First Nation had been part of the Project Committee for the Tulsequah Chief Mine proposal, participating fully in the environmental review process. The court said that the First Nation's views were "put before the decision makers, and the final project approval contained measures designed to address both its immediate and its long-term concerns. The province was not under a duty to reach an agreement with the Tlingit, and there was no evidence that it breached its good faith obligation". Haida Nation v. British Columbia (Minister of Forests), 2004 SCC 73, 3 SCR 511 at para 48: First Nations are "under an obligation not to frustrate the Crown's reasonable good faith attempts, nor to take unreasonable positions to thwart the government from making decisions where an agreement is not reached."

26   Mikisew Cree First Nation v. Canada (Governor General in Council), 2018 SCC 40: "The majority held that when ministers develop policy, they act in a legislative capacity and their actions are immune from judicial review. It deemed the reviewing judge's decision to be inconsistent with the principles of parliamentary sovereignty, the separation of powers, and parliamentary privilege."

27   A list of these agreements can be found at Natural Resources Canada, *Agreements between Mining Companies and Aboriginal Communities or Governments* (Ottawa: Minerals and Metals Sector, 2013). The following are links to some excellent toolkits on negotiating impact benefit agreements: Ginger Gibson and Ciara O'Faircheallaigh, *IBA Community Toolkit: Negotiation and Implementation of Impact and Benefit Agreements* (Toronto: Walter and Duncan Gordon Foundation, 2010); "Nego-

tiating Agreements: Agreements between First Nations and Mining Companies," Fair Mining Collaborative, www.fairmining.ca.

28 "Dependable Project Development," Nuna Group of Companies, nunalogistics.com.

29 Ian Ross, "Forging New Bonds with First Nations," *Northern Ontario Business*, July 5, 2018.

30 "Yukon Zinc Corporation Enters into Socio-economic Participation Agreement with Kaska Nation," news release, July 13, 2005, yukonzinc. com.

31 "Indigenous Engagement," Procon, procongroup.net.

32 "Yukon Zinc Corp," *Canadian Mining Journal*, January 1, 2011; Jacqueline Ronson, "Yukon Zinc Scrambles to Preserve Wolverine Property," *Yukon News*, April 20, 2015; "Wolverine Mine Flooding, Yukon Zinc Not Complying with Agreements," CBC News, March 24, 2015; Justine Davidson, "Firm Admits to Breaching Safety Regulations," *Whitehorse Daily Star*, August 2, 2011.

33 Maura Forrest, "Will Yukon Zinc's Wolverine Mine Ever Reopen?" *Yukon News*, June 30, 2016.

34 See Deranger's corporate biography at Bloomberg.com.

35 See Coon Come's corporate biography at Bloomberg.com.

36 See Fontaine's short biography at riacanada.ca/phil-fontaine and Shawn McCarthy, "First Nations Leader Phil Fontaine: An Angry Radical Embraces Compromise," *Globe and Mail*, May 16, 2014. For more information on Tulsequah Chief Mine, see "About the Region: Taku Watershed," Rivers Without Borders, riverswithoutborders.org.

37 See Nolan's corporate biography at Bloomberg.com.

5: SOCIAL IMPACTS

1 Excellent studies on the social impacts of mining in Canada include Arn Keeling and John Sandlos, eds., *Mining and Northern Communities in Canada: History, Politics and Memory* (Calgary: University of Calgary Press, 2015).

2 Reported in Northwatch and MiningWatch Canada, *The Boreal Below: Mining Issues and Activities in Canada's Boreal Forest* (Ottawa: Northwatch and MiningWatch Canada, 2008), 49.

3 CCSG Associates, *Overburdened: Understanding the Impacts of Mineral Extraction on Women's Health in Mining Communities* (Ottawa: MiningWatch Canada, 2004).

4	G. Gibson, K. Yung, L. Chisholm, and H. Quinn, with Lake Babine Nation and Nak'azdli Whut'en, *Indigenous Communities and Industrial Camps: Promoting Healthy Communities in Settings of Industrial Change* (Victoria: The Firelight Group, 2017), 7, 8, 15.

5	Author's files.

6	A number of these stories can be found in Keeling and Sandlos, *Mining and Northern Communities.*

7	Janis A. Shandro, Marcello M. Veiga, Jean Shoveller, Malcolm Scoble, and Mieke Koehoorn, "Perspectives on Community Health Issues and the Mining Boom-Bust Cycle," *Resources Policy* 36, no. 2 (2011).

8	Todd Godfrey, "Mining and Alcohol Consumption: New Evidence from Northern Canada," (MA thesis, University of Alberta, 2017), era.library. ualberta.ca.

9	L. Reid, "Ghost Town/Boom Town" (Marathon, Ontario), *Equinox* (Fall 1986), 90–95.

10	MiningWatch Canada and Environmental Mining Council of British Columbia, *Mining in Remote Areas: Issues and Impacts* (Ottawa: Min-ingWatch Canada, 2001).

11	Mario Polèse and Richard Shearmur, *The Periphery in the Knowledge Economy: The Spatial Dynamics of the Canadian Economy and the Future of the Non-metropolitan Regions in Quebec and the Atlantic Provinces* (Moncton, NB: Canadian Institute for Research on Regional Development, 2003).

12	For a literature review and more detailed discussion of this subject, see Joan Kuyek and Catherine Coumans, *No Rock Unturned: Revitalizing the Economies of Mining Dependent Communities* (Ottawa: Mining-Watch Canada, 2003).

13	CCSG Associates, *Overburdened.*

14	MiningWatch Canada/MinesAlerte, *On the Ground Research: A Work-shop to Identify the Research Needs of Communities Affected by Large-Scale Mining Activity; Workshop Report* (Ottawa: MiningWatch Canada, 2000).

15	Sudbury mayor John Rodriguez in *The Hole Story*, directed by Robert Monderie and Richard Desjardins (National Film Board, 2011). The film describes the history and impacts of mining in the Greenstone belt in Ontario and Quebec.

16	MiningWatch Canada and Environmental Mining Council of British Columbia, *Mining in Remote Areas.*

17 Anne Marie Mawhinney and Jane Pitblado, *Boom Town Blues: Elliot Lake; Collapse and Revival of a Single Industry Town* (Toronto: Dundurn, 1998).

18 Kuyek and Coumans, *No Rock Unturned.*

6: WORKING IN THE MINING INDUSTRY

1 Christopher Lawson, "Digging Your Career," Job Postings, October 11, 2017, jobpostings.ca.

2 "Donkin Coal Project: Nova Scotia," Mining Technology, mining-technology.com.

3 Elisa Serret and Frances Willick, "'Playing with Fire': Former Donkin Mine Workers Describe 'Scary' Safety Practices," CBC News, March 22, 2017.

4 Serret and Willick, "Playing with Fire."

5 Serret and Willick, "Playing with Fire." These concerns are listed in the story.

6 "Men in the Mines: A History of Mining Activity in Nova Scotia, 1720–1992," Nova Scotia Archives, novascotia.ca.

7 Tom Ayers, "Donkin Mine Punished for Violations under Temporary Foreign Worker Program," CBC News, July 5, 2018.

8 "Minerals Sector Employment: Information Bulletin; Figure 2; Employment by Industry," Natural Resources Canada, January 2019, nrcan.gc.ca.

9 Mining Association of Canada, *Facts and Figures 2017: Facts and Figures of the Canadian Mining Industry* (2017).

10 David Robinson interview, May 30, 2018.

11 See discussion of the Raven Coal Mine Project in chapter 21.

12 Eduardo Regier, "Determinants of Labour Union Membership in Canada: A Study Using Multivariate Regression Analysis of Individual Level Data from the Survey of Labour and Income Dynamics," April 20, 2017, progressive-economics.ca.

13 Unifor, *Mines, Metals, and Minerals: Sector Profile* (2016).

14 Author's files and Oiva Saarinen, "Sudbury: A Historical Case Study of Multiple Urban-Economic Transformation," *Ontario History* 82, no. 1, 14.

15 Four thousand at Vale (see Vale.com) and 1,300 at Glencore with 500 contractors (see Erik White, "'Deep Will Be the New Norm': Glencore

Spends $1B to Find New Ore beneath Sudbury," CBC News, April 5, 2018).

16 John Lang, "One Hundred Years of Mine Mill," in Mercedes Steedman, Peter Suschnigg, and Dieter K. Buse, eds., *Hard Lessons: The Mine Mill Union in the Canadian Labour Movement* (Toronto: Dundurn, 1995), 13.

17 Dieter K. Buse, "Weir Reid and Mine Mill: An Alternative Union's Cultural Endeavours," in *Hard Lessons: The Mine Mill Union in the Canadian Labour Movement*, eds. Mercedes Steedman, Peter Suschnigg, and Dieter K. Buse (Toronto: Dundurn, 1995).

18 "Change at the Top," Christian Labour Association of Canada, March 15, 2017, clac.ca.

19 "I. Profile of Ontario's Mining Sector," Ontario Ministry of Labour, September 10, 2014, labour.gov.on.ca.

20 Canadian Centre for Occupational Health and Safety, ccohs.ca.

21 Brian Dubreuil, "Westray Disaster," Canadian Encyclopedia, thecanadianencyclopedia.ca.

22 Steven Bittle, *Still Dying for a Living* (Vancouver: University of British Columbia Press, 2013).

23 Gowling WLG, "Acquittal in Quebec Bill C-45 Charges," Lexology, April 27, 2011, lexology.com.

7: AFTER THE MINE

1 Quoted in Arn Keeling and John Sandlos, eds., *Mining and Northern Communities in Canada: History, Politics and Memory* (Calgary: University of Calgary Press, 2015), 143.

2 Natural Resources Canada, *Trainer's Manual: Exploration and Mining Guide for Aboriginal Communities* (Ottawa: Natural Resources Canada, 2014).

3 National Orphaned/Abandoned Mines Initiative (NOAMI), abandoned-mines.org.

4 The National Orphaned/Abandoned Mines Initiative (NOAMI) website (abandoned-mines.org) provides links to a map of abandoned mines in Canada and a number of excellent reports on legislative frameworks, case studies, financial assurance, and so on. See also Joan Kuyek, *The Theory and Practice of Perpetual Care of Contaminated Sites: A Literature Review* (2011), sehn.org.

5   Scott Fields, "The Earth's Open Wounds: Abandoned and Orphaned Mines," *Environmental Health Perspectives* 111, no. 3 (2003): 154.

6   "Abandoned Mines," Ontario Ministry of Energy, Northern Development and Mines, mndm.gov.on.ca.

7   "Historic Mines Atlas," British Columbia Ministry of Energy, Mines and Petroleum Resources, empr.gov.bc.ca; Sophie Proulx, "Reclamation of Abandoned Mine Sites Quebec: 2016 Report," Énergie et Ressources naturelles Québec, mern.gouv.qc.ca.

8   Environmental Services Association of Alberta, "Clean-up of Ontario Mining Sites Estimated at $3.1 Billion," *Weekly News*, May 26, 2017.

9   Ed Struzik, "A Deep Pit for Tax Dollars," *Edmonton Journal*, December 21, 2003.

10   "Faro Mine Complex: A Plan for Closure," Faro Mine Project Office brochure (2010).

11   Nancy Thomson, "Ross River Dena Council Faces 'Crisis' of Contaminated Homes," CBC News, October 28, 2016.

12   Independent Peer Review Panel, *Review of Remediation Alternatives for the Anvil Range Complex Final Report* (April 2007), vi.

13   "About Federal Contaminated Sites," Environment and Climate Change Canada, canada.ca.

14   "Action Plan for Contaminated Sites," Environment and Climate Change Canada, canada.ca.

15   Ashley Joannou, "Ottawa Takes over Care and Maintenance at the Faro Mine," *Yukon News*, April 27, 2018.

16   Independent Peer Review Panel, *Review of Remediation Alternatives.*

17   Tim Querengesser, "Faro's Lead Spread Far and Wide," *Yukon News*, March 30, 2007.

18   Natasha Affolder, Katy Allen, and Sascha Paruk, *Independent Environmental Oversight: A Report for the Giant Mine Remediation Environmental Assessment* (University of British Columbia, February 2011), 55–57.

19   "Remediating Faro Mine in the Yukon," Crown-Indigenous Relations and Northern Affairs Canada, aadnc-aandc.gc.ca.

20   The following section is abridged/paraphrased from Independent Peer Review Panel, *Review of Remediation Alternatives.*

21   The members of the panel included: Dr. Laurie Chan, professor, University of Northern British Columbia; Dr. Kenneth Froese, Golder Associates Limited; Dr. Anthony Hodge, professional engineer, Anthony

Hodge Consultants Inc.; Randy Knapp, professional engineer, SENES Consultants Limited (retired); Kenneth Raven, professional engineer, professional geoscientist, Intera Engineering Limited; Dr. Terry Mudder, CHCM, IPRP chairman, TIMES Limited; Dr. Bill Price, Natural Resources Canada; Dr. Andrew Robertson, professional engineer, Robertson GeoConsultants Inc.; Dr. Leslie Smith, professor, University of British Columbia.

22 Independent Peer Review Panel, *Review of Remediation Alternatives*, 28.

23 Independent Peer Review Panel, *Review of Remediation Alternatives*, 30.

24 Kuyek, *Theory and Practice.*

25 Michael Edelstein, Maria Tysiachniouk, and Lyudmila V. Smirnova, eds., "Cultures of Contamination: Legacies of Pollution in Russia and the US," *Research in Social Problems and Public Policy*, vol. 14 (Bingley, UK: JAI Press, 2007).

26 Thomas Leschine, ed., *Long Term Management of Contaminated Sites*, Research in Social Problems and Public Policy, vol. 13 (New York: Elsevier, 2008), 2.

8: THE STRUCTURE AND FINANCING OF THE MINING INDUSTRY IN CANADA

1 Some of the material in this chapter was originally written by the author and published by MiningWatch Canada in November 2007 as *Mining Investors: Understanding the Legal Structure of a Mining Company and Identifying Its Management, Shareholders and Relationship with the Financial Markets* (Ottawa: MiningWatch, 2007). The original is available at on the MiningWatch Canada website. For more on the securities industry and investment concepts, I refer you to Investopedia.com and to the website of the Canadian Securities Administrators, securitiesadministrators.ca. The website Strategiccorporateresearch.com explains how to research a particular company.

2 "Northcliff Resources Ltd.," HDI Companies, hdimining.com.

3 "Northcliff Resources Ltd.," HDI Companies.

4 US Geological Survey, "Tungsten," Mineral Commodity Summaries (2016).

5 Northcliff Resources, "Feasibility Study" (January 2013), 23, 24, sedar. com. A metric ton unit (mtu) is equal to ten kilograms and is the standard weight measure of tungsten. Tungsten prices are generally quoted as US dollars per mtu of tungsten trioxide (WO_3), but can also be

quoted as US dollars per mtu of ammonium paratungstate (APT). APT is a secondary product made from tungsten concentrates.

6 "Trade Log January 2018: Ferro-tungsten, APT," Fastmarkets, metalbulletin.com.

7 Northcliff Resources, *Annual Information Return*, January 29, 2016, 8–10.

8 Northcliff Resources, *Investor Presentation*, December 2015, slide 6.

9 Michael Doggett is principal consultant at Michael Doggett and Associates in Vancouver; he is a director of three public companies and served as director of the Mineral Exploration Master's Program at Queen's University from 1997 to 2007.

10 Paraphrase of a comment from a mining investment lawyer who regularly deals with junior companies.

11 "Canada Directors' Residency Requirements for Companies," Company Formations Canada, companyformations.ca.

12 Practical Law Canada Corporate and Securities, "Yukon Makes a Pitch to Become Delaware of the North," July 7, 2015, ca.practicallaw.thomsonreuters.com.

13 Frik Els, "Top 50 Biggest Mining Companies," Mining.com, April 3, 2017. Anglo American was ranked tenth in 2017.

14 Department of Finance Canada, *Supporting a Strong and Growing Economy* (Ottawa: Financial Institutions Division, August 26, 2016), 18.

15 Nick Hildyard and Mark Mansley, *The Campaigners' Guide to Financial Markets* (Dorset, UK: Corner House, 2003), 15.

16 James Chen, "What Is a Derivative?" *Investopedia*, March 26, 2019, investopedia.com.

17 "Homepage," SEDAR, sedar.com.

18 "British Columbia Securities Commission Asked to Investigate Mining Company's Failure to Disclose Material Facts to Investors," news release, May 23, 2017, miningwatch.ca.

19 Lucy Scholey, "Doug Ford Can't Bulldoze through First Nations to Ring of Fire, Say Indigenous Leaders," APTN National News, June 15, 2018.

20 Auditor General of Ontario, "Chapter 3.11: Mines and Minerals Program," in *2015 Annual Report of the Office of the Auditor General of Ontario* (2015), 440.

21 James Wilt, "What Happens if Imperial Metals Goes Bankrupt?" *The Narwhal*, August 28, 2018, thenarwhal.ca.

22 Deb McCombe, Craig Waldie, and Robert Holland, "NI 43-101 Stan-dards of Disclosure for Mineral Projects," seminar, Ontario Securities Commission, Toronto, March 2, 2007.

23 Companies' Creditors Arrangements Act, R.S.C., 1985, c. C-36; Bank-ruptcy and Insolvency Act, R.S.C., 1985, c. B-3.

24 *Orphan Well Association v. Grant Thornton Ltd.* (*"Redwater"*) 2019 SCC 5. .

25 Poonam Puri and Andrew Nichol, "Beyond Director Liability for Envi-ronmental Remediation," February 9, 2016, cairp.ca.

9: CANADA'S INTERNATIONAL MINING PRESENCE

1   There is considerable material on Canada's international mining pres-ence on the MiningWatch Canada website and at Minesandcommuni-ties.org. A number of books have also been written about this in recent years; see Alain Denault and William Sacher, *Imperial Canada: Legal Haven of Choice for the World's Mining Industries* (Vancouver: Talon-books, 2012); Paula Butler, *Colonial Extractions: Race and Canadian Mining in Contemporary Africa* (Toronto: University of Toronto Press, 2015); and Anthony Bebbington, ed., *Social Conflict, Economic Develop-ment, and Extractive Industry: Evidence from South America* (New York: Routledge, 2012).

2   Prospectors and Developers Association of Canada and Oreninc.com, *State of Mineral Finance, 2018: Gaining Momentum* (Toronto: Prospec-tors and Developers Association of Canada, 2018), 13.

3   Natural Resources Canada, *Exploration and Mining in Canada: An Inves-tor's Brief* (Government of Canada, February 2016). These figures are considerably lower than in 2011–12. In 2011, 90 percent of the shares issued in the mining sector throughout the world were administered by the Toronto Stock Exchange, and in 2012, 75 percent of the world's min-ing companies registered their companies in Canada (see Alain Denault, "At the Heart of the World Mining Industry" in *Extraction Empire*, ed. Pierre Belanger (Cambridge, MA: MIT Press, 2018). Denault also says that two-thirds of the world's mining companies are headquartered in Canada. A serious crash in investment in mining following the 2008 economic crisis played havoc with these investments.

4   Natural Resources Canada, *Exploration and Mining.*

5   Natural Resources Canada, *Exploration and Mining.*

6   Robert Goodland, *Responsible Mining: The Key to Profitable Resource Development*, Research Series A1-2012-4 (Institute for Environmental Diplomacy and Security, University of Vermont, 2012).

7   See Kyla Tienhara, *The Expropriation of Environmental Governance: Protecting Foreign Investors at the Expense of Public Policy* (Cambridge, UK: Cambridge University Press, 2009).

8   "CAFTA Investor-State Cases: Pacific Rim Mining Corp vs. Republic of El Salvador," Public Citizen, citizen.org.

9   Marquita Davis, "UNCITRAL Tribunal Finds Canada's Environmental Assessment Breached International Minimum Standard of Treatment and National Treatment Standard," Investment Treaty News, May 21, 2015, iisd.org; Canada (Attorney General) v. Clayton, 2018 FC 436.

10   "Close but No Cigar: Bilcon Tribunal Rejects Claim on Grounds of Failure to Establish Causation," Tereposky and Derose LLP, March 3, 2019, tradeisds.com.

11   See "Criminalization of Land and Environmental Defenders in the Americas," International Civil Liberties Monitoring Group, iclmg.ca.

12   Justice and Corporate Accountability Project, *The "Canada Brand": Violence and Canadian Mining Companies in Latin America*, Osgoode Legal Studies Research Paper no. 17/2017 (2016).

13   Canadian Centre for the Study of Resource Conflict, *Corporate Social Responsibility: Movements and Footprints of Canadian Mining and Exploration Firms in the Developing World* (October 2009).

14   "Artisanal and Small-Scale Mining," World Bank, November 21, 2013, worldbank.org.

15   Pact Global and Alliance for Responsible Mining, *The Impact of Small-Scale Mining Operations on Economies and Livelihoods in Low- to Middle-Income Countries* (Pact Global and Alliance for Responsible Mining, January 2018).

16   Geoffrey York, "Police Killed 65, Injured 270 at Barrick Mine in Tanzania, Inquiry Hears," MiningWatch, September 26, 2016, miningwatch.ca.

17   Based on "Inequality of Arms," a field assessment brief conducted by RAID (Rights and Accountability in Development) and MiningWatch Canada in June 2017, miningwatch.ca.

18   FAAE Committee Report, "Government Response to the Fourteenth Report of the Standing Committee on Foreign Affairs and International Trade: Mining in Developing Countries; Corporate Social Responsibility," ourcommons.ca.

19   Global Justice Now et al., *Honest Accounts 2017: How the World Profits from Africa's Wealth* (Global Justice Now et al., 2017), 2.

20   See Roger Moody, *The Risks We Run: Mining, Communities and Political Risk Insurance* (International Books, 2005) for an excellent set of case studies on the effects of political risk insurance.

21   Marco Chown Oved, "Ottawa Lent $1 Billion to a Mining Company That Allegedly Avoided Nearly $700 Million in Canadian Taxes," *Toronto Star*, February 5, 2018.

22   "Auditor General Finds Stunning Deficiencies in Risk Management at Canada's Export Bank," Above Ground, May 4, 2018, aboveground.ngo.

23   Alexandra Readhead, *Toolkit for Transfer Pricing Risk Assessment in the African Mining Industry* (Bonn, Germany: Deutsche Gesellschaft für Internationale Zusammenarbeit, 2017), 3.

24   Ian Binnie quoted in Justice and Corporate Accountability Project, *The "Canada Brand,"* 30.

25   Christian Peña, "Canada Mining Murder in Mexico," *Now magazine*, March 5, 2018.

26   Above Ground, *Transnational Lawsuits in Canada against Extractive Companies: Developments in Civil Litigation, 1997–2016* (2016).

27   Paraphrase of Above Ground, *Transnational Lawsuits.*

28   Above Ground, *Transnational Lawsuits,* 4.

29   Cecilia Jamasmie, "Acacia Mining Now Hit with $190 Billion Tax Bill in Tanzania," Mining.com, July 24, 2017.

30   Jamasmie, "Acacia Mining."

31   Yves Engler, "Despite Abuse, Canada Shows Unconditional Love for Mining Company," Rabble.ca, August 2, 2017.

10: EXTERNALIZING MACHINES

1   Arlene Drake, "Canadian Reserves of Selected Major Metals and Recent Production Decisions," Natural Resources Canada, nrcan.gc.ca.

2   This study is summarized in Kevin Dennehy, "Metals Used in High-Tech Products Face Future Supply Risks," Yale News, March 23, 2015, news.yale.edu.

3   *The Report of the High-Level Advisory Group on the Environment to the Secretary-General of the OECD*, November 25, 1997, 10. The need for a 50 percent reduction in material intensity in OECD countries was acknowledged in the October 1994 Carnoules Declaration, endorsed by prominent individuals including the former executive directors of the Business Council for Sustainable Development and the Brundtland

Commission (in Thomas Green, *Lasting Benefits from Beneath the Earth* [Gabriola, BC: H. J. Ruitenbeek Resource Consulting, 1998], 69).

4   Speaking points by environment commissioner Janez Potočnik on circular economy, press conference on Circular Economy and Green Employment Initiative, Brussels, July 2, 2014, europa.eu.

5   Jay Fothergill, *Scrap Mining: An Overview of Metal Recycling in Canada* (Ottawa: Canary Research Institute for Mining, Environment, and Health, October 2004).

6   Fothergill, *Scrap Mining*, 2.

7   Fothergill, *Scrap Mining*, 2.

8   "Minerals Sector Employment: Figure 2; Employment by Industry, 2008–2017," Natural Resources Canada, nrcan.gc.ca. "Education," Canadian Association of Recycling Industries, cari-acir.org. Metal mining and quarrying used to be disaggregated. Quarrying is more labour intensive.

9   MiningWatch Canada and the Green Budget Coalition, presentation before the Senate Banking, Trade, and Commerce Committee on Bill C-48 Regarding the Taxation of Industry and Natural Resources, November 5, 2003, 2.

10   "Coal Phase-Out: The Powering Past Coal Alliance," Environment and Climate Change Canada, canada.ca.

11   Paul R. Epstein et al., "Full Cost Accounting for the Life Cycle of Coal," *Annals of the New York Academy of Sciences* (2011): 73.

12   Epstein et al., "Full Cost Accounting," 93.

13   Epstein et al., "Full Cost Accounting," 93.

14   Environment and Climate Change Canada, "Coal Phase-Out."

15   Environment and Climate Change Canada, "Coal Phase-Out."

16   Mitchell Anderson, "IMF Pegs Canada's Fossil Fuel Subsidies at $34 Billion," *The Tyee*, May 15, 2014, thetyee.ca.

17   Valentina Ruiz Leotaud, "US Blasts Canada over Report on BC Coal Mine," Mining.com, July 8, 2018.

18   Carol Linnitt, "US to Crack down on Pollution from BC Coal Mines," *Elk Valley Coal News*, April 29, 2013, elkvalleycoal.com.

19   Linnitt, "US to Crack Down."

20   "How Much Gold Is in the World? Less Than You May Think," US Money Reserve, July 26, 2017, usmoneyreserve.com.

21   US Geological Survey, "Gold," Mineral Commodity Summaries (2017).

22 Potočnik, Circular Economy and Green Employment.

23 Xianlai Zeng, John A. Mathews, and Jinhui Li, "Urban Mining of E-Waste is Becoming More Cost-Effective Than Virgin Mining," *Environmental Science and Technology* 52, no. 8 (2018).

24 "What Makes Diamonds So Valuable?" The Loupe, June 29, 2017, truefacet.com.

25 "What Makes Diamonds?"

26 Rohin Dhar, "Diamonds Are Bullshit," HuffPost, December 6, 2017, huffingtonpost.com.

27 Gavin Du Venage, "The Lab-Grown Gems Threatening the Diamond Industry," The National, March 18, 2018, thenational.ae.

28 Bill McKibben, *Deep Economy: The Wealth of Communities and the Durable Future* (New York: Holt, 2007), 27.

29 McKibben, *Deep Economy*, 27.

30 Kemess North Mine Joint Review Panel, *Panel Report: Kemess North Copper-Gold Mine Project* (September 17, 2007), publications.gc.ca.

31 Kemess North Mine Joint Review Panel, *Panel Report*.

32 "Whites Point Quarry," Government of Nova Scotia, novascotia.ca.

33 For more information on this case, see Meinhard Doelle, "The Bilcon NAFTA Arbitration: The Damages Ruling," Environmental Law News, Dalhousie University, March 1, 2019, blogs.dal.ca.

34 Mackenzie Valley Environmental Impact Review Board, *Report of Environmental Assessment and Reasons for Decision on Ur Energy Inc. Screech Lake Uranium Exploration Project*, May 7, 2007, and Mackenzie Valley Land and Water Board, "Ur Energy Ltd. Withdrawn Land Use Permit Application," June 27, 2005.

35 Canadian Environmental Assessment Agency, *Report of the Federal Review Panel: New Prosperity Gold-Copper Mine Project* (Ottawa: Minister of the Environment, October 31, 2013), 214.

36 M3 Engineering, *KAM Feasibility Study* (February 28, 2016), 8.

37 M3 Engineering, *KAM Feasibility Study*, 1.

38 M3 Engineering, *KAM Feasibility Study*, 6.

39 M3 Engineering, *KAM Feasibility Study*, 120.

40 Jeannette Jules, Western Mining Action Network Conference, Kamloops, British Columbia, September 30, 2018.

41 Stk'emlupsemc te Secwepemc Nation, "Letter re: SSN Pipsell Decision," news release, October 23, 2017, miningwatch.ca.

42 Stk'emlupsemc te Secwepemc Nation, "Letter re: SSN Pípsell Decision."

43 Not standard practice in British Columbia to include in a feasibility study.

44 M3 Engineering, "Table 21-11: Normalized G&A Operating Costs," in *KAM Feasibility Study* (February 28, 2016), 285.

45 M3 Engineering, *KAM Feasibility Study*, 283. Calculated at 760,200 megawatts/year, $39.67/megawatt using a $1:1.20 exchange rate; based on the estimated cost of new power from the Site C dam project of $110/megawatt.

46 Joan Kuyek and MiningWatch Canada, *Economic Risk Analysis: KGHM Ajax Copper-Gold Mine near Kamloops, BC, Canada* (April 11, 2016), 1.

47 A precursor to our report—which investigated the costs in terms of health, urban planning, and so on, and provided much of the material we needed—was a report prepared by Dennis Karpiak and Ken Blawatt, *Economic, Health, and Environmental Evaluation at Full Cost for the Proposed Ajax Mine* (Kamloops, BC, August 30, 2014).

48 Christopher Klassen and Eugene Ngwenya, *Appendix 3D: Tailings Storage Facility Design Report* (Vancouver: Norwest Corporation, August 26, 2015).

49 See Kuyek and MiningWatch Canada, *Economic Risk Analysis*.

11: THE MINING LOBBY

1 "Members and Partners," Mining Association of Canada, mining.ca.

2 Quotation from an anonymous source who participates in the TSM meetings.

3 "Protocols and Frameworks," Mining Association of Canada, mining.ca.

4 "TSM Verification," Mining Association of Canada, mining.ca.

5 Samantha Wright Allen, "Mining Group Leads July Lobbying," *Hill Times*, August 29, 2018.

6 Prospectors and Developers Association of Canada, pdac.ca.

7 "E3 Plus: A Framework for Responsible Exploration," Prospectors and Developers Association of Canada, pdac.ca.

8   Prospectors and Developers Association of Canada, *Supporting a Competitive and Responsible Canadian Exploration Industry: The Role of the PDA* (January 2017).

9   Mining Matters, miningmatters.ca.

10   Canadian Aboriginal Minerals Association, aboriginalminerals.com.

11   "2018 Supporters," Canadian Aboriginal Minerals Association, aboriginalminerals.com.

12   Mining Association of Canada, Prospectors and Developers Association of Canada, Natural Resources Canada, and Canadian Aboriginal Minerals Association, "Tool Kit to Increase Aboriginal Involvement in Mining," joint news release, March 17, 2004.

13   MiningWatch Canada, *An Insult to Aboriginal People: A Critique of the Mining Information Kit for Aboriginal Communities* (Ottawa: MiningWatch Canada, December 5, 2006).

14   West Coast Environmental Law and Environmental Mining Council of British Columbia, *Undermining the Law: Addressing the Crisis in Compliance with Environmental Mining Laws in BC* (December 2001), 11.

15   MiningWatch Canada, *Submission to BC Ministry of Environment: Mount Polley Mine Permit Application for Long Term Water Management Plan and Discharge into Quesnel Lake* (December 23, 2016), 2.

16   Tŝilhqot'in Nation v. British Columbia, 2014 SCC 44.

17   Tŝilhqot'in Nation v. British Columbia, 2014 SCC 44.

18   "Russell E. Hallbauer," Canadian Institute of Mining, Metallurgy and Petroleum, web.cim.org.

19   Office of the Auditor General of British Columbia, *An Audit of Compliance and Enforcement of the Mining Sector* (Victoria: Office of the Auditor General, May 2016).

20   "BCGEU Calls for More Resources for Regulation and Enforcement in Mining after Auditor General Report," National Union of Public and General Employees, May 9, 2016, nupge.ca.

21   Office of the Auditor General of British Columbia, *An Audit of Compliance.*

22   Mark Hume, "Critics, Officials Disturbed as Taseko Mine Plans to Conduct Test Drilling," *Globe and Mail*, July 26, 2016.

23   Mark Hume, "Controversial Mine Gets Second Chance after Letter to Premier," *Globe and Mail*, November 23, 2016.

24   Taseko Mines Limited v. Canada (Environment), 2017 FC 1099; Taseko Mines Limited v. Canada (Environment) 2017 FC 1100.

25   Taseko Mines federal court citations 2017 FC 1099 and 2017 FC 1100.

26   Jen St. Denis, "Taseko Mines Loses Defamation Suit against Wilderness Committee," Business in Vancouver, January 26, 2016, biv.com.

27   "Court Exonerates Wilderness Committee in Taseko Mines Defamation Suit," Wilderness Committee, January 26, 2016, wildernesscommittee. org.

28   "Wilderness Committee Wins Appeal on Taseko Mines Lawsuit," Wilderness Committee, December 13, 2017, wildernesscommittee.org.

12: CANADIAN MINING LAW AND REGULATION

1   Some sections of this chapter are paraphrased from work previously published by MiningWatch Canada, including Joan Kuyek, *Canadian Mining Law and the Impacts on Indigenous Peoples Lands and Resources* (2005); Ramsey Hart and Dawn Hoogeveen, *Introduction to the Legal Framework for Mining in Canada* (July 2012); and Northwatch and MiningWatch Canada, *The Boreal Below: Mining Issues and Activities in Canada's Boreal Forest* (Ottawa: Northwatch and MiningWatch Canada, 2008). An additional good industry-focused source is Natural Resources Canada's "Roles and Responsibilities of Governments in Natural Resources," nrcan.gc.ca.

2   John Borrows, *Canada's Indigenous Constitution* (Toronto: University of Toronto Press, 2010), 11.

3   Nunavut Tunngavik Inc., *Tukisittiarniqsaujumaviit? A Plain Language Guide to the Nunavut Land Claims Agreement* (Iqaluit: Nunavut Tunngavik Inc., 2004).

4   "Concluding and Implementing Land Claim and Self-Government Agreements," Executive and Indigenous Affairs, eia.gov.nt.ca.

5   Government of Nunavut, Makivik Corporation, and Government of Canada, *Nunavik Inuit Land Claims Agreement* (2006).

6   Government of Nunavut, Makivik Corporation, and Government of Canada, "Article 15," in *Nunavik Inuit Land Claims Agreement* (2006).

7   Government of Nunavut, Makivik Corporation, and Government of Canada, "Part IX: Status and Security of Rights," in *Nunavik Inuit Land Claims Agreement* (2006).

8   Taku River Tlingit First Nation, *Taku River Tlingit First Nation Mining Policy* (March 2007); Northern Secwepemc te Qelmucw Leadership

Council, *Northern Secwepemc te Qelmucw Mining Policy* (November 19, 2014); Anishinabek Nation, *Below the Surface: Anishinabek Mining Strategy Final Report* (January 15, 2009); Kitchenuhmaykoosib Inninuwug, *A Set of Protocols for the Kitchenuhmaykoosib Inninuwug* (July 5, 2011), www.scribd.com.

9   Nunavut Mining Regulations (SOR2014-69).

10   "Environmental Assessments in Canada's North," Crown-Indigenous Relations and Northern Affairs Canada, rcaanc-cirnac.gc.ca.

11   Sections of this chapter are paraphrased from "Basics of Environmental Assessment," Canadian Environmental Assessment Agency, canada.ca.

12   Regulations Designating Physical Activities, Canadian Environmental Assessment Act, 2012.

13   "Environmental Assessment: Questions and Answers," Canadian Environmental Assessment Agency, canada.ca.

14   "Environmental Assessment: Questions and Answers."

15   EPA Caucus, *Achieving a Next Generation of Environmental Assessment: Submission to the Expert Review of Federal Environmental Assessment Processes* (December 14, 2016), 21.

16   The list of the water bodies in Schedule 2, "Tailings Impoundment Areas," can be found at laws-lois.justice.gc.ca.

17   "Reporting Environmental Effects Monitoring Data," Environment and Climate Change Canada, canada.ca.

18   Environment Canada, *Environmental Code of Practice for Base Metals Smelters and Refineries* (Ottawa: Environment Canada, 2006).

19   "Base Metal Smelters Sector: Environmental Performance Agreements Overview; Signatories," Environment and Climate Change Canada, canada.ca.

20   Environment Canada, *Environmental Code of Practice.*

21   Environment and Climate Change Canada, "Code of Practice to Reduce Emissions of Fine Particulate Matter (PM2.5) from the Aluminium Sector," canada.ca.

22   See pollutionwatch.org.

23   For more information, see "National Pollutant Data Finally Released, Sort of," Environmental Law Centre, August 13, 2010, elc.ab.ca; and "Canada's National Pollutant Release Inventory: Data Highlights 2017," Environment and Climate Change Canada, canada.ca. Smelters and refineries report under "manufacturing" not "mining." Environment and Climate Change Canada, *2016 National Pollutant Release Inventory*

Summary Report (Gatineau, QC: Environment and Climate Change Canada, 2017).

24   Commission for Environmental Cooperation, *Taking Stock: North American Pollutant Releases and Transfers* (April 20, 2018).

25   "Marine Protected Areas (MPAs) and Their Regulations," Fisheries and Oceans Canada, dfo-mpo.gc.ca.

26   For more information, see "Chapter 7: Ecological Integrity in National Parks," in *Report of the Commissioner of the Environment and Sustainable Development* (Ottawa: Office of the Auditor General of Canada, 2013).

27   A bond is considered investment grade if its credit rating is BBB- or higher. Bonds rated lower than that are known as "junk bonds." Companies that have a single A- rating (Standard and Poor's) or better are able to fully self-assure for the life of the mine. Companies with a BBB- rating will be able to fully self-assure for the first half of the life of the mine if this first half is at least four years. Companies with ratings lower than BBB- cannot self-assure. Office of the Auditor General of Ontario, "Chapter 3: Mines and Minerals Program," in *2015 Annual Report of the Office of the Auditor General of Ontario* (2015), 438.

28   Montana Trout Unlimited and Earthworks, *Track Record: Montana Modern Hardrock Mining Water Quality Impacts and Reclamation Bonding* (Missoula, MT: Montana Trout Unlimited, 2018).

29   MiningWatch Canada, "BC Encouraging Environmentally Risky Mining and Creating Massive Taxpayer Liability," May 16, 2016, miningwatch.ca.

30   Quebec Ministry of Energy and Natural Resources, *Guidelines for Preparing Mine Closure Plans in Québec* (Quebec City: Government of Quebec, November 2017); and "Mines: Legislative Provisions," Quebec Ministry of Energy and Natural Resources, mern.gouv.qc.ca.

31   Natural Resources Canada, *Exploration and Mining in Canada: An Investor's Brief* (Government of Canada, February 2016), 25–26.

32   Joseph F. Castrilli, *Environmental Regulation of the Mining Industry in Canada: An Update of Legal and Regulatory Requirements* (Toronto: Walter and Duncan Gordon Foundation, 1999).

13: WHY TAXATION MATTERS

1   Detailed resources presenting the industry point of view include KPMG, *A Guide to Canadian Mining Taxation*, 3rd ed. (2016); and "Overview of Main Tax Instruments," Natural Resources Canada, nrcan.gc.ca. Readers

should also refer to the IGF-OECD Program to Address BEPS (Base Erosion and Profit Shifting Practices) in *The Hidden Cost of Tax Incentives in Mining* (2018). Although the report and the BEPS program were developed for African countries, most of the findings are applicable to provinces, territories, and Indigenous governments in Canada.

2   MiningWatch Canada, "What Green Economy? New OECD Report Finds Canada Worst of G7 on Recycling, Minerals Efficiency," December 19, 2017, miningwatch.ca.

3   KPMG, *Guide to Canadian Mining Taxation*.

4   This figure was taken from a technical paper prepared for the Finance Department based on confidential corporate tax data from 1997. A full explanation of how the amount was derived can be found in note 2 in "Understanding Mining Taxation in Canada," written by the author in 2004 and published by MiningWatch Canada. It is available at miningwatch.ca.

5   IGF-OECD, *Hidden Cost of Tax Incentives*.

6   Alexandra Readhead, *Toolkit for Transfer Pricing Risk Assessment in the African Mining Industry* (Bonn, Germany: Deutsche Gesellschaft für Internationale Zusammenarbeit, 2017), 6.

7   Publish What You Pay, publishwhatyoupay.org.

8   Extractive Industries Transparency Initiative, eiti.org.

9   James Wilt, "Canada's Mining Giants Pay Billions Less in Taxes in Canada Than Abroad," *The Narwhal*, July 16, 2018, thenarwhal.ca.

10 For a detailed explanation of marginal effective tax rate, see Duanjie Chen, "Backgrounder: The Marginal Effective Tax Rate," C. D. Howe Institute Backgrounder, August 22, 2000.

11 Auditor General of Ontario, "Chapter 3.11: Mines and Minerals Program," in *2015 Annual Report of the Office of the Auditor General of Ontario* (2015), 440.

12 "Tables on the Structure and Rates of Main Taxes," Natural Resources Canada, nrcan.gc.ca.

13 "Mining and Minerals Tax," Newfoundland and Labrador Ministry of Finance, fin.gov.nl.ca.

14 "Tables on the Structure and Rates of Main Taxes."

15 MiningWatch Canada and Pembina Institute, *Looking Beneath the Surface: An Assessment of the Value of Public Support for the Metal Mining Industry in Canada* (2002), 37.

16 Section 66.1(6) of the Income Tax Act.

17 Brian R. Carr, "Exploration and Development," *Fundamentals of Canadian Taxation,* December 4, 2006.

18 When Royal Oak Mines was in receivership in 2001, the CCEE and CCDE tax pool for the Kemess Mine was over $200 million, and one of the creditors, Northgate, agreed to accept the mine and tax pool in return for its debt. The mine has operated successfully ever since.

19 Section 66.25 of the Income Tax Act.

20 Section 66.25 of the Income Tax Act.

21 Carr, "Exploration and Development," 26.

22 "Canada: Budget 2018; Mineral Exploration Tax Credit Extended and Tax Support for Clean Energy Expanded," Mondaq, March 6, 2018, mondaq.com.

23 Brian R. Carr, "Flow-Through Shares," *Fundamentals of Canadian Taxation*, December 4, 2006.

24 Barrick Gold, *Management Discussion and Analysis* (2004).

25 "Foreign Resource Expense and Foreign Exploration and Development Expense Claims," Natural Resources Canada, nrcan.gc.ca.

26 "Overview of Main Tax Instruments," Natural Resources Canada, nrcan. gc.ca.

27 IGF-OECD, *Hidden Cost of Tax Incentives.*

14: NOTES ON URANIUM

1 George Blondin, quoted in Canada-Délı̨nę Uranium Table, *Action Plan to Address Concerns Raised by the Community of Délı̨nę about Risks to Human and Environmental Health from Exposure to Radiation and Heavy Metals from the Former Port Radium Mine,* 2nd ed. (Great Bear Lake, NWT: Délı̨nę Band Chief and Council and Department of Indian Affairs and Northern Development, December 2002), iv.

2 Hugh S. Spence, "Radium Discoveries in Northwest Canada," quoted in Peter Van Wyck, *The Highway of the Atom* (Kingston/Montreal: McGill-Queen's University Press, 2010), 114.

3 Lorraine Rekmans, *This Is My Homeland: Stories of the Effects of Nuclear Industries by the People of Serpent River First Nation and the North Shore of Lake Huron* (Serpent River First Nation, 2003), xiv.

4 Paul Baton, testimony before the House of Commons Committee on Environment and Sustainable Development, June 11, 1998, parl.gc.ca.

5 "Port Radium (Eldorado Mine)," Ghost Towns, *ghosttowns.com.*

6   Baton, testimony.

7   Cindy Kenny-Gilday, testimony before the House of Commons Committee on Environment and Sustainable Development, June 11, 1998, parl.gc.ca.

8   Van Wyck, *Highway of the Atom*, 40.

9   Van Wyck, *Highway of the Atom*, 49.

10   Van Wyck, *Highway of the Atom*, 49.

11   Andrew Nikiforuk, "Echoes of the Atomic Age: Cancer Kills Fourteen Dene Workers," *Calgary Herald*, March 14, 1998, ccnr.org.

12   Ronald B. Barbour, "Délı̨nę Dene Mining Tragedy," First Nations Drum, December 22, 1998, firstnationsdrum.com.

13   Délı̨nę Dene Band Council, "Dene of Great Bear Lake Call for Federal Response to Radiation Deaths at Great Bear Lake," news release, March 23, 1998.

14   *Village of Widows: The Story of the Sahtu Dene and the Atomic Bomb*, directed by Peter Blow and Gil Gauvreau (Lindum Films, 1999).

15   The following quotes extensively (and selectively) from Canada-Délı̨nę Uranium Table, *Action Plan*.

16   Canada-Délı̨nę Uranium Table, *Final Report: Concerning Health and Environmental Issues Related to the Port Radium Mine* (Government of Canada and Délı̨nę First Nation, 2005), iv.

17   Canada-Délı̨nę Uranium Table, *Final Report*, iv.

18   Van Wyck, *Highway of the Atom*, 184.

19   Van Wyck, *Highway of the Atom*, 185.

20   Van Wyck, *Highway of the Atom*, 186–87.

21   Canada-Délı̨nę Uranium Table, *Final Report*, vi.

22   "Agreement Reached on Assessment of Impacts from Port Radium Mine Tailings," *Northern News Services*, March 10, 2003.

23   Canada-Délı̨nę Uranium Table, *Final Report*, ix.

24   "Contract Awarded for Remediation Work at Former Port Radium Mine," *Northern News Services*, January 8, 2007.

25   "Uranium in Canada," World Nuclear Association, www.world-nuclear. org.

26   "Uranium in Canada."

27   "About Uranium," Natural Resources Canada, nrcan.gc.ca.

28 "Tax Court Battle: The People vs. Cameco," Canadians for Tax Fairness, taxfairness.ca.

29 Jane George, "Areva Pulls out of Baker Lake, Nunavut Uranium Mine Remains Mothballed," *Nunatsiaq News*, May 5, 2017.

30 "Boomerang Project: Review Board Decision," news release, Uravan Minerals, September 17, 2008.

31 "Background," Paladin Energy Ltd., paladinenergy.com.au.

32 "Underground Exploration Program," Strateco, stratecoinc.com.

33 Bertrand Marotte, "Quebec's Plan Nord Project Snubs Uranium Mining in the Province," *Globe and Mail*, July 26, 2015. On December 5, 2013, Strateco filed a motion to invalidate the decision rendered by Quebec's Minister of Sustainable Development, the Environment, Wildlife and Parks, refusing to deliver the certificate of authorization for the underground exploration phase of the Matoush project.

34 This section is abridged from Canadian Nuclear Safety Commission, "Radioactive Waste Management and Decommissioning in Canada," *Report to the OECD* (March 2008).

35 Environmental and Radiation Health Sciences Directorate, canada.ca.

36 "Nuclear Safety Watchdog Head Fired for 'Lack of Leadership': Minister," CBC News, January 16, 2008.

37 Available from Canadian Nuclear Safety Commission, nuclearsafety. gc.ca.

38 Canadian Nuclear Safety Commission, "Radioactive Waste Management."

39 Eric Cline, "The Long-Term Management of Former Uranium Mine Sites," speech given by Saskatchewan Minister of Industry and Resources, World Nuclear Association Meeting, London, 2007.

40 Houston Kempton, Thomas A. Bloomfield, Jason L. Hanson, and Patty Limerick, *Policy Guidance for Identifying and Effectively Managing Perpetual Environmental Impacts from New Hardrock Mines* (Boulder, CO: Center of the American West, 2010), 6.

41 Cline, "Long-Term Management."

42 International Atomic Energy Agency, *Joint Convention on the Safety of Spent Fuel Management and on the Safety of Radioactive Waste Management* (2001).

43 For an excellent analysis of the shortcomings of net present value as a basis for long-term stewardship financial assurance, see Joseph H. Guth,

"Resolving the Paradoxes of Discounting in Environmental Decisions," *Transnational Law and Contemporary Problems* 18, no. 95 (2009).

44 Canadian Nuclear Safety Commission, "CNSC Record of Proceedings Including Reasons for Decision in the Matter of Cameco Corporation Application to Renew the Beaverlodge Mine and Mill Site Waste Facility Operating Licence," November 30, 2009, 9.

45 "Project CLEANS," Saskatchewan Research Council, src.sk.ca.

46 Committee for Future Generations, committeeforfuturegenerations. wordpress.com.

15: STOPPING A MINE BEFORE IT STARTS

1   The account that follows is drawn from the author's own files; David Peerla's *No Means No: The Kitchenuhmaykoosib Inninuwug and the Fight for Indigenous Resource Sovereignty* (Cognitariat Publishing, 2012); and Paula Sherman, "Picking up the Wampum Belt as an Act of Protest," in *Alliances: Re/Envisioning Indigenous–Non-Indigenous Relationships*, ed. Lynne Davis (Toronto: University of Toronto Press, 2010).

2   Jeff Green, "Marilyn Crawford Made a Difference," *Frontenac News*, August 28, 2014.

3   Green, "Marilyn Crawford."

4   Joan Kuyek, "Fighting Free Entry: Ending Mining's Privileged Access to Land," *The Dominion*, November 21, 2008.

5   MiningWatch Canada, "Aboriginal Leaders Face Jail Time in Spreading Disputes over First Nations Rights and Mining Claims," January 28, 2008, miningwatch.ca.

6   Sherman, "Picking up the Wampum Belt," 118.

7   Peerla, *No Means No*, 3.

8   Ardoch Algonquin and Shabot Obaadjiwan news release, July 13, 2007.

9   Peerla, *No Means No*, 3

10 Environmental Commissioner of Ontario, *Annual Report: Reconciling Our Priorities* (Toronto: Environmental Commissioner of Ontario, 2007), 68.

11 Sherman, "Picking up the Wampum Belt," 126.

12 Peerla, *No Means No*.

13 "PATH (People Assessing Their Health)," Antigonish Women's Resource Centre and Sexual Assault Services Association, awrcsasa.ca.

14 Arthur Manuel and Grand Chief Ronald Derrickson, *The Reconciliation Manifesto* (Toronto: Lorimer, 2017), 221.

15 John Borrows, "Crown and Aboriginal Occupations of Land: A History and Comparison," research paper commissioned by the Ipperwash Inquiry (October 15, 2005).

16: DEALING WITH AN OPERATING MINE

1 G. Gibson, K. Yung, L. Chisholm, and H. Quinn, with Lake Babine Nation and Nak'azdli Whut'en, *Indigenous Communities and Industrial Camps: Promoting Healthy Communities in Settings of Industrial Change* (Victoria: The Firelight Group, 2017).

2 Michael Edelstein, Maria Tysiachniouk, and Lyudmila V. Smirnova, eds., "Cultures of Contamination: Legacies of Pollution in Russia and the US," in *Research in Social Problems and Public Policy*, vol. 14 (Bingley, UK: JAI Press, 2007).

3 For further information, see Natasha Affolder, Katy Allen, and Sascha Paruk, *Independent Environmental Oversight: A Report for the Giant Mine Remediation Environmental Assessment* (University of British Columbia, February 2011).

4 Independent Environmental Monitoring Agency, monitoringagency.net.

5 Environmental Monitoring Advisory Board, emab.ca.

6 An excellent example of this problem is described in Council of Canadians, "Council of Canadians in Solidarity with Tŝilhqot'in Nation against Gibraltar Effluent Discharges into the Fraser River," November 12, 2015, canadians.org.

7 Fair Mining Collaborative, fairmining.ca.

8 Centre for Indigenous Environmental Resources, yourcier.org.

9 Mushkegowuk Environmental Research Centre, nafaforestry.org.

10 "What Is Whistleblowing? Guide to Whistleblowing in Canada," KCY at Law, October 25, 2017, kcyatlaw.ca.

11 Robinson-Huron Treaty, rht150.ca; Bill Curry, "Native Band Sues for $550-Billion, Saying Mine Sites Belong to Them," *Globe and Mail*, May 14, 2008.

12 Carl Rhodes and Peter Bloom, "The Trouble with Charitable Billionaires," *Guardian*, May 24, 2018.

13 "Malartic Gold Mine Class-Action Lawsuit Trial Begins," Mining.com, October 27, 2017.

14 "Malartic Gold Mine."

15 See Jane F. McAlevey, *No Shortcuts: Organizing for Power in the New Gilded Age* (New York: Oxford University Press. 2016); and Nora Loreto, *From Demonized to Organized: Building the New Union Movement* (Ottawa: Canadian Centre for Policy Alternatives, 2013).

16 Valentina Ruiz Leotaud, "Secwepemc Protest Imperial Metals and Company's Ties with Government," *Vancouver Observer*, August 12, 2014.

17 Stand for Water, standforwater.org.

18 "Province Halts Private Prosecution against Mount Polley Tailings Spill," CBC News, January 30, 2018; and MiningWatch Canada, "Mount Polley Disaster Stunner: Federal Government Moves to Stop MiningWatch from Presenting Evidence to Court," Cision, January 13, 2017, newswire.ca.

19 Gordon Hoekstra, "Appeal Challenges Discharge of Mt. Polley Mine Effluent to Quesnel Lake," *Vancouver Sun*, August 15, 2018.

20 James Wilt, "What Happens if Imperial Metals Goes Bankrupt?" *The Narwhal*, August 28, 2018, thenarwhal.ca.

21 There is excellent critical debate about risk assessments at the Environmental Research Foundation website, particularly in their *Rachel's Democracy and Health News*—see #470 and #920, rachel.org.

22 National Orphaned/Abandoned Mines Initiative, "A Workshop to Explore Perspectives on Risk Assessment for Orphaned and Abandoned Mines," Vancouver, British Columbia, November 13–14, 2008, abandoned-mines.org.

23 Nicholas D. Martyniak, citing Williams (1998), "The Case of the Pinewood Landfill," in *Long Term Management of Contaminated Sites*, ed. Thomas Leschine, Research in Social Problems and Public Policy, vol. 13 (New York: Elsevier, 2008), 76.

24 Julien Dionne, speaking for SOAR, Sudbury, February 28, 2009.

25 Sudbury Soils Study, sudburysoilsstudy.com.

26 "Sudbury Scientist Leads Deadly Radon Research," *Sudbury Star*, February 8, 2018.

27 SARA Group, "Chapter 7.0: The 2001 Soil Survey," in *Sudbury Area Risk Assessment* (January 2008).

28 Environment Canada and Health Canada, *Canadian Environmental Protection Act: Priority Substances List Assessment Report; Nickel and its Compounds—PSL1* (Minister of Supply and Services Canada, 1994).

29 The preceding discussion is taken from the author's personal files and records.

30 The Better Beginnings project is described in more detail in Joan Kuyek, *Community Organizing: A Holistic Approach* (Black Point, NS: Fernwood, 2011).

31 Myths and Mirrors, mythsandmirrors.wordpress.com.

17: ORGANIZING WHEN THE MINE IS GONE

1 See Joan Kuyek, *The Theory and Practice of Perpetual Care of Contaminated Sites: A Literature Review* (2011), sehn.org.

2 Kevin O'Reilly, "Liability, Legacy and Perpetual Care: Government Ownership and Management of the Giant Mine 1999–2015," In *Mining and Communities in Northern Canada: History, Politics and Memory*, eds. Arn Keeling and John Sandlos (Calgary: University of Calgary Press, 2015). See also Jimmy Thomson, "This Is Giant Mine," *The Narwhal*, June 9, 2018, thenarwhal.ca.

3 O'Reilly, "Liability, Legacy," 344.

4 Actually a lockout in 1992. CASAW was the union, Royal Oak the mine operator. Nine replacement workers were killed in an explosion set by one of the locked-out miners, and the strike deeply divided the city.

5 Kevin O'Reilly interview, June 3, 2018.

6 O'Reilly, "Liability, Legacy," 347.

7 O'Reilly, "Liability, Legacy," 347.

8 O'Reilly, "Liability, Legacy," 358.

9 Kevin O'Reilly interview, June 3, 2018.

10 See Kuyek, *Theory and Practice*.

11 Peter Van Wyck, *Highway of the Atom* (Kingston/Montreal: McGill-Queen's University Press, 2010), 49.

12 Nicholas D. Martyniak, citing Williams (1998), "The Case of the Pinewood Landfill" in *Long Term Management of Contaminated Sites*, ed. Thomas Leschine, Research in Social Problems and Public Policy, vol. 13 (New York: Elsevier, 2008), 76.

13 Eugene A. Rosa, "Long Term Stewardship and Risk Management: Analytic and Policy Challenges," in *Long Term Management of Contaminated Sites*, ed. Thomas Leschine, Research in Social Problems and Public Policy, vol. 13 (New York: Elsevier, 2008), 242.

14 Rosa, "Long Term Stewardship," 242.

15 Natasha Affolder, Katy Allen, and Sascha Paruk, *Independent Environmental Oversight: A Report for the Giant Mine Remediation Environmental Assessment* (University of British Columbia, February 2011).

16 Affolder, Allen, and Paruk, *Independent Environmental Oversight.*

17 Houston Kempton, Thomas A. Bloomfield, Jason L. Hanson, and Patty Limerick, *Policy Guidance for Identifying and Effectively Managing Perpetual Environmental Impacts from New Hardrock Mines* (Boulder, CO: Center of the American West, 2010), 6; Dick Cowan, W. O. Mackasey, and John Robertson, *The Policy Framework in Canada for Mine Closure and Management of Long-Term Liabilities: A Guidance Document* (Sudbury, ON: National Orphaned/Abandoned Mines Initiative, 2010).

18 Saskatchewan Ministry of Energy and Resources, *Institutional Control Program: Post Closure Management of Decommissioned Mine/Mill Properties on Crown Land in Saskatchewan* (Saskatoon: Government of Saskatchewan, December 2009); John Pendergrass and Katherine Probst, *Estimating the Cost of Institutional Controls* (Washington, DC: Environmental Law Institute and Resources for the Future, 2005); Joseph H. Guth, "Resolving the Paradoxes of Discounting in Environmental Decisions," *Transnational Law and Contemporary Problems* 18, no. 95 (2009).

19 Guth, "Resolving the Paradoxes."

20 Indigenous Environmental Network, *Bemidji Statement on Seventh Generation Guardianship* (July 2006); Science and Environmental Health Network and the International Human Rights Clinic at Harvard Law School, *Models for Protecting the Environment for Future Generations* (October 2008).

21 Indigenous Environmental Network, *Bemidji Statement.*

18: INTERNATIONAL SOLIDARITY WORK

1 "Salvadoran Legislature Votes for Water over Gold, Becoming First Country to Ban Metal Mining Outright," MiningWatch Canada, March 30, 2017, miningwatch.ca.

2 Jen Moore interview, May 31, 2018.

3   Two excellent books for further reading about the relationship between mining companies and their critics are Stuart Krisch, *Mining Capitalism: The Relationship between Corporations and Their Critics* (Berkeley, CA: University of California Press, 2014); and Liisa North, Timothy David Clark, and Viviana Patroni, eds., *Community Rights and Corporate Responsibility* (Toronto: Between the Lines, 2006).

4   "Mining, Minerals and Sustainable Development," International Institute for Environment and Development, iied.org.

5   International Institute for Environment and Development, *Breaking New Ground: Mines, Minerals and Sustainable Development* (2003).

6   International Council on Mining and Metals, icmm.com.

7   "Extractive Industries Review," International Finance Corporation, ifc. org; Initiative for Responsible Mining Assurance, responsiblemining. net; Global Compact Network Canada, globalcompact.ca; International Cyanide Management Code, cyanidecode.org; Extractive Industries Transparency Initiative, eiti.org.

8   Mines and Communities, "The London Declaration 2008," Mines and Communities Conference, October 2007, minesandcommunities.org.

9   Mines and Communities, "The London Declaration."

10 Transnational Institute, tni.org; Inter Press Service, ipsnews.net; Center for International Environmental Law, ciel.org; Rights and Accountability in Development, raid-uk.org; Centre for Research on Multinational Corporations, somo.nl.

11 Canadian Network on Corporate Accountability, cnca-rcrce.ca.

12 Above Ground, *Transnational Lawsuits in Canada against Extractive Companies: Developments in Civil Litigation* (February 17, 2016).

13 ECA Watch, ECA-watch.org.

14 Canadian Coalition for Tax Fairness, taxfairness.ca.

15 Kairos Canada, kairoscanada.org.

16 Mining Injustice Solidarity Network, mininginjustice.org.

17 Merle Davis interview, June 20, 2018.

18 Protest Barrick, protestbarrick.net.

19 Merle Davis interview, June 20, 2018.

20 "Report of the International NGO Fact-Finding Mission to Tanzania," MiningWatch Canada, April 16, 2002, miningwatch.ca.

21 "Choc v. HudBay Minerals Inc. and Caal v. HudBay Minerals Inc.,"
    Klippensteins, Barristers and Solicitors, September 15, 2017, chocversu-
    shudbay.com.

22 Tahoe on Trial, tahoeontrial.net.

19: TAKING ON THE COMPANY AND ITS INVESTORS

1   The first part of this chapter is adapted from Joan Kuyek, *Mining Inves-
    tors*, previously published by MiningWatch Canada in 2005, which
    used a lot of material from a UK document published in 2003, *The
    Campaigners' Guide to Financial Markets*, by Nick Hildyard and Mark
    Mansley (Dorset, UK: Corner House, 2003). It has since been revised
    and updated.

2   Hildyard and Mansley, *Campaigners' Guide*.

3   Hildyard and Mansley, *Campaigners' Guide*, 54.

4   Hildyard and Mansley, *Campaigners' Guide*, 13

5   Hildyard and Mansley, *Campaigners' Guide*, 80.

6   Joan Kuyek, *Behind the Pebble Mine: Hunter Dickinson Inc.* (Ottawa:
    MiningWatch Canada, February 2, 2018.

7   Taseko, *Management Information Circular* (April 2017), 37.

8   The only HDI-affiliated company paying taxes to provincial or federal
    governments is Gibraltar Mine, and—other than a portion of the BC
    Mineral Tax—it does not pay taxes unless it earns a profit.

9   Taseko was clearly affiliated with HDI from 1991 until 2016 and contin-
    ues to share a number of directors with HDI and to purchase services
    from HDI. Taseko subsidiaries also share HDI directors.

10 Taseko, "Financial Statements for 2015 and 2016," news release, August
    22, 2017; Taseko, *Financial Statements for 2015 and 2016*, 22. Despite
    the enormous size and risk from the tailings impoundment, in 2017,
    Taseko had only $30,535,000 in a line of credit and a cash deposit of
    $7,500,000 with British Columbia Ministry of Energy and Mines as its
    "provision for environmental rehabilitation" for Gibraltar and the Flor-
    ence Copper Mine in Arizona together.

11 The Bokoni Mine, currently on care and maintenance, is owned by
    Atlatsa Resources (previously known as Anooraq Resources). HDI was
    involved until 2010. Bokoni had previously been called the Lebowa
    Mine. Unanticipated low platinum group metals prices and labour
    unrest forced its closure. Tirisano was to be the flagship of the alluvial
    diamond mines brought into production by Rockwell Diamonds. HDI

was involved with Rockwell until February 2013. Burnstone in South Africa was forced into receivership by its creditors in 2013.

12 The Campo Morado G9 Mine in Mexico was rushed into production by HDI Farallon without a feasibility study. Plummeting zinc prices in 2009 and then violent gang activity led to its closure in early 2015. Nyrstar closed it and sold it for $20 million. Hollister Mine in Nevada was forced into receivership by its creditors in 2013.

13 Ike is opposed by the Tŝilhqot'in as it lies in the heart of Dasiqox tribal park. Sisson is opposed by five of six Maliseet (Wolastoq) communities. Florence is opposed by the Town of Florence and others as they fear for their drinking water aquifer.

14 Kimberley Mok, "Canadian Mining Companies 'Looting' Occupied Tibet," Tree Hugger, March 4, 2009, treehugger.com; and "Tibetan Protests Target Canada Mining Companies," Phayul, June 19, 2006, phayul. com.

15 The Sisson Mine is not currently economically feasible given low commodity prices. Prices in the feasibility study from January 2013 were based on $350/Mtu (USD) for tungsten (much higher than today's market) and $15/lb (USD) for molybdenum (many times higher than today). Heatherdale's Ni-Black (copper-zinc) mine has resource estimates only from 2011. Rathdowney's Olza project is not yet permitted, and until/if zinc prices rise it is highly unlikely to proceed. Ike is a very early stage exploration copper-silver-molybdenum project.

16 Frik Els, "Northern Dynasty Shares Crater after First Quantum Pulls out of Pebble Project," Business in Vancouver, May 28, 2018, biv.com.

17 More information about the Gibraltar Mine can be found in the following: Scott Jones, *Taseko Updated Mineral Reserve Technical Report* (June 15, 2015), 12, intel.rscmme.com; Klohn Crippen Berger, *Gibraltar Mines Ltd.: 2014 Annual Dam Safety Inspection* (November 2014); *Taseko Audited Financial Statements for 2016*, note 19, 28–29; Gordon Hoekstra, "BC's Gibraltar Wants to Increase Amount of Effluent Discharged to the Fraser River," *Vancouver Sun*, September 28, 2015. There is a substantial potential unfunded liability for investors from the Florence Copper Mine, as it is located very close to the drinking water aquifer for Pinal County and the Town of Florence. The consequences of accidents are not covered in the reclamation bond for the mine. Leakage into aquifers from in-situ leach wells—no matter how carefully constructed—is a real concern. Water availability is huge issue in Arizona and there is substantial opposition to the mine from the Town of Florence, from citizens' groups, and from developers South West Value Partners and Pulte Homes, who all believe that the mine endangers the drinking water aquifers.

18   Homestake saw capex (capital costs) more than double once they took over Northern Dynasty in 1986 as the costs had been underestimated. Although the Golden Bear mine operated for only eight years, current owner Goldcorp has had to maintain it since 2005. Placer Dome (PDI) paid $258 million for the HDI Mount Milligan deposit in 1990, and then wrote it off in 1992 when gold prices dropped. This very marginal copper-gold mine was finally brought into production in 2014, but carrying a $782 million gold stream agreement with Royal Gold. In 2016, now carrying $800 million in debt, it was sold again to Centerra, which paid $175.6 million in cash and assumed the debt. The gold stream agreement was renegotiated to include copper. The Bokoni Mine in South Africa struggled for years to be profitable, despite enormous financial assistance from Amplats. It has been on care and maintenance since July 2017. Campo Morado in Mexico was rushed to production by HDI Farallon and sold to Nyrstar for $409 million in 2011. Faced with unpredicted low zinc prices and violence in the state, Nyrstar closed the mine and sold it in 2015 for $20 million.

19   Northern Dynasty, *Financial Statements,* September 30, 2017.

20: SCALING UP

1   Ric Careless, *To Save the Wild Earth* (Vancouver: Raincoast Books, 1997), 169.

2   J. P. Laplante, *Kemess North: Insights and Lessons* (Takla Lake First Nation, 2009).

3 ˙ For two fascinating readings (and two very different points of view) about the early days of Voisey's Bay, see Mick Lowe's *Premature Bonanza* (Toronto: Between the Lines, 1998) and Jacquie McNish's *The Big Score* (Toronto: Doubleday Canada, 1998).

4   Virtual People's Summit on APEC, vcn.bc.ca/summit.

5   Canadian Environmental Network, rcen.ca; Canadian Council for International Co-operation, ccic.ca.

6   Northwatch, web.net/~nwatch; Yukon Conservation Society, yukonconservation.org; Canadian Environmental Law Association, cela.ca; Inter Pares, interpares.ca.

7   Steelworkers Humanity Fund, usw.ca; Canadian Auto Workers Social Justice Fund, caw.ca; Canadian Nature Federation, now renamed Nature Canada, naturecanada.ca; Canadian Parks and Wilderness Society, cpaws.org; Kairos Canada, kairos.ca.

8   "Between a Rock and a Hard Place: Aboriginal Communities and Mining," Ottawa, ON, September 10–12, 1999, miningwatch.ca.

9   "On the Ground Research: A Workshop to Identify the Research Needs of Communities Affected by Large Scale Mining," Ottawa, ON, April 14–16, 2000, miningwatch.ca.

10   Coalition pour que le Québec ait meilleure mine, quebecmeilleuremine. org.

11   Luke Stocking, "Justice after 11-Year Battle to Protect Human Rights in Mining Industry," Catholic Register, February 5, 2018, catholicregister. org.

12   Natural Resources Canada, *Building the Canadian Advantage: A CSR Strategy for the International Extractive Sector* (2009).

13   Devonshire Initiative, devonshireinitiative.org.

14   Sonya Nigam, "Beyond the Fall of Bill C-300," Canadian Lawyer, November 8, 2010, canadianlawyermag.com.

15   Pierre Dagenais, "Canadian Mining Industry Wins with Bill C-300's Defeat," Canadian Mining Journal, December 1, 2010, canadianmining-journal.com.

16   Office of the Extractive Sector Corporate Social Responsibility (CSR) Counsellor, *2011 Annual Report to Parliament, October 2010 to October 2011* (Toronto: Office of the Extractive Sector CSR Counsellor, 2011).

17   Justice and Corporate Accountability Project, *The "Canada Brand": Violence and Canadian Mining Companies in Latin America*, Osgoode Legal Studies Research Paper no. 17/2017 (2016): 37–39.

18   "Minister Oda Announces Initiatives to Increase the Benefits of Natural Resource Management for People in Africa and South America," Republic of Mining, September 29, 2011, republicofmining.com.

19   "The Government of Canada Brings Leadership to Responsible Business Conduct Abroad," news release, January 17, 2018, canada.ca. For more information, see Above Ground, MiningWatch Canada, and OECD Watch, *"Canada Is Back" But Still Far Behind* (November 2016).

20   Jen Moore interview, May 31, 2018.

21: CREATING A NEW STORY

1   Ontarians for a Just Accountable Mineral Strategy, ojams.ca.

2   Iron and Earth, ironandearth.org.

3   Robert Repetto, *Silence Is Golden, Leaden and Copper: Disclosure of Environmental Information in the Hard Rock Mining Industry* (New Haven, CT: Yale School of Forestry and Environmental Studies, 2004).

4   Maya Stano and Emma Lehrer, *Fair Mining Practices: A New Mining Code for British Columbia* (Courtenay, BC: Fair Mining Collaborative, 2013); Glenn M. Grande, *The Mine Medicine Manual: A Community Resource* (Courtenay, BC: Fair Mining Collaborative, 2015).

5   Initiative for Responsible Mining Assurance, responsiblemining.net.

6   International Institute for Sustainable Development, *Seven Questions to Sustainability: How to Assess the Contribution of Mining and Minerals Activities* (Winnipeg, MB: International Institute for Sustainable Development, 2002), 33.

7   There is a whole literature about the social economy, community economic development, and holistic economic development. A good place to start is the Canadian CED Network's "The Social Economy," ccednet-rcdec.ca.

8   From the author's files.

9   Fanny Bay Oysters, fannybayoysters.com, is an example of the shellfish aquaculture industry; Community Tourism Foundation, *Comox Valley Situation Analysis.*

10   From the Ground Up Rural Resource Consultants, *Comox Valley Gap Analysis, 2008: Comox Valley Agri-food Initiative* (2008).

11   On March 14, 2017, the company filed a lawsuit seeking damages from British Columbia for "nuisance, negligence, misfeasance in public office[,] . . . expropriation and interference with its land grant rights." The story continues.

INDEX

Note: Page numbers in italics refer to images/figures.

Canadian Network on Corporate Accountability (CNCA), 272–73; Open for Justice campaign, *301*, 304

Canadian Nuclear Safety Commission (CNSC), 173, 176–77, 187, 211, 213, 21417; Research and Support Program, 214; Uranium Mines and Mills Regulations, 214–15

Canadian Ombudsperson for Responsible Enterprise (CORE), 304–5

Canadian Parks and Wilderness Society, 296, 298

Canadian Securities Administrators, 109, 112

Canadian state: Indigenous dispossession by, 3; role of, 61; violence by, 304

Canadian Union of Public Employees, 79

Canary Research Institute for Mining, Environment, and Health, 141

cancer, 74, 205; lung, 48, 50; radiation-related, 209; and Sudbury soil, 248

cancer-causing pollutants, 45, 49, 87

capital: access to, 160–61, availability of, 280; natural, depletion of, 146, 201; outside, dependence of mining on, 73

capital gains tax, 199, 200

capital movement: removal of national control over, 129–30

carbon-capture and sequestration technologies (CCS), 142

carbon monoxide, 47, 90

carbon pollution, 142

cardiovascular disease: sulphur dioxide and, 48

Careless, Ric, 296

Carnoules Declaration (1994), 140, 339n3

Casa Berardi Gold Mine (Quebec), 52

Casino mine, 44

catastrophic accidents, 244–46, 262–63, 310, 311

Category 1 lands, 170

Cayman Islands: as tax shelter, 107, 132, 201

Center for Research on Multinational Corporations (SOMO), 131, 272

Centerra Gold, 16, 357n18

Central American Free Trade Agreement (CAFTA), 126–27

Centre for Indigenous Environmental Resources (Winnipeg), 241

Centre for International Environmental Law (CIEL), 272

certificate of environmental compliance, 174

CEZinc Refinery (Salaberry-de-Valleyfield), 182

Chalk River nuclear refinery, 214

Chan, Dr. Laurie, 334n21

chemical processing: pollution from, 43–45

Chiapas (Mexico), 133

Chieftain Metals, 67

children: health and behavioural development of, 250–52

chlorine, 43, 45

Choc v. Hudbay, 277

Christian Labour Association of Canada (CLAC), 86

Christian Peacemakers, 225

chromium, 47; and cancer, 49

chronic obstructive pulmonary disease, 86–87

Chub v. Hudbay, 277

Cigar Lake mine (Saskatchewan), 210–11

citizens: rights of, 271; vigilance and mobilization of, 260

Citizens Committee Against Mining Uranium (CCAMU), 227

claims, staking. *See* staking claims

Clark, Christy, 167

climate change, 48, 51, 96, 120; coal and, 142

Eat Local Sudbury, 252

ECA Watch, 273

ecological accounting. *See* economics: ecological

ecological integrity, 183

ecological risk assessment, 95, 252

economic assessment, 15

economic dependence, 239

economic development: non-extractive forms of, 308

economic rights, 273

economics: classical, failure of to address crucial questions, 147; ecological, 145–54; reclaiming, 145–54

economy: costs of coal to, 142; origin of word, 145

ecosystem health, 30, 48

ecosystem services, 146

Edelstein, Michael, 240

"edge effect," 13

Eeyou Istchee: Cree Mineral Exploration Board, 66

EITI. *See* Extractive Industries Transparency Initiative

Ekati diamond mine complex (NWT), 11, 13, 46, 86, 241; Independent Environmental Monitoring Agency, 256

El Dorado gold mine (El Salvador), 127

Eldorado mine (NWT), 204–5, 208

Eldorado Nuclear Limited, 210

electrolysis, 29

electro-winning (SE/EW process), 29

Elliot Lake (Ontario), 75, 204, 210

El Salvador, 126–27; ban on mining in, 127, 265–67, 268, 305, 307

embassy support, 123, 132–34

emergency response, 261–63

employment: alternative, 74; data on, 80–82, 209; Indigenous, 61, 64; mixed, 75; of women, 81

Endangered Species Act, 173, 187

Engler, Yves, 136–37

environmental assessment (EA), 15, 24, 25–26, 38, 64–65, 96–97, 147, 149, 166–67, 172, 173, 174–78, 196, 231, 233, 241, 255, 257–59; federal and provincial, 174–78; Indigenous, 170, 233; regional, 178; by responsible authority, 177; by review panel, 177; strategic, 178, 310

Environmental Assessment Act, 305

Environmental Code of Practice for Base Metals Smelters and Refineries, 181–82

environmental concerns: drilling and, 23; after mine closure, 34; and mine tailings, 30; overlooking, 146

Environmental Defence Canada, 251

environmental degradation and destruction, 3, 128, 240, 281, 311; by coal, 142

environmental disclosure requirements, 311–12

environmental effects monitoring (EEM), 180

environmental harms: liability for, 121–22

environmental impacts, 37–52, 75, 113, 172, 197, 222, 297; lack of investor concern with, 279

environmental impact statement, 174, 231, 281

environmentalists, 21, 178, 296

Environmental Mining Council of British Columbia (EMCBC), 164, 296

environmental monitoring: agreements, 64, 66; independent, 241–42

environmental organizations, 180, 223, 245, 298

environmental protection, 126, 157, 163, 169

environmental rights: violations of, 302

Florence Copper mine (Arizona), 292, 357n13, 357n17

flotation separation, 28

flow-through shares (FTS), 197, *198*, 310

fluorides, 49

fluorite, 30

flux, 31

"follow the money" strategies, 280

Fontaine, Phil, 67, 329n36

footprint: environmental, 148, 253; of exploration, 231; physical, 9–14, 38, 73, 157; political, 253; social, 157

foreign accrual property income, 200

foreign investment and protection agreements, 126

Fort McMurray (Alberta), 205

Fort Resolution, 89

Fort St. James (BC), 16

forward selling, 111

Fothergill, Jay, 141; *Scrap Mining*, 141

Fox, Glen, 252

Frame, Clifford, 20, 88, 321n13

Franco-Nevada, 111

free entry, 17–21, 222, 296; and conflicts, 21; fight to end in Ontario, 223–31

free prior informed consent (FPIC), 223, 271, 308, 310

Free Tibet Committee, 292

free-trade agreements, 126–27

French River, 58

Friedland, Robert, 20, 321n13

Froese, Dr. Kenneth, 334n21

Frontenac Ventures Corporation (FVC), 227, 230

FTS. *See* flow-through shares

Gaian accounting. *See* economics: ecological

Garcia v. Tahoe Resources, 277

gaseous reduction, 29

gas extraction, 47

GDP: Canadian, 2; growth in, 166, 236; Yukon, 92

Geddes Resources, 21, 296

geochemical surveys, 22, 196

Geological Survey of Canada, 174

geological surveys, 17

geophysical surveys, 22, 196

Ghana, 297, 300

Giant Mine (Yellowknife), 49, 91, 186, 297, 321n13; arsenic contamination from, 255–59; cleanup and long-term care of, 257; closure of, 255, 257; environmental assessment of remediation plan, 96–97, 255–59; Oversight Board, 241, 259

Gibraltar Mine (BC), 10, 150, 292, 356n8, 357n17

Glencore, 69, 172, 181–82; Belledune smelter, 182; CCR copper refinery, 182; Horne smelter, 182; Sudbury smelter, 9, 50, 86

Glencore-Noranda Income Fund, 182

Global Affairs Canada, 114

Global Compact, 163, 269

globalization, 123

Global South: bauxite ore from, 182; Canadian mining companies in, 127–28, 137, 162, 301; criminalization of land and water protectors, 236; EITI requirements in, 192; impact of corporate tax loopholes on, 126; much to learn from, 267, 299

global warming, 49, 317

Goderich (Ontario), 86

Godfrey, Todd, 73

God's Lake Resources, 21

gold: artisanal mining of, 128; geological belt of, 243; grade of, 10; increase in reserves of, 140; lack of real need for, 139, 144, 315; mining of, 16, 18, 20,

40–41, 43, 243, 255; recovery of, 29; rich deposits of, 123; trade in, 55, 111

Goldcorp, 67, 268, 357n18; corporate structure of, *133*; tax paid by, 191

Goldcorp Coffee Project, 44

Goldcorp tailings (Balmertown), 50

Golden Bear (BC), 293, 357n18

Gold Fields Act of British Columbia, 18

gold roasters, 49, 255

gold rushes, 18, 57

Grande, Glenn M., 312

Gratton, Pierre, 160

gravity separation, 28

Great Basin Gold, 292

Great Bear Lake (NWT), 204–5, 207, 209

Great Slave Lake (NWT), 255

greenhouse gases (GHG), 13, 39, 47, 142; emissions management, MAC and, 159

Green Lake (Ontario), 221, 224

green mining, 308

Grenville-sur-la-Rouge (Quebec), 232

Gros Rosebel gold mine (Suriname), 131

groundwater: contamination of, 92, 147, 184; seepage into, 50

guardianship, intergenerational, 264

Guatemala, 113, 135, 267; Supreme Court, 113; Xinka population in, 113

Gunnar mine (Saskatchewan), 217

habitat loss, 13, 30, 149. *See also* fish/fish habitat; wildlife

Haida Gwaii, 64

Haida/Taku case, 170

Hallbauer, Russell, 166–68, 291

Hanmer (Ontario), 250

Hanslinger, Richard, 16

Harper, Stephen, 179, 302

Hatch consultancy, 322n2

hazardous pollutants, 33

hazardous wastes: import and export of, 173, 187

Hazeltine Creek (BC), 51, 164, 319n1 (intro.)

HDI Farallon, 356nn11–12, 357n18

health: risk assessment, 233, 246, 249–51, 257, 261; social determinants of, 233. *See also* human health

health and safety. *See* human health; occupational health and safety

Health Canada: First Nations and Inuit Health Branch, 249; Radiation Protection Bureau, 213

health care, 49, 189

heap leaching, 29, 44

Heatherdale, 357n15

heavy metals, 30, 42, 47–49

hedge funds, 111

hedging, 111

helicopter surveys, 22

Hemlo mine (Ontario), 192

Henderson, Hazel, 146

Hidden Cost of Tax Incentives in Mining (IGF-OECD), 191, 201

Highland Valley Copper Mine (BC), 31, 32, 150, 166

Hildyard, Nick, 109

Hiroshima (Japan): atomic bomb dropped on, 205; Dene visit to, 207

Hodge, Dr. Anthony, 334n21

The Hole Story, 330n15

Hollister Mine (Nevada), 292, 356n12

homelessness, 71

Honest Accounts 2017, 130

Horne smelter (Rouyn-Noranda), 182

housing crisis: as result of influx of workers, 26; among Ross River Dena, 92

Hudbay Minerals Inc., 135, 182; smelter (Flin Flon), 47, 182

human health, 23, 30, 75, 95; costs of coal to, 142; effects of elevated levels of metals on, 249; and former mine workers, 74; hazardous pollutants and, 33, 74; preservation of, 315; risk assessment, 249–51, 257, 261

human health risk assessment (HHRA), 249–51

human rights: violations of, 302

Hunter Dickinson Inc., 104, 286, 290–93

Hupacasath people, 316

hydraulic fracturing, 29

hydrocarbons, 30

hydrochloric acid, 43, 45

hydrometallurgy, 32–33

hyper-masculinity, 240

"If Only We Had Known" (oral history), 209

Ike mining exploration project (BC), 292, 357n13

immigrants: and income disparity, 73

impact benefit agreements (IBAs), 61, 64, 65–66, 172, 242–43, 281

Imperial Metals, 159, 164–65, 244, 246; tax paid by, 191

Inco, 69, 84, 163, 296–97, 319n2 (intro.)

income disparity, 73, 74, 240

income inequality, 240

Income Tax Act, 194

income taxes, 121; corporate, 190, 194–98

independent environmental monitoring, 241–42, 259, 263

Independent First Nations Alliance, 56

independent qualified person (QP), 118

India: mining company violations in, 128

Indian and Northern Affairs Canada, 95

Indian Mining Regulations, 18

Indigenous and Northern Affairs Canada, 18, 173, 186

Indigenous Environmental Network, 63

Indigenous governments: and control over traditional lands and waters, 63; and corporations, 107; and development moratoriums, 224; and environmental assessment, 65, 177–78; and environmental monitoring, 241; and joint ventures with mining companies, 107; and resource development, 170; and revenue sharing, 65–66, 199; and staking claims, 18–20; and staking rushes, 221

Indigenous lands: and Canadian mining companies abroad, 127; and contaminated sites, 97; control over, 63; exploration on, 19–20; mines on, 56, 61; non-Aboriginal blockades and occupations of, 57; and Robinson-Huron Treaty, 57–60; transfer of title for, 170; unceded, 58

Indigenous law, 170–72; as separate from Canadian law, 170

Indigenous Leadership Initiative, 64

Indigenous Network on Environment and Trade, 63

Indigenous peoples: advancing participation of in mining industry, 157, 161; benefits to, 148; blocking company access to land, 234; cheated, 242; consultation with, 196; on corporate boards, 67; and defence of right to land, 235; different approaches to mining industry by, 62–67; displacement and dispossession of, 3, 57, 70, 72, 127, 316; education of, 61; effects of Canadian mining companies on, 162, 168; employment of in mining and exploration, 61, 64, 66, 81, 222, 308; and environmental assessment, 25, 233; and Global South, 267; governance responsibilities of, 63; impact of mining and colonialism on, 55–67; impoverishment of, 3, 61; and income disparity, 73; lack of economic alternatives for, 61; lands being stolen from, 3; leadership of, 299; marginalization of, 72; after mine closure, 75, 91, 260, 264; mineral discoveries of, 56; and mining companies, 66; and prospecting licences, 19; reparations for, 310, 311; representation of at policy tables, 65; resistance by, 61, 63, 127–28, 223; revenue sharing with, 199–200; and Ring of Fire, 115; sovereignty of, 169; strength of when financial institutions are vulnerable, 280; struggles of, 240, 298

Indigenous rights, 127, 162, 170–71, 225, 234, 315; to free prior informed consent, 223, 271, 308, 310; guarantee of, 271; non-assertion of, 172

Indigenous treaties, 170, 225, 243; map of, 58; mining companies and obligations to, 308

Indigenous waters, control over, 63

Indigenous women, 71

Indonesia, 116

industrial deafness, 86

industrial disease, 56, 74, 87, 244, 252, 316

inequality, 3; income and gender, 240

infrastructure support, 114–16

initial public offering (IPO), 112

Initiative for Responsible Mining Assurance (IRMA), 269; Framework for Responsible Mining, 312

injuries, 56, 74; critical, 87; from violence, 276

Innu Nation, 64, 296–97, 298

insider information, 242

Institutional Control Plan (ICP). *See* Saskatchewan Institutional Control Plan

Inter-American Commission on Human Rights, 128

intergenerational equity, 264

inter-jurisdictional conflict, 262

internal rate of return (IRR), 119

international aid: cuts to, 302

International Atomic Energy Agency: Joint Convention on the Safety of Spent Fuel Management and on the Safety of Radioactive Waste Management, 216

International Council on Mining and Metals, 162, 269

International Cyanide Code (ICC), 44, 269

international financial accounting rules, changes to, 311

international forums, Indigenous participation in, 63

International Institute for Environment and Development, 315

International Joint Commission, 143

International Monetary Fund, 143

international presence, Canada's, 123–37, 265; and taxation, 200–201

international solidarity work, 265–78

international trade, 272

international treaties and agreements, 126–27, 272

Internet staking, 17

Inter Pares, 297, 298

Inter Press Service (IPS), 272

Intertec Management Limited, 208–9

intervenor funding, 176

intrusive rentier syndrome, 73–74

Inuit, 297; benefit to, 172; lands owned by, 170; land title of, 18

Inuit Tapirisat of Canada, 297

investment activities, 26; dealers and brokers, 111–12

Investment Industry Regulatory Organization of Canada (IIROC), 109

investor campaigning, 280, 311; framework for, 281–85

investors: questions asked by, 286–90; strategies for taking on, 279–93, 311–12

mineral exploration, 22, 281; risky nature of stocks in, 279; tax incentives for, 189

mineral industry: cancellation/renegotiation of contract/licences in, 271; federal government role in, 174; funds raised for, 126; infrastructure for, 271; jobs in, 141; promotion of, 271; responsible, 308

mineralization, 22; metal sulphide, 40

mineral potential, 18; estimating, 116–20

mineral processing, 45

mineral reserves, 117; depletion of, 140

mineral resources, 117, 196; provincial responsibility for management of, 186; rent for use of, 194

mineral rights, 17–19, 223; severance of from surface rights, 130

minerals: conservation and recycling of, 189, 201; cost of, 189; exhaustible nature of, 3, 73; pillaging earth for, 3

mineral strategy, new, 308–9

Mineral Tax Credits for Exploration (METCs), 197

mineral tenures, granting of, 18

mine reclamation trust contributions, deduction of, 197–98

miners/mine workers: agency of, 311; differences between mining companies and, 78–80; health and safety acts for, 169; lives of, 3; pride of, 3; protection of, 170; support for, 244; working in mining industry, 77–88

mines: advice for those taking action to stop, 231–36; demonstrations against, 234; eating the cities that feed them, 243–44; economic value of, 139; economic viability of, 147; operating, dealing with, 239–54; physical footprint of, 9–14, 38, 73, 157; stopping before they start, 221–37

Mines and Communities Network, 270, 299; London Declaration (2008), 270–72

mine shafts: collapsing of, 243; excavating of, 196; sinking of, 24, 26, 196

mining: aggregation of data on, 190; as assault on earth, 10–11; building alternatives to dependence on, 315; and community resistance, 1–5; for compensation, 21–22; as dangerous and destructive work, 74, 77–78, 244; de-emphasizing, 201; environmental impacts of, 37–52, 75; environmental monitoring paid for by, 241; green, 308; Indigenous employment in, 61, 64, 66, 81, 222, 308; internalizing full costs of, 309–10; as male-dominated industry, 81; putting in its place, 307–17; regulatory framework for, 172–74; responsible, 157, 312; social impacts of, 69–75; sustainable, 308; as ultimate expression of violence of colonialism, 3; as waste management industry, 10, 197; and water, 246; wealth created by, 74, 242

Mining Act, 19

Mining Association of British Columbia, 162, 166

Mining Association of Canada (MAC), 91, 158–60, 165; *Facts and Figures 2017*, 60; as "progressive" voice of industry, 159; Towards Sustainable Mining (TSM), 159–60, 165

mining camps, 15, 23, 25, 26, 27, 77, 240; construction of, 23; effect of on women, 71; labour shortages at, 64

mining codes, 129, 137

mining companies, 22, 25; access of to ore bodies, 222; accountability of, 128, 295, 300–306, 313; and availability of labour/funds, 222; blocking access of to land, 234; branches vs. foreign subsidiaries of, 200; code of conduct for, 301; colonial, 56;

communications people, 240; conflict of interest in, 281; contracting out by, 80; as corporations, 105–6; credit rating of, 184; and CSR, 163; differences between miners and, 79–80; disclosure of environmental information, 311–12; donations by, 158, 240, 243; externalized costs of, 139–54, 158; finance strategies of, 280; and full bonding in realizable securities, 310; and full costs of mining, 308–10; funding of NGOs by, 268; Indigenous peoples holding shares in, 66; Indigenous supply and service to, 66; international operations of, 1, 123–37, 307, 313; junior, 79, 105, 286, 290–93; kinds of, 104–9; lawsuits against, 277; lies of, 269, 276–77; mandatory disclosure of taxes paid by, 192; mine closure and, 35; misinformation of, 276–77; myths/lies about, 269; onus on to prove economic viability, 222; owners of, 3, 284; pillage by/pollution of, 269; poor management decisions by, 280; power imbalances between communities and, 74; predatory nature of in Global South, 127; public availability of information on, 285; regulation of behaviour of, 27; reputation of, 157, 281; respect and fair treatment from, 82–86; rights of, and Indigenous law, 170; rules of operation of, 101–22; scandals of, 281; secrecy of, 242; strategies for taking on, 279–93; and Sudbury soils study, 249; suits against, 134–35; sustaining mining industry as they know it, 308; taxing international operations of, 200–201; tax paid by, 190–91, 194–96, 242; theft by, 136–37; undertaking research on, 281, 284–85; violations by, 128; violence of, 123, 127–29, 269, 272; vulnerability of, 61, 281; as wealth creation activity, 104, 242; world's publicly traded, 126

mining equity: total global, 126

mining industry: associations, 158–62; Canada's international presence, 123–37; cancellation/renegotiation of contracts/licences in, 271; control of discourse by, 308; data on employment in, 80–82; different approaches to, 62–67; externalized costs of, 311; federal expenses and adjustments specific to, 196–98; federal government promotion of, 123; government subsidization of, 310; as heavy user of water and energy, 201; and Indigenous peoples, 308; lobbying in, 157–68; opposition of to EITI, 192; power of, 166; pressure on, 269; profits, 308; public funding of, 114–16; shaping of taxation policy by, 189–90; social footprint of, 157; structural causes of problems in, 276; structure and financing of, 101–22; value of government support for, 190; vulnerability of, 307; working in, 77–88, 276

Mining Industry Human Resources Council, 81

Mining Injustice Solidarity Network (MISN), 274–76

mining investment, 126, 310

mining investors, 286. *See also* investors

mining law and regulation, 169–88, 295–306

mining leases, 22, 24, 185, 225

Mining, Minerals, and Sustainable Development initiative, 269

mining permits, 20, 187

mining policies, 61, 172; Indigenous, 63

mining-reliant communities: economic vulnerability of, 75; number of, 70; organizing to effect change in, 239–54, 300

mining sequence, 15–35

Mining Suppliers Trade Association, 162

mining support activities industry, 80

new mines: proposals for, 63, 72, 102, 147; tax holidays for, 195–96

New Prosperity Mine (BC), 165–68, 292

Ni-Black Mine (Alaska), 292, 357n15

Nicaragua, 297

Nichol, Andrew, 121

nickel, 33, 47, 296; and cancer, 49, 250; contamination by, 248–51; decline in reserves of, 140; mining of, 40; plumes, 50; as pollutant, 179; smelters, 181; toxicity of, 181

Nikiforuk, Andrew, 206

Nishnawbe Aski Nation (NAN), 224

nitrate, 44

nitrogen oxides, 47

noise pollution, 14; camps and, 26

Nolan, Glenn, 67, 268

non-governmental organizations (NGOs), 113, 245, 297, 299, 301; funding by mining companies, 268, 302; human rights and environmental, 304, 312; substitution of own agenda for community's, 280; working in, 276

Norman B. Keevil School of Mining Engineering, 16

Noront Resources, 67

North American Free Trade Agreement (NAFTA), 106, 114, 127, 148

Northcliff Resources, 101–2, 104

Northern Dynasty Minerals, 291, 293, 357n18

The Northern Miner, 285

Northern Secwepemc te Qelmucw Mining Policy, 63, 172

Northgate, 347n18

North Mara Mine (Tanzania), 129, 131

Northstar Aerospace, 121

Northwatch, 296, 297–98, 320n8

Northwest Territories, 11–14, 149; contaminated site cleanup in, 94; diamond mines in, 46, 145, 241;

environmental assessment and permitting, 172; Indigenous law in, 171; *Mackenzie Valley Resource Management Act*, 172; *Mineral Resources Act*, 172; permitting, 187; Supreme Court, 120; unions in, 86; uranium mine proposals in, 212

Nova Scotia: coal mining in, 78; exploration in, 22; gold mineral exploration in, 311; mining tax in, 195; moratorium on uranium mining in, 213; requests for proposals for exploration in, 20; Supreme Court, 120; unions in, 86

N'Swakamok Native Friendship Centre, 253

Nuclear Safety and Control Act (NSCA), 173, 213–15

nuclear waste, 97

Nuna Logistics, 66

Nuna Management Company, 66

Nunatsiavut: Assembly, 212; Inuit land in, 18

Nunavik, 171–72

Nunavut, 64; Court of Justice, 120; Impact Review Board, 171, 212; Indigenous law in, 171; Inuit land in, 18; Land and Water Board, 173; Land Claim Agreement, 171; mining industry employment in, 80; Mining Regulations, 173; uranium mine proposals in, 212

Nuu-chah-nulth Nation, 316

Nyrstar, 357n18

Obed Coal Mine (Alberta), 52

O'Brien, Chris, 257

occupational health and safety, 77, 78, 82, 86–88, 209, 244; MAC and, 159

Occupational Health and Safety (OHS) Act, 87

occupations (of land), 57, 235–36

OceanaGold, 127

Oceans Act, 173, 183

Oda, Bev, 304

Office of the Extractive Sector Corporate Social Responsibility Counsellor, 303–4

Office of the Public Sector Integrity Commissioner of Canada, 134

oil extraction, 47

Olza Mine (Poland), 292, 357n15

ombudspersons, 301, 304–5

Ondaatje, Michael, 230

Ontarians for a Just Accountable Mineral Strategy, 308–9

Ontario: abandoned mine sites in, 91; bulk sampling laws in, 24; business corporations act of, 106; Court of Appeal, 230–31; disputes between First Nations and exploration companies, 21; environmental assessment rules in, 25, 174, 176; *Environmental Bill of Rights*, 187; Environmental Commissioner, 228; exploration in, 22, 221; *Far North Act*, 231; fight to end free entry in, 223–31; gold rushes in, 57; investor disclosure in, 285; mine closure regulation in, 184; Mineral Development Strategy, 224, 308; mineral rights in, 17; *Mining Act*, 223–25, 227, 230–31; mining for compensation in, 21; mining sector employment in, 80; mining tax in, 194–95; Ministry of Northern Development and Mines, 24, 184, 186, 193–94; Ministry of the Environment, 248, 250; prospecting licences in, 19; revenue sharing with Indigenous peoples in, 199; *Securities Act*, 113, 285; smelters and refineries in, 33; Superior Court, 135, 225, 226; Supreme Court of Justice, 120; tax holidays for new mines in, 195; value for money audit, 193–94

Ontario Nature, 225

Ontario Securities Commission, 285

Opemiska Mine (Quebec), 52

open-pit mines, 9, 11, 24, 127, 129, 240; awesome size of, 11; construction of, 26; cost of, 104; dangers in, 77–78; noise and light pollution from, 14; slope of walls in, 12; waste from, 12; waste rock material in, 27; and water removal, 46

options (stock), 110–11

oral history, 209

ore: crushing and grinding of, 26, 28, 40; separation of, 26, 28

ore bodies, 10–11, 17, 46, 163, 222; credible, 116; depletion of, 73; grade of, 10; identification of, 123; inadequacy of, 222, 310; nature of, 11

ore concentration, 29

O'Reilly, Kevin, 256–59, 297; *Mining and Communities in Northern Canada*, 257

Organisation for Economic Co-operation and Development (OECD), 189, 201

organizing: after mine closure, 255–64

organochlorines, 45

Orkin, Andrew, 206

orphaned mines. *See* mine abandonment

Osisko Mining, 243

overburden, removal of, 10, 23, 26, 27, 196

oxidation, 40

Oyu Tolgoi mine (Mongolia), 131

Pacific Rim Cayman LLC, 126–27

Paladin Energy (Australia), 212

Panama Papers, 132

Papua New Guinea, 276

Parks Canada, 183

Parry, Roger, 88

Parsons Corporation, 94

participation agreements, 65–66, 102

"small mines," 25
smallpox, 58
smelters, 46, 47, 49, 247; distribution of, 33; ferro-chrome, 115; fumes and dust from, 39; toxins from, 249
smelting, 31–33, 47, 80, 86, 141, 181, 190, 248; environmental impacts of, 126
Smith, Dr. Leslie, 334n21
Snyder, John, 317
SOAR (Steelworkers Organization of Active Retirees), 247–48
social accounting. *See* economics: ecological
social fabric: changes in, 240; destruction of, 70; rebuilding and maintaining, 70, 72; strengthening, 253–54
social hierarchy, 75
social impacts, 69–75, 113, 148, 281, 297; during exploration and construction, 70–71; at mine closure, 74–75; during mine operations, 72–74
social justice, 163; organizations, 223
social licence, 310, 315
social rights, 273
social unionism, 84–85, 253
sodium chloride, 45
soil: contamination of, 30, 38, 48, 209, 239, 247; risk management level of, 250; sampling of, 22, 248, 250; Sudbury soils study, 246–52
solidarity work, international, 265–78; lessons learned about, 267–69
solid waste: storage for, 25
SOQUEM, 22, 195
Soros, George, 192
South Africa, 292; diamonds in, 144–45
Sparrow case, 170
speculative bubbles, 118
"spot" market prices, 118
stakeholder activities, 26

staking claims, 15, 17–22, 222, 230; "fatal flaws" in, 222
"staking rush," 24, 221, 224, 286
Standing Committee on Foreign Affairs, 300–301
Stanley (New Brunswick), 101
Stano, Maya, 312
steel: manufacturing of, 47
Steelworkers Humanity Fund, 298
Stk'emlúpsemc te Secwépemc Nation (SSN), 65, 150–51
St. Lawrence River, 49
stock exchanges. *See* financial markets, 109
stock instruments, forms of, 110–11
Strateco, 213, 349n33
strategy, vs. tactics, 234
strikes, 82–83, 281; wildcat, 83
stripping, 23
Struzik, Ed, 93
subsistence, 71
subsurface rights, 17, 64, 171, 223
Sudbury (Ontario), 1, 9, 11, 14, 49, 50, 59–60, 69, 72, 80, 84, 182, 184; Better Beginnings, Better Futures, 253–54; City of, 249; Donovan/Flour-Mill neighbourhood, 73, 253; mining camp in, 15; Myths and Mirrors, 253–54; pollution in, 247; soils study, 246–52; unions in, 84–85
Sudbury and District Health Unit, 249, 252
Sudbury Area Risk Assessment (SARA) Group, 249, 252
Sudbury Community Legal Clinic, 86
sulfide compounds, 30
sulphur: separation of from gold, 255
sulphur dioxide, 30, 32, 33, 47–49, 182; damage to trees from, 257; toxicity of, 181
sulphuric acid, 29, 30, 40, 43, 44, 47

Westray Bill, 87–88, 313
Westray Mine disaster, 20, 78, 87–88, 244, 321n13
whistle-blowers, 242, 311
white hand, 74, 86
Whites Point Quarry (Nova Scotia), 127, 148
Wilderness Committee, 168
wildfires, 96, 168
Wildlands League, 46
wildlife: effects on, 39, 43, 48, 147, 149, 231
Williams, Chief Roger, 166
Williams Lake (BC), 246, 292
Wilt, James, 192–93
Windy Craggy Mine (BC), 21, 296
withholding taxes, 114, 200
Witte, Peggy (aka Margaret Kent), 20, 21, 257, 321n13
Wolastoq First Nation, 101–2, 357n13
Wolf Lake First Nation, 221–22
Wolf Minerals Drakelands Mine (UK), 104
Wolverine Mine (Yukon), 66
women: effect of camps on, 71; employment of in mining, 81; and family employment after mine closure, 75; and income disparity, 73; Indigenous, 71; violence against in camps, 26
worker fatigue, 87
Workers' Compensation Board (WCB), 86
Workers' Memorial Day, 85
workplace fatalities, 87
World Bank, 114, 129–32; Extractive Industries Review (2004), 269; International Court for the Settlement of Investment Disputes (ICSID), 126; International Development Association (IDA), 271; International Finance Corporation (IFC), 271

World Gold Council, 144, 162
World Health Organization, 233
World Nuclear Association, 210, 216
World Vision, 302

Xat'sull First Nation, 165, 246
Xstrata Copper-Kidd/Timmins Glencore, 182
Xstrata Nickel (Sudbury), 182, 249

Yellowknife (NWT), 72; City Council, 256–58; Giant Mine: see under Giant Mine
Yellowknives Dene, 255, 257–59
Young, Alan, 296
youth: as effective guardians, 264; and income disparity, 73; MISN and, 276
Yukon, 19–20, 50; abandoned mine sites in, 91; business corporations act of, 106; Environmental and Socio-Economic Assessment Board, 95, 173; Faro Mine in, 91–96; GDP of, 92; gold rushes in, 57; permitting, 187; placer deposits in, 39; *Placer Mining Act*, 173; porphyry copper mines in, 44; *Quartz Mining Act*, 173; Supreme Court, 120
Yukon Chamber of Mines, 162
Yukon Conservation Society (YCS), 93, 296, 298
Yukon Water Board, 94
Yukon Zinc, 66

Zambia, 137
zinc: contamination by, 90; decline in reserves of, 140; extraction of, 90; plumes, 50; as pollutant, 179; refineries, 182; smelters, 181; solubility of, 41; toxicity of, 42

Joan Kuyek is a community-focused mining analyst and organizer living in Ottawa. She was the founding national coordinator of MiningWatch Canada from 1999 to 2009 and continues to do work for MiningWatch and for a number of communities affected by mining.